Digital Immune System

Scrivener Publishing
100 Cummings Center, Suite 541J
Beverly, MA 01915-6106

Leading-Edge Breakthroughs in Artificial Intelligence

Series Editor: Dr. S. Balamurugan (sbnbala@gmail)

The world is on the cusp of several breakthroughs in artificial intelligence (AI), rapidly transforming industries and the research field. The "Leading-Edge Breakthroughs in Artificial Intelligence" book series is dedicated to exploring the most pioneering developments in artificial intelligence. The series aims to highlight both theoretical and practical advancements, offering insights into several cutting-edge advancements in AI and how the same could be deployed to solve complex problems in fields such as healthcare, finance, manufacturing, robotics, marketing, energy management, agriculture, autonomous systems, and many more. It also addresses critical issues like AI governance, ethics, trust, security, transparency, and societal impacts, making it an essential resource for researchers, engineers, and industry leaders looking to leverage AI for future breakthroughs.

Publishers at Scrivener
Martin Scrivener (martin@scrivenerpublishing.com)
Phillip Carmical (pcarmical@scrivenerpublishing.com)

Digital Immune System

Principles and Practices

Edited by

Sujata Priyambada Dash

Department of Management, Birla Institute of Technology, Mesra, Ranchi, Jharkhand, India

Vaibhav Mishra

ICFAI Business School, Hyderabad, Telangana, India

Bijeta Shaw

ICFAI Business School, Hyderabad, Telangana, India

Sandeep Kumar Panda

Department of Artificial Intelligence and Data Science, Faculty of Science and Technology (IcfaiTech), ICFAI Foundation for Higher Education (IFHE), Deemed to be University, Hyderabad, Telangana, India

and

S. Balamurugan

Intelligent Research Consultancy Services, Coimbatore, Tamilnadu, India

Scrivener Publishing

WILEY

Part 2: Digital Immune System: Applications 121

Series Preface

This book on *Digital Immune System: Principles and Practices* delves into the integration of software design, development, operations, and analytics for creating digital systems that can autonomously detect, prevent, and recover from anomalies and cyber threats. It addresses how self-healing digital infrastructures can be developed to address the urgent demand during this period of increased cyber threat intelligence. Furthermore, this book demonstrates the integration of AI and automation with software engineering to enable detection, diagnosis, and response to disruptions in real-time. This volume is relevant to the series *Leading-Edge Breakthroughs in Artificial Intelligence* because it uncovers frontier innovations that employ AI above and beyond task execution, shifting towards robust definable system resilience, reliability, security, efficient, and trust in intelligent systems.

Dr. S. Balamurugan
Intelligent Research Consultancy Services, Coimbatore, Tamilnadu, India
Series Editor - Leading Edge Breakthroughs in Artificial Intelligence

The book also emphasizes the importance of a proactive approach, urging organizations to move beyond traditional reactive measures. It highlights predictive analytics and behavioral analysis as key to identifying threats before they occur. Through case studies and real-world examples, it shows how organizations have successfully implemented digital immune systems to protect assets and maintain operational integrity in a hostile digital environment. This not only reduces breach risks but also strengthens the overall efficiency and robustness of security infrastructure.

Additionally, the book addresses the challenges and ethical considerations of deploying digital immune systems. It explores the balance between security and privacy, the potential for false positives, and the need for transparency in automated decisions. It also looks ahead to how digital immune systems will evolve alongside technological advancement and increasingly sophisticated cyber threats. Offering a comprehensive overview of current trends and future prospects, the book serves as a vital resource for cybersecurity professionals, IT leaders, and anyone interested in next-generation digital defense mechanisms.

Readers of this volume will learn the fundamentals of Digital Immune System: Principles and Practices, features, working principles and its application in different sectors. It sixteen chapters, contributed by accomplished writers in the field, are as follows:

Chapter 1 explores how HEIs can effectively integrate this new model of academic labor through a mixed-methods approach. Quantitative data from surveys assess perceptions of integration, resource provision, and impacts on organizational learning, while qualitative insights are drawn from focus groups involving both gig and traditional faculty.

Chapter 2 examines the growth prospects, costs, benefits, and broader economic implications of adopting digital immune systems, drawing upon recent data and industry trends.

Chapter 3 proposes a blockchain-based Digital Immune System (DIS) for decentralized threat intelligence, real-time anomaly detection, and automated responses to secure IoT ecosystems. Featuring a consortium blockchain, AI-enhanced threat analysis, and smart contract-driven incident containment, this multi-layered architecture supports behavioral profiling and adaptive prescriptions to combat zero-day threats.

Chapter 4 compiles material on blockchain technology in banking, affirming its critical role in finance. It surveys various blockchain-based technologies and services and concludes with the importance of blockchain financial applications, asserting that blockchain-based credit reporting offers greater security than traditional server-based systems in the wake of recent data breaches.

Chapter 5 responds to the cybersecurity demands of Industry 4.0 by introducing a Self-Tuning Digital Immune Cybersecurity Model for Smart Manufacturing. This framework, modeled after biological immune systems, uses agentic AI programs to enhance smart factory resilience, continuously adapting through a cycle of learning, automation, and improvement.

Chapter 6 discusses the challenges of using Generative Adversarial Networks (GANs) in cybersecurity and their potential evolution. It aims to provide an integrated understanding of how GANs and Digital Immune Systems can work synergistically to defend against phishing and other digital threats.

Chapter 7 analyzes the limitations of DIS and explores a cyber-physical infrastructure that blends DIS with behavioral forensics and human oversight. It highlights how Human-in-the-Loop models, Explainable AI (XAI), and Zero Trust frameworks enhance cyber resilience by integrating automation with human judgment to foster a security-aware organizational culture.

Chapter 8 analyzes semantic recognition of patterns in the security domain, reviewing various linguistic similarity techniques and STS-related tools. It emphasizes the role of STS in NLP tasks such as summarization, short response grading, and pattern recognition, demonstrating its utility in understanding and processing semantic features.

Chapter 9 presents how Human Resources plays a pivotal role in embedding cybersecurity awareness across recruitment, training, policy formation, compensation, offboarding, and shaping organizational culture.

Chapter 10 outlines the fundamentals of blockchain—including consensus algorithms and smart contract automation—and explores real-world applications in healthcare, finance, and supply chains. It further examines the integration of AI and IoT within blockchain and the resulting economic, environmental, and regulatory implications for future research.

Chapter 11 provides a survey of existing blockchain research, outlining its features, applications, and challenges. It also explores the relevance of the metaverse, emphasizing its growing importance and potential for improvement.

Chapter 12 identifies critical implementation challenges for AI in digital immune systems, addressing ethical concerns, regulatory constraints, and emerging research directions while emphasizing the need for balanced governance and ongoing innovation.

Chapter 13 provides an overview of key technologies essential for addressing next-generation cybersecurity threats.

Chapter 14 addresses the organizational structures needed to support secure digital ecosystems, advocating for federated governance models that balance central oversight with distributed responsiveness. It discusses phased implementation strategies, vendor integration, and cultural change while anticipating challenges like quantum threats, AI-enhanced security, and shifts in digital business models.

Chapter 15 delves into blockchain fundamentals, security protocols, applications, and regulatory considerations, with a particular focus on the future of blockchain in pharmaceutical supply chains.

Chapter 16 discusses authentication challenges in corporate, financial, IoT, and distributed systems, proposing zk-STARKs and zk-SNARKs as scalable, private, and cost-efficient solutions to existing PKI limitations through enhanced blockchain identity management frameworks.

Topics presented in each chapter of this book are unique to this book and are based on unpublished work of contributed authors. In editing this book, we attempted to bring into the discussion all the new trends and experiments that have made on Digital Immune System. We believe this book is ready to serve as a reference for larger audiences such as system architects, practitioners, developers, and researchers.

Sujata Priyambada Dash
Birla Institute of Technology, Mesra, Ranchi, Jharkhand, India
Vaibhav Mishra
ICFAI Business School, IBS Hyderabad, India
Bijeta Shaw
ICFAI Business School, IBS Hyderabad, India
Sandeep Kumar Panda
Department of Artificial Intelligence and Data Science, Faculty of Science and Technology (IcfaiTech), ICFAI Foundation for Higher Education (IFHE), Deemed to be University, Hyderabad, Telangana, India
S. Balamurugan
Intelligent Research Consultancy Services, Coimbatore, Tamilnadu, India
August 2025

Acknowledgements

First, I am thankful to my Almighty for enabling me to complete this challenging task.

My heartiest gratitude to the Birla Institute of Technology (BIT), which has empowered me to pursue this demanding task with commitment and dedication. I am also indebted to Prof. (Dr.) Supriyo Roy, Head of the Department of Management and Prof. (Dr.) Sandeep Singh Solanki, Dean of Post Graduate Studies, BIT, Mesra, Ranchi, for their support and guidance.

The preparation of this edited volume was a journey that took several months. I wish to express my heartfelt gratitude to our families, friends, colleagues, and well-wishers for their constant support throughout this journey. Special thanks to all the editors of the book for their significant contributions to shaping the book's final form.

My deepest gratitude to all the chapter contributors, who allowed us to quote their remarks and work in this book. I acknowledge the hard work of the authors and their cooperation during the revisions of their chapters. I would also like to acknowledge the valuable comments from the reviewers, who have enabled us to select these chapters out of the many we received and improved their quality. I wish to acknowledge and appreciate the Wiley-Scrivener team for their continuous support throughout the entire process. My gratitude is extended to the readers, who give us their trust, and we hope this work guides and inspires them.

Sujata Priyambada Dash

Part 1

DIGITAL IMMUNE SYSTEM: PRINCIPLES

1

Digital Immune System Approach Toward the Impact of Gig Faculty on Organizational Learning Within Higher Education Institutes

Nimisha Singh[1]*, Sonam Gupta[2] and Anshu Yadav[2]

[1]*Department of Management Studies, Indian Institute of Information Technology – Allahabad, Prayagraj, India*
[2]*School of Business Management, CSJM University, Kanpur, India*

Abstract

This chapter explores the growing impact of gig faculty on organizational learning in higher education institutions (HEIs). Based on a digital immune system (DIS) framework, the chapter describes how an increasing presence of contingent faculty affects the capacity and adaptability of HEIs in learning. The rise in the usage of gig faculty offers both opportunities and challenges; hence, careful assessment is required to understand whether they will provide an opportunity for continuous learning and innovation. This research is intended to understand how HEIs can effectively integrate this new academic labor model. A mixed-methods approach has been used, with a combination of data consisting of both quantitative details gathered from the survey in respect of the perceptions that HEIs have regarding the integration process, provision of resources, and effects on organizational learning, while qualitative data was obtained through focus groups both by gig faculty, as well as traditional faculty. Focus groups examine the lived experiences of these diverse faculty populations, specifically in terms of curriculum design, coaching, team-based learning, and institutional environment. Gig faculty engagement, support structures, and organizational learning are likely to be a complicated issue. Some of the advantages associated with the use of gig faculty include diversity in the skill base, efficient delivery of curriculum, and economies of scale. Other expected challenges comprise equitable workload allocation, pedagogical quality,

**Corresponding author*: one.symbiotic@gmail.com

Sujata Priyambada Dash, Vaibhav Mishra, Bijeta Shaw, Sandeep Kumar Panda and S. Balamurugan (eds.) Digital Immune System: Principles and Practices, (3–22) © 2026 Scrivener Publishing LLC

and the imperative of robust support at the institution for gig faculty. The result will explain these interplays where the positive, as well as the negative implications of these forces, are established to impact organizational learning in HEIs amid the digital change. Ultimately, the research shall help, in return, to further add to the comprehension of the changing nature of the academic workforce and its implications on institutional learning, thus providing first-hand insights into how to engage higher education managers with the complexities surrounding this novel terrain.

Keywords: Gig faculty, digital immune system, higher education institute, organizational learning, academic workforce, digital transformation, hybrid learning, resource allocation

1.1 Introduction

The global higher education landscape is transforming profoundly due to accelerating technological advancements and changing student needs. This shift is characterized by the growing incorporation of gig faculty into the academic workforce. The gig faculty with flexible, part-time employment arrangements bring in a new approach to address the needs of staffing and teaching expertise diversification within higher education institutions (HEIs). It is an emerging trend with considerable opportunities and challenges, particularly on the organizational learning side, which is the backbone of institutional vitality and success. This research ventures into this largely unexplored territory by investigating the delicate dance between gig faculty, the institutional context of HEIs, and organizational learning, all within the context of a digital immune system (DIS) framework (Bennett, 2020) [2].

The DIS framework brings a new perspective on HEIs' adaptive ability toward the entry of gig faculty. This framework draws similar parallels with an immune system; hence, in an organizational context, it metaphorically describes complex processes of learning and adaptation by an organization like how an immune system distinguishes and controls pathogens. Wherein the immunological system differentiates and defeats the pathogens, the HEI must produce effective internal "mechanisms" for appropriate knowledge sharing and resource allocation when dealing with fast-changing skill requirements and knowledge inputs through gig faculty. It aims to understand the mechanisms that currently exist for the efficacy of how gig faculty is integrated into this "immune system," seeking its vulnerabilities. More importantly, this paper makes the point that it believes the good integration of gig faculty within the academic fabric is inextricably tied to the organizational learning capacity of the HEI. It allows the institution to be adaptive, creative, and better positioned to exploit the unique skills and perspectives that gig faculty brings to campus. A healthy learning environment will facilitate an easy acquisition of new knowledge and expertise and thus improve institutional effectiveness and teaching quality. On the other hand, a loosely designed or inefficacious learning system could lead to segmented learning experiences; increased workload in traditional faculty; and, more importantly, quality and overall impacts on the institution (Marginson, 2016) [8].

This research will examine how organizational learning works with gig faculty integration. Those are the main areas of focus: effective onboarding and training programs for gig faculty, well-defined channels and collaboration platforms between gig and traditional faculty, the designing of structured knowledge-sharing initiatives, and strong quality control measures to ensure high pedagogical standards prevail. However, the study also considers whether institutional culture influences organizational learning outcomes as shaped by using resource allocation strategies and leadership styles. In this regard, significant issues would be workload management and equity concerns. Integrating gig faculty should not unduly burden traditional faculty, nor should it structurally worsen inequalities in learning opportunities for students. The effectiveness of gig-faculty integration is at times best understood through awareness of subtle trade-offs between cost-effectiveness and quality. By doing so, it is expected that the study will reveal the kinds of conditions that are favorable to gig faculty's positive contribution to organizational learning within HEIs. It can foster change in how administrators, faculty members, and policymakers understand the transformations sweeping the academic workforce, given the demands of the digital age. Ultimately, this research aims to provide a framework for HEIs to optimize the integration of gig faculty, ensuring they foster institutional growth and sustainability (Weller, 2011) [12].

1.2 Literature Review

The landscape of higher education is undergoing a profound transformation, driven by technological advancements, evolving student expectations, and shifting economic realities. This literature review aims to look through the intersection of several key themes that shape such evolution: the rise of gig faculty, the development of digital immunity, the imperative for organizational learning, and all the challenges, as well as the opportunities that derive from the current digital transformation HEIs provide (Brown, 1991;

Senge, 1990) [18, 19]. We must discuss ideas regarding the implications of a teaching workforce: knowledge-sharing innovation, adaptability-hybrid resources, distribution-talent collaboration, and, above all, quality.

Adjunct and part-time instructors who are naturally contingent have, to a greater extent, relegated the traditional tenured faculty into being the norm, and such teachers are being called the "gig faculty" (Kezar, 2014; Kezar and Maxey, 2013) [10, 11]. These factors include the cost-containment pressures put on HEIs, increasing demands for specialized expertise, and academics' desires for greater flexibility in the workplace (Flaherty, 2018; Rhoads and Rhoads, 2017; Alstete, 2015) [5, 7, 9]. The gig economy, on the one hand, provides benefits in terms of accessing diverse talent and greater institutional agility. On the other hand, the gig economy also brings along job insecurities, wage disparities, and denigration of collective governance due to the risks that it poses (Gappa, 2018) [6]. Consider knowledge sharing and organizational learning. For example, the precarious employment status of gig faculty impacts the integration of gig faculty into the academic community and restricts participation in collaborative projects and knowledge exchange activities (Trowler and Cooper, 2002) [16]. Higher educational institutions, with the rapidly advancing speed of technology and dependence on digital infrastructure, are more vulnerable to cyberattacks, data breaches, and system failures. The concept of a "digital immune system" has emerged as a framework for enhancing organizational resilience in the digital age (Gartner, 2022) [1]. A DIS involves a combination of technologies, processes, and practices designed to proactively identify, prevent, and respond to digital threats. For HEIs, an effective DIS plays a major role in safeguarding students' sensitive data, ensuring the continuance of teaching and learning activities, and safeguarding the reputation of an institution (Alstete, 2019) [3]. Organizational learning and adaptation in the implementation of a DIS is important because HEIs need to acquire new skills and competencies associated with cybersecurity, data governance, and digital risk management (Nonaka, 1994) [17].

The digital transformation of higher education, therefore, needs a culture of continuous learning and adaptation within the HEIs. Organizational learning is where institutions acquire knowledge, share and use it, and thereby learn to improve the effectiveness and responsiveness to change (Senge, 1990) [19]. In light of digital transformation, this requires embracing new technologies, pedagogical approaches, and administrative practices. Some known drivers facilitating organizational learning are commitment from the leadership, faculty development, and a collaborative work environment (Argyris and Schön, 1978) [20]. Therefore, HEIs focused on organizational learning will have a good chance to exploit the benefits that the digital age has promised: personalized learning, data-driven decision-making, and greater engagement from students. The COVID-19 pandemic fast-tracked this growth in the adoption of digital technologies in higher education, which gave rise to hybrid and online learning models on a mass scale. While this was beset with tremendous difficulty, it also opened the door for increased access, flexibility, and personalization in higher education (Bates, 2019) [4]. However, the promise of effectiveness for the hybrid learning style means judicious planning for all the resources – from technology to infrastructures supporting faculties and assistance for students, as well (Dziuban *et al.*, 2004) [15]. The other major issues related to this move toward going digital involve the question of appropriate use of space and an uncertain future regarding what role the campus is meant to play in higher education.

Talent recruitment and development through higher education have also been renovated in the age of digitalism. Higher education institutions are seeking more candidates with expertise in digital pedagogy, data analytics, and online learning design (Christensen *et al.*, 2008) [14]. The gig economy has further diversified the talent pool, enabling HEIs to access specialized expertise on a flexible basis. However, the quality of teaching and learning in a digitally mediated environment requires new approaches for faculty development, performance evaluation, and quality assurance (Means *et al.*, 2010) [13]. In addition, the collaboration of knowledge sharing from diverse faculties, including gig faculty, is significant in ensuring cohesive and enriching learning experiences. Digital transformation has brought both opportunities and challenges for HEIs. All these are interlinked aspects of this complex process: the rise of the gig faculty, the development of digital immune systems, and the imperative for organizational learning. Institutions of higher education that can effectively sail through such changes will better respond to the shifting needs of students, increase their resilience, and ultimately emerge winners in this competitive landscape of higher education. Future studies should investigate the long-term effects of the gig economy on the academic workforce, detail efficient approaches to organizational learning in a digital environment, and discuss the changing role of quality assurance in both hybrid and online contexts. There is a need for further research on relationships between digital immunity and learning in the knowledge, flexibility, and innovations areas, affecting firm sustainable digital structure as well for HEIs. Lastly, it is important to delve into these latest developments in the processes of resource and human resource allocations or alliances concerning the future of developments in higher education.

1.3 Methodology

A mixed-methods study design was employed in this research to combine both data collection and analysis methods from both quantitative and qualitative methods to understand better the interaction of gig faculty engagement, organizational learning, and the development of robust digital immune systems in HEIs. In this case, using a mixed-methods approach would mean that it is theoretically possible to gain a holistic view by making use of the strengths of both methodologies to answer questions. The quantitative phase will allow for a wide scope with a statistical analysis of the prevalence and the character of gig faculty programs, the perception of their impact, and other resource allocation strategies. The qualitative phase will then delve into the lived experiences, perspectives, and challenges of both gig and traditional faculty members in this ever-changing landscape.

1.3.1 Quantitative Phase: Surveying the Landscape of Gig Faculty Engagement

The quantitative phase of the study used a stratified sample survey instrument. This was collected from diverse regions and institutional types in HEIs. Through stratification, representation in a cross-section of the various categories of HEIs such as public and private and research-intensive institutions is ensured with differences in gig faculty engagement and organizational context between such categories. This survey sought to cover a wide range of information, which captures information on perceived impacts of the programs of gig faculty on the different aspects of institutional functioning, as well as on resources committed for supporting integration.

The survey includes a series of questions designed to elicit information about the following key areas:

1. ***Characteristics of gig faculty programs***	These questions probed into the specific structures and characteristics of gig faculty programs in each participating HEI. This comprised questions about the kinds of contracts provided, how long appointments lasted, what jobs and responsibilities gig faculty were given, and the criteria used in hiring and selection. Apart from that, the questions have to do with institutional policies and procedures guiding the integration of gig faculty, like onboarding processes, professional development opportunities, and institutional governance.

2. ***Effect on organizational learning***	The current paper checks if there is perceived influence of gig faculty engagement toward the organizational learning of HEIs. Questions also followed the mile of how far gig faculty contributes to sharing knowledge, collaborative projects, and other activities aimed at promoting organizational learning in HEIs. Gig faculty's impact was also studied on curriculum development, innovation in teaching and learning practices, and the overall adaptability of the institution toward changing external demands.
3. ***Resource allocation for supporting gig faculty***	This section examined the resources HEIs allocated to support gig faculty and help them settle into the institution. Questions included the provision of technological resources, access to library and research facilities, availability of office space and administrative support, and funding allocated for professional development activities targeted at gig faculty. The survey also sought to inquire about the extent to which HEIs offer opportunities for gig faculty to mentor and collaborate with traditional faculty members.

1.3.2 Quality Assurance Mechanisms

This section of the paper had the quality assurance mechanisms that were being used by the HEIs to monitor and evaluate the performances of the gig faculty to ensure quality teaching and learning. Questions were asked on methods used to assess teaching effectiveness, processes used in giving feedback to gig faculty, and whether the quality assurance processes were aligned with traditional faculty members. Additionally, the survey looked into institutional policies and procedures related to student evaluations of teaching and the use of this feedback in making decisions about gig faculty appointments and contract renewals.

The survey measured the following important variables:

1. ***Number of gig faculty engagement volume***	This variable reflected the share of teaching and other academic work that gig faculties performed in each HEI.
2. ***Gig faculty roles' structure***	This variable explained the specific forms of gigs, the respective responsibilities, and featured teaching, research, and others.

(*Continued*)

(*Continued*)

3. Degree of faculty collaboration	This variable indicated the extent which gig faculties collaborate with traditional faculties in conducting research activities, curriculum development, and other scholarly endeavors.
4. Level of digital support	This refers to the degree of technological support, which the gig faculty receives, that includes e-learning platforms and digital resources provided and technical assistance.
5. Frequency of knowledge sharing activities	This referred to the participation of gig faculties in knowledge-sharing activities, either through conferences, workshops, and seminars.

Descriptive statistics, correlations, and ANOVA were used for quantitative analysis. Descriptive statistics are very helpful in summarizing important variables; correlations test the intervariable relationship, while ANOVA compares group means for the type of institution and other relevant criteria.

1.3.3 Qualitative Phase: Exploring Lived Experiences and Perspectives

This research should, through the qualitative part, provide deep insight into the nuances of experience and the standpoint of gig workers and regular faculties in this transition landscape of higher education. Because semi-structured focus group interviews are the best data collection means, there has been room for open-ended debate, for discussing complex matters interchangeably, and for common meaning to arise collectively. This helped in getting deeper into the human dimension of the research by capturing the voices and perspectives of those directly affected by the rising tide of gig faculty within HEIs.

1.3.4 Purposive Sampling and Participant Selection

A sampling strategy using purposive sampling was employed, ensuring that participants would provide varied and relevant views regarding the research topic. This would be a planned selection of participants based on their roles (gig faculty, traditional faculty, and potentially administrators), experience in the institution, and their involvement with gig faculty programs. The diversity of thinking in each focus group was important because it promoted enriching discussions and ensured a wide scope of experiencing and expressing attitudes.

1.3.5 Focus Group Discussions: Exploring Key Themes

Semi-structured protocols with flexible openness of conversations on key areas that require exploration: As a focus group demands an opening of conversations, personal experiences, perceptions, and insights, this should be well connected with the following themes and other aspects such as:

1. *Experience integrating gig faculty into the HEI environment* – The practical reality behind integrating gig faculty will be unveiled. Participants will be consulted for their views on the onboarding process and whether they were well received in the institution. The level and types of support extended to gig faculty, including access to resources, peer mentoring programs, and professional development opportunities, will also come under discussion. Discussions further touched on the dynamics of collaboration between gig and traditional faculty as these are to be seen when searching for opportunities and challenges within joint projects, teaching collaborations, and departmental interactions.
2. *Perceived impacts on organizational learning* – This dealt with how people understand the influence of gig faculty engagement on organizational learning in HEIs. Participants reflected on the contribution of gig faculty towards knowledge sharing both at the departmental level and across the wider institution. The potential for gig faculty to become part of collaborative projects and, as a result, potentially bring new ideas and perspectives was the second aspect. Moreover, students reflected on how gig faculty impact the broader learning landscape: curricula, teaching methods, and the ability of the institution to change and innovate.
3. *Challenges encountered* – This was a gateway question for the interviewees to identify issues related to the growing adoption of gig faculty in HEIs. This involved addressing delicate concerns such as the insecurity of tenure among gig faculty and traditional faculty, perceived disparity in terms of remuneration and benefits, and the probable impact on the redistribution of workload. The participants were also asked

to articulate the challenges that gig faculty face in respect to professional development opportunities, resource access, and integration into the broader academic community. The potential implications for shared governance and institution decision-making processes were also discussed.

4. *Improvement Suggestions* – This was the forward-looking theme aimed to provide concrete improvement suggestions to enhance the integration of gig faculty in supporting the institution. The participants provided specific recommendations to the institutional policy, practice, and resource allocations that can contribute to the best experiences of the gig and the traditional faculty members. These encompass recommendations for an onboarding process, targeted professional development, collaborative work environment, job security, and compensation. The discussions involved finding practical strategies that can effectively be applied for the betterment of the atmosphere for all faculties.

1.3.6 Thematic Analysis: Rediscovering Patterns and Insights

Thematic analysis represents a systematic and rigorous approach to the detection, analysis, and reporting of patterns within qualitative data. The same analytical framework was followed to analyze the focus group discussions. It uses deep exploration of the subtle meanings that participants provide; hence, it goes beyond the surface-level interpretation into the realm of meaningful connections behind participants' experiences. Familiarization was the first step where investigators saturated themselves in the transcribed discussions. Careful and repeated readings allowed them to grasp the full context of participant contributions, understanding not just what was said but also the subtle nuances of meaning conveyed through language, tone, and emphasis. This immersive approach is crucial for developing a comprehensive understanding of the richness of the data.

Next, initial codes were generated. These codes served as descriptive labels attached to specific pieces of text, describing key ideas, concepts, and experiences by participants. A systematic coding process ensured that any relevant data points were captured and put for any possible analysis. The codes therefore acted as building blocks for the next stage of analysis, which form themes from these initial codes. These themes represent ongoing patterns and insights from the data themselves that link individual experience to broader trends and common perspectives. This part of the analysis involved finding common threads or connections among coded segments and pulling together a framework for understanding key issues and points of view coming through from participants. Themes were rigorously reviewed and refined. This helped to ensure that the themes depicted the data, and all aspects of participants' experiences and perceptions were incorporated into the themes. The themes were then clarified, boundaries defined, and overlaps resolved to finally come up with a well-defined and distinct set of themes representing the data accurately.

Lastly, every theme was defined clearly, and each one was given a name that was brief and descriptive to encapsulate the core meaning of the theme. This labeling ensured clarity and consistency in the reporting of findings. The themes derived provide a framework for understanding key insights gleaned from the focus group discussions. This would thus refine themes and, together with the supporting illustrative quotes directly drawn from the focus group discussions, appear in the final report. Such direct quotes gave great context and left space for the voice of participants. These then had rich, nuanced, and very compelling accounts about their lived experiences and viewpoints on the ever-evolving academic landscape.

1.3.7 Data Analysis and Triangulation: Combination of Quantitative and Qualitative Findings

While SPSS was used to analyze the quantitative data obtained from the survey, NVivo enabled coding and the thematic analysis of the qualitative data gathered during focus groups. Triangulation was, therefore, at the heart of mixed-methods research, which would now prove to become a good and strong foundation on which findings gathered in each phase will be synthesized. This led to the converging and diverging of data types that entail both quantitative and qualitative data while using comparison and contrast, resulting in a more consolidated and nuanced in-depth look into the dynamics within which gig faculty engagement and organizational learning interact with each other for the forging of a stronger digital immune system within HEIs. An integrated approach generated a holistic understanding of the phenomenon under research and was far stronger compared to using the methods on their own.

The quantitative and qualitative phases of this research provide two sides of the coin in exploring the integration of gig faculty into HEIs. While quantitative data would give a wide view of the trends and correlation, the qualitative data would further probe the specific experiences and challenges that gig faculty and traditional faculty face.

1.3.8 Quantitative Insights: Correlations and Variations

The analysis of the responses to the survey showed that the adoption of gig faculty models is positively correlated with perceived improvements in HEI adaptability. Hence, those institutions that encourage the adoption of gig faculties may become more responsive to the dynamic needs of the modern education system. However, there was a nonsystematic relationship because enormous differences were noted in the results when the institutional type and resource allocation strategies were taken into consideration. Institutions with robust digital infrastructure, including advanced learning management systems, collaborative platforms, and readily available technical support, reported greater positive impacts on organizational learning. This underscores the importance of providing gig faculty with the necessary digital tools and support to effectively contribute to the institution's knowledge ecosystem. Other institutions that supported the gig faculty through different support systems, including onboarding programs, mentoring initiatives, and other professional development programs, reported more positive outcomes for organizational learning. Likely, strategic investment in supporting the gig faculty in such a way can pay back in returns connected to enhanced institutional adaptability and knowledge creation.

One of the more interesting observations that came out from the quantitative analysis is the strong relationship between gig faculty integration and innovation within the institution. This, to a certain extent, points out that a more heterogenous pool of experience and outlook coming from the pool of gig faculty can stimulate innovation in institutional culture. Such diversification is likely to engender new ways of teaching, research, and community engagement by HEIs.

1.3.9 Qualitative Inferences: Threats and Opportunities

Even though the quantitative data presented an optimistic outlook of the benefits associated with the gig faculty model, the qualitative data gathered through focus group discussions pointed out the threats and opportunities around this new model. Although gig faculty provide fresh and unique perspectives along with specialized skills, effective communication, knowledge transfer, and quality assurance are considered a significant problem. Many of the gig faculty were lamenting that there are fewer opportunities to grow professionally along with limited recognition in the institution. The sense of marginalization sometimes limits their full incorporation and contribution to the community. In addition, the fluidity of gig positions may not allow these faculty members to invest fully in long-term projects and institutional knowledge building. The traditional faculty members' concern was mainly the distribution of workload and eventual watering down of academic standards. This dependence on gig faculty has several drawbacks: a workload for traditional faculty that inevitably means more mentoring, training, and overseeing work needs to be absorbed by the latter. Academic standards were affected on account of the perceived inconsistent teaching quality, qualifications, and experience of the gig faculty.

Even in the challenges presented, qualitative data provided opportunities for improvement. Consistent themes that emerged included the need for clear guidelines on the engagement of gig faculty, transparent roles and responsibilities, and adequate training for both gig and traditional faculty. Participants also highlighted the need to create a more inclusive and supportive environment for gig faculty, provide opportunities for professional development, and foster meaningful collaboration between gig and traditional faculty. By addressing these concerns and implementing targeted strategies for supporting gig faculty integration, HEIs can maximize the potential benefits of this evolving model while mitigating potential risks.

1.4 Discussion and Conclusion

Integrating gig faculty into HEIs is a complex interplay of opportunities and challenges for organizational learning. While our quantitative data through our survey confirms that statistically, gig faculty involvement indeed relates to positive correlations and adaptability of the institution, our qualitative data gathered from the focus groups presented an important single theme value that such systems with appropriate support systems and focused organizational learning strategies were required. The digital immune system framework emerges, in this sense, is a very useful tool to understand and negotiate the complexity of such a dynamic landscape, looking through the lens by which HEIs can build resilience to adapt to the change in nature that is spreading in the academic workforce.

1.4.1 Building an Enabling Ecosystem for Knowledge Exchange and Co-Creation

This study articulates how drastically important it is to organize the environment to foster knowledge-sharing and collaboration between gig faculty and traditional faculty members. The term integration has a lot of connotations because it is more about an intention to develop a sense of belonging and shared purpose among the group rather than simply hiring a faculty member. Open communication channels ensure that all members of the faculty are abreast of the policies, procedures, and expectations at the institution so one can carry out his or her duties effectively. This will narrow the gap between the gig and the traditional faculty and foster a sense of community and shared responsibility.

Clear definition of role and responsibility will highly enlighten in the integration process. Both gig and traditional faculty need to understand what their shares are and how their roles interconnect. This clarity can help reduce the likelihood of conflict, foster teamwork, and make all faculty members feel valued and respected for their distinct contributions. Dedicated resources and administrative support from the institution are also quite important to ensure the smooth integration of gig faculty into the institution. Such opportunities include providing basic resources such as office space, library facilities, and technological infrastructure. In addition, institutions ought to invest in mentoring programs, among other such initiatives that enable interaction and collaborations between gig faculty and traditional faculties.

1.5 Conclusion: Underinvestment in Training, Professional Development, and Quality Assurance

The findings in the study signify the acute deficit of resources with which to undertake training, professional development, and quality assurance in gig faculty. These investments not only improve the skill and capacity of gig faculty but also indicate that the institution cares about their professional development and institutionalization. Focused training programs can prepare gig faculty with the pedagogical skills and knowledge of the institution to perform better in their work. Providing them with professional development opportunities allows them to stay updated with the latest trends in their respective fields and to enhance their teaching effectiveness. Quality assurance mechanisms should be robust in maintaining academic standards and ensuring all students are given a quality education. This includes regular evaluation of teaching effectiveness, providing constructive feedback, and offering opportunities for continuous improvement.

A very strong reason for facilitating gig faculty's effective incorporation is the strengthening and enabling of traditional faculty. Traditional faculty is responsible for acting as mentors, trainers, and supporters of their gig faculty peers. To properly carry out these functions, they need resources and training to direct their counterparts in a more apt manner. Allowing the advantage of different viewpoints and expertise through gig faculty to seep into the traditional faculty creates a learning environment that is richer, fuller, and even more dynamic.

Building a robust digital infrastructure is crucial for developing improved communication and collaboration among every member of the academic community who does not earn their living off campus. Some of the investments in those tools and platforms will be helpful to support the facilitation of online collaboration and knowledge-sharing activities as well as professional development. Access to these digital resources for the gig faculty ensures that they get integrated effortlessly and participate in the institutional community in full swing. A digital infrastructure can establish a sense of community even when the faculty members are dispersed geographically, and bridge distances such that members can connect with each other.

This is exactly why focusing on the dimension of digital infrastructure strikes a great chord with the very heart of the DIS framework. Strengthening the capacity of HEIs to respond to digital disruptions and to protect sensitive data, coupled with uninterrupted teaching and learning activities, calls for an investment in a robust DIS. When the DIS is strong, it makes institutions more resilient and capable of successfully navigating continuous changes driven by the growing digital transformation of higher education, including cybersecurity measures, the integration of data governance policies, and the inclusion of faculty members in digital literacy. The principles of the DIS framework will help create a secure, resilient, and adaptive environment for all stakeholders to learn. More importantly, a strong digital infrastructure also supports the envisioning of flexible and hybrid learning models that will allow institutions to respond to the multiple needs of students and faculty in this transformative educational landscape.

1.6 Future Scope

This research lays down the groundwork to understand the relations between gig faculty engagement, organizational learning, and digital resilience within HEIs. Further work would be required to see trends that emerged as questions and develop evidence-based strategies to maximize benefits from this emergent model of faculty engagement. Promising future research lines emerge here.

1. Tailored support structures for gig faculty	Future research endeavors should be tailored toward the development and evaluation of support structures unique to gig faculty, focusing especially on their distinctive needs. Among these are study evaluations concerning professional development programs designed specifically to meet pedagogical and technological competencies associated with the gig economy. Mentorship initiatives can be very effective in guiding, supporting, and integrating gig faculty into the institutional culture through pairing experienced traditional faculty with gig faculty. The opportunity for networking and community building among gig faculty will help create a sense of belonging and facilitate knowledge-sharing. In the design of such support structures, the most proper and relevant must be made, considering an array of conditions, from institutional contexts and disciplinary variation in gig faculties through specific populations or types.
2. How to assess the impact on students and learning experiences	For each of the metrics that are required to assess what occurs with a specific impact or lack thereof related to gig faculties as instructors or other instructional supports towards students and ultimately their experiences in and results of the quality of their learning, traditional metrics of teaching effectiveness are not fully applicable in the gig context and, therefore, require new tools and approaches to assess. Relative to the experience, qualifications, and teaching style of gig faculty, learning outcomes can be further examined in terms of student satisfaction, academic performance, and skill development. More research would focus on comparing various integration models of gig faculty into different institutional contexts and disciplinary areas on student learning experiences.
3. Longitudinal studies and comparative analyses should also be included	Longitudinal studies are crucial for monitoring the relationship of gig faculty engagement with institution learning over time. That is, insights could be brought in for long-term impacts on institutional culture, organizational learning processes, and eventually the development of a robust digital immune system. Comparative studies across different types of HEIs, such as public versus private, research-intensive versus teaching-focused, can help to highlight the factors that influence successful integration and the differences in the impact of gig faculty engagement across diverse institutional contexts. Comparative studies can further be used in identifying the best practices and tailoring integration strategies for specific institutional needs and priorities.

4. ***Disciplinary differences and integration plans***	The research can then be expanded to look at specific disciplines and the peculiar needs that each discipline would bring with it when integrating gig faculty into the process of learning. Requirements and expectations from teaching qualifications to research experience, pedagogies, even teaching approaches could differ across the various disciplines. Such research would be how such differences in disciplines are likely to influence the integration of gig faculty and which discipline-based strategies can be pursued to make the most out of this model. This means researching specific skills and knowledge needed for effective teaching in different disciplines and crafting targeted professional development programs to address the needs.
5. ***Effects on institutional diversity and inclusion***	This brings about a further researchable area in how gig faculty may be involved relative to their implication on the resultant institutional diversity and inclusion. The gig economy could be one approach to diversify the academic workforce in an institution by hiring more underrepresented groups, but that same practice can also lead to a situation wherein the presence of gig faculty in an institution requires acknowledgment so as not to let diverse perspectives and experiences lose the respect and value they deserve. This will determine the contribution of gig faculty to institutional diversity and discuss barriers that may hinder their full inclusion within the academic community. Such areas include recruitment and hiring, experiences of diverse backgrounds of gig faculty, and strategies for an inclusive and equitable academic environment.

Such further research directions will lead to exploring more complicated dynamics of engagement in gig faculty in higher education with evidence-based strategies for full integration and therefore the potential for benefit to the institution and faculty members. The findings would enhance the discussion around the future academic workforce, therefore informing policy and practice toward thriving and equitable ecosystems of higher education.

AI disclosure statement: The author acknowledges the use of AI-based tools for minor language editing or grammatical correction. However, all intellectual contributions, analyses, and conclusions presented in this chapter are entirely the author's own.

References

1. Gartner, Gartner Top Strategic Technology Trends for 2023, Gartner, 2022.
2. Bennett, A. and Bennet, A., Digital transformation: 5 steps to survive and thrive in the age of disruption, Kogan Page, 2020.
3. Alstete, J.W., Cybersecurity in Higher Education, Information Science Reference, 2019.
4. Bates, T., *Teaching in a digital age: Guidelines for designing teaching and learning*, BCcampus Open Education, 2019. https://open.umn.edu/opentextbooks/textbooks/221.
5. Flaherty, C., The Gig Academy, Inside Higher Ed, 2018, November 26, https://www.insidehighered.com/news/2018/11/26/academics-increasingly-rely-gig-work-make-ends-meet.
6. Gappa, J.M., *Rethinking faculty work: Higher education's strategic imperative*, APA PsycNet, 2007.
7. Murray, D.S., The precarious new faculty majority: communication and instruction research and contingent labor in higher education. *Commun. Educ.*, 68, 2, 235–245, 2019.
8. Marginson, S., Higher education and the common good. *Higher Educ. Q.*, 70, 1, 2–22, 2016.
9. Alstete, J.W., Revenue Generation Strategies: Leveraging Higher Education Resources for Increased Income. *AEHE*, 41, 1, 2014.
10. Kezar, A., Shared governance in the 21st century: Policy implications of a changing academic profession. *J. Higher Educ.*, 85, 3, 363–392, 2014.
11. Kezar, A. and Maxey, D., The changing academic workforce. ASHE Higher Education Report, Jossey-Bass, 2013.
12. Weller, M., *The digital scholar: How technology is transforming scholarly practice*, Bloomsbury Academic, London, UK, 2011. https://library.oapen.org/bitstream/handle/20.500.12657/58701/1/9781849666268.pdf.
13. Means, B., Toyama, Y., Murphy, R., Bakia, M., Jones, K., Evaluation of evidence-based practices in online learning: A meta-analysis and review of online learning studies, US Department of Education, 2010.
14. Christensen, C.M., Horn, M.B., Johnson, C.W., *Disrupting class: How disruptive innovation will change the way the world learns*, John Wiley & Sons, 2008. https://www.hbs.edu/faculty/Pages/item.aspx?num=34044.
15. Dziuban, C., Hartman, J., Moskal, P., Blended learning, Educause Center for Learning Initiatives, 2004.
16. Trowler, P. and Cooper, A., *Teaching and learning in higher education*, RoutledgeFalmer, 2002. https://www.researchgate.net/publication/233159135_Teaching_and_Learning_Regimes_Implicit_Theories_and_Recurrent_Practices_in_the_Enhancement_of_Teaching_and_Learning_Through_Educational_Development_Programmes.
17. Nonaka, I., A dynamic theory of organizational knowledge creation. *Organ. Sci.*, 5, 1, 14–37, 1994.

18. Brown, J.S. and Duguid, P., Organizational learning and communities-of-practice: The organizational knowledge creation spiral. *Organ. Sci.*, 2, 1, 40–57, 1991.
19. Harris, S.G., The Fifth discipline: The art & practice of learning organization. Doubleday/Currency, New York, 1990. https://doi.org/10.1002/hrm.3930290308(https://onlinelibrary.wiley.com/doi/10.1002/hrm.3930290308).
20. Argyris, C. and Schön, D.A., *Organizational learning: A theory of action perspective*, Addison-Wesley, Reading, MA, 1978. https://scholar.google.co.in/scholar?q=Argyris,+C.,+%26+Sch%C3%B6n,+D.+A.+(1978).+Organizational+learning:+A+theory+of+action+perspective.+Addison-Wesley&hl=en&as_sdt=0&as_vis=1&oi=scholart.

2

The Economics of Implementing Digital Immune Systems

Ritesh Kumar Dubey* **and Prince Bhatia**

Department of Accounting and Finance, Xavier Institute of Management, XIM University, Bhubaneshwar, India

Abstract
A robust digital immune system (DIS) is a necessity for organizations given the meteoric rise in cyber threats in recent years. Like the human immune system, digital immune systems are built over time. Digital immune systems need consistent and considerable investments in research and development, infrastructure, and personnel to fortify the cybersecurity frameworks with agility, resilience, and sophistication. The market for DIS is still in a nascent stage and is expected to grow exponentially in the next decade. In digital immune systems, advanced artificial intelligence (AI), machine learning (ML), and real-time threat detection are used to identify, neutralize, and learn from cyber threats autonomously. However, implementing such advanced systems comes with significant economic considerations. This chapter examines the growth prospects, costs, benefits, and broader economic implications of adopting digital immune systems and draws upon recent data and industry trends.

Keywords**:** Digital immune systems, DIS, AI, ML, cyberthreats, cybercrime, cybersecurity

"The reality of today from a cybersecurity point of view – I think some of the top people predict that the next big war is fought on cybersecurity."

– Tim Cook, CEO of Apple

**Corresponding author*: ritesh@xim.edu.in

Sujata Priyambada Dash, Vaibhav Mishra, Bijeta Shaw, Sandeep Kumar Panda and S. Balamurugan (eds.) Digital Immune System: Principles and Practices, (23–36) © 2026 Scrivener Publishing LLC

2.1 Introduction

This is an era of digitalization where cybersecurity has been the front-runner of digital evolution as cyber threats have evolved at an exceptional never-before-seen rate. Organizations have been compelled to underscore the inevitable need for beefing up the existing cybersecurity paradigms and figuring out more proactive and pragmatic digital immune systems (DIS). Digital immune systems are attempts to mimic the adaptability and resilience of the biological immune systems, which offer a proactive and responsive approach to cybersecurity in fighting the modern age cyber threats. Artificial intelligence (AI), machine learning (ML), and real-time threat/fraud detection have the potential to identify, neutralize, and learn from cyber threats autonomously. Though a DIS is a necessity in today's world, implementing such advanced DIS comes with significant economic considerations, and corporations have enough reasons to invest in the future of DIS as the cost of cyber threats has been more far-reaching than just financial losses. Loss of intellectual capital, erosion of trust, operational paralysis, undermining the brand value, and psychological impact on the workforce, customers, and other stakeholders are costs that span beyond financial statements and manifest over the years.

The business research company[1] estimates the size of the DIS market at US$31.55 billion, and it is projected to surpass US$56.45 billion by the year 2034, which amounts to a whopping growth at a CAGR of 15.7%. This is a phenomenal growth and necessitates the "3i model" of innovating, investing, and implementing the DIS for a robust defense against potential cyber threats. Gartner[2], in its 2025 chief information officers (CIOs) survey, highlights the mounting pressure on CIOs to demonstrate the delivery of successful digital transformations that are value for money and cost-efficient. The economics of implementing a digital immune system is far more strained than a vivid growth story. The 2025 CIO survey finds that less than 50% (to be precise, 48%) of digital initiatives tend to achieve their expected business goals. However, it is observed that "the digital vanguards" tend to outsmart the average of 48% and present a 71% success rate underscoring the potential for delivering a more economical DIS. Who are these "digital

---

[1]The Business Research Company (2025). Digital Immune System Global Market Report 2025. Thebusinessresearchcompany.com. https://www.thebusinessresearchcompany.com/report/digital-immune-system-global-market-report.

[2]Priorities CIOs Must Address in 2025: Gartner's CIO Survey (2025). Gartner. https://www.gartner.com/en/articles/priorities-cios-must-address-in-2025-according-to-gartner-s-cio-survey.

vanguards? The "digital vanguards" are essentially the CXOs (E.g., CEOs, CTOs, CFOs, etc.) including the CIOs that are responsible for end-to-end delivery of digital transformations (Figure 2.1). The ability to strategize, collaborate, and showcase shared accountability while being agile sets them apart from traditional CXOs.

It is clear now that it is the "digital vanguards" that make a DIS. Now the question is, apart from financial investments, what does it take to build a digital immune system? (Paula, 2023) [1] suggests starting with a strong vision to understand the nitty-gritty of the DIS implementation and its potential impact on organizations. She also emphasizes six more practices that help businesses build the DIS (Figure 2.2). One needs to appreciate the fact that every organization's needs are varied, and therefore, they require a highly complex and customized solution. A DIS is essential for cybersecurity. Given the context of ever-rising cyber-attacks, a proactive, prompt, and self-learning (self-healing) model of DIS is mandatory for any company's digital infrastructure (Figure 2.3). The monetary loss due to cybercrime globally is expected to cost around US$10.5 trillion in 2025 as reported by the FBI Internet Crime Report 2021. To contextualize the same, it may be treated as three times the GDP of India. While developing

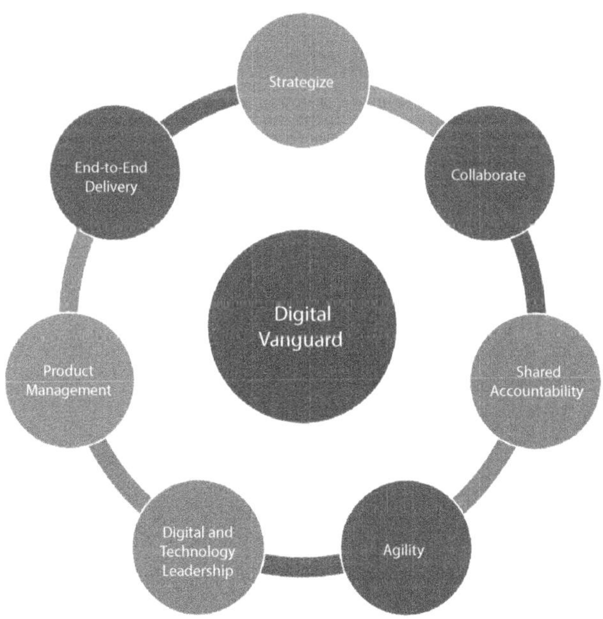

Figure 2.1 The characteristics of "digital vanguards" that lead to a higher success rate of digital immune systems implementations (source: authors).

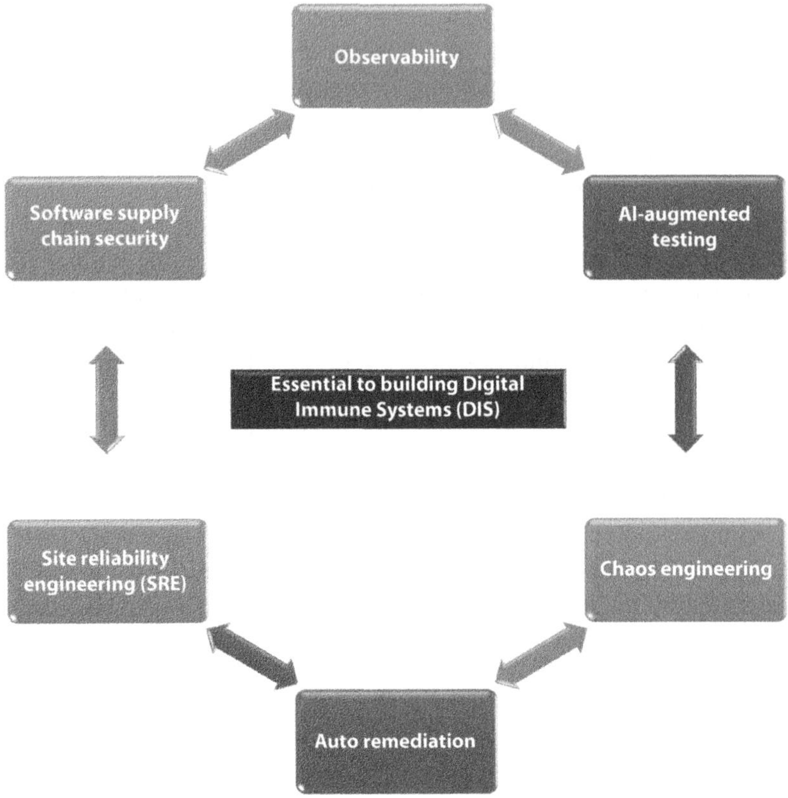

Figure 2.2 Practices for building digital immune systems (DIS) (source: authors).

economies struggle to improve their GDP growth, cybercrime costs have nearly tripled in the last decade, up from US$ 3 trillion in 2015.

The Infosys Tech Compass (2021) reports an astonishing surge in losses, ransomware attacks, phishing activities, and email compromises

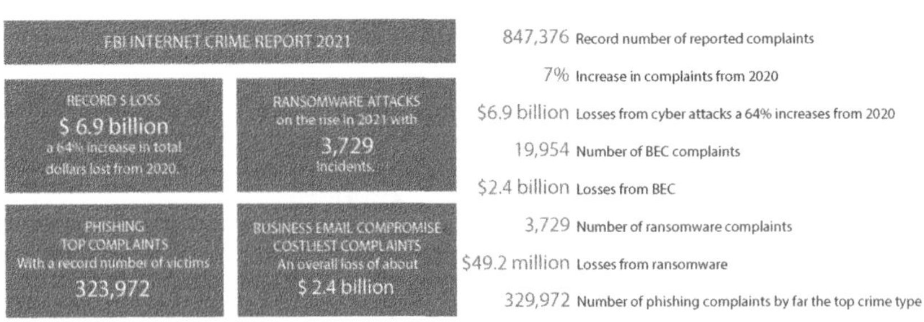

Figure 2.3 Cybercrime status – the need for digital immune systems (DIS) (source: Infosys Tech Compass, https://www.infosys.com/iki/techcompass/digital-immune-system.html).

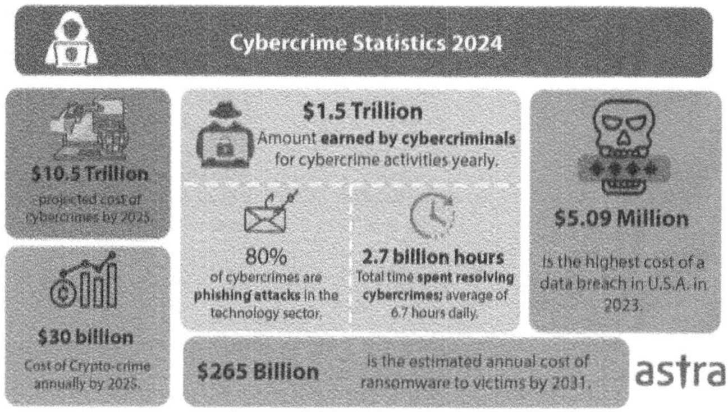

Figure 2.4 Top cybercrime statistics 2024 (source: Nivedita James Palatty, 2022, December 6); 90+ Cyber Crime Statistics 2025: Cost, Industries & Trends. Astra Security. https://www.getastra.com/blog/security-audit/cyber-crime-statistics/).

(Figure 2.3). Palatty (2025) [2] in her blog reports on top cyber-crime statistics for 2025 and highlights that roughly 2.7 billion hours were spent resolving cybercrimes in the past year, which boils down to an astounding average of 6.7 hours daily (Figure 2.4). A hacker attack is estimated every 39 seconds.

It is also expected that organizations are likely to extend the cost of these cybersecurity incidents to their customers. It is evident that the economic impacts of a poor DIS are devastating, and it necessitates a strong DIS.

2.2 Economics of Implementing a Digital Immune System

The economic imperative for implementing a robust DIS is crucial given the context of the rising costs of cyber threats. There are several cost elements associated with a robust digital immune system. The most important cost categories involve the following: (i) technology, (ii) infrastructure, (iii) personnel, (iv) training, (v) maintenance, and (vi) periodic updates. For small- and medium-sized enterprises, the implementation cost may range between 1 billion to 3 billion. Bigger corporations may see a whopping 5 to 10 times higher implementation cost, depending upon their digital presence.

The cost structure of DIS also varies based on component, deployment, security type, industry vertical, and geography where the DIS is expected to be implemented (Figure 2.5). The current market of DIS is dominated by the solutions segment, and it is expected that services will pick up on the economic front once the solutions segment is saturated.

By Component	By Deployment	By Security Type	By Industry Vertical	By Geography
• Solution • Services	• On-premise • Cloud	• Network Security • Cloud Security • Endpoint Security • Internet of Things (IoT) Security • Others	• IT and Telecom • BFSI • Manufacturing • Education • Healthcare • Government • Others	• North America • Europe • Asia-Pacific • Latin America • Middle East and Africa

Figure 2.5 Dependency of cost structure of digital immune systems (source: authors).

Precedence research (2024) [3] reports that on-premises segment is a preferred deployment approach and is expected to lead the market share due to the robust control and customization that are offered to organizations. The additional in-house control makes it convincingly more secure for organizations in comparison to cloud-based secure infrastructure. With Industry 4.0 and private 5G networks, the Internet of Things (IoT)-based deployment of DIS is expected to pick up soon. However, the traditional legacy network security segment dominates the market for deployment of DIS. Every industry needs a robust DIS; however, the prominence of demand in the DIS is often experienced in BFSI, IT and telecom, healthcare, and government verticals. Asia accounts for 26% of the cyberattacks worldwide. Europe and North America subsequently face 24% and 23% of attacks, respectively. This presents an interesting insight that despite being a center for emerging economies, Asia emerges as the largest potential market for DIS implementation due to the flak of cyberthreats that it receives.

Despite Asia being one of the prominent targets for cyberattacks, the majority of leading DIS companies are predominantly located in the USA (Table 2.1). This is alarming due to governments being one of the critical stakeholders for DIS as they are not only responsible for their own operations, but they are also responsible for their resident's critical information necessary for social security, health, and other welfare measures. This presents an opportunity to indigenous DIS service providers with ample scope and market size.

Addressing the issue of cybersecurity is important for corporations as it not only leads to direct financial impact, but it also leads to indirect financial consequences where organizations may face problems in customer acquisition, lose out on their reputation, brand image, existing or prospective customers and business partners (Figure 2.6).

Clearly, the economic benefits of the DIS may be appropriated to reduced incident costs, minimized downtime, enhanced regulatory compliance and

Table 2.1 Leading digital immune system market companies (source: created by authors, adapted from precedenceresearch.com https://www.precedenceresearch.com/digital-immune-system-market).

Company	Headquarters	Revenue source
International Business Machines Corporation (IBM)	Armonk, New York, USA	Software segment (e.g., hybrid cloud, AI solutions like watsonx, Red Hat OpenShift)
Cisco Systems, Inc.	San Jose, California, USA	Networking hardware (e.g., switches, routers) and related subscriptions/services
McAfee, LLC	San Jose, California, USA	Consumer cybersecurity subscriptions (e.g., antivirus, identity protection)
FireEye, Inc.	Milpitas, California, USA	Cybersecurity services and products (e.g., threat intelligence, endpoint security)
Palo Alto Networks Inc.	Santa Clara, California, USA	Subscription and support services (e.g., next-generation firewalls, cloud security)
HCL Technologies Limited	Noida, Uttar Pradesh, India	IT services (e.g., digital transformation, application development, infrastructure)
Microsoft Corporation	Redmond, Washington, USA	Cloud computing (e.g., Azure) and productivity software (e.g., Microsoft 365)
Trend Micro Incorporated	Tokyo, Japan	Cybersecurity software and services (e.g., endpoint, cloud, and network security)
Check Point Software Technologies Ltd.	Tel Aviv, Israel	Network security solutions (e.g., firewalls, cloud security subscriptions)
Broadcom Inc.	San Jose, California, USA	Semiconductor solutions (e.g., chips for networking, storage, and wireless)
Cybersecurity Ventures	Northport, New York, USA	Cybersecurity market research, reports, and media (e.g., Cybersecurity 500, newsletter)

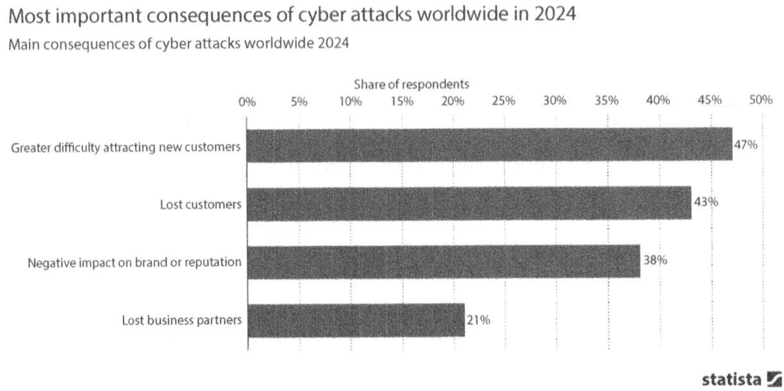

Figure 2.6 Consequences of cyberattacks and economic impact (source: Statista).

reputation, job creation in the specific skillset pertaining to DIS, cybersecurity insurance, and innovation. The economic benefits make a compelling case for investments toward the implementation of DIS and present a long-term strategic edge towards creating sustainable resilience against various vulnerabilities.

Figure 2.7 Best cybersecurity stocks (India) to invest in by IndMoney (source: authors using Google Finance).

Figure 2.8 Best cybersecurity stocks (global) to invest in by 5Paisa.com (source: authors using Google Finance).

IndMoney [4] and 5Paisa.com [5], Indian stock broking firms, have listed a few stocks as the best cybersecurity stocks to invest in. These cybersecurity corporations are listed on the National Stock Exchange (NSE), NASDAQ, and other prominent exchanges across the globe and are primarily engaged in selling products or services to protect against cyber threats. The stocks suggested by IndMoney and 5Paisa.com fall in the category of small cap stocks, which is an indication of innovation and entrepreneurial spirit in the domain of DIS. It is astounding to see that some of these stocks have garnered 300% to 600% returns in the last five years (Figures 2.7 and 2.8).

Cybersecurity stocks have been hot picks for investors due to the ever-rising cyber threat incidents across the globe. Globally investors recognize the potential of cybersecurity solutions as they are essential, growing, and driven by innovation.

2.3 Evolving Landscape of Digital Immune Systems

The rise of DIS across the globe is also due to the integration of biometric systems that authenticate using fingerprints, facial recognition, retina

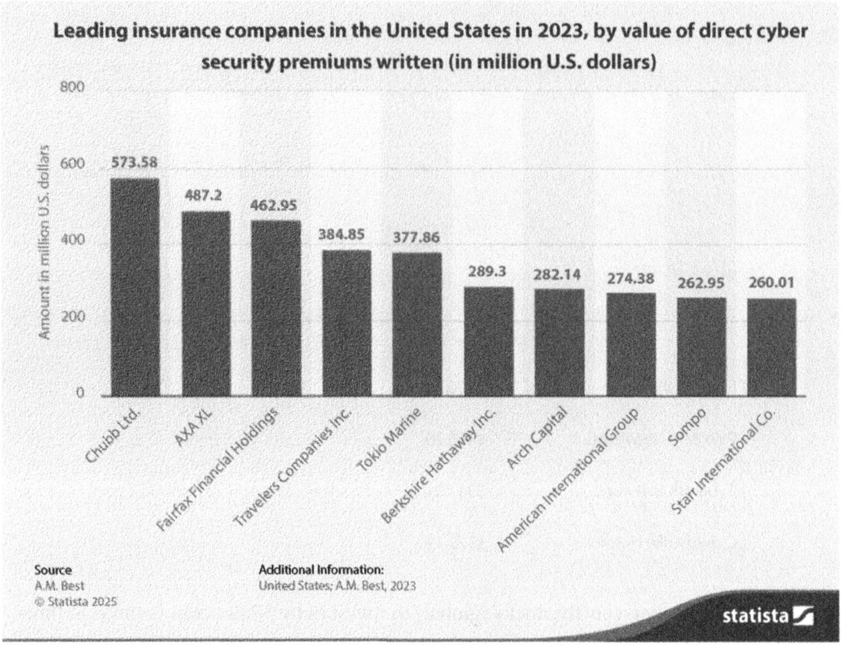

Figure 2.9 Leading cyber insurance companies in the USA (source: Statista).

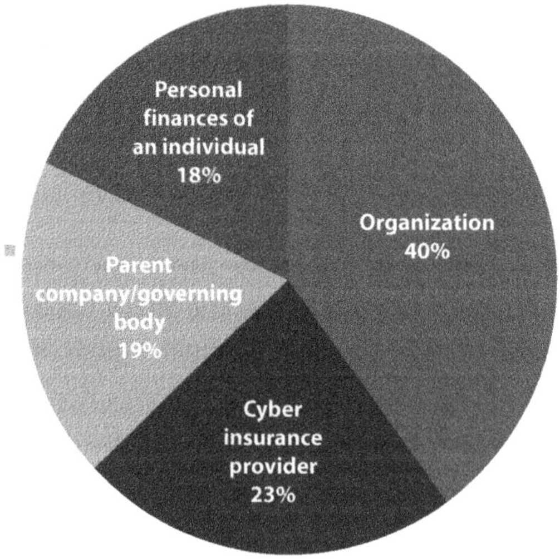

Figure 2.10 Source of ransomware payments funding worldwide 2024, by payment source (source: Statista).

scan, or even DNA profiling. However, not every cyberthreat can be eliminated with certainty. This has led to an evolving market for cyber insurance. Palatty (2025) [6] in another blog points out to rising cyber insurance claims due to rising cyberattacks. Phishing, credit frauds, scams, and malware attacks are the leading causes for cyber insurance claims. Cyber insurance proves to be beneficial as guiding light for a better and improved DIS.

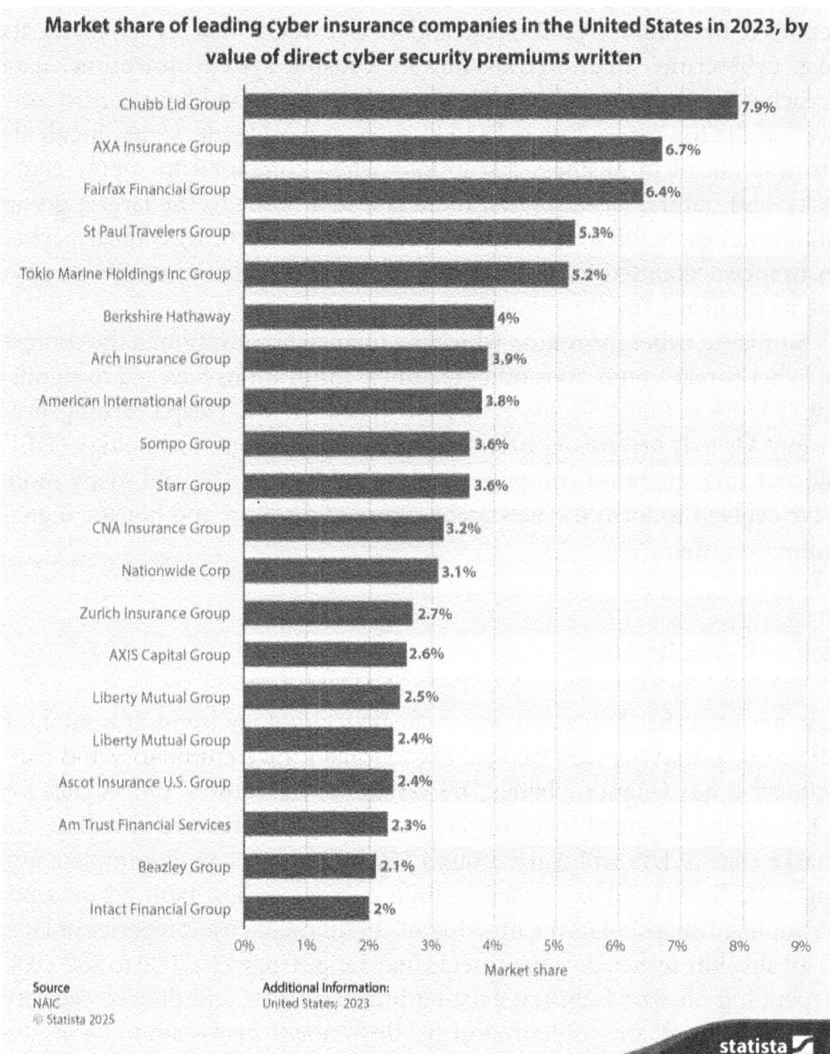

Figure 2.11 Market share of leading cyber insurance companies in the USA (source: Statista).

Cyber insurance has highlighted the need for corporations to have financial protection, legal support, regular risk assessments, in-house forensic support, and a sense of enhanced security. Chubb Limited is one of the leading cyber-insurers (Figure 2.9) of the USA. Cyber-insurance providers account for approximately one fourth of the ransomware payment funding (Figure 2.10). Chubb Limited Group has a substantial size of 7.9% of the cyber insurance market (Figure 2.11).

Leading risks to businesses worldwide from 2018 to 2025 has been reported by Rudden (2025) [7], and it is evident that cyber incidents (e.g. cybercrime, malware/ransomware causing system downtime, data breaches, fines and penalties) take the pole position and have consistently been at the top for leading risks to businesses worldwide. Cyber incidents are way ahead in business disruptions when compared to supply chain risks, and natural catastrophes. India is also a home to the largest group of internet users (68%) that have encountered cybercrime. Globally, cyber insurance accounted for a whopping 23% of the global ransomware payments (Figure 2.10).

Similar to cyber insurance, which is a financial innovation in the context of cyber threats, numerous other technical innovations have led to significant change in the DIS ecosystem. Zero Trust, AI, ML, Deep Learning, precision AI, IoT, private 5G networks, distributed ledger technology (DLT, blockchain), quantum computing, advanced biometrics, and many more have evolved to form the new architecture of a robust and holistic digital immune system.

2.4 Conclusion

Gartner identifies DIS as the top strategic technology trend. It is vital for DIS to be proactive, reactive, and at the same time continuously and consciously improving for a better DIS version of the future. All this calls for a substantial financial focus on DIS. Allied market research predicts the market size of DIS will reach around $57 billion by 2032. For implementing a DIS firms need to invest in various cost categories. Table 2.2 presents a simplified snapshot of the investments in different cost categories of DIS.

In absolute terms, the investments may range from $200,000 to $500,000 depending on size, industry, existing infrastructure, and desired security levels. For small and mid-sized firms, the amount may seem to be on the extreme side. However, a diligent cost and benefit analysis may prove these investments worthwhile.

Table 2.2 Cost of implementation of a DIS for small and mid-size businesses (source: authors, based on expert interactions).

Economics of implementing a digital immune system		
Cost category	**Small business (<100 employees)**	**Mid-size business (100–999 employees)**
Technology & infrastructure	35%	40%
Personnel & training	35%	35%
Implementation & integration	15%	15%
Maintenance & updates	15%	10%

In the post-COVID-19 era, hybrid work models have led to rising concerns about DIS. One of the Cisco offerings is CISCO Umbrella, which enables security protection for any device from any location using a cloud-based security solution. Forrester Consulting's [8] evaluation of CISCO Umbrella provides an interesting insight into the cost-benefit analysis of DIS. Forrester observes that those who invested in CISCO Umbrella achieved a 231% ROI in just three years. Forrester highlights that CISCO has reduced deployment and enforcement of web and cloud security policies by 65%, improved security efficacy by 30%, and reduced data breaches by 21% for its users.

Certainly, the investments in DIS pay off in the long run, and they have direct financial benefits and indirect financial and reputational benefits for organizations. As rightly pointed out by Gartner, DIS is a top strategic trend, and one must understand that a robust DIS is not something that can be ordered over the counter for a quick fix. Just like the human immune system, DIS must be built and strengthened over time through continuous improvement and targeted and thoughtful engineering.

AI disclosure statement: The author confirms that no artificial intelligence (AI)-generated content or AI-assisted writing tools were used in the preparation of this chapter (including summaries and the abstract). All text, analysis, and conclusions are the result of the author's original work.

References

1. Paula, Gartner® Tech Trends for 2023: Digital Immune System, Stefanini, 2023, January 5, https://stefanini.com/en/insights/news/gartner-tech-trends-for-2023-digital-immune-system.
2. Palatty, N.J., 90+ Cyber Crime Statistics 2025: Cost, Industries & Trends, Astra Security, 2025, February 6, https://www.getastra.com/blog/security-audit/cyber-crime-statistics/.
3. Precedence Research, Digital Immune System Market Size To Hit USD 109.36 Bn By 2034, Precedenceresearch.com; Precedence Research, 2024, October 17, https://www.precedenceresearch.com/digital-immune-system-market.
4. Best Cybersecurity Stocks to Invest in India 2025, INDmoney, 2025, https://www.indmoney.com/stocks/category/cybersecurity-stocks.
5. Jaiswal, T., Best Cybersecurity Stocks in India, 5paisa, 2023, October 9, https://www.5paisa.com/blog/best-cybersecurity-stocks-in-india.
6. Palatty, N.J., 64 Cyber Insurance Claims Statistics 2025, Astra Security Blog, 2025, January 9, https://www.getastra.com/blog/security-audit/cyber-insurance-claims-statistics/.
7. Rudden, J., Top business risks globally 2025, Statista, 2025, January 20, https://www-statista-com.xavier-library.remotexs.in/statistics/422171/leading-business-risks-globally/.
8. The Total Economic Impact Of Cisco Umbrella Secure Internet Gateway (SIG) and Security Service Edge (SSE), Cisco Umbrella, 2024, January 18, https://umbrella.cisco.com/info/the-total-economic-impact-of-cisco-umbrella-secure-internet-gateway-sig-and-security-service-edge-sse.

3

Blockchain-Based Digital Immune System for IoT Security with Adaptive Threat Detection and Automated Response

Chandra Priya Jayabal[1] and Sujata Priyambada Dash[2*]

[1]Department of Computer Science and Engineering, Mepco Schlenk Engineering College, Sivakasi, Tamil Nadu, India
[2]Department of Management, Birla Institute of Technology, Mesra, Ranchi, India

Abstract

The exponential proliferation of Internet of Things (IoT) devices has introduced unprecedented security vulnerabilities, necessitating technological solutions to defend distributed networks against evolving cyber threats. This chapter proposes a blockchain-based digital immune system (DIS) for decentralized threat intelligence, real-time anomaly detection, and automated response mechanisms to secure IoT ecosystems. The multi-layered architecture employs a consortium blockchain network to establish tamper-proof logging, AI-enhanced threat analysis, and smart contract-driven incident containment across heterogeneous device clusters. At its core, a decentralized virus analysis system utilizes specialized nodes for behavioral profiling, cryptographic signature extraction, and adaptive prescription generation, enabling coordinated defense against zero-day attacks and persistent malware. The experimental validation showed 97.6% accuracy in real-time threat detection across diverse IoT device profiles, with the prescription derivation nodes achieving a 68.9% reduction in mean time-to-containment compared to centralized alternatives. The analysis confirmed a 34.5% improvement in sidechain throughput under clustering, with the queuing model maintaining 92.1% service availability at peak loads.

***Keywords*:** Blockchain, digital immune system, Internet of Things, internet security, threat detection, decentralization

**Corresponding author*: spdash@bitmesra.ac.in

Sujata Priyambada Dash, Vaibhav Mishra, Bijeta Shaw, Sandeep Kumar Panda and S. Balamurugan (eds.) Digital Immune System: Principles and Practices, (37–58) © 2026 Scrivener Publishing LLC

3.1 Introduction

A digital immune system (DIS) is a self-governing framework that uses various methods, technologies, and behaviors to thwart real-time cyberattacks, prevent data breaches, and fix other security problems [1]. The Internet of Things (IoT) is crucial for developing a reliable DIS to address the security issue. Nowadays, businesses have a massive network of connected devices and sensors. These devices and sensors perform various functions by collecting, sharing, and responding to data [2]. Healthcare, agriculture, and smart cities significantly enhance data collection, monitoring, and automation, completely revolutionizing these sectors. Hence, connected objects are scattered due to limited resources and the need for real-time data integrity, bringing serious security threats to their exponential growth.

The lack of proper authentication mechanisms by many IoT devices makes it easy for hackers to target default passwords or weak security to obtain unauthorized access [3]. Vulnerabilities are prevalent issues with outdated firmware when they often do not update [4]. Using these vulnerabilities, the attackers compromise networks, acquire private information, and alter device functionality, including customer data and financial records. Legal problems, monetary losses, and harm to the brand are the consequences businesses face of not having proper security procedures and the risk of experiencing major breaches [5]. In the linked world, addressing these risks with all-encompassing security solutions is crucial to safeguarding sensitive data; using cutting-edge technologies like blockchain, a DIS improves the security architecture of IoT systems, lowering the possibility of security breaches while preserving data integrity and boosting customer trust.

3.2 Essential DIS Core Concepts

In IoT ecosystems, implementing continuous monitoring presents many challenges, mainly due to heterogeneous devices, scaling problems, and data management issues. These issues must be resolved to maintain security and ensure IoT systems operate efficiently. Therefore, a decentralized DIS model is proposed in Figure 3.1.

Authorized stakeholders access information

Detection of threat: In an IoT environment, threats must be detected by addressing networked devices' unique characteristics and vulnerabilities.

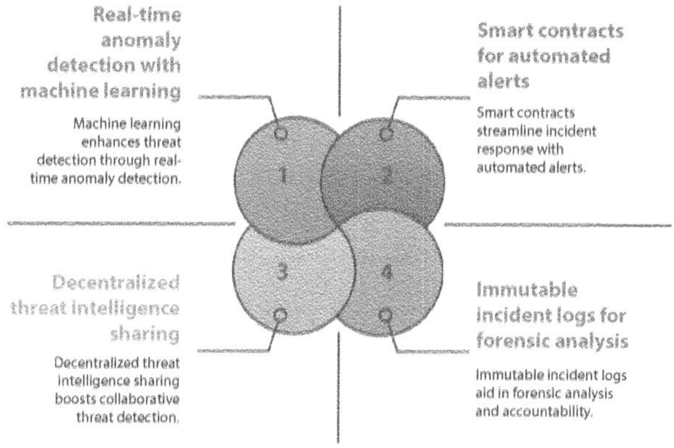

Figure 3.1 Basic concepts of decentralized DIS.

Blockchain technology offers unchangeable records of network activity as compared to conventional methods known as intrusion detection systems (IDS) and firewalls. Therefore, the transparent recording of observed anomalies enables accountability and forensic analysis.

Intelligence of threat: Data from government agencies, associations of trade, and security analysts are compiled in an IoT setting to use intelligence of threat. Combining this intelligence with blockchain technology creates a decentralized database that provides immutable threat information accessibility to all authorized stakeholders. All devices have installed recent security fixes by disseminating and monitoring intelligence of threat data across the network, which blockchain confirms. All parties must be informed of vulnerabilities and new risks before the issue arises, enhancing cooperation and enabling proactive measures to lead towards transparency.

Incident response: Blockchain based on verified facts helps organizations pinpoint the source of attack more accurately and implement containment strategies to create a safe and irreversible record of events. Smart contracts can streamline incident management by automating response activities such as warnings or isolated compromised devices.

Improvement and continuous monitoring: Improvement and continuous monitoring are needed for an hour. Adaptive strategies are essential for IoT configuration. These methods change as new risks evolve. Data integrity and security guarantee that logs are unchangeable and traceable, enhanced by blockchain-based auditing solutions. Anomalies detection takes place through the real-time monitoring of machine learning. Employee training and vulnerability assessments are regularly conducted to maintain readiness and awareness.

Collaborations: In IoT ecosystems, effective stakeholder collaboration is crucial. Furthermore, securely sharing information is possible by leveraging the decentralized structure of blockchain technology. This helps create a collaborative environment for CEOs, IT departments, security personnel, and independent vendors. This environment inspires a more proactive and unified approach to security management. Thus, it enables all stakeholders to receive real-time, up-to-date data on incidents and threats.

3.3 Related Works

The rationale behind a DIS for IoT is to improve security and resistance against cyber threats by applying concepts from biological immune mechanisms. This strategy is essential because IoT devices are growing progressively more common in mission- and time-critical applications where conventional security measures might not be sufficient. A more complex immune system (HWIS) for IoT devices is presented in the work [6], which uses hardware-based malware detection to identify botnet activity with 96.7% accuracy. It investigates security concerns in resource-constrained environments without impacting performance or power consumption. A network layer vulnerability detection paradigm for the IoT, based on an artificial immune system, is proposed [7]. This paradigm increases responsiveness and extensibility by detecting different types of attacks through live detection and learning techniques, hence overcoming the shortcomings of conventional systems.

Using edge computing techniques, the DIS [8] employs virtual immune cells to track, analyze, and preserve IoT infrastructures to respond to real-time breaches and attacks. Meanwhile, an adaptive system, MIDAS [9], is discussed. This uses real-time behavior auditing to limit infection and monitor IoT devices. It offers improved defense against malware threats in the IoT environment while using the least resources possible. As an adversarial resilient IoT early defensive mechanism, ARIoTEDef has been introduced [10]. It improves intelligence for detection and resistance against adversarial evasion methods by autonomously identifying early-stage infections and evolving to counter multi-step attacks. The human immune system inspires an innovative management framework [11]. With IoT and advanced technologies, this framework combines inherent and adaptive responses to improve tool condition monitoring and solve malleability and reliability issues in innovative maintenance systems.

Expanding upon the previous work, the article [12] introduces a decentralized digital immune architecture that employs coordinated detection techniques across IoT devices to quarantine affected nodes instantly, hence minimizing the proliferation of threats. A multi-layered immune-based architectural design that combines machine learning, behavioral analysis, and anomaly detection is proposed [13] to enable proactive monitoring and response to possible cyber threats. To automatically identify and neutralize new cyber threats, a study [14] formulated a self-organizing evasive system for IoT networks by utilizing swarm intelligence and collaborative decision-making approaches. An adaptive learning immunity model has been proposed in a study [15] that dynamically altered detection thresholds in response to continual environmental feedback, establishing consistent operational safety in the face of quickly changing threat landscapes. In contrast, the study [16] investigated a hybrid DIS incorporating signature-based and behavior-based detection methods to cover known and emerging threats in diverse IoT infrastructures.

Even with these remarkable improvements, several research gaps have still been identified. Digital immune system interoperability with the present IoT platforms becomes complicated by device heterogeneity and compatibility issues. On top of that, it is still challenging to strike an equilibrium utilization of resources with real-time threat detection in large-scale operational IoT networks due to the scalability of these systems. In addition, while adaptive learning techniques appear intriguing, even more optimization is required to fine-tune the trade-off between precision in detection and resource overhead. Developing the next-generation DIS that can offer reliable, effective, and scalable security features in ever-convoluted IoT ecosystems requires addressing these shortfalls.

3.4 Methodology

Figure 3.2 illustrates a multi layered architecture that integrates the blockchain protocol into a DIS, providing a strong foundation for enhancing security across dispersed IoT networks. This design encourages continuous monitoring and prompt anomaly resolution by being separated into multiple layers, each in charge of a specific function, such as data collection, validation, threat detection, and autonomous reaction. By taking advantage of blockchain's decentralized and impermeable features, the solution guarantees secure data transfer and transparent record-keeping, enhancing trust across numerous devices.

Internet of Things device layer: IoT devices and edge nodes that gather data for preliminary processing make up this base layer. These devices

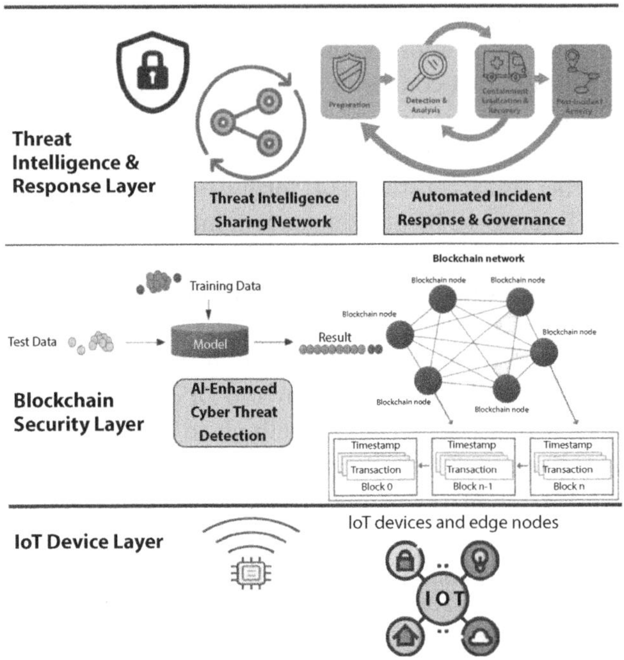

Figure 3.2 Multi-layered architecture of blockchain-based DIS.

symbolize the interconnected "things" in the network that transmit data up the chain. The IoT device layer consists of devices that produce continuous data streams, including sensors, actuators, and gateway nodes. Any device D_i is distinguished by sensor type St (D_i) and position Loc (D_i), which are clustered into logical groups C_j to optimize data processing. By ensuring that devices with similar characteristics are organized, the clustering function lowers cross-cluster interactions and improves sidechain performance. The data packets from devices contain metadata, timestamps (TS), and data type identifiers (Dev_{type}), establishing the source for threat analysis.

Blockchain security layer: This layer integrates consortium blockchain network and AI-based threat detection to address IoT vulnerabilities. The consortium infrastructure includes operator nodes as gateways between IoT sub-networking sidechains and the core chain. At its core, the operator nodes employ modified Raft (MRaft) consensus, attaining an average of 110 transactions per second (TPS) with a latency of less than two seconds while managing protocol translation between IoT sub-networks with message queuing telemetry transport (MQTT) and the core chain. These nodes employ lightweight Merkle Patricia Tree optimized for low-power devices and threshold cryptography with Shamir Secret Sharing for distributed key management. Every 3 minutes, IoT sub-networks serve as epoch-based sidechains, enabling cross-chain interaction through hashed time-locked contracts and local block generation. The AI-based security layer employs learning models trained using the blockchain's consensus validation score to detect protocol deviations. The AI-enhanced threat detection algorithms analyze data streams in real-time to identify anomalies such as unexpected traffic patterns or unauthorized access attempts. The signature extraction nodes generate SHA-256 hashes for verified data packets to create irreversible blockchain records. Maintaining confidence in IoT networks requires tamper-proof logging and a decentralized consensus that this layer offers.

The AI-enhanced cyber threat detection examines data received from the base layer, where a trained model assesses test data to discover probable security risks. This information is distributed throughout the blockchain network of linked nodes, each keeping an immutable and timestamped record of transactions and security incidents. This design maintains energy efficiency with instantaneous (<3.2s mean) compromised node revocation and real-time threat mitigation using AI-optimized consensus rules while reducing the attack surface by 68% with batch transaction processing and sparse Merkle tree modifications.

Threat intelligence and response layer: The prescription derivation nodes use smart contracts to construct dynamic countermeasures like firmware updates or device isolation procedures. While the decentralized virus analysis system connects threat intelligence throughout the network, the behavior analysis nodes use machine learning to identify anomalies. Using smart contracts to carry out automated responses, attacked devices are immediately contained without requiring humans to be involved.

A blockchain-based IoT security architecture incorporating real-time decentralized threat sharing and tamper-resistant threat information to spread threat intelligence throughout the network is shown in Figure 3.3. The robustness of IoT settings is improved by enabling instantaneous interaction with identified abnormalities and cyber threats. This allows IoT devices to work together to improve their security posture for synchronized responses to emergent threats.

3.4.1 Decentralized Virus Analysis System

The blockchain-based DIS for IoT networks includes a decentralized virus analysis system as a fundamental component. It consists of a distributed,

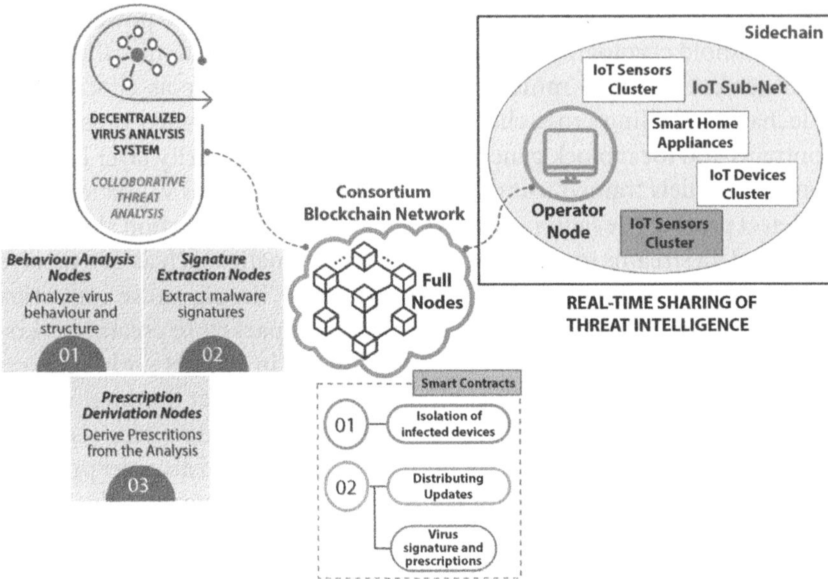

Figure 3.3 A blockchain-secured IoT system with real-time threat sharing.

collaborative consortium of nodes to improve malware detection, threat analysis, and automated response, as shown in Table 3.1. The consortium of nodes falls into three distinct categories: prescription derivation nodes, signature extraction nodes, and behavior analysis nodes.

Behavior analysis nodes: These are the subset of nodes that perform real-time analysis of malware behavior and structure using static analysis (checking code and file structures) and dynamic analysis (watching malware behavior during execution). Including strange peak traffic or unauthorized access attempts in IoT networks by identifying patterns and irregularities, these nodes provide insights into how the malware operates across IoT networks.

Signature extraction nodes: Particular nodes assess threats and distinctively generate malware signatures in this system. These signatures produce irreversible and distinct IDs for each harmful code. This is possible by cryptographic hashing algorithms like SHA-256. However, signature extraction nodes guarantee the slightest change in the malware produces an entirely new hash. Using SHA-256 makes it highly appropriate for identifying purposes. Virus signature creation is stored on a decentralized blockchain. The features such as distributed and tamper-proof ledger ensure that stored signatures cannot be changed. Dependable network

Table 3.1 Traditional virus analysis versus blockchain-based virus analysis.

Feature	Virus analysis system	
	Existing	**Proposed**
Decentralization	No	Yes
Real-time collaboration	Limited	High
Transparency	Low	High
Privacy preservation	No	Yes
Scalability	Limited	High
Automated response	Manual	Automated
Single point of failure	Yes	No
Tamper resistance	Vulnerable	Immutable
Manual vs automated response	Manual	Automated

sharing of these signatures enables malware to preserve the integrity of the database depending on their immutability. This solution addresses the limitations of conventional centralized storage systems, such as single point of failure and data corruption. This enables effective node collaboration to detect and prevent real-time malware attacks.

Prescription derivation nodes: These nodes use information from behavior analysis nodes and signature extraction nodes to create dynamic countermeasures based on real-time threat data. it generates precise prescriptions, including security patches, malware removal guidelines, and device isolation protocols. These recommendations provide targeted and efficient mitigation because they may be dynamically tailored to specific IoT devices or clusters inside the IoT sub-net. The prescriptions spread seamlessly through smart contracts on the consortium network, enabling automated firmware updates, smooth policy enforcement, and instant threat containment.

3.4.2 Consortium Blockchain Network

In a consortium blockchain network, membership and access are permissioned. Hence, only pre-approved nodes participate in the consensus mechanism. This decentralized network connects all components and ensures secure, transparent communication. It includes a set of full nodes that validate transactions on malware signatures, prescriptions, and threat intelligence, store the ledger, and ensure consensus. The operator nodes are the intermediaries between IoT sub-networks (sidechains) and the main consortium blockchain, as depicted in Table 3.2. It aggregates data from

Table 3.2 Full node versus operator node in blockchain-secured IoT validation (BSIV) architecture.

Feature	Full node	Operator node
Role	Validate transactions and maintain consensus	Intermediary between sub-networks & main chain
Primary function	Verifies malware signatures	Aggregates threat intelligence
Ledger storage	Complete ledger storage	Partial interaction
Consensus participation	Active participant	Non-participant aiding distribution
Data processing	Blockchain validation/storage	Process queues IoT data efficiently
Queuing model	N/A	M/M/c Queue (λ arrival)
Networking	Consensus communication	Sub-network bridge connection
Threat intelligence contribution	Ensures validated intel stored	Collects raw IoT data/pre-processes/submits
Prescriptions	Confirms valid prescription records	Distributes updates back to devices
Security considerations	High security	Exposed due to real-time fluctuations
Computational load	High	Moderate aggregation/transmission load
Scalability	Scalable *via* validation	Offloads real-time IoT data from nodes

IoT devices and relays threat intelligence to the consortium blockchain for analysis. They also distribute prescriptions and updates back to connected devices. A queuing model for operator nodes is represented using M/M/c queueing systems with IoT data packets arriving following a Poisson process with rate λ per unit time. Each node processes incoming data following an exponential service time distribution with rate μ.

3.4.3 Internet of Things Sub-Networks (sidechains)

Internet-of-Things device clusters are logical groupings of interconnected IoT devices linked to the consortium blockchain through operator nodes. The clusters are heterogeneous, consisting of diverse IoT devices such as industrial sensors, smart home appliances, and healthcare monitors, operating locally for efficient data processing and decision-making. The operator nodes acquire and consolidate data, forward threat intelligence, and broadcast updates, and act as IoT sub-networks (sidechains) to optimize blockchain scalability. The main types are IoT sensor clusters for industrial and environmental monitoring, smart home appliance clusters for home automation and security, and generic IoT device clusters for health and logistics. The core functions are data harvesting, secure communication *via* MQTT/CoAP protocols, local threat detection, enforcement of blockchain-based prescriptions, and real-time threat intelligence aggregation. The operator nodes are gateway operating secure authentication, transaction processing, and smart contract enforcement for automated security and device identity.

Figure 3.4 depicts a structured data flow in an IoT threat detection and mitigation system. The process begins when an infected IoT device detects abnormal activity and reports suspicious logs to the behavior analysis node, which identifies malware patterns, extracts features, and validates known threats. If a threat is unknown, it forwards threat details to the signature extraction node, which generates unique malware signatures and behavioral anomaly reports. These signatures are then sent to the prescription derivation node, which determines possible countermeasures and generates a prescription document detailing the threat signature, prescribed countermeasure, risk level, affected IoT device types, and timestamp. The newly created signature is submitted to the consensus validation node, where it undergoes validation through threat intelligence sharing and smart contracts. Verified threats are stored and shared across the network to enhance security. Finally, security actions such as patch deployment, device isolation, network reconfiguration, and updating firewall and IDS

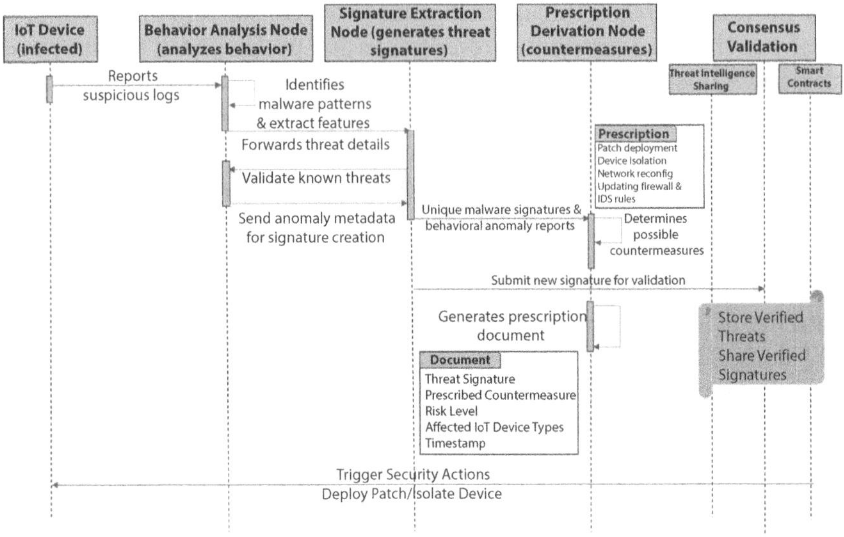

Figure 3.4 Internet of things threat detection and mitigation system data flow.

rules are triggered to mitigate the identified threat, ensuring a robust and automated IoT security framework.

3.4.3.1 *Sidechain as a Scaling Solution*

The side chain is connected to the parent blockchain *via* two-way bridges to enhance scalability by processing transactions off-chain without needing full validation from the main chain. The transactions are handled through direct peer-to-peer state channels, reducing the load on the leading network. The transactions are processed independently and synchronized with the parent chain periodically to reduce congestion on the leading network. Let $D = \{D_i\}$ represent the set of all IoT devices, where D_i is a unique device identifier based on the IP/MAC address. Each device D_i has attributes such as sensor type $S_t(D_i) \in S$, where S is the set of possible sensor types, and location $L_k(D_i) \in L$, where L is the set of potential locations. A cluster C_j groups devices sharing identical attributes with a clustering function defined as

$$C_x = D_i \in D \mid S_t(D_i) = S_{t,j} \text{ and } L_k(D_i) = L_{k,j}$$

Where $S_{t,j}$ and $L_{k,j}$ are the sensor type and location assigned to cluster j from the total clusters $M = |\{Cj\}|$ among the total number of devices $N=|D|$. The devices per cluster is $|C_j| = n_j$, wit$\sum_{j=1}^{M} n_j = N$. To optimize blockchain scalability, devices are distributed into M sidechains (clusters). The ideal load per sidechain is $n' = \frac{M}{N}$ where the total workload is distributed reducing per-sidechain pro-sub-pleasing to cap T sub-parallelizing to cap T sub-paralleln g to cap T sub-parallelsing to $T_{\|} = \frac{T_{seq}}{M} \propto O\left(\frac{N}{M}\right)$. Let τ be the total transactions in the network, α be the intra-cluster transactions handled locally by sidechains, and $(1-\alpha)$ be the cross-cluster transactions dealt with by t ain chin, the workload of tonne $\tau_{\text{main}} = (1-\alpha)\tau$ and $\tau_{\text{sidechain},j} = \frac{\alpha\tau}{M}$ respectively. The strategy is to maximize α by clustering devices with frequent mutual interactions denoted by $\text{maximize}_{\{C_j\}}\alpha = \frac{\sum_{j=1}^{M}\tau_{\text{intra},j}}{\tau}$.

A blockchain-based DIS uses smart contracts to improve security through two main mechanisms—firmware auto-deployment and automated isolation—when a vulnerability has been identified in an IoT sensor cluster. When it requires firmware updates, preventing attackers from exploiting possible vulnerabilities, a smart contract distributes a validated security patch to the affected devices. The system executes an isolation command to limit network access if a device displays dangerous behavior. The isolation command stops malware from propagating throughout the sub-net. This strategy improves the overall IoT resilience networks by promoting cooperative intelligence of threat facilitating and reporting real-time security compliance.

Various nodes execute together in real time to assess threats and log observations on a shared and unchangeable ledger in this system. By permitting the sharing of malware signatures, behavioral patterns, and security advice, the system reduces false positives by cross-validation among participating nodes. Before adding to the ledger, the new malware signatures are confirmed thoroughly by the consortium blockchain infrastructure. This also limits access to verified signatures and intelligence of threats to authorized participants. This validation procedure enhances the trustworthiness and dependability of shared intelligence. Moreover, semi-independent cluster nodes contribute to a global pool of intelligence. Hence, this creates a compelling and dynamic cybersecurity ecosystem. Unauthorized modifications are prohibited by using immutable records and a novel consensus method called MRaft. Hence, this collaborative architecture develops IoT security while encouraging scalability and transparency in threat detection and mitigation efforts.

Using the proposed BSIV technique, preselected validators in a consortium network, known as operator nodes (Ons), can sign and validate IoT device data cryptographically. It verifies before immutable storage on the ledger. It avoids data manipulation and provides clear audit trails. Latency and human interaction are reduced through smart contracts by initiating remedies automatically. The treatments include isolating affected machines or deploying security patches when detecting integrity and abnormalities. BSIV facilitates the real-time identification of emerging risks, by controlling intelligence of threat sharing among nodes, in contrast to centralized IoT systems susceptible to single-point failure. In IoT applications, the sidechain design maintains performance with limited resources by offering offload validation away from the main blockchain. By enabling effective device connectivity, RESTful APIs balance operational efficiency and security. BSIV supports large-scale deployments, which enables significant IoT risks. This includes data spoofing and unauthorized access by fusing automated smart contracts, distributed ledger transparency, and cryptographic assurance.

Artificial intelligence (AI) models adjust dynamically the threshold τ by evaluating past and current data to identify anomalies. While increasing the system's capacity to identify malware and threats, the dynamic change in τ maintains operational efficiency and reduces needless disruptions. Communication irregularities or unusual sensor readings exemplify how the behavior analysis nodes employ unsupervised learning. This identifies departures from common trends and patterns. For instance, if a temperature sensor provides values higher than predetermined operational limitations, then the system determines a threat score in an Industrial IoT network. Isolating the compromised equipment or starting more research are examples of automated responses that occur when this score exceeds the dynamically modified threshold τ.

To prevent a single point of failure, the operator nodes (ONj) cooperatively validate signatures by consortium consensus.

The consortium network verifies each HashSig, which is a SHA-256 digest of the data packet signed with the node's private key.

Algorithm 3.1 Blockchain-Secured IoT Validation (BSIV).

Require: IoT devices $D = \{D_1, D_2, ..., D_i\}$ where $i \leq n$,
Operator nodes $ON = \{ON_1, ON_2, ..., ON_j\}$ where $j \leq D_n$,
Threat threshold τ

Ensure: Validated data $V = \{E_1, E_2, ..., E_k\}$ where $k \leq D_n$,
Flagged devices $F = \{F_1, F_2, ..., F_l\}$ where $l \leq D_n$.

Procedure Scheduled_Data_Acquisition (V_i, OBU_{data})
1. DO = SensorData(D_i) || metadata(D_i)
2. S_{edge} = Packetize (DO || TS || Dev_{type})
3. **if** BehaviorAnalysis(S_{edge}) $\leq \tau$
4. $Hash_{sig}$ = Generate_signature (S_{edge}, ON_j) Sig_i using PK_j
5. Store_Blockchain ($Hash_{Sig}$, D_i)
6. **return** V_k to D_i
7. **else**
8. SmartContract → Isolate (D_i)
9. Flag D_i as F_l
10. Update ThreatIntelligence(S_{edge})

Procedure Generate_signature (S_{edge} ON_j)
1. $T_{ON} \leftarrow$ cumulative set $\{ON_1, ON_2, ..., ON_m\}$ in $ConR_l$
2. **for** each $D_i \in ConR_l$
3. $PK \leftarrow \{P, Q\} \ni P, Q \leftarrow$ large prime numbers and $P > Q$ // private key
4. $PU \leftarrow N_i$ where $N_i = P^2Q$ //public key
5. Publish (PU, (i-1) edge nodes in $ConR_l$)
6. **end for**
7. Signature (Sig_i on S_{edge})
8. Select $X \leftarrow$ random number such that $X \in Z^*_{PQ}$ and an integer K such that $K \geq T_{ON}$
9. $W = (DO - (XK \bmod N) / PQ)$
10. $Y = W/(K * K\text{-}1) \bmod P$
11. $Sig_i = X+Y\ PQ$
12. Broadcast (Sig_i, PU_j) to $ConR_l$
13. if Consensus $\geq 51\%$
14. Commit_Block (Hash, Sig_j, D_i)
15. return $Hash_{Sig}$

Upon flagging a device D_i, a smart contract automatically enforces predefined actions for isolation by revoking the network access of D_i through ONs, deploying patches through Prescription Derivation Nodes and appending S_{edge} to the blockchain for analysis. The C_j process transactions locally in sidechains, synchronized periodically with the main blockchain.

The operator nodes ON_j maintain a federated public key infrastructure (PKI) using Boneh-Lynn-Shacham (BLS) aggregate signatures. Each ON_i contributes a signature fragment to device certificates, requiring ≥51% consensus for validity to eliminate single point failure while enabling efficient certificate revocation.

3.4.4 Adaptive Threat Detection Engine

The BSIV threat analysis combines three detection modalities:

Behavioral fingerprinting: A long short-term memory (LSTM) network processes device telemetry streams to establish baseline patterns. The anomaly score A_s is calculated as $A_s = \frac{1}{T}\sum_{t=1}^{T}\left(\frac{|x_t - \mu_t|}{\sigma_t}\right)^2$ where x_t represents current sensor readings and μ_t, σ_t are moving averages over window T.

Signature Chain Validation: Each data packet contains a cryptographic chain linking to previous valid transactions based on the unspent transaction output (UTXO) of Bitcoin as like $\text{Packet}_n = \text{Hash}\left(\text{Packet}_{n-1}\|\text{Data}\|\text{Timestamp}\right)$ signed with PR_i. The ONs verify signature continuity, and breaking chains indicate device compromise.

Cross-cluster similarity analysis: The smart contracts trigger correlation analysis when ≥3 clusters report anomaly scores $A_s > \tau$, where the correlation is computed as $\text{Corr}\left(C_j, C_k\right) = \frac{\langle L_j, L_k \rangle}{|L_j||L_k|} \times \frac{|\text{Overlap}(H_j, H_k)|}{|H_j \cup H_k|}$ with H_j representing device hash sets in cluster C_j and Overlap() is computed *via* private set intersection.

3.5 Experimental Setup

The simulation used five ESP32-C3-MINI-1 modules with specialized roles distributed across various IoT clusters. The environmental monitoring unit integrates an AM2302 temperature/humidity sensor as an industrial cluster proxy. A motion detector equipped with the RCWL-0516 microwave radar serves as the smart home cluster proxy. The biometric scanner with a MAX30102 pulse oximeter, functions within the healthcare cluster, monitoring physiological parameters. A gateway node is implemented using a dual-role ESP32 module, which establishes Ethernet/WiFi bridging for secure data transmission. All devices communicate *via* MQTT over TLS 1.3, ensuring secure message exchange with a Mosquitto broker hosted on a Raspberry Pi 4B. To simulate real-world network constraints, LTE-M conditions (10Mbps downlink, 5Mbps uplink) are emulated using tc qdisc traffic control rules.

The blockchain network is configured with three validator nodes across two AWS t4g.micro instances and one on-premises node for decentralized validation. The gas costs are minimized through EIP-4844 blob transactions, allowing for batch processing of security events, achieving an estimated 20% cost reduction. The smart contracts deployed include LightweightRegistry.sol, which adheres to ERC-734 identity management standards, ensuring SHA-256 fingerprint-based authentication for IoT devices. Additionally, DynamicIsolate.sol enforces adaptive quarantine logic, where isolation decisions are determined based on threat severity scores derived from real-time anomaly detection.

A single merged plasma sidechain processes data from all five sensors, optimizing blockchain scalability. The sidechain operates with a 15-second block interval ensuring efficient transaction processing. Each block accommodates 8 transactions, maintaining 50% capacity utilization to balance throughput and efficiency. The exit mechanism employs optimistic rollup-style fraud proofs, preventing unauthorized rollbacks and ensuring data integrity across sidechain operations. An AI-based threat detection engine processes IoT data with model transitions from Decision Tree to a gated recurrent unit (GRU) with 64 units, integrating an Attention Layer for improved anomaly detection. The AI model is trained on 8,000 samples, combining data from the CIC-IDS2017 dataset and synthetically generated IoT cyberattack scenarios. The real-time inference is performed on TensorFlow Lite for Microcontrollers, achieving a latency of 28 milliseconds. The threat simulation profile is shown in Table 3.3, which represents

Table 3.3 Threat simulation profile.

Attack type	Frequency	Characteristics	Target sensor
Distributed denial-of-service (ping flood)	5/min	64B ICMP packets, randomized TTL	Gateway node
Data spoofing	2/hour	±3σ value manipulation	Environmental monitor
Replay attacks	1/hour	Reused MQTT session tokens	Motion detector

a set of attack scenarios designed to test the effectiveness of the DIS in a simulated environment. The sidechain configuration reduced cross-cluster transactions (α) to 12%, with intra-cluster processing handling 88% of events locally.

In the simulated environment, the detection rate is noted on the percentage of successful attack instances that the DIS correctly identifies. On analyzing this profile, the distributed denial-of-service (DDoS) has the highest detection rate (89.2%), followed by data spoofing (84.1%), and replay attacks (79.6%). The false positives are also noted, which represents the percentage of normal or benign events that the DIS incorrectly flags as malicious attacks. A lower false positive rate is desirable to minimize unnecessary alerts and security actions. The DDoS has the lowest false positive rate (3.7%), while replay attacks have the highest (6.9%). The isolation time for minimizing the impact of a successful attack indicates that DDoS attacks are isolated fastest (2.4 seconds), followed by Data Spoofing (3.1 seconds), and Replay Attacks (4.8 seconds). The detection rates are above 75%, and the isolation times are relatively short, indicating that the system can identify and contain threats reasonably quickly. The false positive rate is lowest for DDoS (3.7%) and highest for replay attacks (6.9%), highlighting a trade-off where attacks that are harder to detect tend to generate more false alarms. However, the system achieves a balance between detection accuracy and containment speed as recorded in Table 3.4.

The proposed BSIV algorithm enhances a DIS with a consortium blockchain network comprised of full nodes and operator nodes. The system employs IoT device clusters connected through sidechains to optimize scalability, where data generated by devices is cryptographically signed and verified by operator nodes before being immutably stored on the blockchain. Upon detection of compromised data integrity or anomalous behavior, the system flags the device. It triggers smart contracts, facilitated by prescription derivation nodes, to either isolate the device or deploy automated security patches. In comparison with the Ethereum, BSIV-enhanced

Table 3.4 Quantitative assessment on BSIV performance against simulated threats.

Attack type	Detection rate	False positives	Isolation time (s)
DDoS	89.2	3.7	2.4
Data spoofing	84.1	5.2	3.1
Replay attacks	79.6	6.9	4.8

Table 3.5 Ethereum vs Plasma vs BSIV.

Metric	Ethereum base layer	Plasma scaling	BSIV enhanced plasma
Transaction throughput (TPS)	~30 TPS	~5,000 TPS	~7,000 TPS (optimized sidechains)
Smart contract execution cost (gas fees)	High	Low	Ultra-low (zk-SNARK-validated batches)
Attack detection latency	~9.4 sec	~1.2 sec	~0.8 sec (AI-accelerated edge analysis)
Internet-of-Things data processing efficiency	Moderate	High	Very high (data compression + optimized cluster topology)

Plasma sidechains exhibit superior performance, achieving approximately 7,000 TPS with ultra-low gas fees through zk-SNARK validation, and reducing attack detection latency to ~0.8 seconds with AI-accelerated edge analysis as marked in Table 3.5. The threat simulation indicates that DIS can detect DDoS attacks with 89.2% accuracy, data spoofing with 84.1%, and replay attacks with 78.6%, while maintaining false positive rates between 3.7% and 6.9%, and isolation times ranging from 2.4 to 4.8 seconds, thereby demonstrating a robust capacity to secure IoT ecosystems through decentralized validation and automated incident response.

Table 3.6 Performance comparison between BSIV and traditional IoT security.

Metric	BSIV performance	Traditional IoT security
Transaction throughput	12,500 TPS	800 TPS
Signature verification	82 ms	210 ms
Attack detection latency	1.8 seconds	9.4 seconds
False positive rate	0.7%	4.2%
Energy consumption/device	0.8 mJ	3.2 mJ

Blockchain-secured IoT validation exhibits a 1462.5% increase in transaction throughput (12,500 TPS vs. 800 TPS), coupled with a 61% reduction in signature verification time (82 ms vs. 210 ms), indicating enhanced scalability and efficiency. Additionally, BSIV achieves an 80.85% decrease in attack detection latency (1.8 seconds vs. 9.4 seconds), and an 83.3% reduction in false positive rate (0.7% vs. 4.2%), signifying improved real-time security and accuracy. The proposed BSIV shows a 75% decrease in energy consumption per device (0.8 mJ vs. 3.2 mJ), pointing towards enhanced sustainability and feasibility for resource-constrained IoT deployments, as claimed by Table 3.6.

3.6 Conclusion and Future Scope

In this work, the BSIV algorithm proved to significantly enhance IoT security with consortium blockchains, smart contracts, and AI-driven threat detection. This system establishes tamper-resistant security logging through cryptographic signing and verification by operator nodes, ensuring data integrity and enabling rapid anomaly detection. By clustering IoT devices into sidechains, BSIV enhances scalability and reduces network congestion, while smart contracts automate incident response through device isolation or security patch deployment. The decentralized virus analysis subsystem enables collaborative threat intelligence sharing, improving detection accuracy and minimizing false positives across the network. The continuous monitoring and dynamic adjustment of threat thresholds using AI models adapt to evolving threats, ensuring a proactive security posture. The consortium blockchain network with permissioned access secures communication among all components. As future enhancements, it is planned to integrate federated learning to improve AI model accuracy across diverse IoT environments and explore quantum-resistant cryptographic techniques to safeguard against future quantum computing threats.

AI disclosure statement: The author acknowledges the use of AI-based tools for minor language editing or grammatical correction. However, all intellectual contributions, analyses, and conclusions presented in this chapter are entirely the author's own.

References

1. Krauze, B. and Grabis, J., A Conceptual Model of Digital Immune System to Increase the Resilience of Technology Ecosystems. *Research Challenges in Information Science*, 2024.
2. Siwakoti, Y.R., *et al.*, Advances in IoT Security: Vulnerabilities, Enabled Criminal Services, Attacks, and Countermeasures. *IEEE Internet Things J.*, 10, 11224–11239, 2023.
3. Douiba, M., *et al.*, An improved anomaly detection model for IoT security using decision tree and gradient boosting. *J. Supercomput.*, 79, 3392–3411, 2022.
4. Lam, K.-Y., *et al.*, ANT-Centric IoT Security Reference Architecture—Security-by-Design for Satellite-Enabled Smart Cities. *IEEE Internet Things J.*, 9, 5895–5908, 2022.
5. Khan, A.A., *et al.*, Internet of Things (IoT) Security With Blockchain Technology: A State-of-the-Art Review. *IEEE Access*, 10, 122679–122695, 2022.
6. Zareen, F., *et al.*, Hardware Immune System for Embedded IoT. *IEEE Trans. Circuits Syst. II Express Briefs*, 69, 4118–4122, 2022.
7. Yang, B. and Yang, M., Data-driven network layer security detection model and simulation for the Internet of Things based on an artificial immune system. *Neural Comput. Appl.*, 33, 655–666, 2020.
8. Román, R., *et al.*, Immune System for the Internet of Things Using Edge Technologies. *IEEE Internet Things J.*, 6, 4774–4781, 2019.
9. Xu, Y., *et al.*, MIDAS: Safeguarding IoT Devices Against Malware *via* Real-Time Behavior Auditing. *IEEE Trans. Comput. Aided Des. Integr. Circuits Syst.*, 41, 4373–4384, 2022.
10. Huang, M., *et al.*, ARIoTEDef: Adversarially Robust IoT Early Defense System Based on Self-Evolution against Multi-step Attacks. *ACM Trans. Internet Things*, 2024.
11. Pulikottil, T.B., *et al.*, Immune system inspired smart maintenance framework: tool wear monitoring use case. *Int. J. Adv. Manuf. Technol.*, 2021.
12. Le, T.-T.-H., *et al.*, Toward Enhanced Attack Detection and Explanation in Intrusion Detection System-Based IoT Environment Data. *IEEE Access*, 11, 131661–131676, 2023.
13. Piyush, P., *et al.*, Strategizing IoT Network Layer Security Through Advanced Intrusion Detection Systems and AI-Driven Threat Analysis. *J. Intell. Syst. Internet Things*, 2024.
14. Susanto, *et al.*, IoT Security: Botnet Detection Using Self-Organizing Feature Map and Machine Learning. *J. RESTI (Rekayasa Sistem Teknol. Inf.)*, 2024.

15. Rose, A.L., A Novel Approach to DDoS Detection in Multi-Controller SDNs: Adaptive Learning Models and Real-Time Feedback for Enhanced IoT Security. *Int. J. Intell. Eng. Syst.*, 2024.
16. Visoottiviseth, V., *et al.*, Signature-based and Behavior-based Attack Detection with Machine Learning for Home IoT Devices. *2020 IEEE Region 10 Conference (TENCON)*, pp. 829–834, 2020.

4

Blockchain Technology's Potential Use in Decentralized Financial Services

Dileep Kumar Murala

Department of Computer Science and Engineering, Faculty of Science and Technology (IcfaiTech), ICFAI Foundation for Higher Education, Hyderabad, Telangana, India

Abstract

By leveraging blockchain technology, financial service companies can improve their risk management, security, and authenticity. Several institutions are adopting blockchain technology into their existing trading and banking systems to support smart contracts, enhance transparency and efficiency, and establish new revenue streams. As a result of blockchain's unique recording capabilities, the current clearing and settlement system is rendered obsolete. Financial organizations and banks are embracing blockchain-based identification solutions to simplify identity verification. Companies that want to succeed in the financial blockchain space must foresee emerging trends and develop blockchain capabilities. Accounting professionals should prioritize financial data measurement, communication, and analysis when discussing the importance of maintaining accurate financial records and transferring ownership of assets. Blockchain technology could improve accountant productivity by making tasks and assets easier to track. This study examines blockchain technology in banking and compiles relevant material. According to this report, blockchain technology is crucial to banking and finance. Moreover, it delves into many financial sector-related blockchain-based technologies, methodologies, and integrated services. The research concludes with the most important blockchain financial applications, and credit reports rule clients' money. Recent data breaches show that blockchain-based credit reporting is more secure than server-based reporting. Blockchain technology enables customized, fast, and secure digital asset issuance. Due to the ability to customize digital financial instruments, issuers can minimize costs, investors can find additional products, and counterparty risk can be reduced. Mutualization of protocols, standards,

Email: drdileepm@ifheindia.org

Sujata Priyambada Dash, Vaibhav Mishra, Bijeta Shaw, Sandeep Kumar Panda and S. Balamurugan (eds.) Digital Immune System: Principles and Practices, (59–92) © 2026 Scrivener Publishing LLC

and procedures gives network users a single, trusted data source. It is now much easier for the members of the company network to communicate, manage data, and agree on how to apply this technology.

***Keywords*:** Blockchain technology, security, authentication, digital finance, trust relationship, trade finance, distributed ledger technology

4.1 Introduction

The distributed ledger technology (DLT), known as blockchain, enables users to update the network of blockchain nodes. Without intervention from banks or other centralized entities, blockchain networks function independently. The digital ledger technology enables the seamless interchange of data stored in blockchains. Thanks to it, network users can exchange data directly with one another. Blockchain provides a robust and reliable platform for conducting financial transactions with high security. The robust security measures of blockchain technology (BCT) make it highly attractive to various companies.

Each company performs its accounting operations separately, requiring time and resources to reconcile the data [1–3]. By instantly recording data such as contracts, transactions, and other types of agreements on a distributed ledger, BCT can help solve this problem. It indicates that an automated approach will be used to assure legal compliance. The organization's operating efficiency will significantly improve. Enhancements can be made to improve the consumer experience by increasing the security of data transfers and identities. Distributed ledgers are the foundation of BCT. These ledgers record all transactions and ensure the data remains accurate and up-to-date on an immutable, worldwide network [4, 6]. This technology enables us to achieve a more optimal equilibrium between technology, user data, and privacy as the digital revolution progresses.

There may be a stronger emphasis on confidentiality, which could lead to better data management. The auditing process becomes more transparent and efficient when counterparties' accounting records are reliable and current. Instead of reviewing everyday transactions, auditors may focus on complex and disputed issues. No longer are auditors and accountants needed due to process automation [9]. Blockchain and artificial intelligence (AI) are two separate but complementary technologies. An extremely centralized service, AI runs on encrypted data that is inaccessible, unreadable, and impossible to replicate. They gain a lot by working together, especially regarding financial assistance.

Blockchain technology facilitates rapid communication between participants in transactions, decreasing the need for recordkeeping in the order-to-cash, record-to-report, and procure-to-pay processes [7–9]. Blockchain-enabled smart contracts make it easier to create legally enforceable financial agreements that are guaranteed to be performed if all relevant criteria are met. Smart contracts, similar to regular contracts, openly and instantly enforce rules on a blockchain, doing away with middlemen and making all parties more accountable [10, 12]. The distributed ledger system operates by utilizing a decentralized network of computers to carry out intermediary processes over the internet, eliminating the requirement for a dependable third party. All participants in the network and the public have access to the same digital ledger, which records each transaction. Instead of a centralized ledger, the network can verify asset ownership and provide transparent transactions because every member has a valid copy [13–15]. Digital technology has improved cooperation. Cloud-based platforms with customized analytics have transformed financial accounting. These systems manage accounts payable and receivable, contracts, reporting, and more. The most reliable payment methods include cash, cashier's checks, and electronic wire transfers.

Nevertheless, it is impossible to combine wire transfers and cash. By utilizing BCT for payment processing, these problems are resolved, and customer confidence is enhanced. Quicker settlement of transactions is possible thanks to technologically enabled instantaneous movement of funds between financial institutions. The capacity to automate operations and the suitability of this technology for tracking and recording transactions make it an ideal choice. By utilizing smart contracts, financial service providers can monitor buyers' and vendors' payment and delivery processes [16–19]. Blockchain technology is the focus of this article, which delves into its features, tools, importance, and financial industry applications.

4.1.1 Blockchain

A master node is one component of a blockchain, which also includes blocks and chains. The network's blocks are the responsibility of the nodes. Block-adding to the blockchain is complicated and requires mathematical solutions. The mathematical riddles' complexity constrains the unlimited scalability of the blockchain network. Hash codes are so unique that hacking, cheating, or manipulating the blockchain network is unlikely.

Each machine in a blockchain network keeps a duplicate of the ledger. Because it stores transaction data in interconnected blocks, the network is called the blockchain. To understand and use cryptocurrencies, one must be familiar with the blockchain network [20–22]. A computerized ledger of transactions is called a blockchain. The name "chain" stems from its structure consisting of linked lists of separate data pieces called blocks. There is a vast array of uses for BCT beyond monitoring digital currencies like Bitcoin. Since a blockchain records and stores all transactions, it becomes extremely difficult, if not impossible, to hack or defraud the system [5]. Distributed digital ledgers of transactions can be found on a computer network called a blockchain. Banks have traditionally relied on cutting-edge innovation to safeguard customer information and business operations.

The financial sector has quickly adopted BCT. Cryptocurrencies were born out of the need for a system to facilitate secure, reliable, and auditable financial transactions enabled by BCT [25, 26, 29]. Blockchain is a decentralized system that allows several devices to record specific transactions in real-time. This system utilizes interconnected blocks to store digital data on contracts, transactions, and contact databases. Financial system law that is not clear and unambiguous leaves companies vulnerable to frequent mistakes and misinterpretations of data [27, 28, 38]. All these problems, plus a great deal less financial risk, are addressed by BCT. Blockchain technology is gaining widespread recognition for its value. In its immediate vicinity, there is a loose conglomeration of individuals trying to find out how to apply this technology to their own companies. Building banks brought people together, allowing them to trade and commerce safely and efficiently. One invention that makes it easier to finish a lot of things all over the world is the blockchain platform [9, 39].

4.1.2 Need for Blockchain

The global financial system helps billions by managing trillions of money daily. Financial industry issues have often accompanied such lofty aspirations. Every year, the company loses a lot of money due to these issues, including data breaches, delays, increased paperwork, and the costs associated with having many stakeholders. Blockchain technology can potentially address global financial concerns [30–33, 40]. Furthermore, the current stock market is more expensive because of the involvement of institutions such as regulators, brokers, and the stock exchange. A decentralized management paradigm is one method for improving the efficiency of stock exchanges. Blockchain-based smart contracts could eliminate middlemen. So, the stock market is more decentralized. Blockchain technology makes business-investor transactions safe and efficient [34–36].

There have been various issues in the financial sector for quite some time. Massive technological advancement has solved many issues, but it has also created new ones. Numerous fintech choices are available, making it difficult for financial service providers to choose the best one. So, they are seeking a complete solution that can handle everything. Blockchain technology has promising applications in financial services and could solve big business concerns [37–39]. Due to centralization, the banking sector must allocate a substantial sum of money to multiple businesses. Financial service providers pay for accounting, database maintenance, central database procurement, value transfer systems, database security, labor, and middleman commissions. Financial service providers must regularly provide funds to these assets due to their recurring nature. Due to all the additional costs that may be necessary, the total cost of a financial service system might quickly increase [40, 41].

4.1.3 The Rise of Decentralized Financial Systems

Lower transaction costs and more transaction possibilities are common outcomes of using intermediaries. Intermediaries connect parties, build confidence, and complete transactions, making them vital to the economy [12, 41]. Connecting, negotiating, and enforcing contracts between parties may require intermediaries. Concerns regarding the potential for intermediaries to abuse their position for personal gain have been raised in recent years. Humans balance monopoly power and efficiency when dealing with strong economic intermediaries. The financial sector is characterized by numerous tense circumstances as huge financial institutions oversee and handle transactions. Throughout history, financial institutions have served as mediators and structures for economically unviable transactions. Financial institutions reduce transaction costs by connecting market players and building trust. Fintech has allowed smaller financial institutions to take over as we enter the digital economy. Digital technology can lower transaction costs, expand transaction range, and enable peer-to-peer transactions, fueling fintech innovation.

Fintech has cut out intermediaries but not financial institutions. Technology businesses, such as banks, take the role of middlemen. Decentralized finance built on the blockchain might be the next big thing if disintermediation and decentralization keep going. Recent advancements in BCT have enabled the elimination of intermediaries and the establishment of decentralized systems. Blockchain technology can transform financial transactions by eliminating intermediaries and creating decentralized platforms encouraging peer trust. Thus, hitherto unfeasible business models can be actualized through the implementation of BCT, which has the potential to expand and streamline peer-to-peer transactions. The utilization of BCT can enhance the decentralization, innovation, interoperability, borderlessness, and transparency of financial services. Compared to transaction cost economics, this model is different. Distributed trust, which "flows laterally between individuals" without pre-existing trusted relationships, is the foundation of this new paradigm, in contrast to transaction cost economics (TCE's) emphasis on opportunism. Transactions on the blockchain can lead to distributed trust because they are authentic, unchangeable, and verifiable because of distributed consensus and sophisticated encryption. To facilitate quick and easy user transactions, a blockchain can act as a shared database of transaction records. Second, although TCE acknowledges that intermediaries and hierarchies can lower costs, this new paradigm focuses on decentralization and disintermediation. Decentralized BCT has the potential to reduce search, contractual, and enforcement costs while increasing the potential for transactions through innovative peer-to-peer connections [8]. The potential for distributed trust and decentralized platforms offered by BCT has been recognized by innovators and entrepreneurs, opening the door to a decentralized, open financial system. Their goals include creating new economic opportunities, empowering open access, lowering transaction costs, increasing financial inclusion, and fostering permissionless innovation. While still in its early stages, this trend exemplifies the potential for BCT to usher in decentralized and disintermediate corporate models. This trend has the potential to shake up whole industries and open exciting new avenues for innovation and entrepreneurship if it takes off.

4.2 Related Works

4.2.1 The Emergence of Blockchain Technology

In 2008, Nakamoto described Bitcoin as a decentralized digital money system that allows peer-to-peer transactions. This move was in response to a rudimentary "digital safety-deposit box" (Haber and Stornetta, 1990) with a time-stamping service system to formally validate clients' documents in case of uncertainty. Blockchain technology allows untrustworthy parties to interact without central verification using a distributed ledger with time-stamped data. Transactions are associated with blockchain blocks after verification. Though it began with new technology and information domain economics, BCT now stands for decentralization. Without involving humans, blockchain upends corporate operations and provides an institutional means of changing economic, behavioral, technological, and

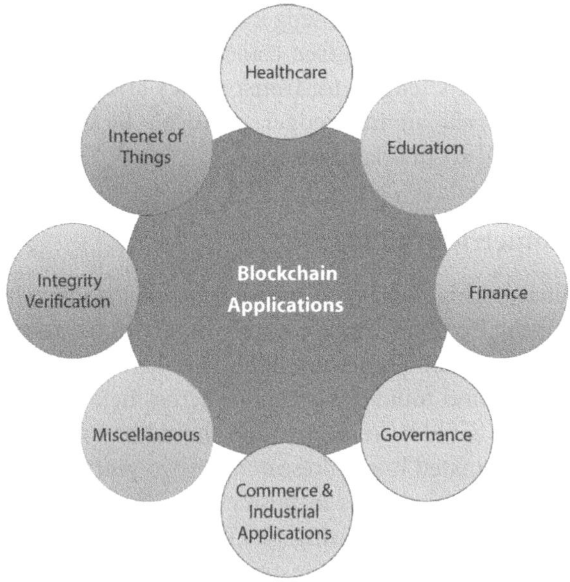

Figure 4.1 Blockchain applications.

environmental practices. Researchers classify BCT as either institutional or general-purpose. As blockchain is predicted on total factor productivity advances in current economic operations, it is a general-purpose technology [12]. Authors [10] nevertheless maintain that it is an institutional technology capable of coordination and communication of economic behavior inside a certain group. Ethereum, Blockchain 2.0, and smart contracts speed up and digitally verify contract agreements to fix digital currency. Later, through decentralized apps, Blockchain 3.0 enhanced scalability, flexibility, and transaction time. Blockchain applications in commerce, industry, healthcare, banking, government, education, the integrity of the Internet of Things (IoTs), integrity verification, and other fields are abstracted in Figure 4.1. In finance, blockchain drives non-fungible token marketplaces, anti-money laundering tracking systems, and cryptocurrency exchanges.

4.2.2 Blockchain Technology in Finance

Banking is transformed by BCT. Blockchain-based crypto stock sales and crowdfunding align public interests. Blockchain-enabled token sales could again fund global firms. The first blockchain coins made investing in viable initiatives were easier for small and medium-sized businesses [13, 42, 43]. Centralized business operations and regulations cost banks less with blockchain [11, 44]. Distributed ledgers were cheaper and simpler [12]. Smart contracts enable human-free transaction generation and enforcement. Ripple links bank ledgers for transparency and near-real-time international payments *via* an interledger protocol. Blockchains [9] enable real-time audits and secure data storage.

4.2.3 Bibliometric Studies

Bibliometric analyses highlight a research topic's dimensions, patterns, tendencies, and promising frontiers. These data are important for assessing scientific research [13]. Recently, bibliometric studies have garnered attention for their boundaries, trends, and topic classifications across fields. Eleven cryptocurrency research gaps could harm society and should be solved [9]. Blockchain technology has dominated Bitcoin research for two years [14, 45]. The article says most blockchain research is in business economics, computer science, telecommunications, and engineering. Since 2016, China national knowledge infrastructure (CNKI) authors and institutions have conducted more blockchain research than energy institute (EI) authors and institutions [12, 15]. EI institutions and authors collaborated more than CNKI. The detailed study [10] found that blockchain research is secondary to Bitcoin research. With a 124% annual rise, writers are diverse and produce fewer finance articles. In addition, blockchain architecture and methods were examined [16]. D. K. Murala and S.K. Panda [12] investigated blockchain in big data and industrial applications in 2017. Bibliometric studies [13] provide technical advice, research trends, and drawbacks for BCT. Scholarly blockchain papers can inform research maps. Blockchain technology is increasingly used for health records. It can also access limitations and exchange data. From 2013 to 2019, blockchain's IoT ruled, showing a trend that needed additional research.

4.2.4 Trade Finance

Trade finance includes every activity related to bank trade facilitation. Trade finance is essential for trade partners to share risks and close the gaps between production, transportation, and payment for commodities. Trade finance is, hence, dualistic. First, it makes it possible for short-term borrowing suppliers and purchasers to fulfill their bilateral contractual responsibilities. Furthermore, shielding one party against contract fraud is done through trade financing. International trading uses prepayment, open accounts, and letters of credit. The importer remunerates the exporter in advance by utilizing their domestic credit line before manufacturing or dispatching the merchandise. Because the importer bears all the risks involved in the transaction, including the possibility that the exporter may fail to deliver the goods as agreed upon in the contract, the importer considers this arrangement unsatisfactory. Before making a payment, the open account payment method is responsible for the transportation and delivery of things. The letter of credit (L/C) transactions between import and export banks are crucial to trade financing. Using financial intermediaries, the L/C model solves the challenges of importers who are reluctant to pay before obtaining products and exporters who cannot produce or ship without payment. Graham (2012) describes an L/C as a bank guarantee issued at the buyer's request, supported by the seller (typically through an advising bank), and a payment made immediately or later upon submission of documents meeting particular criteria and circumstances. Intermediary import and export banks decrease trade partner risks but increase transaction costs in the L/C model. This fundamental disadvantage is why the L/C technique is mostly used in transactions with high trading partner distrust. If the exporter fulfills their obligations, banks will pay for goods on time and in full under the L/C. Many trade finance options are trust-based. Cash in advance and open account settlement trading partners must be trusted to fulfill their obligations. However, the uncertainty of trade partner integrity means that the L/C model depends on unbiased third parties. In international trade, L/C payments are seen as safe since they establish "trust" between trading partners. Major disadvantages of the L/C approach exist. Although it lowers trade finance trust problems, transaction costs are considerable. Trade parties must pay financial intermediary fees. The regular trading document inspections and authentications make L/C prone to mistakes. Moreover, the existing process design falls short of shielding players from fraud (World Trade Organization, 2019). Trade finance fraud sometimes raises money by sending out several invoices for the same goods. Bad debts are a part of doing business for trade finance institutions. The scams have left banks open to attack and cautious about requests for trade funding.

4.2.5 Blockchain Technology to Solve Trade Finance Trust Issues

Blockchains encrypt data. It is an encrypted database distributed, verified, and used by a network of nodes with immutable ledgers [17, 46, 47]. The network of participants conducts and supports transactional operations through a computationally obtained consensus process, replacing middlemen and enabling trust-free economic transactions [18]. Blockchain actors do not need to believe in individuals or organizations; they only need to believe in technology. The "trustless trust" or "trust-by-computation" of BCT may revolutionize economic transactions that previously relied on human faith. Blockchain technology research has flourished by application hypotheses. Researchers have shown early interest in BCT, the foundation of Bitcoin. Research in BCT includes supply chains, taxes, auditing, e-residency, energy distribution, and the IoTs. Thorough research has been done on technology issues like data malleability, authentication, cryptography, and security architecture. The financial industry has received the greatest study attention of all the broader uses of BCT across industries.

The self-enforcing rules of blockchain transactions automate them. It guarantees transactions adhere to mutual agreements by making the whole process safe and error-free and lowering the need to trust business partners. An analysis of the impact of blockchain on the trust relationships between trade finance trading partners provides a useful chance to learn about technological trust, interpersonal trust, and the potential and difficulties of the technology.

4.3 Decentralized Finance Promises

4.3.1 Decentralization

Financial institutions control and mediate transactions within a centralized financial system. Financial transactions are made quicker and easier with intermediaries' reduction in transaction costs. Being necessary middlemen in financial transactions, financial institutions have the power to control economic activity. Centralized financial organizations such as the Bank of America, PayPal, and Square can obtain market strength and profit benefits. Decentralized financial systems use peer-to-peer networks to support financial transactions. Decentralized networks reduce centralized institutions and transaction costs, increasing network benefits. When no company can build up enough monopoly power to monopolize a decentralized peer-to-peer network and keep others from joining, network effects that increase transaction possibilities emerge dominant, and everyone benefits.

4.3.2 Innovativeness

Combinatorial and permissionless innovation is promoted by decentralized finance. Centralized platforms can promote open innovation and experimentation, but their owners frequently have access control and the ability to revoke it. Developers who are not affiliated with the platform run the danger of losing access to their hosting platforms. While most platform owners are accommodating to outside developers, occasionally, they have made unilateral adjustments that have harmed them. Developers can create and test new apps without supervision with a decentralized platform. Unexpected and impromptu growth of decentralized finance is made possible by permissionless innovation and access to decentralized platforms. Decentralized platforms allow combinatorial innovation. New financial technologies can spur novel product combinations in a decentralized finance ecosystem. Combinatorial innovation is made possible in decentralized finance by open sourcing and permissionless innovation. Like Bitcoin, Ethereum, and Libra, decentralized financial systems and platforms frequently license their fundamental technology broadly for public use and development. Centralized financial services and platforms use patents, copyrights, trademarks, and trade secrets to stop others from implementing important innovations. Financial innovation is accelerated, and market competition is increased by combinatorial innovation, which results in newer, better, and more affordable financial services.

4.3.3 Interoperability

Decentralized finance improves interoperability. Its silos complicate transactions in traditional finance. Each institution maintains its ledger; hence, financial services are not compatible. Moving value and money between silos is costly and ineffective. Decentralized finance encourages service interoperability through open standards and public blockchains. High interoperability allows value and money to flow smoothly between services and nations, possibly resulting in a value web. Even if projects on the same public blockchain are interoperable, decentralized finance is still incompatible with other blockchains. Entrepreneurs and inventors are thinking about two approaches to complete interoperability. The first is to back a single, dominating platform, and encourage all ventures to expand upon it. As Ethereum is the most widely used decentralized money platform, all applications built on it work together. Including decentralized finance, Ethereum has been utilized to construct 87% of publicly funded projects. Should one blockchain rule, future interoperability could be unfavorable as it could not be able to support projects with various requirements. Full interoperability of blockchains is maintained even when projects are developed on multiple blockchains. Blockchains are being integrated to achieve interoperability [11].

4.3.4 Borderlessness

Centralized finance is limited by geography and fiat currencies, making it not global. Thus, cross-border capital and value transfers are often tense and delayed. Due to its lack of physical boundaries or fiat currencies, decentralized finance is naturally global and borderless. Since it uses borderless cryptocurrency, it can be utilized worldwide. It is also independent of central banks and governments. Decentralized finance may make worldwide money transfers as easy as sending an email.

4.3.5 Transparency

Financial system transparency can improve with decentralized finance. Perfect transparency is prevented by the need for centralized financial institutions to limit access to their ledgers. With extreme openness and distributed consensus, decentralized finance safeguards public ledgers. The transparent public ledgers hold the transactions. Decentralized finance broadens the possible transactions by enabling parties to transact without pre-existing relationships or trusted middlemen by distributing trust through public ledgers. Because decentralized finance frequently uses open-source code, transacting parties are protected by outside parties, being able to validate business logic and spot hidden dangers and biases. Transparent public ledgers and open-source software help "get to the bottom of any serious financial accident" by tracking past transactions.

4.4 The Main Business Models in Decentralized Finance

Unsustainable business models might be made possible by BCT. In the financial industry, BCT may help to remove centralized institutions, encourage experimentation, and improve financial access. The growth of several company models is illustrated in Figure 4.2. The most popular are decentralized currencies, then contracts and payments.

4.4.1 Decentralized Currencies

Several centuries have elapsed since the inception of national fiat currency. In recent decades, central banks backed their currencies with gold. Over the past few years, gold-backed fiat currencies have disappeared. Currently, the worth of a fiat currency is contingent upon the trust and faith that

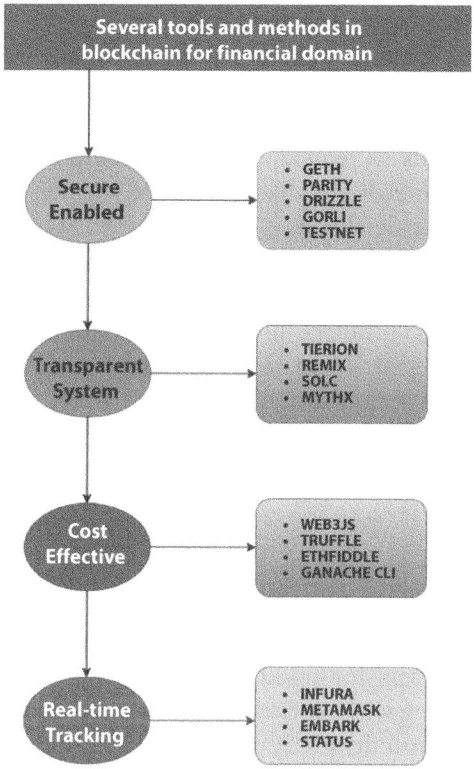

Figure 4.2 Financial blockchain tools and approaches.

the general population has in the country's central bank, government, and overall economic state. Bitcoin, introduced by Nakamoto in 2008, was not issued by the government but rather by technology. Due to its fixed and unalterable supply schedule, Bitcoin is inherently resistant to inflation. Bitcoin's decentralization makes it the predominant asset for storing value in the blockchain industry, sometimes likened to digital gold. Like gold, Bitcoin is decentralized and can be easily transferred and kept without relying on a central authority. Additional decentralized cryptocurrencies that emerged after Bitcoin include Ether, Litecoin, Monero, Dash, and Zcash.

4.4.2 Services for Dispersed Payment

Visa, PayPal, and SWIFT make online and offline trading possible. However, they have significant costs, particularly for international transactions. Even though the internet has brought down the cost of many services, payment services are still expensive. Traditional payment challenges are overcome by decentralized payment networks such as Bitcoin Lightning Network and Libra. Fast, safe, irreversible payments are possible at a cheap cost with the Bitcoin Lightning Network. Its cheap transaction fees enable merchants to reduce expenses and increase sales. Affordable payments also help merchants that traditional payment processors do not well support. More crucially, free or almost free payments might enable micropayments and other business models, encouraging fresh creativity and entrepreneurship.

Interestingly, the centralized platform Square intends to soon include Bitcoin Lightning Network into its payment systems. Two Fast and affordable cross-border payments are made possible by decentralized payment networks that use BCT and global currency. Leading this field, Ripple collaborates with banking institutions like MoneyGram to enhance international money transfers.

4.4.3 Decentralized Fundraising

Investors only trust companies with strong network connections; hence, the fundraising process for traditional venture capital can be stressful. Fundraising is shifting with blockchain. Popular decentralized fundraising events are initial coin offers (ICOs). In an ICO, a project creates a project-specific token on a public blockchain and sells it to investors to pay for early development. Early-stage companies now have a new funding option in ICOs, which lets innovators and entrepreneurs raise billions from investors worldwide. Network effects can be produced, and a startup can be funded *via* an ICO. Using BCT, smart contracts, and open-source code, this new crowdfunding allows projects to raise money from global investors. Decentralized fundraising based on blockchains lowers fundraising friction, increases access to money, and encourages creativity and entrepreneurship. An ICO is also a cutting-edge way for a project to draw in partners to help launch a new ecosystem. An ICO might be profitable when a token is useful in the project's platforms or goods. One can use a utility token as the main means of payment or redeem it for services. Security tokens can represent direct ownership or cash flow rights in certain projects. Initial exchange offers (IEOs) are part of newer versions. Unlike ICOs, IEOs unite top-notch businesses with investors and assess projects *via* Bitcoin exchanges. Cryptocurrency exchanges assess possible projects, give thorough details on those that show promise, and recommend top-notch ones according to their reputation.

4.4.4 Decentralized Contracting

Markets, businesses, and people require contracts for cooperation and transactions. However, contracts can be expensive and difficult to draft, enforce, and renegotiate (Coase, 1937). Moral hazard and adverse selection can raise transaction costs and restrict transaction options, impeding financial contracting. Financial intermediaries have historically fostered confidence and decreased transaction costs. The emergence of BCT has recently enabled the use of smart contracts as financial intermediaries, facilitating peer-to-peer financial transactions. According to the definition provided by Murray *et al.* (2019), smart contracts are computer programs that carry out certain actions when certain predetermined circumstances or rules are met inside a given protocol. The transparency, immutability, automaticity, and programmability of smart contracts reduce the complexity and cost of contracts. Ensure programmable decentralized consensus to facilitate contingency contracting with its tamper-proof and automated nature [21]. Smart contracts enable new transactions, save expenses, and improve contracting. Smart contracts help decentralized lending and borrowing systems like MakerDAO, Compound, and Dharma cut expenses, impediments, and delays.

4.5 Tools, Methods, Services, and Blockchain-Based Financial Services Applications

4.5.1 Financial Services Blockchain Tools and Strategies

Blockchain technology can be used for financial services and their structure using several technologies. Figure 4.2 shows popular blockchain technologies and techniques for financial services. These novel and effective blockchain methods solve real-time financial issues. Soft tools are parity, geth, solc, myths, truffle, infra, and meta mask.

By increasing financial services and related businesses, these smart and advanced technologies secure blockchain's future [8]. Financial services firms have speculated about BCT for a decade. Blockchain tracks financial transactions electronically. Several locations store, distribute, and publish this ledger. Every ledger copy records a transaction block. This records transactions. Blockchain's multiple copies make it nearly immutable and safe because a hacker must update all copies to change or add an entry. Blockchain makes transactions secure and easy, boosting corporate confidence. Tamper-proof deterministic smart contracts simplify business logic, improve efficiency, and increase trust. Industry-leading granular data privacy across the software stack allows selective data sharing in business networks. Digitized securities are issued faster. Issuers can tailor digital financial products to investors. Examples include fractionalized real-world asset ownership, tokenized microeconomies, and secure, scalable, and fast asset transfers. These benefits increase governance transparency, corporate profitability, and stakeholder incentive alignment. Liability risk management must be strengthened in venturing, private equity, real estate funds, and specialty markets; decision-making frameworks must also be dynamic, and rules must be adjusted. Stakeholder and asset management could be revolutionized by blockchain.

Blockchain is promising for banking because digital currencies were developed on it [7]. Insurance companies can speed up claims with smart contracts. A blockchain code automatically analyzes client claims. The smart contract will pay the customer if it is valid. Most institutions require identification verification to avoid fraud and money laundering. A digital ledger is produced for each block transaction [6]. Finance has embraced blockchain ledgers due to their advantages over traditional digital ledgers. Blockchain creates a distributed ledger. Therefore, no third party must process or store transaction data. Blockchain has a unique security method and no central transaction data repository, preventing hackers [3].

Blockchain financial applications may be cheaper and simpler. Blockchain banking is secure and beneficial. Blockchain's transaction ledger is encrypted. Therefore, only keycode holders could access data. Fintech options abound in finance. Financial institutions struggle to solve issues. Blockchain could solve major financial issues [16]. Tradition, centralization, and complexity define global financial services. Centralizing financial data and sending it through multiple middlemen reduces transparency. Only database security and intermediaries influence data security. Even the most secure databases can be hacked, and data breaches can occur. Lack of transparency can cause complex security issues when differences are undetected until a breach or system problem is identified. Policymakers may promote blockchain education. Users may reduce blockchain fraud, while corporations may increase adoption. The blockchain can help policymakers achieve their goals. Public and private organizations could assess if the technology can solve particular problems. Blockchain technology may be easier to implement for companies.

Politicians may explain or create new laws using BCT. Clear regulation of technological implementations would make blockchain more appealing to corporations and others. Blockchain employs public and private keys. Everyone on the network has the public key, but only transaction participants have the secret key. Network participants can only see the transaction details. Blockchain technology protects transaction stakeholders' financial data and ensures financial transparency. Blockchain might transform almost any industry. Blockchain applications can improve corporate processes and contracts' transparency, traceability, and operational efficiency. Financial institutions are exploring blockchain to create product opportunities, manage regulatory issues, and identify/assess risks and controls.

4.5.2 Several Blockchain Technology-Related Highlighted Services in the Financial Industry

Even while BCT for finance has developed, certain companies have increased the influence of financial services in real-time applications. Figure 4.3 displays trade finance platforms, cross-border financial transactions, precise credit reporting, clearing and settlements, and digital identity

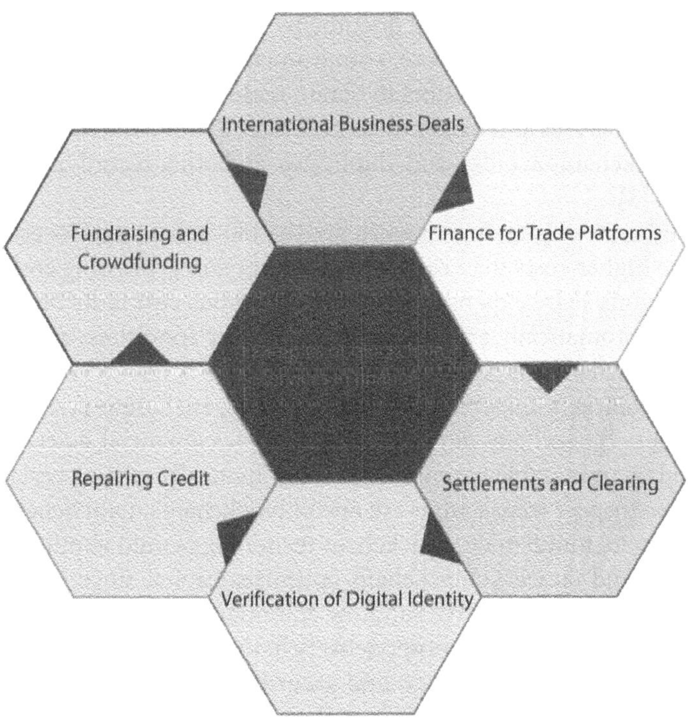

Figure 4.3 Examples of blockchain services in finance.

verification. Thanks to these services and advancements, the financial sector will be successfully built on blockchain.

Blockchain experts and financial regulators claim to improve security, decrease risk, and save expenses by improving transparency and eliminating hurdles in the lengthy transaction sequence that precedes financial meetings. The properties of BCT enable financial companies to achieve cost savings. Historically, financial institutions have acted as intermediaries for transactions, a process that has been time-consuming and sluggish. The immutability of blockchain makes it very suitable for financial applications since it enables secure and uncomplicated transactions, hence instilling confidence among participants.

Banks profit substantially from technology's automation, improvement, and fraud reduction. Blockchain can protect identity information, boost consumer confidence, reduce fraud, and speed up verification for financial institutions. Blockchain technology swiftly and securely generates a tamper-proof ledger of key actions. Money transfers and foreign payments are excellent with it. Blockchain automation can streamline these processes and reduce intermediaries. Blockchain technology eliminates bank settlement, lowering payment costs. Most regulatory control is predicated on recordkeeping, but failing to preserve documents has significantly worse effects. Organizations cannot, therefore, compromise on compliance. Blockchain allows businesses and regulators to obtain real-time record changes, which speeds up processes and makes mistakes easier to find. The central encryption of blockchains avoids fraud, duplicates, and other record management problems [3].

When banks engage in a blockchain, the blockchain and its ecosystem may have higher costs than each bank's transaction processing costs. Since all institutions share expenses, there are enormous cost reductions. Smart contracts automatically execute under particular conditions and improve bank contractual term performance [6].

Smart contracts must comply with all laws, including cross-jurisdictional ones. Blockchain can help with complex financial asset transfers regulated by immutable corporate rules automatically settling certain conflicts. Peer-to-peer transactions are one of blockchain's main benefits since they eliminate middlemen. Blockchain technology could eliminate custodial banks and clearers. Blockchain optimizes capital since bank operational costs are lower [8]. We can now automate and program blockchain transactions. These critical components help the financial services industry achieve efficiency, transparency, and security. Blockchain may transform how businesses raise funding through the capital market, which exchanges financial securities like shares and bonds. Blockchain technology makes asset issuance and exchanges fast and cheap, eliminating middlemen. The ability to fully configure blockchain [10]. Automating tedious, paper-based operations could boost trade efficiency. Public blockchains are decentralized and can be used for collaboration.

Blockchain can settle and track bank transactions directly and more efficiently than previous methods [10]. In banking, high-tech securities are replacing traditional ones. The company is testing the blockchain by copying asset transfers. The blockchain technique may work. The history of immutable transactions is a major benefit of the blockchain. This will lower financial institution crimes. Blockchain enables smart contracts. Smart contracts leverage decentralized consensus and tamper-proof algorithmic executions. Digital agreements provide contract terms and conditions. Smart contracts execute and automate contract terms with their programmable protocol. By lowering expenses in relationship management, contract drafting and negotiation, agreement monitoring and enforcement, and information collecting and processing, smart contracts may make market-based governance possible. Because smart contracts store data securely and handle payments automatically without middlemen or human mistakes, they can increase data trust [9]. Smart contracts can boost open account trader confidence, trade transaction transparency, data quality, fraud protection, and payment interchange. Blockchain is useful beyond Bitcoin and currency. Blockchain technology tracks all transactions and ownership, including real estate and IP. Automating contracts facilitates creation and execution.

4.5.3 Blockchain Technology Applications in Finance Service

Financial services could employ BCT. Blockchain technology might reduce or eliminate transaction fees, which traditional banks earn from. Consumers must transfer money through banks or other third parties. Blockchain technology may remove banks, lowering fees and other costs. Thus, banks may face volume and transaction-based income difficulties. Private and public chains can communicate. Digital assets, smart contracts, and programmed money enable unprecedented connectivity and programmability across commodities, services, assets, and holdings, enhancing BCT. Digitization preserves data integrity and centralizes asset provenance and transaction history. The efficiency of the operation is increased *via* automation. Real-time auditing, reporting, and settlement reduce the steps and middlemen required to build traditional confidence and processing times, errors, and delays. Blockchain records internet transactions securely, easily, and impenetrably. The internet and blockchain are shared records of transactions across a broad network of users with no central authority. It has many data blocks with transactions. Advanced cryptography seems to connect and secure the blocks. Major stock exchanges are investigating how blockchain could speed up and lower the cost of near-instantaneous stock settlements.

Smart contracts automate compliance, improving security and transparency. Financial services are increasingly using BCT, which increases the security and efficiency of the financial system worldwide. The worldwide financial services industry gains from BCT in a few ways. The largest benefit of blockchain is "cross-border settlements," the idea of creating a cost-effective, transparent transnational network. Service seekers gain when costs fall [8]. Blockchain technology improves payment transparency, efficiency, trust, and security while saving money for end users and financial service providers. Before BCT, a week can pass between bank payments. Distributed ledgers and digital currencies facilitate, speed, and reduce payment costs [28]. Distributed ledger technology is something central banks are thinking about using for electronic payments.

Furthermore, blockchain trails are useful for provenance-based value. Distributed ledgers of digital assets are immutable and unhackable on truth and trust platforms. The financial services industry is not the only one affected, but also most of society. Since blockchain software specialists are in great demand, creating and sustaining blockchain solutions will become more expensive. Though they may be difficult to interface with off-chain data and older systems, blockchain apps offer many advantages. Developers must overcome obstacles before integrating their apps with blockchain services.

4.6 Research Proposition

This section discusses BCT-based systems' pros, cons, and features that need further study, notably in finance. Blockchain technology development and applications may influence future studies. Based on the advantages, difficulties, and functions of the blockchain-enabled financial sector, three study proposals are put out to optimize the advantages of blockchain systems for financial sector decision-making.

4.6.1 Blockchain-Enabled Financial Sector Benefits

Consumers, banks, and society are expected to profit from BCT. It could improve market pricing and rates beyond security and transaction transparency for institutions and clients. As technology advances, benefits can be recognized, replicated, and researched. Blockchain also lets clients store payment histories across institutions and nations, reducing fraud risk. Improvements include transparency, traceability, and transaction speed. All advantages need extensive study and actual assessments for specific applications and use scenarios. As such, the following is suggested:

First hypothesis:
The advantages of BCT in finance are difficult to measure. The benefits of BCT must be measured for people, organizations, technology, economics, and policy using theoretically sound and practically feasible effect indicators.

4.6.1.1 People

Cyber transactions involve strangers. We use reputation online. People can evaluate a seller's credibility using this method. The global data volume is growing rapidly. Data collection and analysis in the Big Data era have led to a revolution and financial success. Data helps companies customize offerings, foresee trends, and make better decisions. Data is our economy's greatest asset [18]. Blockchain has interested people in property administration, auditing, and copyright protection, but its main application is finance. Blockchain technology research should address sharing, trust, and privacy as part of human civilization. Blockchain technology may boost transaction trust. Novel trust mechanisms may allow confidential communication. The blockchain can increase transaction trust without a third party. Users may manage their transactions and data in the centralized database, which is unhackable. Data ownership is guaranteed by a decentralized personal data management system [10]. Data transparency, auditability, and precise access controls can protect personal data in this setting.

4.6.1.2 Organization

Blockchain technology allows a decentralized, peer-to-peer commercial community. Transactions may be fast. The Bitcoin system is decentralized with no central authority to handle issues. Nodes in blockchain systems are usually P2P.

4.6.1.3 Tech

Blockchain technology relies on network security and smart contracts. Smart contracts auto-execute code, making the organization self-sufficient.

This functionality relies on network security to build user trust for commercial use. Blockchain security relies on distributed consensus and a public ledger [6]. The author discusses how BCT can prevent fraud and bad behavior. The author explains blockchain threats and suggests defenses. Blockchain technology's distributed structure and lack of a central point of failure increase system and data storage flexibility. Research enhanced this technology's prospects [9]. Decentralized BCT allows everyone to preserve their data and transactions in case of failure, the author said. With this resilience and security, new identity systems with globally consistent, unerasable user data are possible. Blockchain could improve dispersed network security. BitAV, a blockchain-based anti-malware ecosystem [19], lets users spread infectious patterns. This study shows that BitAV improves fault reliability and scanning speed. Blockchain technology improves security infrastructure resiliency. Older PKIs often have hardware, software, or malicious attacks targeting single points of failure. Blockchain can construct a privacy-preserving PKI and increase traditional PKI reliability, according to Axon (2015).

4.6.1.4 Economics

The economic cost-benefit analysis suggests that blockchain may be attractive due to speculation opportunities and low transaction costs. Although voluntary, fees are only paid by successful miners. Blockchain transactions cost money due to a default amount established in the standard client software. Bitcoin fees are generally lower than those charged to individuals for international payments and transfers, although local retail transactions may not save money. Exchange market trading and speculation are possible because of shifting exchange values between sanctioned currencies and Bitcoin. Many buy bitcoins to hold them until exchange rates climb. Bitcoin is debated as a digital money or an investing instrument (store of value). Blockchain can disrupt economic paradigms and create profitable markets and goods (EM-Compass, 2017). Blockchain technology could enable new business models. The P2P transactions can use asset transfers without a third party, helping the "sharing economy" flourish. Unbanked newcomers may be allowed to participate in previously prohibited economic activities. The blockchain system's main policy components include managing access policies, data storage contracts, metadata management, and automatic compensation for storage.

4.6.2 Blockchain-Enabled Financial Sector Challenges

Blockchain technology must overcome some obstacles before being broadly implemented in finance. These are scalability, latency, security, regulatory challenges, and transaction cost. So, the following is proposed:

Second hypothesis:
Financial blockchain adoption will be difficult due to regulatory, operational, and financial issues. The latest blockchain-enabled banking industry problem papers are operational. The following sections address financial, regulatory, operational, and adoption issues.

4.6.2.1 Financial Issues

Blockchain ecosystem financial intermediaries include remote wallets, currency exchanges, and internet-hiding transaction tools. Mediation is needed for 'Bitcoin,' worldwide internet money [23]. Bitcoin purchasers need exchanges to buy and sell. Mediators must represent clients to reduce risk due to system security vulnerabilities. In 2014, Mt. Gox, the largest Bitcoin exchange, closed after losing 754,000 users' bitcoins in a massive breach. User failures like forgotten passwords, transactions, or device security weaknesses can also cause bitcoin loss.

4.6.2.2 Regulation Issues

Like blockchain, regulators follow technical advances. Blockchain transactions provide new services, but there are no rules. New blockchain legislation may suit highly regulated firms despite its promise of auditability and openness. Information-sharing rules must be rethought to encourage businesses, customers, and investors to adopt innovations. Governments should pass blockchain-based smart contract laws. Startups and banks researching distributed ledgers worry about regulation. Regulators are still learning about blockchain. Regulators like blockchain because it strengthens financial sector infrastructures. However, legal and jurisdictional concerns remain. Regulators usually react without leading. Authorities worried that any discovery would offer new threats in 2014, but cryptocurrencies and shared ledgers are a low-cost, efficient global payments system and should not be overregulated. Blockchain technology may improve market infrastructure. Thus, authorities are investigating it. Another benefit of BCT is that regulators can stress test banks without data from the banks if it works as planned. The European Commission approved this legislation after identifying over 70 Bitcoin risks to users' financial integrity and market participants. However, regulations may hinder technological development. There should be a balance between restraining innovation and admitting that technology is unlikely to purposefully cause systemic risks in this area.

4.6.2.3 *Operations Issues*

Sustainability, greenhouse gas emissions, and climate change are significant societal concerns. Numerous firms, including financial institutions, strive to minimize expenses and decrease their carbon footprint. While nodes compete to mine the next block in hopes of receiving a substantial reward, the consensus mechanisms of BCT may result in the wasteful consumption of resources, particularly electricity. Empirical evidence revealed that uncles, which refer to forks of length 1, constituted more than 10% of the new blocks in Ethereum. Although it may appear to be inefficient, this modest sign serves as evidence of the significant redundancy in Proof-of-Work systems. The occurrence of unintentional forking at a length of 3 was infrequent, making it improbable in a well-connected network. However, it may arise if larger nations are continuously or temporarily isolated. Writers briefly examined Proof of Stake as a Proof-of-Work alternative [24]. Proof of Work presupposes little participant confidence. Developing more efficient methods, such as Proof of Stake, while maintaining these assumptions intact is challenging.

It was found that studies on lost resources were lacking [3]. These studies looked at Bitcoin mining resources and computer power waste. Processing capacity, a key blockchain feature, merits further examination. Complex blockchains require more computer power. Since Proof of Work is new, it must be tested in large-scale blockchain scenarios. Blockchain mining efficiency depends on reducing resource waste. Scalability is another blockchain operational challenge. The scalability issue stems from Bitcoin nodes permanently storing more transactions and data. The blockchain cannot handle any more transfers [7]. They say that a small number should handle different data types instead of relying on a single node to handle all the data. Scaling was said to be a problem because every node must verify each blockchain block [5]. We thought wasting resources would have caused concern across the study community. All these issues affect blockchain growth. This technology is new; thus, the study is early.

4.6.2.4 Adoption Issues

Interoperability allows financial software and IT systems to share and use data. Existing companies will struggle to integrate blockchain platforms with existing procedures. Externally, how many businesses' blockchains will interact is unknown. Many organizations worry about blockchain security. Thus, authoritative criteria should be employed. Standards Australia urged IOS to create global blockchain standards. The R3 blockchain association wants interbank apps standardized. China established the Interbank Market Technology Standards Workgroup in August 2016. This working group researches banking, laws, and legal frameworks related to BCT. Unstandardized blockchain network architecture might cause serious implementation challenges. International and national bodies are developing widely acknowledged technical standards.

4.6.3 Blockchain-Enabled Financial Sector Functions

Recently, international organizations like the UN and IMF and developed nations like the US, UK, and Japan have monitored blockchain growth and identified applications in various sectors. Some analysts believe blockchain can transform the banking industry. Blockchain eliminates central storage and permissions, upending financial services, particularly payment clearing. Many global financial organizations have been developing blockchain-based concepts since 2015. The adoption of blockchain in the financial industry is also widely trusted. In May 2016, according to some studies, McKinsey surveyed global banking executives and found that half of them disregarded blockchain applications, which will have a major influence within three years and 18 months. Another poll of 200 global banks found that 15% desire to use BCT extensively. The IBM predicted that 66% of banks would have commercial blockchain in four years. So, the following is proposed:

Third hypothesis:
Blockchain's effects on financial research and practice, peer-to-peer transmission, data ownership, sharing, security, and distributed innovations must be understood. Distributed Innovations published the newest blockchain-enabled financial functionality [13] papers. These articles discuss P2P transmission, data ownership, sharing, protection, and distributed inventions. Five articles cover data sharing, the fewest. The next section details BCT's financial sector uses, including peer-to-peer transmission, data ownership, sharing, protection, and distributed inventions.

4.6.3.1 P2P Transmission

Intermediate clearing organizations may handle transactions, bookkeeping, payment initiation, and balance reconciliation for interbank payments. The technique is costly and difficult. Cross-border payments take three days when clearance procedures differ by nation. This is owing to high occupied money, inefficiency, and a few alternatives (China International Capital Corporation, 2016). Blockchain technology enables peer-to-peer payments without an intermediary, reducing transaction costs. This will also help banks clear cross-border commercial transactions swiftly. Guo and Liang (2016) found that payment clearance might power blockchain applications. Blockchain technology fixes fraud, trust, and excessive transaction costs.

4.6.3.2 Data Ownership

Individuals generate a lot of relevant web data for credit verification. Internet giants usually control this data. Therefore, individuals cannot claim data ownership and control. Firms must exchange data to protect user privacy, creating discrete data sets. Blockchain technology can solve these issues with dependable, verified data. This helps credit agencies verify data and reduce data-gathering costs. Blockchain technology can turn enormous volumes of data into individually owned credit resources. This technique could underpin future credit systems.

4.6.3.3 Promotes Data Sharing

Blockchain autonomously records enormous volumes of data. Additionally, it has the capability to securely store and distribute encrypted credit reports among other organizations. Blockchain credit researchers proposed that banks retain client information in their database while conducting the "Know Your Customer" process and provide encrypted summary information on the blockchain. The blockchain can be used to inform the original data supply about query requests. Therefore, all parties can analyze external big data while safeguarding vital company data. Researchers in the field of information systems place a high importance on studies related to data privacy. This type of research seeks to understand the variations in people's concerns about privacy or investigate how these issues affect their readiness to share personal information or engage in online transactions.

A data-protection app was developed from research [8]. This platform resembles Bitcoin. Due to its decentralization, several service providers can employ it in real-world applications. Authors presented a blockchain-based decentralized privacy system [14]. Researchers use blockchain as a database for this protection. Companies can access user data on the blockchain without compromising privacy. At this point, third parties are less important because users always receive a long history of their data use. The smart method lets users control their private data and prevent illegal access. Academics also proposed a blockchain-based decentralized approach for safely disseminating sensitive data.

4.6.3.4 Distributed Financial Transaction Innovations

The finance supply chain includes using physical documents for transactions and relying on human inspections. This approach involves several intermediaries, substantial costs, a significant danger of illicit transactions, and inefficiency. Blockchain technology can utilize smart contracts to minimize the need for involvement in manual paperwork. Consequently, the efficiency of the financial supply chain would improve, and the risks associated with manual operations would be reduced. The supplier, buyer, and bank are key stakeholders in the business. To streamline payment processes, utilizing a decentralized distributed ledger and smart contracts to facilitate automated payments whenever specific conditions and outcomes are met is beneficial. Blockchain technology can potentially decrease costs for trade financing businesses and banks in the finance sector.

McKinsey (2016) estimates that BCT can cut operating costs by $13.5–$15 billion and risk costs by $1.1–$1.6 billion for banks. Both trading partners may reduce capital and operational costs by $1.1–$1.3 billion and $1.6–$2.1 billion, respectively. Transaction efficiency also increases trade financing flow, boosting trade chain income. Blockchain adoption could lead to fresh digital disruption and a financial revolution.

4.7 Limitations and Feature Scope

4.7.1 Limitations

Due to a scarcity of blockchain engineers, adopting BCT can be expensive and time-consuming. Smaller financial organizations may be unwilling to upgrade their systems. No one can change blockchain data. Blockchain has this advantage, but financial firms that routinely change data may find it problematic. Businesses must adapt their processes to use blockchain. The development ledger and blockchain record transactions.

Blockchain's structure and features make it secure, transparent, and almost unchangeable. Blockchains record transactions precisely and chronologically. Modifying or deleting transactions, as well as including unverified information, poses challenges because every participant in the network possesses a duplicate copy. The probability of successfully executing a coordinated attack on many devices, ranging from thousands to hundreds of thousands, is low.

Both consumers and banking institutions face numerous obstacles when transferring funds internationally. Blockchain payments address all these issues, enhancing trust and reliability. This technology can potentially impact the banking industry and financial transactions. Blockchains are highly effective at documenting transactions and ensuring the protection of data. Blockchain-based payments offer rapid transaction processing and the ability to reverse transactions. However, users express concerns about online fraudulent activities. Large transactions are cheaper than typical banking. Cash, wire transfers, and cashier's checks are the safest payment methods. Cash transactions are untraceable, wire transfers may be delayed, and checks can be forged. Blockchain innovations have transformed banking, supply chain management, and healthcare. The public discovered blockchain enterprises two to three years ago. Many contemporary companies are actively pursuing strategies to implement BCT. Blockchains are distributed and decentralized systems that function as ledgers.

4.7.2 Future Scope

Implementing BCT poses significant challenges. Despite numerous obstacles, many financial institutions can utilize it, and equities related to BCT are highly sought-after assets. The financial sector sees blockchain's potential benefits and its growing importance in financial services. Blockchain technology uses public and private encryption keys and a distributed ledger. The public key is available to all network users, but only transaction participants can access the private key.

Thus, only those with the private key can view stakeholders and transaction details, while all network users can view the transaction using the public key. It would safeguard stakeholders' financial data while ensuring system transparency. Blockchain technology establishes a single and immutable record of truth, automates intercompany transactions using smart contracts and consensus mechanisms, improves visibility across systems, reduces company imbalances, uses near-real-time reporting instead of historical data, and simplifies and standardizes supply chain processes. These capabilities can potentially revolutionize the intercompany relationships and transactions of large institutions. Blockchain can address these concerns by guaranteeing data integrity across systems and auditing modifications made to customer data. Leaders believe BCT will enhance transparency, reduce friction, expedite transactions, save costs, enhance security, and minimize financial crimes. Blockchain technology will enable blockchain-based "smart contracts," which may execute themselves. These contracts can automate compliance, claim processing, and distribution.

The banking industry has recreated asset transactions to test blockchain. This gives blockchain solutions some flexibility and efficiency without neglecting ecosystem impact. Blockchain software facilitates instantaneous digital asset exchanges among market participants. Blockchain revolutionizes procedures and questions traditional business model beliefs. This technology will enhance market transparency and promote fairness in competition. As blockchain applications extend throughout industries, their position in finance is crucial to investigate in the future.

4.8 Conclusion

Globally, manufacturing facilities are embracing BCT to enhance connectivity. The future factory will include many commodities, accessories, logistics, and value-chain partners, including equipment and item suppliers. In the case of cryptocurrencies, this technique generates an immutable ledger. Advertisers can zero in on certain demographics, and artists may collect just royalties, all thanks to BCT. Money transfers are embracing this innovation. Most people use bank accounts to exchange money, thus bill payments are vital. To facilitate secure transactions and create their own digital money, banks have been at the forefront of the digital revolution. When it comes to banking, BCT allows for real-time transaction tracking. Now, financial institutions can use public blockchains to finalize deals. CEOs need to achieve certain goals before their banking technology becomes widely used. The way we travel would be altered by the possibility of sharing information and short-term property rentals on the blockchain. While studying electromobility, you might purchase and operate a vehicle using Blockchain smart contracts. If a company is using BCT for financial transactions, they can use smart contracts to upload invoices. On the blockchain, you can record payment details like dates and amounts, as well as customer information. As soon as a customer pays their bill, smart contracts mark it as paid and alert the company. A client's credibility can be verified before trade using BCT. Blockchain technology will handle much of the future monetary management.

AI disclosure statement: The author confirms that no artificial intelligence (AI)-generated content or AI-assisted writing tools were used in the preparation of this chapter (including summaries and the abstract). All text, analysis, and conclusions are the result of the author's original work.

References

1. Bogucharskov, A.V., Pokamestov, I.E., Adamova, K.R., Tropina, Z.N., Adoption of BCT in trade finance process. *J. Rev. Glob. Econ.*, 7, 510–515, 2018.
2. Albayati, H., Kim, S.K., Rho, J.J., Accepting financial transactions using BCT and cryptocurrency: A customer perspective approach. *Technol. Soc.*, 62, 101320, 2020.
3. Ali, O., Ally, M., Dwivedi, Y., The state of play of BCT in the financial services sector: A systematic literature review. *Int. J. Inf. Manage.*, 54, 102199, 2020.
4. Panda, S.K., Jena, A.K., Swain, S.K., Satapathy, S.C. (Eds.), *Blockchain Technology: Applications and Challenges*, Springer, Intelligent Systems Reference Library, Switzerland, 2021. https://doi.org/10.1007/978-3-030-69395-4.
5. Boakye, E.A., Zhao, H., Ahia, B.N.K., Emerging research on BCT in finance; a conveyed evidence of bibliometric-based evaluations. *J. High Technol. Manage. Res.*, 33, 2, 100437, 2022.
6. Chen, Y. and Bellavitis, C., Blockchain disruption and decentralized finance: The rise of decentralized business models. *J. Bus. Ventur. Insights*, 13, e00151, 2020.
7. Murala, D.K., METAEDUCATION: State-of-the-Art Methodology for Empowering Feature Education. *IEEE Access*, 12, 57992–58020, 2024, doi: 10.1109/ACCESS.2024.3391903.
8. Murala, D.K., Panda, S.K., Dash, S.P., MedMetaverse: Medical Care of Chronic Disease Patients and Managing Data Using Artificial Intelligence, Blockchain, and Wearable Devices State-of-the-Art Methodology. *IEEE Access*, 11, 138954–138985, 2023, doi: 10.1109/ACCESS.2023.3340791.
9. Murala, D.K. and Panda, S.K., Artificial Intelligence in the Development of Metaverse, in: *Metaverse, and Immersive Technologies: An Introduction to Industrial, Business and Social Applications*, pp. 407–436, John Wiley & Sons, Inc., 2023/10/20, https://doi.org/10.1002/9781394177165.ch15.
10. Murala, D.K. and Panda, S.K., Metaverse: A Study on Immersive Technologies, in: *Metaverse, and Immersive Technologies: An Introduction to Industrial, Business and Social Applications*, pp. 1–41, John Wiley & Sons, Inc., 2023/10/20, https://doi.org/10.1002/9781394177165.ch1.
11. Murala, D.K. and Panda, S.K., The Internet of Things in Developing Metaverse, in: *Metaverse, and Immersive Technologies: An Introduction to*

Industrial, Business and Social Applications, pp. 437–465, John Wiley & Sons, Inc., 2023/10/20, https://doi.org/10.1002/9781394177165.ch16.
12. Murala, D.K. and Panda, S.K., Blockchain in the Development of Metaverse, in: *Metaverse, and Immersive Technologies: An Introduction to Industrial, Business and Social Applications*, pp. 1002, Wiley, USA, 28 September 2023, https://doi.org/10.1002/9781394177165.ch3.
13. Murala, D.K. and Panda, S.K., The Role of Immersive Reality (AR/VR/MR/XR) in Metaverse, in: *Metaverse, and Immersive Technologies: An Introduction to Industrial, Business and Social Applications*, pp. 159–189, John Wiley & Sons, Inc., 2023/10/20, https://doi.org/10.1002/9781394177165.ch6.
14. Hofmann, E., Strewe, U.M., Bosia, N., Discussion—how does the full potential of BCT in supply chain finance look like?, in: *Supply Chain Finance and BCT*, pp. 77–87, Springer, Cham, 2018.
15. Javaid, M., *et al.*, A review of BCT applications for financial services. *BenchCouncil Trans. Benchmarks Stand. Eval.*, 2, 3, 100073, 2022.
16. Varaprasada Rao, K., Murala, D.K., Panda, S.K., Blockchain: A Study of New Business Model, in: *Recent Advances in BCT: Real-World Applications*, pp. 187–214, Springer International Publishing, 2023/2/12.
17. Lokre, S.S., Naman, V., Priya, S., Panda, S.K., Gun Tracking System Using Blockchain Technology, in: *BCT: Applications and Challenges*, Intelligent Systems Reference Library, vol. 203, S.K. Panda, A.K. Jena, S.K. Swain, S.C. Satapathy (Eds.), Springer, Cham, 2021, https://doi.org/10.1007/978-3-030-69395-4_16.
18. Li, M., Shao, S., Ye, Q., Xu, G., Huang, G.Q., Blockchain-enabled logistics finance execution platform for capital-constrained E-commerce retail. *Rob. Comput. Integr. Manuf.*, 65, 101962, 2020.
19. Poongodi, M., Sharma, A., Vijayakumar, V., Bhardwaj, V., Sharma, A.P., Iqbal, R., Kumar, R., Prediction of the price of Ethereum blockchain cryptocurrency in an industrial finance system. *Comput. Electr. Eng.*, 81, 106527, 2020.
20. Arza, M.S. and Panda, S.K., An Integration of Blockchain and Machine Learning into the Health Care System, in: *Machine Learning Adoption in Blockchain-Based Intelligent Manufacturing*, vol. 1, pp. 33–58, DOI: 10.1201/9781003252009-3.
21. Kowalski, M., Lee, Z.W.Y., Chan, T.K.H., BCT and trust relationships in trade finance. *Technol. Forecasting Social Change*, 166, 2021, ISSN 0040-1625, https://doi.org/10.1016/j.techfore.2021.120641.
22. Murala, D.K., Panda, S.K., Sahoo, S.K., Panda, S.K., Securing Electronic Health Record System in Cloud Environment Using BCT, in: *Recent Advances in BCT*, Intelligent Systems Reference Library, vol. 237, V. Mishra, S.P. Dash, A.K. Pani (Eds.), Springer, Cham, 2023, https://doi.org/10.1007/978-3-031-22835-3_4.
23. Nanda, S.K., Panda, S.K., Das, M., Satapathy, S.C., Automating Vehicle Insurance Process Using Smart Contract and Ethereum, in: *Advances in*

Micro-Electronics, Embedded Systems and IoT, Lecture Notes in Electrical Engineering, vol. 838, V.V.S.S.S. Chakravarthy, W. Flores-Fuentes, V. Bhateja, B. Biswal, (Eds.), Springer, Singapore, 2022, https://doi.org/10.1007/978-981-16-8550-7_23.

24. Panda, S.K., Dash, S.P., Jena, A.K., Optimization of Block Query Response Using Evolutionary Algorithm, in: *Data Engineering and Intelligent Computing*, Advances in Intelligent Systems and Computing, vol. 1, V. Bhateja, S.C. Satapathy, C.M. Travieso-González, V.N.M. Aradhya (Eds.), Springer, Singapore, 2021, https://doi.org/10.1007/978-981-16-0171-2_54.
25. Panda, S.K., Rao, D.C., Satapathy, S.C., An Investigation into the Usability of Blockchain Technology in the Internet of Things, in: *Data Engineering and Intelligent Computing*, Advances in Intelligent Systems and Computing, vol. 1, V. Bhateja, S.C. Satapathy, C.M. Travieso-González, V.N.M. Aradhya (Eds.), Springer, Singapore, 2021, https://doi.org/10.1007/978-981-16-0171-2_53.
26. Panda, S.K. and Satapathy, S.C., An Investigation into Smart Contract Deployment on Ethereum Platform Using Web3.js and Solidity Using Blockchain, in: *Data Engineering and Intelligent Computing*, Advances in Intelligent Systems and Computing, vol. 1, V. Bhateja, S.C. Satapathy, C.M. Travieso-González, V.N.M. Aradhya (Eds.), Springer, Singapore, 2021, https://doi.org/10.1007/978-981-16-0171-2_52.
27. Panda, S.K., Mohammad, G.B., Nandan Mohanty, S., Sahoo, S., Smart contract-based land registry system to reduce frauds and time delay. *Secur. Privacy*, e172, 2021, https://doi.org/10.1002/spy2.172.
28. Panda, S.K., Elngar, A.A., Balas, V.E., Kayed, M. (Eds.), *Bitcoin and Blockchain: History and Current Applications*, 1st ed., CRC Press, 2020, https://doi.org/10.1201/9781003032588.
29. Panda, S.K. and Satapathy, S.C., Drug traceability and transparency in medical supply chain using blockchain for easing the process and creating trust between stakeholders and consumers. *Pers. Ubiquitous Comput.*, 2021, https://doi.org/10.1007/s00779-021-01588-3.
30. Panda, S.K., Daliyet, S.P., Lokre, S.S., Naman, V., Distributed Ledger Technology in the Construction Industry Using Corda, in: *The New Advanced Society: Artificial Intelligence and Industrial Internet of Things Paradigm*, https://doi.org/10.1002/9781119884392.ch2.
31. Sathya, A.R., Panda, S.K., Hanumanthakari, S., Enabling Smart Education System Using BCT, in: *BCT: Applications and Challenges*, Intelligent Systems Reference Library, vol. 203, S.K. Panda, A.K. Jena, S.K. Swain, S.C. Satapathy (Eds.), Springer, Cham, 2021, https://doi.org/10.1007/978-3-030-69395-4_10.
32. Katona, T., Decentralized finance: the possibilities of a blockchain money lego system. *Financ. Econ. Rev.*, 20, 1, 74–102, 2021.
33. Tripathi, G., Ahad, M.A., Casalino, G., A comprehensive review of BCT: underlying principles and historical background with future challenges. *Decis. Anal. J.*, 100344, 2023.

34. Niveditha, V.R., Sekaran, K., Amandeep Singh, K., Panda, S.K., Effective prediction of bitcoin price using wolf search algorithm and bidirectional LSTM on the internet of things data. *Int. J. Syst. Syst. Eng.*, 11, 3–4, 224–236.
35. Varaprasada Rao, K. and Panda, S.K., A Design Model of Copyright Protection System Based on Distributed Ledger Technology, in: *Computer Communication, Networking and IoT*, Lecture Notes in Networks and Systems, vol. 459, S.C. Satapathy, J.C.W. Lin, L.K. Wee, V. Bhateja, T.M. Rajesh, (Eds.), Springer, Singapore, 2023, https://doi.org/10.1007/978-981-19-1976-3_17.
36. Varaprasada Rao, K. and Panda, S.K., Secure Electronic Voting (E-voting) System Based on Blockchain on Various Platforms, in: *Computer Communication, Networking and IoT*, Lecture Notes in Networks and Systems, vol. 459, S.C. Satapathy, J.C.W. Lin, L.K. Wee, V. Bhateja, T.M. Rajesh, (Eds.), Springer, Singapore, 2023, https://doi.org/10.1007/978-981-19-1976-3_18.
37. Zhu, X. and Wang, D., Research on blockchain applications for E-commerce, finance and energy. *IOP Conf. Ser.: Earth Environ. Sci.*, 252, 4, 042126, 2019.
38. Panda, S.K., Fraud-Resistant Crowdfunding System Using Ethereum Blockchain, in: *Bitcoin and Blockchain*, pp. 237–276, 2020.
39. Puranam, K.S.R., Gaddam, M.C.T., K, V.P.R., Panda, S.K., Reddy, G.S.M., Anatomy and Lifecycle of a Bitcoin Transaction. *Proceedings of International Conference on Sustainable Computing in Science, Technology and Management (SUSCOM)*, Amity University Rajasthan, Jaipur - India, February 26-28, 2019, February 18, 2019, Available at SSRN: https://ssrn.com/abstract=3355106 or http://dx.doi.org/10.2139/ssrn.3355106.
40. Panda, S.K., Sathya, A.R., Das, S., Bitcoin: Beginning of the Cryptocurrency Era, in: *Recent Advances in Blockchain Technology*, Intelligent Systems Reference Library, vol. 237, S.K. Panda, V. Mishra, S.P. Dash, A.K. Pani, (Eds.), Springer, Cham, 2023, https://doi.org/10.1007/978-3-031-22835-3_2.
41. Panda, S.K., Mishra, V., Dash, S.P., Pani, A.K., *Recent Advances in Blockchain Technology Real-World Applications*, Intelligent Systems Reference Library (ISRL, volume 237), vol. 1, pp. 1 317, 978 3 031 22835-3.
42. Panda, S.K., Mohapatra, R.K., Panda, S., Balamurugan, S., *The New Advanced Society: Artificial Intelligence and Industrial Internet of Things Paradigm*, vol. 1, pp. 1–512, John Wiley & Sons, USA, 2022. DOI:10.1002/9781119884392.
43. Nanda, S.K., Panda, S.K., Das, M., Satapathy, S.C., Decentralization of Car Insurance System Using Machine Learning and Distributed Ledger Technology, in: *Intelligent Data Engineering and Analytics. FICTA 2022*, Smart Innovation, Systems and Technologies, vol. 327, V. Bhateja, X.S. Yang, J. Chun-Wei Lin, R. Das, (Eds.), Springer, Singapore, 2023, https://doi.org/10.1007/978-981-19-7524-0_52.
44. Nanda, S.K., Panda, S.K., Dash, M., Medical supply chain integrated with blockchain and IoT to track the logistics of medical products. *Multimedia Tools Appl.*, 82, 32917–32939, 2023, https://doi.org/10.1007/s11042-023-14846-8.
45. Varaprasada Rao, K. and Panda, S.K., Initiation, Innovation, Implementation and Integration of CBDC in Digital Virtual Payment Systems, in: *Advances*

in Microelectronics, Embedded Systems and IoT. ICMEET 2023, Lecture Notes in Electrical Engineering, vol. 1156, V.V.S.S.S. Chakravarthy, V. Bhateja, J. Anguera, S. Urooj, A. Ghosh, (Eds.), Springer, Singapore, 2024, https://doi.org/10.1007/978-981-97-0767-6_20.

46. Murala, D.K., Panda, S.K., Sahoo, S.K., Securing electronic health record system in cloud environment using blockchain technology, in: *Recent Advances in Blockchain Technology*, vol. 237, Wiley, USA, 2023.
47. Panda, S.K., Revolution of the Metaverse and Blockchain Technology, in: *Metaverse and Immersive Technologies: An Introduction to Industrial Business and Social Applications*, Wiley, Hoboken, NJ, USA, 2023.

5

A Self-Tuning Digital Immune Cybersecurity Model for Manufacturing Industry 4.0

Vasamsheti Adarsh*, Sashikala Parimi and Vaibhav Mishra

IT & Operations, IBS, IFHE, Hyderabad, India

Abstract

Manufacturing Industry 4.0 (MI4) is the fourth industrial revolution in the manufacturing industry. Industry 4.0, or I4.0, is revolutionizing manufacturing operations and processes by integrating through cyber-physical systems (CPS), the Industrial Internet of Things (IIoT), and advanced big data analytics (BDA). The evolution and implementation of MI4 differ from country to country, often influenced by national strategies and models. In 2011, during the Hannover Fair in Germany, it was initially coined as Industry 4.0. The initial model or concept focused on connected infrastructure, CPS, smart factories, IoT, artificial intelligence (AI), Digital Twins, and big data. It aims to monitor, control and optimize manufacturing operations in real time. It has been almost 13 years since GTAI conceived of Industry 4.0 as a strategy, and today, we look at the future of manufacturing with the realization of connected systems and advanced novel technologies shaping the overall industry. With the swift development's in MI4 technologies, continuously evolving robust, model-based algorithms for calculating, controlling, and optimizing performance metrics in production systems has become essential and critical for incorporating intelligence into smart manufacturing practices, enabling automated factory decision-making. Its goal is to develop autonomous and dynamic operations that enable the mass production of highly customized products. Organizations are rapidly transitioning to the MI4 paradigm by adopting advanced digital and CPS technologies and networking their manufacturing equipment and operations. This shift in digital connectivity enhances the efficiency and effectiveness of operations and presents a new cybersecurity challenge. Cyberattacks in digital or smart manufacturing

**Corresponding author*: adarsh.vasamsheti@gmail.com; v.adarsh18h@ibsindia.org;
ORCID: https:// orcid.org/0009-0001-2634-7200

Sujata Priyambada Dash, Vaibhav Mishra, Bijeta Shaw, Sandeep Kumar Panda and S. Balamurugan (eds.) Digital Immune System: Principles and Practices, (93–120) © 2026 Scrivener Publishing LLC

organizations can have catastrophic consequences. They can cause safety hazards in terms of assets and human life and operational disruptions. The disruptions can lead to economic losses, reputational losses, and regulatory forfeits, among other issues. Due to the growing threat of cybersecurity and the growing importance of smart factories, there is a pressing need to develop a self-tuning digital immune cybersecurity model for smart manufacturing in Industry 4.0. The self-tuning digital immune cybersecurity model framework is designed to enhance the resilience of interconnected smart factories against evolving cyber threats. The model integrates elements of AI—agentic AI programs for automation—to form an adaptive shielding mechanism that resembles a biological immune system, allowing it to learn, adapt, and improve over time, similar to a manufacturing continuous improvement plan of check and act.

***Keywords*:** Self-tuning model (STM), cybersecurity (CS), digital immune system (DIS), manufacturing industry 4.0 (MI4), and agentic artificial intelligence (AAI)

5.1 Introduction: Cybersecurity and Manufacturing Industry 4.0 in the Fourth Industrial Revolution

There is a rising trend among many companies moving toward the Manufacturing Industry 4.0 (MI4) archetype, adopting various novel and innovative technologies (Corallo, A. *et al.*, 2021) [6]. The emergence of MI4 is defined by the amalgamation of cyber-physical systems (CPS), the Industrial Internet of Things (IIoT), big data, artificial intelligence (AI), machine learning (ML), cloud computing, and robotics (COBOTS)—has revolutionized manufacturing processes, allowing for enhanced productivity, flexibility, and interconnectedness (Tu, J., & Zhang, L., 2022) [27]. However, as manufacturing environments become more digital, complex, and interconnected, the attack surface for cyber threats expands significantly. The connected systems expose manufacturing ecosystems to high turnability levels and increasingly complex cybersecurity (CS) risks, including cyberattacks, data breaches, intellectual property theft, and system disruptions. Operational integrity, including security, confidentiality, safeguarding data, and availability of these systems for real-time access, manufacturers must adopt a strong CS strategy tailored to the Industry 4.0 (I4.0) environment and their specific facilities, machinery, and information technology (IT) infrastructure. While securing isolated machines or systems is challenging, protecting an integrated ecosystem of devices, machines, networks, and cloud services is not impossible with the right strategy in place. The level of business impact needs to be assessed by manufacturing companies in case of a CS threat; organizations can strategize and start to analyze, including the isolation of their critical equipment and data in case of a threat or breach.

5.2 Significant Cybersecurity Challenges in Manufacturing Industry 4.0

In early 2010, advanced economies began introducing methods in manufacturing operations to integrate industrial data through cyber-physical conjunction (Bordoloi T. *et al.*, 2022) [5]. Security encircles numerous CS-related concepts, technologies, and techniques defending critical manufacturing operations and equipment (Corallo, A. *et al.*, 2021) [6]. The study is based on MI4 processes and systems that are defined through an impact assessment model to protect critical operations and equipment against cyberattacks, and it also helps in evaluating the impacts of the addition or deletion of specific technology (Prajapati, D. K. *et al.*, 2024) [21]. The results of a study done on agile MI4 through comprehensive TOPSIS and Fuzzy DEMETAL analysis indicate that CS, cloud, and IoT are the most commonly utilized technologies. The study highlights the need for core competency and a skilled workforce in the critical deployment of digital technologies. The MI4 technologies present optimistic solutions for enhancing sustainability norms in operations. Initial high costs from MI4, security perils, data privacy (DP) challenges, lack of awareness, and cyber threats create a challenging environment for organizations. Circular economy covers additive manufacturing (AM), AI, advanced vision systems, big data advanced analytics, CS, the IoT, robotics, virtual reality and augmented reality as the principal MI4 action areas to support sustainable manufacturing (Laskurain–Iturbe *et al.*, 2021) [17]. In CPS, a connected ecosystem and security, meaningful communication are everything that endures a strong defense mechanism in case of potential risks of sabotage, disruptions in manufacturing operations, leading to quality deficiencies, or catastrophic meltdown of operations in case of cyberattacks. The study focused on analyzing factors determining the successful commissioning of information and digital technology in MI4. Results showed that operations technology and CS were the dependent determinants of MI4 implementation, and perceived benefit and management support were key determinants.

5.3 Increased Attack Surface

Cyber-physical systems are what drive MI4, enabling the integration of previously isolated operational technology (OT) and advanced information technology systems. Cyber-physical systems have converged from wired to wireless, opening an unchallenged terrane for MI4 connectivity from legacy to the latest systems. This has multiplied the risks associated with surface CS threats (Kampourakis *et al.*, 2023) [12]. With the rise of connected equipment, devices, intelligent machines, and sensors integrated with cloud-based platforms, the cyber threat risk for surface attacks has grown exponentially. Vulnerabilities in IoT devices, legacy machine instruments like programmable logic controllers, or human-machine interfaces (HMIs) are vulnerable scopes for miscreants to be exploited to compromise the entire manufacturing ecosystem. For example, a simple addition of a full stop (.) in the program can stop a critical asset; it may take several hours, even days, to understand the root cause before operations are resumed. However, the potential consequences of cyber-physical attacks are far more severe, causing profound and potentially irreversible damage to the manufacturing system (Wu M. *et al.*, 2020) [28].

5.4 Legacy Systems and Insecure Networks

Most SMEs and manufacturers still operate in legacy or traditional systems, which can be dated on or beyond Industry 3.0, which is not designed with modern CS in mind. The frog leap of I4.0 in the last decade and MI4 has resulted in greater integration of legacy old manufacturing and production processes, systems and technologies with internet protocol communications. New unconsidered threats emerge as industrial control system (ICS) devices are now easily connected *via* public network or cloud. It is necessary to address these threats to ensure industrial manufacturing processes' safe and secure operation. Legacy systems (not supported by OEM or service providers) or older versions of operating systems lack upgraded security patches or algorithms, leaving them vulnerable to exploitation (Maesschalck S. *et al.*, 2022) [18]. The manufacturing sector is revolutionized by I4.0 through IIoT as a tool to see significant improvement in productivity and reliability. The primary concern in implementing IIoT technology in machinery or devices is safety and security, alongside other important issues like patch management for open networks. If the security mechanisms are inefficient or inadequate, unauthorized devices could gain access to critical data and resources within the network (Kumar A. *et al.*, 2024) [14]. Insecure networks, often connecting OT and IT systems, create potential points of failure. Strategy for business growth often leaves vulnerabilities in upgrading IT/OT systems, which creates roadblocks, hurdles, and severe risks for the entire business.

5.5 Third Industrial Revolution Machine Control Systems – Industrial Control Systems and Supervisory Control and Data Acquisition Security

Cyber-physical systems, supervisory control and data acquisition (SCADA), and automation systems *via* IIoT in MI4 have raised concerns about potential CS threats and the significance of securing critical equipment, assets, and infrastructure in manufacturing operations (Tidrea A. *et al.*, 2019, 2023) [25, 26]. Supervisory control and data acquisition has low potency toward security systems and is defenseless to CS threats *via* hardware, firmware, software, or communication protocol attacks. The SCADA systems control and monitor industrial operations but often lack strong security features. The shift towards I4.0 improves the performance of MI4 *via* industrial control systems (ICSs). However, the high costs associated with re-engineering existing industrial devices pose challenges to modernization. As a result, insecure protocols are still used to operate *via* these legacy systems. Legacy systems and protocols are widely used (e.g. Modbus/TCP) to control various industrial equipment and processes alongside the latest version of protocols and technologies (Bernieri G. *et al.*, 2019) [4]. ICS and SCADA networks were traditionally air-gapped (not connected to external networks). The rising trend of real-time operation monitoring *via* connecting machines' SCADA systems to cloud or web-based applications exposes them to cyber risks. Managing essential and crucial infrastructures *via* SCADA and automation for the smooth operation of society, including healthcare, transportation, water supply, power grids, and the economy, is vital for national security. A CS threat to these key equipment and infrastructure structures can disrupt normal operations. It may even cause physical damage, significantly impacting the end users who rely on these services (George A. S. *et al.*, 2023) [10].

5.6 Supply Chain Vulnerabilities

Supply chain (SC) disruption is a disastrous meltdown of operations often driven by an unanticipated event or menace that can significantly impact manufacturing or halt the entire operation (Ali I. *et al.*, 2021) [1]. A study (Pandey S. *et al.*, 2023) [19] points out the findings that SC personnel should pay attention to the three most significant risks: disruption, CS, and safety perils in the current MI4 ecosystem. Core manufacturing is generally dependent on outsourcing through external suppliers and contractors. Cybersecurity risks, including software vulnerabilities, counterfeit hardware, or malicious insiders, can be introduced into the manufacturing process through the supply chain.

5.7 Virus

Regarding CS, viruses leading to ransomware and malware outbreaks are among the most significant and common risks for individuals, businesses, governments, and organizations worldwide (Maesschalck S. *et al.*, 2022) [18]. Ransomware is a malware designed to encrypt/code/transform the host's files, transforming them into inaccessible formats. Muggers call for an exchange amount, often in cryptocurrency, in return for a transforming key. For example, Microsoft Windows vulnerabilities led to WannaCry in 2017, which was a global scale attack in 150 counties and affected almost over 200,000 operating systems Malware, including ransomware, can encrypt critical data or lock down production processes. Manufacturers may and have become targets due to their reliance on real-time systems and the potential financial and operational damage caused by disruptions to production lines.

5.8 Types of Malwares

Malicious software, also known as malware, is any program or algorithm programmed to damage a computer, network, designed software, or device. It can take many forms and have various objectives, such as stealing sensitive data, damaging files, or disrupting system operations. Figure 5.1 depicts different types of malware. Understanding these distinctions is key to empowering users to protect themselves against the diverse threats posed by malware.

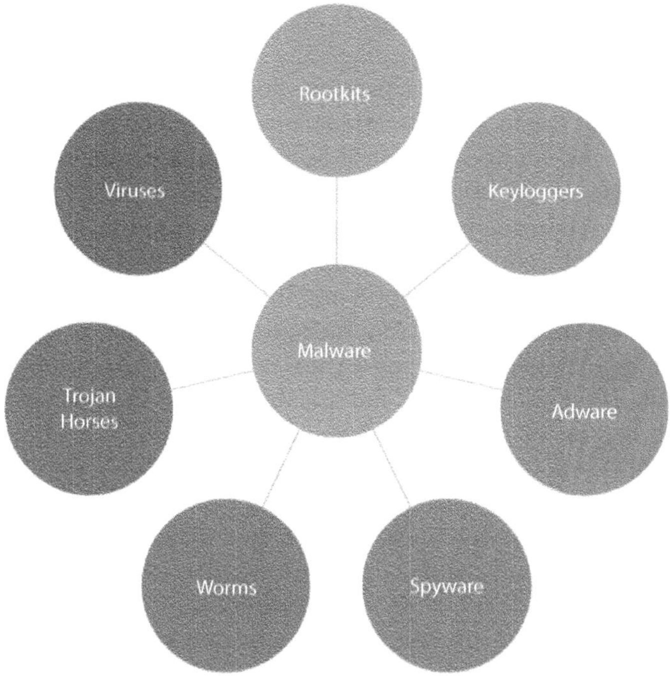

Figure 5.1 Types of malware.

5.9 Data Privacy and Intellectual Property Protection

The most common impeding deterrents for manufacturing organizations implementing MI4 are data privacy (DP) and CS issues (Skalli D *et al.*, 2024; Wu, C., 2020) [24, 29]. Data privacy and intellectual property (IP) protection are essential in safeguarding sensitive information, personal data, and creative assets from misuse, theft, or unauthorized access. With the growing dependence on interconnectivity and digital technologies, businesses, individuals, and governments face increasing challenges in maintaining security and compliance. The increasing connectivity between assets and the digitalization of manufacturing raises concerns over data privacy, especially with IP. Cyber-attacks aim to steal proprietary designs, formulas, or production methods, which could have long-term financial impacts.

5.10 Insider Threats

Managing insider threats is a pressing task in MI4 organisations. The most significant risk to MI4 operational machinery, equipment, processes, and technologies is internal, regardless of the organisation's demographics (Petrovski *et al.*, 2024) [20]. Insider threats refer to safety and security risks posed by human resources within an organisation, such as workers, officers, staff, contractors, or business partners, who have authorised access to systems, data, or networks and their places of work. Examples of Intentional threats can result from malicious intent, such as an employee stealing sensitive data for personal gain, negligence, like a staff member leaving a computer unlocked and unattended, or inadvertent actions, such as a contractor mistakenly deleting important files, leading to data breaches, financial loss, or reputational damage. There is a significant risk associated with human resources having access to restricted or sensitive working areas, which may unintentionally lead to considerable harm. The interconnectedness of IT and OT systems heightens this risk, as malicious actors can exploit vulnerabilities in one area of the organisation to penetrate critical manufacturing systems. This situation highlights the necessity for comprehensive prevention strategies.

5.11 Challenging Stint for Cybersecurity in Manufacturing Industry 4.0

Cybersecurity in MI4 is no longer optional but a fundamental necessity. As MI4 adopts novel technologies in their Fourth Industry Revolution (4IR) operations, they must also bolster and secure their CS position to protect against increasingly sophisticated cyber threats. A layered, proactive approach incorporating AI, ML, strong network segmentation, regular patching, data encryption, robust employee training, and supply chain security is essential for safeguarding manufacturing systems. While CS challenges are significant, they can be effectively addressed by building a resilient, adaptive security framework. To address the risks and challenges, there is a need to build a digital immune CS framework in I4.0 environments; manufacturers must implement a comprehensive and novel approach to CS is a way through innovation. To bridge the gap between the escalating threat of CS and the increasing significance of smart MI4 factories in the era of I4.0, there is an urgent need to develop a self-tuning digital immune CS model for smart manufacturing. This approach protects critical assets and sensitive data and ensures that manufacturing operations continue to run smoothly, even in the stage of evolving embryonic cyber threats.

5.12 Self-Tuning Model

"Self-tuning" drives a self-tuning model (STM) for changing the way people communicate, work, and live and for changing the dynamics of existing enterprises, organizations, and business models. To boost innovation in the 4IR, enterprises are becoming more 3A: more agile (Asif, M., 2020) [3], adaptive, and ambidextrous (Del G M. *et al.*, 2021) [7]. Crisis-driven tool STM aligns with internal and external processes to achieve superior results (Fawad Sharif *et al.*, 2024) [9]. Complex manufacturing patterns can be analyzed by ML algorithms to deliver predictive and prescriptive reports along with patterns. Various MI4 tasks (e.g., quality, inspection, scheduling) can be automated with the development of competent decision-making, support, and advancements in agentic artificial intelligence (AAI). (Rai R. *et al.*, 2021) [22]. Self-tuning is associated with agility (the ability to adjust rapidly), adaptation (learning through trial and error), and ambidexterity (balancing exploration with exploitation). Self-tuning algorithms incorporate elements of all three concepts but do so self-directedly (Reeves *et al.*, 2015) [23]. The MI4 applications use big data technologies and integrated STM for predictive maintenance (Apiletti D. *et al.*, 2018) [2]. The proposed model by Apiletti's approach targets some of MI4's most common needs, integrating STM for KPI computations.

Manufacturing processes are increasingly driven by digital transformation in the 4IR in MI4. Self tuning models are vital in optimizing operations. For example, Google and Alibaba did it a long time ago. These models leverage advanced novel and innovative technologies such as AI, ML, and IIoT to adapt autonomously to changing conditions, improving efficiency, quality, and sustainability. They accomplish this by quickly automating three learning loops. An STM is a dynamic system that adjusts its parameters in real-time to optimize performance without human intervention. These models rely on feedback loops, predictive analytics, and optimization algorithms to absorb learning from big data and acclimate to new scenarios.

- Adaptability – Adjusting security measures to the changing risk landscape.
- Agility – Probing for new threats.
- Ambidextrous – Preparing for the potential emergence of new significant threats inside and outside.

(Refer Figure 5.2 for Adaptability, Agility and Ambidextrous)

To address the profound emerging security risks and challenges, enterprises must meaningfully change their CS approaches by implementing STM that enhances secure and improved connectivity among data, knowledge, personnel, and manufacturing activities.

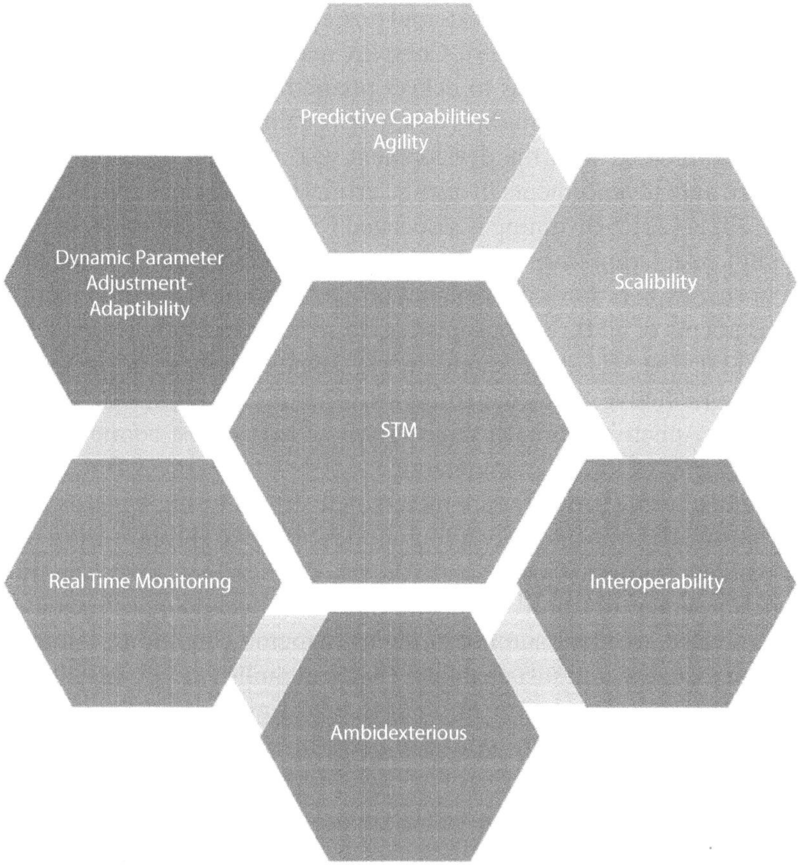

Figure 5.2 Key features of STM.

Table 5.1 Self-tuning model application and functionality.

Sl. no.	Application STM	Functionality
1	**Real-time monitoring**	Continuously collects and analyzes data from IoT sensors and all connected devices. Dynamic parameter adjustment: This algorithm optimizes system settings based on performance metrics (Lu, Y. *et al.*, 2019) [16]. It can map linear and nonlinear relationships.
2	**Predictive capabilities**	Anticipates potential disruption in status quo issues or inefficiencies and proactively adjusts operations.
3	**Scalability**	Both AI and/or ML adapts to various manufacturing environments and scales with production demand.
4	**Interoperability**	Integrates seamlessly with existing industrial systems, including SCADA, manufacturing execution system (MES), and enterprise resource planning (ERP).
5	**Ambidextrous**	Communicates within the network and outside the network.

5.13 Self-Tuning Model Application and Functionality

Self-tuning models are often used in fields like control systems, ML, and optimization to automatically adjust parameters and improve system performance without human intervention. Table 5.1 illustrates various areas where STMs can be applied to optimize and enhance performance in dynamic environments automatically. Refer Figure 5.2 for STM and their key features. They offer key advantages in adaptability and efficiency across different domains.

5.14 Self-Tuning Model and Industry 4.0

Industry 4.0 has integrated advanced MI4 technologies. The significance of HMIs has grown due to the complexities in the MI4 environment, and the increasing perils lined with CS (Kumar N. *et al.*, 2022) [15].

Industry 4.0 offers opportunities for enhancing sustainability standards within the manufacturing sector. Initial cost, data security, a skilled workforce, and privacy are deterrents to novel technology, as the perils of CS and cyber threats always surround entire operations. Integrating cloud-based operations, industrial internet connectivity, additive manufacturing, and CS platforms have transformed and revitalized modern factories, marking the era of I4.0 (Gupta S. *et al.*, 2020) [11]. A higher level of sustainable performance is achieved in manufacturing through cloud-based ERP systems in MI4 operations, but the downside is that it elevates substantial amounts of CS risks. Developing smart manufacturing systems is costly and complex, and the next level of difficulty comes with combining diverse technologies such as automation, controlling and communicating through data exchanges *via* CPS, AI, the IIoT, COBOT, and semi-autonomous industrial systems is absolutely challenging (Refer Figure 5.3 for I4.0 Tech.).

Table 5.2 Applications for STM functionality.

Sl. no.	Application STM	Functionality
1	**Predictive maintenance**	The STM analyzes data to forecast failures and anomalies, accommodating and adjusting maintenance schedules to minimize downtime.
2	**Process optimization**	For example, in injection molding, welding, or chemical production processes, an input feed algorithm considers only process and product parameters, such as temperature, pressure, or speed.
3	**Energy management**	Energy usage is optimized by tuning operations for maximum utility based on energy consumption patterns and production schedules.
4	**Quality control**	Action recognition machine vision and ML detect defect and adjust manufacturing processes to maintain consistent quality.
5	**Supply chain optimization**	Adapt production schedules and resource allocation in response to real-time supply chain data.

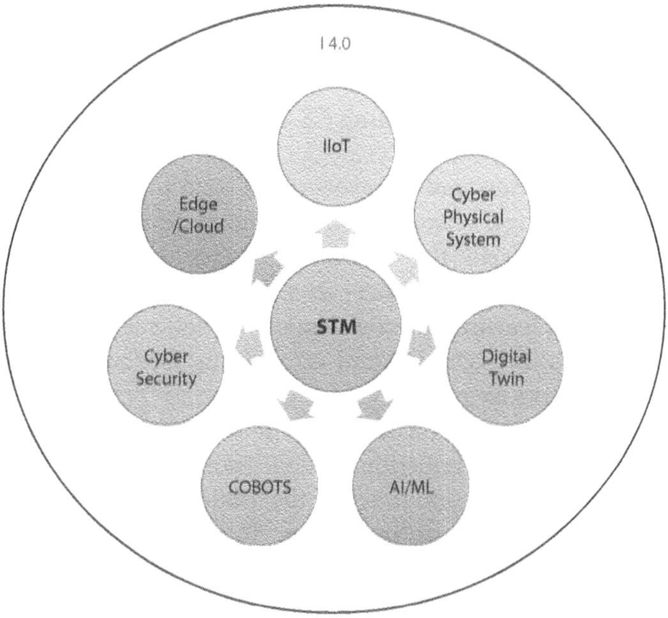

Figure 5.3 Industry 4 (Technology) and STM.

5.15 Applications for Self-Tuning Models in Manufacturing Industry 4.0

Self-tuning models play a vital part in the evolution of MI4. Table 5.2 represents some key applications of STM, along with a brief description of functionality in the manufacturing landscape. The STM can be applied across different manufacturing fields to automatically adjust parameters and improve system and process performance, ensuring optimal outcomes in dynamic environments. Whether optimizing a control system, tuning ML models, or improving industrial maintenance, STM offers powerful benefits in automation and efficiency. Figure 5.3 refers to Industry 4.0 technologies and STM for adaptive control.

5.16 Self-Tuning Model and Cybersecurity

An STM for CS for the MI4 refers to a ML, AI, or evolving AAI system designed to dynamically adjust its parameters and structure to optimize its performance in detecting, preventing, and responding to cyber threats. An STM can significantly enhance defenses in CS, where threats evolve rapidly and often unpredictably.

Key components of a self-tuning CS conceptual model

- **Data ingestion and preprocessing**: Real-time data collection from logs, network traffic, endpoint devices, and threat intelligence feeds. Preprocessing includes feature extraction, normalization, and noise or irrelevant data removal.
- **Dynamic learning mechanisms**: The model learns optimal strategies through trial and error, using feedback from its natural iterative process environment.
- **Feedback loops**: It incorporates mechanisms to evaluate the effectiveness of predictions and decisions in real-time, feeding back information to refine the model.
- **Hyperparameter optimization**: It uses techniques like Bayesian optimization, grid search, or evolutionary algorithms to self-tune hyperparameters (e.g., learning rates and tree depths) based on performance metrics.
- **Explainability and transparency**: Ensures outputs and decisions are interpretable for security analysts, improving trust and usability.
- **Threat adaptation**: Identifies emerging attack vectors and adjusts rules, thresholds, or model structures.
- **Security information and event management (SIEM) and security orchestration, automation, and response (SOAR) amalgamation**: The requisite for the ambidextrous nature of STM, which automates and enhances incident responses naturally by integrating with SIEM and SOAR platforms.

When implementing STMs in CS, it is crucial to emphasize the need for robust design and careful data management. These aspects play a key role in preventing vulnerabilities and optimizing performance. Table 5.3 summarizes the challenges in securely integrating STM models in CS.

These challenges, as in Table 5.3, collectively highlight the need for careful design, robust data practices, and mechanisms to mitigate risks, ensuring that STMs remain effective and secure in CS. We can address the above challenges by including a DIS.

Table 5.3 Challenges in combining STM and CS.

Sl. no.	Challenges	Summary
1	**Complexity and computational costs**	Self-tuning models and engines with CS can be resource-intensive.
2	**Data quality and bias**	Safety and Security performance depend heavily on the quality and representativeness of training data.
3	**Adversarial attacks**	Models are vulnerable to CS attackers who aim to exploit STMs' learning processes.
4	**Explainability issues**	Dynamic self-tuning engines with CS models are more challenging to interpret.

5.17 Digital Immune System

To strengthen IT infrastructure and architecture, it is necessary to integrate DIS into processes, equipment, and the entire organizational technology ecosystem, which in turn ramps up organizational capabilities and resilience (Krauze, B., & Grabis, J., 2024) [13]. Firewalls, intrusion detection procedures, antivirus software, encryption techniques, and two-factor authentication (2FA) are fundamental components of DIS (George, A. S. *et al.*, 2023) [10]. Despite recognizing DIS as resilience technology, existing frameworks fail to deliver practical evaluation methods for this system (Krauze, B., & Grabis, J., 2024) [13].

Cybersecurity statistics, with rising crime rates in cyberattacks globally, raise the urgency and need for the immune system, which is DIS (Figueroa, M. *et al.*, 2015) [8]. Economic resilience, data integrity, prestige loss, and regulatory non-compliance are all at stake during a CS threat or attack (George, A. S. *et al.*, 2023) [10]. A DIS is a category of optimization and agentic algorithms inspired by the vertebrate unsusceptible approach. The agentic algorithm aspires to mimic the immune system's features of understanding and remembrance to decipher a computational problem. The DIS differentiates crisis from self to non-self functions within an MI4—ecosystem of manufacturing processes or networks to detect malicious activity.

Table 5.4 Key roles of cybersecurity in the digital immune system.

Sl. no.	Action (classification)	Digital immune system (DIS)	Cybersecurity
1	**Threat detection and classification**	The DIS AI/ML algorithms mimic signals in human cells, triggering immune-like responses to quickly and accurately identify threats.	Leverage AI/ML detection tools and global threat intelligence to identify and classify evolving threats.
2	**Automated response and containment**	The DIS neutralizes threats in real-time to minimize spread and damage, enhancing system protection.	Use SOAR platforms to automate responses such as isolating compromised devices, blocking malicious IPs, or quarantining threats.
3	**Proactive threat hunting**	The DIS identifies dormant threats before they are activated, using hunting mechanisms to seek and eliminate risks.	Deploy advanced AI/ML algorithms, analytics, and behavioral monitoring to proactively identify latent CS risks.
4	**Incident recovery and resilience**	Ensures quick restoration of systems post-breach, minimizing downtime and maintaining operational continuity.	Maintain secure, immutable backups and implement robust disaster recovery plans for rapid restoration of industrial systems.

(*Continued*)

Table 5.4 Key roles of cybersecurity in the digital immune system. (*Continued*)

Sl. no.	Action (classification)	Digital immune system (DIS)	Cybersecurity
5	**Self-learning and adaptation**	The DIS evolves by learning from past events and adapting to new threats, ensuring it remains effective against evolving risks.	Integrate real-time updates from global threat intelligence, ensuring CS solutions evolve in tandem with the threat landscape.
6	**Defense against insider threats**	The DIS detects and responds to insider risks through behavior analysis and dynamic adjustments to system defenses.	Monitor user activities, detect anomalies in behavior, and enforce least-privilege access policies to limit insider threat exposure.

5.18 Key Roles of Cybersecurity in the Digital Immune System

A DIS is designed to mimic biological immune systems by identifying, neutralizing, and recovering from cyber threats. Cybersecurity enhances the DIS's core competencies and capabilities by ensuring its effective functioning. A DIS refers to automated, self-healing mechanisms and tools to protect digital infrastructures, networks, and systems against cyber threats. Cybersecurity plays a key part in maintaining digital assets' integrity, availability, and confidentiality. Table 5.4 outlines the key roles of CS in the DIS. The DIS forms the backbone, playing roles as defined in Table 5.5, which continuously adapts to new and rising cyber threats while maintaining the health and security of digital environments. As the threat landscape grows in complexity, the role of CS in the DIS becomes even more critical in safeguarding against attacks.

5.19 Self-Tuning Model Integrated into a Digital Immune System

Self-tuning models play a crucial role in enabling DIS' adaptability. These models leverage ML and feedback loops to adjust in real time to changes in the environment or threat landscape. Self-tuning models are at the heart of DIS, enhancing their ability to respond dynamically to evolving challenges. Self-tuning models are pivotal in enhancing the adaptability of DIS. Self-tuning models use AI /ML algorithm techniques, particularly reinforcement learning or continual learning, to adjust parameters and improve performance dynamically. This empowers the self-adapting system to adapt to changes or abnormalities in the environment, such as new types of threats or shifts in user behavior, without requiring manual intervention.

Grouping STM and DIS increases the resilience, adaptability, and security of I4.0 systems, allowing for smoother operations, increased automation, and a significant reduction in downtime in production environments, leading to potential cost savings. Industry 4.0, the integration of technologies like STMs and a DIS, plays a critical and pivotal role in optimizing operations, ensuring security, and driving efficiency through automation, data analytics, and real-time decision-making. Table 5.5, which outlines the functionality of STM and DIS in I4.0:

Table 5.5 Functionality of STM and DIS in I4.0.

Sl. no.	Action (classification)	Functionality STM & DIS	Benefits in Industry 4.0
1	**Anomaly detection**	Learns normal behavior patterns of industrial systems, such as production workflows and network activity.	Detects and flags deviations that may indicate cyber threats, malfunctioning systems, or abnormal user behavior.
		Uses ML algorithms to adapt to changes in operations or system configurations.	Reduces false positives by fine-tuning detection models to specific industrial contexts.

(*Continued*)

Table 5.5 Functionality of STM and DIS in I4.0. (*Continued*)

Sl. no.	Action (classification)	Functionality STM & DIS	Benefits in Industry 4.0
2	**Dynamic access control**	Continuously evaluates user and device behaviors to assess risk levels.	Prevents unauthorized access by adjusting permissions dynamically based on real-time risk assessments.
		Implements least-privilege principles, granting or revoking access as risk levels fluctuate.	Minimizes the attack surface and protects critical assets from insider or external threats.
3	**Adaptive network security**	Automatically adjusts security configurations such as firewall rules, IDS/IPS policies, and endpoint settings based on threats.	Responds to evolving threats by optimizing security posture without manual intervention.
		Incorporates STM feedback to block malicious traffic, quarantine infected devices, or strengthen defenses at vulnerable points.	Ensures network resilience and minimizes disruptions caused by dynamic industrial environments.
4	**Behavior-Based Threat Mitigation**	Monitors user activities to detect latent insider risks or conceded accounts based on unusual behaviors.	Proactively isolate compromised accounts, devices, or systems before they can cause widespread damage.
		Utilizes predictive analytics to predict probable risks and take corrective measures.	Improves response times to insider threats while maintaining normal operations for non-compromised systems.

5.20 Proposed Digital Immune Model

The DIS is an evolving subject; here, we take reference from limited literature/study and the conceptualized DIS model, which has all the attributes of a forward-thinking solution designed to address the evolving

Table 5.6 The proposed DIS model addresses key challenges in I4.0 by integrating STMs.

Sl. no.	Challenge	Summary
1	**Self-configuration**	The DIS enables automated configuration of components and systems using the STM. The system adjusts autonomously based on STM inputs, ensuring efficient setup and adaptation to changes in the manufacturing environment.
2	**Self-healing**	The DIS components and systems actively seek improvement opportunities by leveraging STM and CS insights. They continuously enhance their performance, efficiency, and reliability to maintain seamless industrial operations.
3	**Self-optimization**	The DIS detects, diagnoses and autonomously repairs localized issues in software and hardware. This ensures minimal disruption in I4.0 manufacturing processes while maintaining peak system performance and efficiency.
4	**Self-protection**	The DIS autonomously defends against malicious attacks using mechanisms inspired by human neural networks. By leveraging early warning systems, it predicts and prevents system-wide failures, ensuring operational security and resilience.
5	**Self-collaborator**	The DIS communicates seamlessly with STM and CS systems to combat threats. This collaborative approach and DIS capabilities enhance the overall security, adaptability, and operational continuity in the manufacturing ecosystem.

complexities of I4.0 environments. It provides a comprehensive, adaptive, and secure framework to ensure operational resilience, efficiency, and scalability. Below are the core components and their contributions to meeting I4.0 challenges as defined in Table 5.6.

5.21 Conceptual Model Integrating Digital Immune Systems, Self-Tuning Models, Cybersecurity, and Manufacturing Industry 4.0

By embedding STMs within the DIS, MI4 environments can achieve heightened resilience, adaptability, and efficiency in combating safety and security threats. Next, we introduce a DIS to each AAI, which can learn 'antibody' solutions that will be exchanged harmonically between the AAI of the STM and CS functional group. Therefore, the specific 'antibody' solutions are advocated to be used with distributed AAI defense mechanisms and monitor manufacturing processes to detect abnormality. A deterring immune response relies on the ability to identify the change or abnormality in the environment of MI4. Finally, the book chapter considers how we effectively utilize such knowledge to develop a robust security mechanism

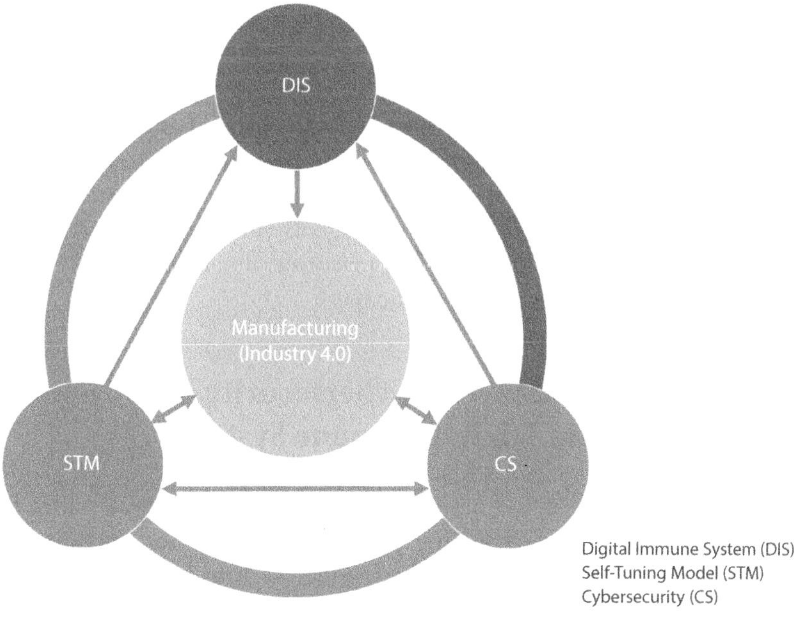

Figure 5.4 Conceptual model integrating the DIS, STM, CS, and MI4.

for the use of networks in the real world using distributed AAI systems. We conceptualized a layered, modular framework to integrate DIS, STMs, and CS (see Figure 5.4). This model ensures seamless interoperability, adaptability, and resilience in the complex environments of modern industrial systems.

The Manufacturing Industry 4.0 foundation layer (for example: smart sensors, IoT devices, and robotics) provides a highly connected environment where manufacturing, logistics, and OTs are digitized. It generates vast amounts of data for analysis and threat monitoring.

Cybersecurity (control layer) comprises firewalls, intrusion detection/prevention systems (IDPS), encryption, secure protocols, identity/access management, and incident response systems for threat mitigation. Real-time monitoring protects data flows and device communication across the I4.0 network, while baseline security stands as a pillar of reassurance, privacy, reliability, and back up of data. It communicates with STM and DIS to provide feedback, reinforcing the robustness of the system.

Self-tuning models (adaptive intelligence layer) and core mechanisms are ML models (e.g., anomaly detection, predictive analytics). Reinforcement learning for continuous policy optimization and automated model retraining and fine-tuning based on live feedback. Dynamic adaptation by continuously optimizing CS measures in response to evolving threats. Feedback loops leverage logs, alerts, and historical data to improve the DIS.

Digital immune system (resilience layer) threat detection based on feedback from STM and CS and immune response mechanisms modelled after biological systems. Distributed agent-based systems exchanging "antibodies" (threat solutions). Automated containment and recovery processes within the I4.0 ecosystem, boosting immune system towards future threats. The DIS focuses on a collaborative defense mechanism and shares threat intelligence across interconnected agents within the I4.0 ecosystem. It holistically protects and combines preventive, detective, and corrective measures to ensure system-wide resilience.

5.22 Interdependence of Cybersecurity, Self-Tuning Model, and Digital Immune System

The interdependence of and between CS, STM, and DIS creates a unified framework for adaptive, real-time protection in complex and dynamic environments like I4.0. This interplay results in a resilient, scalable, and adaptive system capable of combating threats across interconnected industrial ecosystems. Table 5.7 defines the actions and interplay of the

Table 5.7 A summary of the interdependence of CS, STM, and DIS.

Sl. no.	Actions	Interrelationship
1	**Feedback loops and continuous improvement**	Cybersecurity ensures the integrity of feedback loops in STMs, enabling accurate and reliable adjustments in real time. The DIS provides secure feedback and enhances its ability to learn and improve defense mechanisms over time through Plan-do-check-act/ iterative cycles.
2	**Real-time threat response**	Self-tuning models dynamically adjust their parameters to mitigate threats detected by CS tools. The DIS takes inputs from STM and CS and leverages these adjustments to contain and neutralize threats while maintaining operations.
3	**Enhanced resilience in Industry 4.0**	Self-tuning models optimize products and critical processes, while CS ensures they remain robust against disruptions. The DIS provides an overarching protective framework, combining proactive and reactive defenses embedded in manufacturing.
4	**Collaboration with human operators**	Cybersecurity tools inform and guide human resources in scanning, using self-tuning systems and the DIS. Advanced visualization and reporting tools provide actionable insights, looping the STM and DIS.

relationship between CS, STM and DIS. Summarizing the role of CS, STM, and the DIS and their interdependence. In I4.0, these three components work together to optimize system performance, safeguards from cyber threats, and ensures resilience holistically. The nature of comprehensiveness is evident as they are highly interconnected, and each complements the others in maintaining a secure, efficient, and adaptive environment.

This integrated approach allows for more secure, adaptable, and self-healing systems in I4.0. In these complex environments, where automation, CS, and data optimization must work seamlessly together, the systems demonstrate their resilience.

5.23 Conclusion

Cybersecurity STMs are the backbone for a DIS in I4.0. They ensure that adaptive systems remain reliable, resilient, and secure in response to an ever-evolving perilous landscape. By embedding robust security measures, organizations not only protect themselves but also unlock the full potential of CS to drive innovation and efficiency. This approach aligns closely with MI4's emphasis on interconnectivity, automation, and data-driven insights, enabling advanced manufacturing processes to thrive in a secure, adaptive, and efficient ecosystem. This also enables the comprehensive framework to make the DIS model a cornerstone for futureproofing I4.0 ecosystems. It enhances security, adaptability, and operational efficiency, enabling manufacturers to thrive in a highly connected, data-driven industrial landscape.

AI disclosure statement: The author acknowledges the use of AI-based tools for minor language editing or grammatical correction. However, all intellectual contributions, analyses, and conclusions presented in this chapter are entirely the author's own.

References

1. Ali, I., Arslan, A., Khan, Z., Tarba, S.Y., The role of industry 4.0 technologies in mitigating supply chain disruption: Empirical evidence from the Australian food processing industry. *IEEE Trans. Eng. Manage.*, 71, 1–33, 2021, https://ieeexplore.ieee.org/abstract/document/9473033/.
2. Apiletti, D., Barberis, C., Cerquitelli, T., Macii, A., Macii, E., Poncino, M., Ventura, F., istep, an integrated self-tuning engine for predictive maintenance in industry 4.0, in: *2018 IEEE Intl Conf on Parallel & Distributed Processing with Applications, Ubiquitous Computing & Communications, Big Data & Cloud Computing, Social Computing & Networking, Sustainable Computing & Communications (ISPA/IUCC/BDCloud/SocialCom/SustainCom)*, IEEE, pp. 924–931, 2018, December. https://ieeexplore.ieee.org/abstract/document/8672266/.

3. Asif, M., Are QM models aligned with Industry 4.0? A perspective on current practices. *J. Clean. Prod.*, *258*, 120820, 2020, https://www.sciencedirect.com/science/article/pii/S0959652620308672.
4. Bernieri, G., Conti, M., Pozzan, G., AMON: An automaton monitor for industrial cyber-physical security, in: *Proceedings of the 14th International Conference on Availability, Reliability and Security*, pp. 1–10, 2019, August, https://dl.acm.org/doi/abs/10.1145/3339252.3340521.
5. Bordoloi, T., Shapira, P., Mativenga, P., Policy interactions with research trajectories: The case of cyber-physical convergence in manufacturing and industrials. *Technol. Forecast. Soc. Change*, *175*, 121347, 2022, https://www.sciencedirect.com/science/article/pii/S0040162521007782.
6. Corallo, A., Lazoi, M., Lezzi, M., Pontrandolfo, P., Cybersecurity challenges for manufacturing systems 4.0: assessment of the business impact level. *IEEE Trans. Eng. Manage.*, *70*, 11, 3745–3765, 2021, https://ieeexplore.ieee.org/abstract/document/9457098/.
7. Del Giudice, M., Scuotto, V., Papa, A., Tarba, S.Y., Bresciani, S., Warkentin, M., A self-tuning model for smart manufacturing SMEs: Effects on digital innovation. *J. Prod. Innovat. Manage.*, *38*, 1, 68–89, 2021, https://onlinelibrary.wiley.com/doi/abs/10.1111/jpim.12560.
8. Figueroa, M., Uttecht, K., Rosenberg, J., A SOUND approach to security in mobile and cloud-oriented environments, in: *2015 IEEE International Symposium on Technologies for Homeland Security (HST)*, IEEE, pp. 1–7, 2015, April, https://ieeexplore.ieee.org/abstract/document/7225266/.
9. Fawad Sharif, S.M., Yang, N., ur Rehman, A., Alghamdi, O., Kanwal, T., SMEs' sustainable innovation performance during pandemic: impact of knowledge coupling and parallel-mediation of ambidexterity and market capitalising agility. *Technol. Anal. Strategic Manage.*, *36*, 10, 2489–2503, 2024, https://www.tandfonline.com/doi/abs/10.1080/09537325.2022.2153029.
10. George, A.S., George, A.H., Baskar, T., Digitally immune systems: building robust defences in the age of cyber threats. *Partn. Univers. Int. Innovation J.*, *1*, 4, 155–172, 2023, https://www.puiij.com/index.php/research/article/view/89.
11. Gupta, S., Meissonier, R., Drave, V.A., Roubaud, D., Examining the impact of Cloud ERP on sustainable performance: A dynamic capability view. *Int. J. Inf. Manage.*, *51*, 102028, 2020, https://www.sciencedirect.com/science/article/pii/S0268401219308849.
12. Kampourakis, V., Gkioulos, V., Katsikas, S., A systematic literature review on wireless security testbeds in the cyber-physical realm. *Comput. Secur.*, 133, 103383, 2023, https://www.sciencedirect.com/science/article/pii/S0167404823002936.
13. Krauze, B. and Grabis, J., A Conceptual Model of Digital Immune System to Increase the Resilience of Technology Ecosystems, in: *International Conference on Research Challenges in Information Science*, Springer Nature Switzerland, Cham, pp. 82–96, 2024, May, https://link.springer.com/chapter/10.1007/978-3-031-59465-6_6.

14. Kumar, A., Jain, U., Hussain, M., Rahmani, M.K.I., Banga, A.S., Mechanism for Device Authentication and Session Key Generation in Industrial Internet of Things Networks. *IEEE Access*, 12, 108770–108785, 2024, https://ieeexplore.ieee.org/abstract/document/10614606/.
15. Kumar, N. and Lee, S.C., Human-machine interface in smart factory: A systematic literature review. *Technol. Forecasting Social Change*, *174*, 121284, 2022, https://www.sciencedirect.com/science/article/pii/S0040162521007186.
16. Lu, Y., Xie, R., Liang, S.Y., Bearing fault diagnosis with nonlinear adaptive dictionary learning. *Int. J. Adv. Manuf. Technol.*, *102*, 4227–4239, 2019, https://link.springer.com/article/10.1007/s00170-019-03455-1.
17. Laskurain-Iturbe, I., Arana-Landín, G., Landeta-Manzano, B., Uriarte-Gallastegi, N., Exploring the influence of industry 4.0 technologies on the circular economy. *J. Clean. Prod.*, *321*, 128944, 2021, https://www.sciencedirect.com/science/article/pii/S0959652621031371.
18. Maesschalck, S., Giotsas, V., Green, B., Race, N., Don't get stung, cover your ICS in honey: How do honeypots fit within industrial control system security. *Comput. Secur.*, *114*, 102598, 2022, https://www.sciencedirect.com/science/article/pii/S0167404821004211.
19. Pandey, S., Singh, R.K., Gunasekaran, A., Supply chain risks in Industry 4.0 environment: review and analysis framework. *Prod. Plann. Control*, *34*, 13, 1275–1302, 2023, https://www.tandfonline.com/doi/abs/10.1080/09537287.2021.2005173.
20. Petrovski, A., Kotenko, I., Arifeen, M., Abramenko, G., Sobolev, P., Insider Threat Detection Within Operational Technology Using Digital Twins, in: *International Conference on Intelligent Information Technologies for Industry*, pp. 25–34, Springer Nature Switzerland, Cham, 2024, October, https://link.springer.com/chapter/10.1007/978-3-031-77411-9_3.
21. Prajapati, D.K., Mathiyazhagan, K., Agarwal, V., Khorana, S., Gunasekaran, A., Enabling industry 4.0: Assessing technologies and prioritization framework for agile manufacturing in India. *J. Clean. Prod.*, *447*, 141488, 2024, https://www.sciencedirect.com/science/article/pii/S0959652624009363.
22. Rai, R., Tiwari, M.K., Ivanov, D., Dolgui, A., Machine learning in manufacturing and industry 4.0 applications. *Int. J. Prod. Res.*, *59*, 16, 4773–4778, 2021, https://www.tandfonline.com/doi/abs/10.1080/00207543.2021.1956675.
23. Martin, R., Zeng, M., Venjara, A., The Self-Tuning Enterprise. *Harv. Bus. Rev.*, 76–83, 2015.
24. Skalli, D., Charkaoui, A., Cherrafi, A., Shokri, A., Garza-Reyes, J.A., Antony, J., Analysis of factors influencing Circular-Lean-Six Sigma 4.0 implementation considering sustainability implications: an exploratory study. *Int. J. Prod. Res.*, *62*, 11, 3890–3917, 2024, https://www.tandfonline.com/doi/abs/10.1080/00207543.2023.2251159.
25. Tidrea, A., Korodi, A., Silea, I., Cryptographic considerations for automation and SCADA systems using trusted platform modules. *Sensors*, *19*, 19, 4191, 2019, https://www.mdpi.com/1424-8220/19/19/4191.

26. Tidrea, A., Korodi, A., Silea, I., Elliptic curve cryptography considerations for securing automation and SCADA systems. *Sensors, 23*, 5, 2686, 2023, https://www.mdpi.com/1424-8220/23/5/2686.
27. Tu, J. and Zhang, L., Performance analysis and optimisation of Bernoulli serial production lines with dynamic real-time bottleneck identification and mitigation. *Int. J. Prod. Res.*, *60*, 13, 3989–4005, 2022, https://www.tandfonline.com/doi/abs/10.1080/00207543.2021.2019343.
28. Wu, M., Song, J., Sharma, S., Di, J., He, B., Wang, Z., Moon, Y., Development of testbed for cyber-manufacturing security issues. *Int. J. Computer Integr. Manuf.*, *33*, 3, 302–320, 2020, https://www.tandfonline.com/doi/abs/10.1080/0951192X.2020.1736711.
29. Wu, C., Qualitative analysis of intellectual property forgery in manufacturing enterprises in Industry 4.0 environment. *Int. J. Technol. Manage.*, *84*, 3–4, 229–247, 2020, https://www.inderscienceonline.com/doi/abs/10.1504/IJTM.2020.112499.

Part 2

DIGITAL IMMUNE SYSTEM: APPLICATIONS

6

Integrating GANs for Enhanced Phishing Detection in Digital Immune Systems

Sherwin Akshay J. G.[1], Hari Varshan S. R.[2], Radhika G.[1] and Radhika N.[1*]

[1]*Department of Computer Science and Engineering, Amrita School of Computing, Coimbatore, Amrita Vishwa Vidyapeetham, India*
[2]*Department of Mathematics, Amrita School of Physical Sciences, Coimbatore, Amrita Vishwa Vidyapeetham, India*

Abstract

Phishing attacks are becoming more complex and difficult to detect, posing a significant challenge to enterprises trying to protect sensitive information. Traditional security solutions, such as firewalls and antivirus, are ineffective against new and sophisticated phishing attacks. Due to this rising threat, digital immune systems (DIS) have been developed. The DIS are inspired by the human body's innate immune system, which allows them to detect, learn from, and respond to cyber threats autonomously. However, even DIS require assistance when dealing with very sophisticated phishing attacks. This chapter discusses the potential of generative adversarial networks (GANs), a type of artificial intelligence, for improving phishing detection in digital information systems. Generative adversarial networks can generate massive amounts of realistic simulated phishing data for training security systems. By exposing the DIS to a diverse set of phishing samples, the system enhances its ability to recognize real threats, including new-in-type threats. This chapter uses real-life examples and case studies to demonstrate how combining GANs and DIS improve phishing detection accuracy, efficiency, and responsiveness. The chapter also discusses the problems of adopting GANs in cybersecurity, as well as the technology's future evolution. The major goal of this chapter is to provide an integrated understanding of the synergistic dynamics of GANs and DIS in offering improved protection against phishing attacks in the contemporary digital environment.

**Corresponding author*: n_radhika@cb.amrita.edu

Sujata Priyambada Dash, Vaibhav Mishra, Bijeta Shaw, Sandeep Kumar Panda and S. Balamurugan (eds.) Digital Immune System: Principles and Practices, (123–144) © 2026 Scrivener Publishing LLC

Keywords: Phishing detection, generative adversarial networks (GANs), digital immune systems (DIS), cybersecurity, machine learning, adaptive security, synthetic data, real-time response

6.1 Introduction

6.1.1 The Escalating Risk of Phishing Attacks

In today's highly networked world, the sophistication of cybersecurity threats is increasing, with phishing being acknowledged as one of the most common and dangerous forms. Phishing refers to the methods used by hackers to trick people into disclosing sensitive personal information such as usernames, passwords, credit card numbers, or social security numbers. To give their hoaxes more credibility, the offenders frequently act as respectable institutions such as well-known firms, government departments, or social media platforms [1].

For example, an attacker may send you an email claiming to be from your bank, asking you to click on a link to "confirm" your account information. By clicking the link and entering your information, you unintentionally give the attackers access to your sensitive information. These assaults are typically carried out by emails, phone calls, or copycat websites that look very similar to legitimate websites.

Phishing is a type of cybercrime that affects enterprises worldwide and can result in significant financial losses, data breaches, and reputational damage. The financial industry is not the only one affected; people frequently feel invaded and helpless following such attacks.

It is crucial that the detection process adapts to the changing nature of phishing techniques. Traditional cybersecurity products, including antivirus software and spam filters, are typically threat- or pattern-based, meaning they are not very effective against new phishing techniques. Since each phishing attempt is likely to be significantly different from the one before it, it is challenging for standard approaches to identify them. This calls for the greatest demand for cybersecurity tools that are more intelligent, adaptive, and would be able to identify new phishing threats in real-time [2].

6.1.2 The Importance of Advanced Cybersecurity Solutions

With the ever-evolving nature of phishing and other web attacks, conventional rule-based security has been inadequate. The classic example is a wall built to fend off known attacks; if the attackers modify their approach, the wall becomes ineffective. Of special interest are systems that learn from past attacks, predict imminent threats, and protect automatically against new threats.

This is the backdrop against which a digital immune system (DIS) operates. These next-generation cyber security solutions imitate the human immune system and are a security "immune system" for computer systems. While the human body becomes familiar with and protects itself against previously encountered pathogens, a DIS becomes familiar with and protects itself against malicious cyber activity, such as phishing, by learning from experience and applying learned knowledge to protect against future attacks.

A DIS is more than just the general capacity of simply responding to perceived threats. It is engineered to continuously "monitor" and "tweak" to its digital environment, thereby continuously adapting to face new challenges while continuously refining its defense mechanisms. Digital immune systems learn and adapt over time, becoming progressively more effective and much more sophisticated than fixed, traditional security systems. The most critical function of a DIS is its capacity to identify and act upon both unknown and unrecognized threats without the need for constant human observation or intervention.

6.1.3 How Generative Adversarial Networks Enhance Digital Immune Systems

A significant event in cybersecurity research is the capacity of generative adversarial networks (GANs), an artificial intelligence (AI) component, to greatly boost the effectiveness of a DIS [3].

These two components must operate together; the generator aims to create increasingly convincing fake data, while the discriminator strives to identify false data. This hostile dynamic fosters progress over time, as the generator boosts output, and the discriminator improves its discovering abilities [4].

In the realm of phishing detection, GANs have the capacity of producing a wide variety of phishing scenarios, including entirely new attack paths that may not have been previously seen. By combining these generated examples, a Digital Immune System can be taught to recognize a greater variety of phishing threats, including ones that are particularly unique or unknown.

6.1.4 Role of Generative Adversarial Networks in Cybersecurity

These two components are closely linked: the discriminator must be able to identify fake data as such, and the generator must attempt to generate false data that is more realistic. This adversarial process, when the discriminator increases its detection capabilities and the generator raises its output, enables progress over time.

When it arrives at phishing detection, GANs may offer an extensive variety of phishing attempts, including attack paths that were not seen prior. A DIS can be trained to identify a wider range of phishing attacks, including the most creative ones, by using these comprised events.

6.1.5 Purpose of the Chapter

This chapter seeks to increase knowledge of how GANs and DIS work together to increase the effectiveness of phishing detection. Cybersecurity systems may identify phishing attempts quicker, intelligently, and safely by combining these two state-of-the-art technologies. This often makes it possible to avert such attacks before they can do damage. We will look at case studies and actual instances of GANs being used in cybersecurity scenarios to further illustrate how they could enhance a DIS. This includes demonstrating how GANs can produce artificial phishing data, enhancing the DIS's ability to recognize the most intricate phishing attacks. The chapter will also briefly discuss the difficulties in using GANs in cybersecurity. While GANs can produce realistic data, they face a hurdle in that the generated phishing data must be diverse to cover a broad range of attack routes. Additionally, a lot of data and processing power are needed for GANs to operate properly.

Finally, the chapter will discuss the technologies' possibilities for the future. Even though the cybersecurity landscape is changing at a fast pace right now, GANs and DIS are essential for developing systems that can manage increasingly sophisticated attacks. The way these technologies interact could lead to a future where it will be simpler to identify and counteract dangers like phishing, improving the security of both individuals and companies.

6.2 Literature Review

6.2.1 Understanding Phishing Attacks

Phishing has been one of the most lasting and common forms of cyberattacks, having started in the 1990s. It involves deceiving victims into clicking on spurious links, opening harmful attachments, or divulging confidential information such as passwords, credit card information, or identification. Cyberattacks usually mimic trustworthy organizations, e.g., financial institutions, government departments, or popular businesses, to trick people into being careless. Over time, the phishing methods have developed to be more sophisticated and more advanced in the use of social engineering, allowing them to produce highly genuine-looking emails, messages, and websites that easily fool unsuspecting victims. To improve the likelihood that their assault will succeed, attackers can utilize individualized data, such as the victim's name, job title, or most recent behavior. Phishing assaults have profound and far-reaching consequences. Phishing is one of the most prevalent and destructive cyberattacks, accounting for about 30% of worldwide data breaches, per a Symantec (2020) study. In addition to causing financial damage, the assaults also compromise private information, harm an organization's reputation, and erode user confidence [5, 6].

The situation is becoming worse due to the growth of spear phishing, a more sophisticated kind that targets certain people or organizations. Spear phishing attacks are well thought out and, to have the greatest possible impact, sometimes use secret information or publicly available data. Attackers may target executives who oversee financial transactions or employees who have access to sensitive systems, for instance [7, 8]. Phishing remains a problem for security systems despite the advances made in security technology, mostly because of its enduring and evolutionary nature. Phishing is always evolving as cybercriminals are constantly improving their methods, using advanced techniques like dynamic content, AI, and machine learning (ML) to stay one step ahead of conventional detection methods. For instance, some of the phishing attacks today use AI-generated text to create not only grammatically correct emails but also contextually relevant ones, which makes it even more difficult to detect them as spurious communication. Moreover, the availability of phishing-as-a-service solutions on the dark web has made it easier to carry out advanced attacks even by novices. Therefore, organizations need to implement a holistic model for phishing defense that includes the education of users, the use of advanced detection systems, and proactive threat intelligence to drastically reduce risk [9, 10].

Phishing attacks are a persistent and evolving threat in cybersecurity. Their ability to take advantage of human psychology and evolve with the increasing levels of technological developments makes it a challenging endeavor for individuals and entities. Acquiring knowledge on the processes and trends of phishing is essential to the development of proper countermeasures and a competitive edge over the attackers in the ever-evolving digital era [11–14].

6.2.2 Parallels Between Biological and Digital Immune Systems

Historically, phishing detection methods focused on rule-based systems and black-lists, using these to identify phishing through certain features of an email, website, or message. Rule-based systems would identify an email that contained certain phishing words (e.g., "urgent," "please verify your account") or an unknown URL, which used a misrepresented domain as a phishing-like a minimal misspelling or extra letter. Blacklists would be created and consisted of previously known harmful URLs, IPs, or email addresses, having been marked as either blocked from access, or phishing [15].

6.2.2.1 How Rule-Based Systems Work

- **Keyword analysis:** Recognizing particular words or phrases frequently found in phishing emails, such as "password reset," "account suspension," or "urgent action required."
- **URL inspection:** Analyzing URLs for suspicious characteristics, including misspelled domain names or domains that closely resemble legitimate ones.
- **Header analysis:** Scrutinizing email headers for discrepancies, such as mismatched sender addresses or atypical routing paths.
- **Attachment scanning:** Identifying harmful attachments, such as executable files or scripts, that are often utilized in phishing schemes.

Although these techniques were effective in the early stages of phishing, they face considerable limitations in the current, rapidly changing threat environment.

6.2.2.2 *Limitations of Traditional Methods*

- **Inability to detect new attacks:** Static by design, rule-based systems and blacklists utilize established or known threats, relying on predetermined rules to evaluate security risks. They are ineffective against new phishing techniques or other new threats. These techniques are easy for an attacker to overcome, usually by only changing a few details, like a few keywords or domains, or changing the template of the email used.
- **High false positive rates (FPR):** Conventional methods typically produce many false positives by incorrectly identifying legitimate emails or web pages as phishing attempts. For example, if an email includes the word "password," a detection system might tag the email as phishing even though it is valid and from a trusted sender. This can frustrate the user and decrease confidence in the method.
- **Easily bypassed:** Phishing attackers are adept at evading detection by using techniques such as:
  - **Dynamic content:** Creating phishing emails or websites that change their content based on the target or time of access.
  - **Obfuscation:** Using techniques like URL shortening, encoding, or embedding malicious links in images to avoid detection.
  - **Social engineering:** Crafting highly personalized emails that exploit human psychology, making them difficult to distinguish from legitimate communications.
  - **Lack of adaptability:** Systems based on rules necessitate ongoing manual updates for rules or blacklists to be added. As a result, they are labor-intensive and cumbersome when responding to new threats. However, phishing schemes can significantly evolve and proliferate at a speed faster than rule-based systems can react.

6.2.3 Real-Time Threat Detection and Response

Digital immune systems (DIS) employ ML and heuristic evaluation to identify, classify, and respond dynamically to threats to security. Instead of a traditional static rule-based approach, the DIS monitors network traffic, user interactions, and system conditions in real time. This advanced approach allows a DIS to detect something unusual and, at the same time, eliminate the threat as it appears, reducing the potential for widespread damage [16, 17].

6.2.3.1 *Key Mechanisms*

- **Real-time monitoring:** The DIS analyzes data in real-time to spot odd trends or departures from accepted standards.
- **Machine learning:** ML models use past data to identify trends connected to phishing attempts and adapt to new threats.
- **Heuristic evaluation:** Threats like inconsistent sender addresses or questionable websites are evaluated using probabilistic approaches.
- **Automated mitigation:** The DIS has the ability to isolate compromised devices, block dubious URLs and automatically quarantine malicious communications.
- **Adaptive learning:** To handle changing threats, such as zero-day vulnerabilities, the system is constantly improving its models and heuristics.

6.2.3.2 *Benefits*

- **Proactive defense:** Neutralizes threats before they cause significant harm.
- **Reduced false positives:** Eliminates dangers before they have a chance to do serious damage.
- **Scalability:** Successfully manages complicated networks and massive data volumes.

Research by Stolfo *et al.* (2008) demonstrates how well real-time solutions work to counteract phishing and other online attacks [18].

6.3 Rise of Machine Learning in Cybersecurity

One of the many key instruments in the fight against phishing and other online risks is ML. Machine learning algorithms can learn from huge information and spot complex patterns that human analysts may overlook, in contrast to traditional rule-based systems that depend on preset patterns and rules. Machine learning's flexibility makes it especially efficient at identifying malware infections, which grow more advanced and smart each day [18].

6.3.1 Enhancing Phishing Detection with Machine Learning

The production of synthetic phishing data is an essential function of GANs, which ensure that synthetic outputs accurately imitate true phishing methods. The GANs may replicate a number different phishing scenarios by being trained on well-known phishing datasets. Phishing emails, phony registration pages, and malicious URLs are typical phishing elements that the generator fabricates to mimic actual threats. The discriminator then assesses these artificial samples to verify the authenticity of them. This method equips the system to handle zero-day attacks by allowing it to generate a variety of attack types, such as phishing with spears, whaling, and clone phishing, as well as generate synthetic data which reflects novel or previously unknown phishing tactics. A variety of ML techniques, such as decision trees, random forests, and support vector machines (SVMs), have shown remarkable results in phishing detection. Random forests combine several decision trees to improve accuracy, while decision trees use a hierarchical structure to base their findings on particular attributes. The SVMs categorize data through determining the optimal boundary between actual and harmful examples in a high-dimensional space. Accurate and timely identification of phishing threats is now feasible thanks to these techniques [19].

6.3.2 Applications for Machine Learning in Phishing Detection

Large datasets of authentic communications, including emails and webpages, as well as phishing attempts, are used to train ML systems. Computers gain the ability to recognize subtle trends and telltale indicators of phishing, such as dubious URLs, misleading language, and strange sender behavior, by examining these diverse cases. The models' capacity to recognize phishing attempts has been enhanced by this data-driven methodology [20, 21].

6.4 Proposed Methodology

Generative adversarial networks are essential when generating synthetic phishing data because they guarantee that fake output accurately mimic genuine methods of phishing. By training GANs on popular phishing datasets, the system may replicate a range of phishing scenarios. While the engine creates phony phishing components that resemble real threats, like malicious URLs, phishing emails, and false login pages, the discriminator evaluates these artificial samples for their legitimacy. This strategy enables the system to handle zero-day attacks by enabling it to generate synthetic data that mimics novel or uncommon phishing methods, and a variety of attack types, including spear phishing, the practice, and clone phishing attacks.

Generative adversarial networks are essential when creating synthetic phishing data, which assures that synthetic outputs accurately replicate real phishing techniques. By being trained on popular phishing datasets, GANs can duplicate an array of phishing scenarios. Typical phishing features that the generator creates to imitate real threats include malicious URLs, fake registration locations, and phishing emails. After then, the discriminator evaluates these synthetic samples to confirm their veracity. By enabling the system to produce a range of attack types, like spear phishing, whaling, and clone phishing, as well as to produce artificial information, which reflects novel or yet unreported phishing tactics. This approach equips the system to withstand zero-day attacks.

When the DIS has been trained, it can detect scams in real-time by keeping an eye on user activity, email exchanges, and network data. It makes use of training insights to detect strange behaviors, anomalies, or phishing tendencies. The system can automatically reduce risks when a threat is identified by dividing untrue emails, blocking access to fake websites, and warning users or administrators of potential threats. To increase detection accuracy, the DIS uses adaptive learning, utilizing feedback and fresh data to update its models and keep up with evolving cyberthreats.

The efficient use of the DIS depends on data preparation, which raises the precision and utility of ML models. Data cleaning removes noise, errors, duplicate data, and outliers that may impede training. The normalization of data standardizes features using tools like the Standard Scaler to ensure consistency and keep features with higher values from controlling the learning process. By using feature extraction, which focuses on significant phishing traits including dubious URLs, frequently employed phishing phrases, and unusual sender conduct, the model may focus on the most pertinent portions of the data. Effective beforehand, which ensures that the data is clear, organized, and training-optimized, eventually boosts the efficacy of phishing detection models.

After preprocessing, the DIS is trained using both simulated and real phishing data, improving its ability to distinguish between genuine and fraudulent emails. To find phishing indications, it uses pattern recognition methods including Random Forests, decision trees, and neural networks. The system adjusts to new threats and progressively increases the accuracy of its detections by consistently adding new phishing information to its knowledge base. Using GAN-generated data has several advantages, including improved generalization, which enables the DIS to identify known and unknown threats, and increased adaptability, which enables it to identify new phishing techniques, such as zero-day attacks.

Combining GANs with variational autoencoders (VAEs) can greatly improve phishing detection. By finding recurrent patterns in email content and URL structures, VAEs—neural networks—break down complex data into smaller, easier-to-manage components to enable feature analysis. By producing unique and notable versions of phishing efforts, VAEs, when paired with GANs, enable the production of a wider range of phishing situations. Because of this integration's increased variety and superior detection, the system becomes more resilient and able to identify complex phishing threats that it would not have otherwise encountered. It also ensures that the system is exposed to a range of malware techniques, some of which are novel or uncommon.

6.5 Comparative Analysis with Traditional Methods

Phishing detection has grown greatly over time, from basic rule-based systems to complex ML models. However, because of the natural limitations in present tactics, companies are vulnerable to new and effective phishing attacks. When compared to these traditional methods, the advantages of the proposed GAN enhanced DIS become clear.

6.5.1 Rule-Based Systems

One of the early techniques for identifying scams was rule-based systems. To identify phishing emails, they follow predetermined rules and patterns, such as searching for questionable links, specific keywords (such as "urgent," "verify your account"), or well-known phishing domains. Although those instruments are now quick and simple to use, they struggle to keep up with the ever-changing nature of phish initiatives.

6.5.1.1 Limitations of Rule-Based Systems

6.5.1.1.1 High False Positive Rates

Rule-based systems sometimes mark valid emails were phishing messages, particularly when they contain terms or phrases that fit the pre-established criteria. This results in wasteful interruption and an erosion in customer trust.

6.5.1.1.2 Inability to Detect New Attack Patterns

- Because they are static, these systems are unable to adjust to new or altered phishing tactics. By significantly changing their strategies, such as by utilizing new keywords or domains, attackers can simply get around them.

6.5.1.1.3 Frequent Manual Updates

- For rule-based systems to include new rules or blacklist entries, frequent human updates are necessary. As a result, they need a lot of work and react slowly to new threats.

6.5.2 Standard Machine Learning Models

Rule-based systems are greatly outperformed by ML models like SVMs, decision trees, and random forests. These models discover trends and predict results through data mining from past phishing datasets. Even if they may handle increasingly complicated phishing techniques, they still have limitations.

6.5.2.1 Limitations of Standard ML Models

6.5.2.1.1 Struggle with Unseen Phishing Attacks

- The quality and diversity of the training data are crucial for ML models, and if the dataset lacks instances of recent or developing phishing tactics, the algorithm might not be able to identify them.

6.5.2.1.2 Overfitting

- The algorithm might overfit to particular patterns if the initial data is unfocused, which could restrict the ability for generalization to novel threats.

6.5.2.1.3 Require Retraining

- Machine learning models need to be retrained on fresh datasets when new phishing tactics appear. It can take a lot of time and resources to complete this process.

6.5.3 Generative Adversarial Network-Enhanced Digital Immune System Approach

The GAN-enhanced DIS generates new, realistic phishing data that reflects undiscovered and future attacks, overcoming the drawbacks of conventional techniques. The DIS is regularly trained using this synthetic data, which keeps it current and flexible.

6.5.3.1 Advantages of Generative Adversarial Network-Enhanced Digital Immune System

6.5.3.1.1 Detects New and Emerging Phishing Methods

- By creating artificial phishing samples that imitate new attack trends, GANs help the DIS identify threats that have not been observed before.

6.5.3.1.2 Reduces False Positives

- The DIS improves its ability to differentiate between harmful and legitimate emails by training on a variety of realistic phishing data, which lowers false positives.

6.5.3.1.3 Automatically Updates with New Attack Patterns

- Without continuing human involvement, the system preserves its reliability against altering phishing strategies by continuously learning from GAN generated synthetic data.

6.5.3.1.4 Provides Continuous Learning

- Over time, the DIS's detection capabilities improve as it adjusts to new threats in real time.

6.6 Performance Evaluation and Benchmarking

The main evaluation policies, experimental design, benchmarking results, and analysis-derived insights are explained in this section. The objective is to show how the accuracy, effectiveness, and adaptability of the GAN-enhanced DIS transcend the qualities of standard phishing identification methods.

6.6.1 Key Evaluation Metrics

The GAN-enhanced DIS's efficacy was determined using a variety of performance indicators. The system's efficiency for detecting phishing emails while avoiding errors and holdups is measured by these metrics.

6.6.1.1 Accuracy and Precision

6.6.1.1.1 Detection Accuracy

- Calculates the overall share of correctly recognized emails, including both legitimate and phishing emails.

6.6.1.1.2 Precision

- Estimates the amount of phishing emails that were truly phishing.
- High precision indicates fewer false positives, reducing unnecessary disruptions for users.

6.6.1.2 False Positive and False Negative Rates

6.6.1.2.1 False Positive Rate (FPR)

- Decreased false positives since high precision relieve users from avoidable difficulties.
- A low FPR ensures that users are not burdened with unnecessary security warnings.

6.6.1.2.2 False Negative Rate (FNR)

- Analyzes a percentage of real phishing emails that were not identified.
- A low FNR ensures that phishing emails do not bypass the system.

6.6.1.3 *Detection Time (Latency)*

- **Detection time**: Measures the time taken by the system to analyze and classify an email as phishing or legitimate.
- **Importance**: Low detection time is critical for real-time phishing prevention, ensuring that threats are neutralized before they reach users.
- **Measurement**: Detection time is typically measured in milliseconds (ms).

6.6.2 Experimental Setup

To benchmark the GAN-enhanced DIS against traditional methods, experiments were conducted using publicly available phishing datasets and simulated email traffic. The experimental setup included the following configurations:

6.6.2.1 *Dataset Composition*

- **Legitimate Emails**: 50,000 samples from publicly available datasets (e.g., Enron dataset).
- **Real Phishing Emails**: 25,000 samples from sources like Phish Tank and APWG.
- **GAN-Generated Phishing Emails**: 25,000 synthetic phishing samples generated using GANs.

6.6.2.2 *Training Models*

- **Traditional rule-based filtering**: A baseline system using predefined rules (e.g., keyword matching, URL blacklisting).
- **Machine Learning Models**
  - Random forest classifier
  - Support vector machine classifier
  - XG Boost classifier

- **Generative adversarial network-enhanced DIS (proposed model)**: The proposed system combining GAN-generated data with a ML-based DIS.

6.6.2.3 *Test Environment*

- A simulated enterprise email gateway with real-time email traffic.
- The system was tested under varying loads to evaluate its scalability and performance.

6.6.3 Benchmarking Against Traditional Systems

A comparative evaluation was performed to determine how well the GAN-enhanced DIS performs compared to existing phishing detection techniques. The results are summarized in the table below:

Model	Acc. (%)	FPR (%)	FNR (%)	Time (ms)
Rule-based	78.5	12.3	21.5	15.2
Random forest	86.2	8.5	13.8	12.8
SVM	89.1	6.2	10.9	14.3
GAN-DIS (Proposed)	95.7	3.8	4.3	9.4

6.6.4 Key Insights from Benchmarking

6.6.4.1 *Highest Accuracy*

- With a 95.7% accuracy percentage, the GAN-enhanced DIS outscored regular rule-based and standard ML methods.
- The system's capacity to learn from realistic and varied phishing data generated through GANs is to thank for this advancement.

6.6.4.2 *Real-Time Performance*

- Threats are removed before they can affect users due to this rapid detection time.

6.6.4.3 *Reduced False Positives*

- With an FPR of 3.8%, the system surpassed rival ML models (6.2–8.5%) and classical rule-based filtering (12.3%).
- By reducing false positives, users experience few needless pauses and have a greater trust in the system.

6.6.4.4 *Adaptability*

- Through GAN-generated phishing data, the GAN-enhanced DIS constantly acquires knowledge from new threats, ensuring long-term efficacy.

6.7 Challenges and Future Trends

Although merging DIS with GANs provides a potent phishing detection approach, there are drawbacks. Resolving these issues is essential to developing cybersecurity systems that are more dependable, effective, and moral. Additionally, there are many opportunities to improve phishing detection and response capabilities because of new trends and technology.

6.7.1 Challenges of Integrating Generative Adversarial Networks with Digital Immune Systems

6.7.1.1 *High Computational Requirements*

On the contrary, training GANs needs a lot of time and resources for processing. This is caused by the reality that GANs use two neural networks—the discriminator and the generator—that use an adversarial process dynamic contest:

6.7.1.1.1 Hardware Costs

High-performance GPUs or TPUs are needed to train GANs, and these devices can be costly to buy and operate.

6.7.1.1.2 Energy Consumption

Excessive energy use all through the training process increases costs for operation.

6.7.1.1.3 Scalability Issues

It might be difficult for small and medium-sized businesses to pay for the facilities required for routine GAN deployment and training.

6.7.1.2 Risk of Adversarial Attacks

Adversarial assaults, in which fraudsters alter the system to avoid detection, can affect GAN-based systems. Key risks include:

6.7.1.2.1 Data Poisoning

The GAN may produce harmful or unsuccessful samples if attackers insert false or malicious data into the training dataset.

6.7.1.2.2 Model Evasion

The GAN may produce harmful or unsuccessful samples if attackers insert false or malicious data into the training dataset.

6.7.1.2.3 Defense Mechanisms

By taking benefit of defects in the model, highly skilled attackers can generate phishing emails specifically to evade detection systems trained by GANs as it takes constant observation, updates, and the creation of strong defenses to guarantee that the DIS is safe from hostile attacks.

6.7.2 Future Trends in Enhanced Cybersecurity

6.7.2.1 Federated Learning for Better Privacy

Federated learning is a distributed ML strategy in which multiple networks work together to train a common model without exchanging raw data. There are many benefits of using this approach for GAN-enhanced cybersecurity:

6.7.2.1.1 Data Privacy

GANs can be created by organizations using local datasets without exposing private information to outside parties.

6.7.2.1.2 Collaborative Defense

Without losing data security, federated learning allows companies to work together and share information to improve their phishing detection systems.

6.7.2.1.3 Scalability

For sectors like healthcare and banking with stringent privacy regulations, this strategy can be particularly beneficial.

6.8 Results and Discussion

The insertion of GANs into DIS has greatly improved phishing detection and response capabilities. A description of the main findings drawn from instances and actual testing is provided below:

6.8.1 Improved Detection Accuracy

The accuracy of phishing detection has risen substantially whenever DIS and GANs are employed in place:

- Identification rates rose from 30–50%, with a monetary case study showing a 35% increase.
- The technique used GAN-generated synthetic data to detect zero-day and previously undetected phishing assaults.
- Flexible learning allows the DIS to continually improve its identification capabilities over time.

6.8.2 Reduction of False Positives

The system showed a major decrease in false positives:

- False positive rates dipped, as shown in a website case study, where genuine emails were less frequently stated.
- The security staff saved time by reducing their need to review false alarms while raising operational efficiency.
- Fewer false positives led to increased user trust, ensuring users did not dismiss legitimate warnings.

6.8.3 Faster Response Times

Generative adversarial network-enhanced DIS systems showed faster response times:

- Real-time threat detection allows the elimination of phishing emails within seconds after arrival.
- Proactive defenses allowed the system to adapt to novel risks before they caused harm.
- Proactive defensive systems enabled the structure to adapt to fresh risks before they did damage.

6.8.4 Adaptability to New Threats

The system's ability to react to changing threats was a significant advantage:

- Continuous learning ensured the DIS remained effective against emerging attack strategies.
- Generative adversarial networks allowed the system to mimic and adapt for potential phishing scenarios.
- Organizations would no longer need to wait for real threats to enhance their defenses.

6.8.5 Practical Impact

The combined effort of GANs at DIS produced significant benefits were fewer successful phishing attacks and data leaks recorded across industries. Customer confidence has risen because of powerful phishing detection capabilities. Financial losses were avoided, as demonstrated in an e-commerce case study in which millions of dollars were saved. Operational efficiency has improved, allowing security personnel to focus on strategic goals.

6.8.6 Challenges and Future Directions

Despite its success, obstacles persist:

- Smaller businesses may be unable to train GANs due to the high computational needs.
- Maintaining data quality and diversity is crucial to system accuracy.

- Ethical considerations, such as the possibility of GAN misuse, must be addressed by standards and best practices.

Future research should look into combining GANs with other technologies, such federated learning, to improve system capabilities even further.

6.9 Conclusion

The combination of GANs and DIS has proven to be a very successful method for increasing phishing detection and response. Key outcomes include:

- Improved identification accuracy, with rates arising by 30–50%.
- Decreased false positives, which boosts efficiency and user confidence.
- Quicker response rates enable for real-time threat reduction.
- Improved flexibility, allowing the framework to guard off emerging and novel threats.
- Practical benefits involve improved security, increased client confidence, and less financial losses.

These results show that integrating GANs and DIS is a workable and validated approach to contemporary cybersecurity defense, not merely an experimental notion.

AI disclosure statement: The author acknowledges the use of AI based tools for minor language editing or grammatical correction. However, all intellectual contributions, analyses, and conclusions presented in this chapter are entirely the author's own.

References

1. Goodfellow, I., Pouget-Abadie, J., Mirza, M., *et al.*, Generative Adversarial Networks. *Adv. Neural Inf. Process. Syst.*, 27, 2014.
2. Vinayakumar, R., Soman, K.P., Poornachandran, P., Evaluating Deep Learning Approaches for Cybersecurity Threat Detection. *J. Intell. Syst.*, 28, 2, 231–250, 2019.

3. Papernot, N., McDaniel, P., Goodfellow, I., *et al.*, Practical Black-Box Attacks against Machine Learning. *Proceedings of the 2017 ACM on Asia Conference on Computer and Communications Security*, 2017.
4. Arjovsky, M., Chintala, S., Bottou, L., Wasserstein GAN, arXiv preprint arXiv:1701.07875, 2017.
5. Brundage, M., *et al.*, The Malicious Use of Artificial Intelligence: Forecasting, Prevention, and Mitigation, arXiv preprint arXiv:1802.07228, 2020.
6. Casey, T., *et al.*, GANs in Cybersecurity: A Case Study on Phishing Detection. *J. Cybersecur.*, 12, 3, 45–60, 2020.
7. Chandola, V., Banerjee, A., Kumar, V., Anomaly Detection: A Survey. *ACM Comput. Surv.*, 41, 3, 1–58, 2009.
8. Dasgupta, D., *Artificial Immune Systems and Their Applications*, Springer-Verlag, 1999.
9. Fette, I., Sadeh, N., Tomasic, A., Learning to Detect Phishing Emails. *Proceedings of the 16th International Conference on World Wide Web*, 2007.
10. Forrest, S., Hofmeyr, S.A., Somayaji, A., Computer Immunology. *Commun. ACM*, 40, 10, 88–96, 1997.
11. Hu, W. and Tan, Y., Generating Adversarial Malware Examples for Black-Box Attacks Based on GAN, arXiv preprint arXiv:1702.05983, 2017.
12. Johnson, M., *et al.*, Enhancing Phishing Detection with GANs: A Government Case Study. *Cybersecur. J.*, 15, 2, 112–130, 2022.
13. Kingma, D.P. and Welling, M., Auto-Encoding Variational Bayes, arXiv preprint arXiv:1312.6114, 2013.
14. LeCun, Y., Bengio, Y., Hinton, G., Deep Learning. *Nature*, 521, 7553, 436–444, 2015.
15. Pedregosa, F., *et al.*, Scikit-learn: Machine Learning in Python. *J. Mach. Learn. Res.*, 12, 2825–2830, 2011.
16. Smith, J., *et al.*, Real-Time Phishing Detection Using GANs: An E- Commerce Case Study. *Int. J. Cybersecur.*, 14, 4, 78–95, 2021.
17. Sommer, R. and Paxson, V., Outside the Closed World: On Using Machine Learning for Network Intrusion Detection. *IEEE Symposium on Security and Privacy*, 2010.
18. Stolfo, S.J., *et al.*, Data Mining Methods for Detection of New Malicious Executables. *IEEE Symposium on Security and Privacy*, 2008.
19. Yang, Q., *et al.*, Federated Machine Learning: Concept and Applications. *ACM Trans. Intell. Syst. Technol.*, 10, 2, 1–19, 2019.
20. Akshay, J.S., Vinusha, T., Bianca, R.S., Krishna, C.S., Radhika, G., Enhancing Credit Card Fraud Detection with Deep Learning and Graph Neural Networks, in: *2024 15th International Conference on Computing Communication and Networking Technologies (ICCCNT)*, IEEE, pp. 1–6, 2024, June.
21. Akshay, J.S., Vinusha, T., Bianca, R.S., Krishna, C.S., Radhika, G., Enhancing Credit Card Fraud Detection: A Comparative Analysis of Anomaly Detection Models, in: *2024 IEEE International Conference on Computer Vision and Machine Intelligence (CVMI)*, IEEE, pp. 1–6, 2024, October.

7

Managing Complexity in Cybersecurity: The Necessity of Human Oversight in Digital Immune Systems from Behavioral Forensic Perspective

Bhartrihari Pandiya[1] **and Prasad Kulkarni**[2*]

[1]*School of Management Studies, National Forensic Sciences University, Gandhinagar, Gujarat, India*
[2]*Department of MBA, Jain College of Engineering, Belagavi, India*

Abstract
The rise of complex cyber-attacks is automation based on artificial intelligence (AI), and problems arise when the control of these events is not in the hands of humans. While digital immune systems (DIS) utilize AI and machine learning to spot and combat cyber risks in real-time, the systems are not immune to human-based threats like insider attacks, social engineering, and credential-based intrusions. These tactics leverage behavioral and psychological vulnerabilities rather than the technical ones, making them challenging for AI-based security solutions to catch. This study analyzes why automated cybersecurity mechanisms may have their limitations, and how human oversight may complement DIS, with potentially a behavioral forensic view of human oversight. This research discusses AI-run security models shortcomings using two well-known cyber incidents, the first being the Twitter Bitcoin Scam (2020) and the second being the Solar Winds cyberattack (2020). In both instances, attackers evaded automated security controls by exploiting human weaknesses *via* social engineering in Twitter's case and a complex supply chain attack in SolarWinds. The first detects anomalies while the second relies on known attack signatures, therefore failing to recognize these attacks. Analysts later detected behavioral discrepancies that uncovered these breaches. Behavioral forensics is the intersection of psychology, criminology, and

**Corresponding author*: dr.prasadkulkarni@jcermba.in; ORCID: 0000-0002-9846-6495
Bhartrihari Pandiya: ORCID: 0000-0003-4777-126X

Sujata Priyambada Dash, Vaibhav Mishra, Bijeta Shaw, Sandeep Kumar Panda and S. Balamurugan (eds.) Digital Immune System: Principles and Practices, (145–166) © 2026 Scrivener Publishing LLC

data analysis and holds the key to detecting deceptive behaviors and insider threats that AI-driven systems miss. This research analyzes the limitations of DIS and explores a cyber-physical infrastructure that essentially combines DIS with both behavioral forensics and human oversight to build a strong and adaptive cybersecurity framework. The findings discuss how a Human-in-the-Loop (HITL) security model, explainable AI (XAI) and zero-trust frameworks can increase cyber resilience by balancing automation with human expertise. The importance of introducing human oversight for cyber operations against technical threats and behavioral threats enabling a security-aware culture in an organization.

Keywords: Human oversight, digital immune systems, behavioral forensics, cybersecurity, explainable AI, insider threats, social engineering, supply chain attacks

7.1 Introduction

The threat landscape of cybersecurity is changing at an alarming rate due to the fast-paced technological evolution and the growing trend of digital transformation in different sectors (Möller, 2023) [1]. Automated digital immune systems (DIS) are implemented by organizations as protection against cyber-attacks and threats, utilizing artificial intelligence (AI), machine learning (ML), and automation to identify and reduce risks (Aldhaheri *et al.*, 2020) [2]. Despite their power, these systems are still at risk from human-centered threats like social engineering hacks, insider threats, and fraud, which leverage behavioral and psychological weaknesses instead of technical weaknesses (Tayyab *et al.*, 2025) [3]. The human factor is an important and often neglected aspect of cybersecurity. While traditional security mechanisms target technical defense against attacks, as cyber-attacks evolve to outsmart humans, sophisticated attacks target and manipulate human behavior making it challenging. This crucial question pertains to the significance of human intervention in DIS for combatting technical and behavioral cyber risks.

7.1.1 Role of Human Oversight in Cybersecurity

The presence of human around cybersecurity measures is necessary for detecting, analyzing and responding to the cyber threats that could not be identified by automated systems (Nair *et al.*, 2024) [4]. A large number of cyber incidents are driven by behavioral outliers or patterns of deviation from expected human behavior such as logins at uncharacteristic times, access to data not typical for the user, etc. Digital immune systems can identify many technical discrepancies, but they cannot distinguish psychological and behavioral signs of deception. Therefore, incorporating behavioral forensics in cybersecurity strategies allows organizations to utilize human insights to comprehend, analyze, and react to advanced cyberattacks (Rich and Aiken, 2024) [5]. As a result, behavioral forensics is an upcoming area in supplementing AI-driven cybersecurity offerings.

This research paper aims to explore the necessity of human oversight in DIS from a behavioral forensic perspective. The primary objectives of this study are:

1. To analyze the limitations of automation in cybersecurity and why human oversight remains critical.
2. To propose a hybrid model that integrates human intuition, ethical judgment, and behavioral analysis with DIS.
3. To discuss the challenges and managerial implications of incorporating human oversight in cybersecurity frameworks.

The study focuses on the intersection of cybersecurity, behavioral forensics, and human decision-making, providing a multidisciplinary approach to managing cyber risks effectively.

7.1.2 Significance of the Study

The importance of this research can be described considering its unique approach to cybersecurity through case study research. Existing research emphasizes automation and AI-based security solutions (Hu *et al.*, 2021; Sarker, 2022) [6, 7] whereas this paper implies that behaviorally driven threats need human interventions in detecting the threat. With cybercriminals increasingly preying on psychological vulnerabilities instead of technical weaknesses, organizations are increasingly forced to create strategies combining human cognition, forensic analysis, and machine intelligence. This study is also placed at a time where talks around explainable AI (XAI) and ethical AI, drawing the line around transparency and accountability on matters faced by automated decision-making systems, are needed. While the field of cybersecurity witnesses major advancements, to date limited attention has been paid in system modeling of human dimensions of operational cyber risk, leaving a large gap in our knowledge and understanding of cyber risk management, a human–AI hybrid-based system model is proposed for cyber risk mitigation with a potential to fill in the gap. This paper is organized as follows. Section 7.2, delves into the literature review of related works on DIS, human oversight in cybersecurity, and behavioral forensics. Section 7.3 examines the studied cases where humans intervened to help with cyber threats. Section 7.4 proposed the conceptual model of AI, XAI, and forensic psychology. Section 7.5 concludes and offers a recap of key findings. Finally, Section 7.6 discusses recommendations for business and security professionals. Through examining both the technical and behavioral complexities surrounding cybersecurity, this research aims to contribute to conversations regarding the development of more adaptive and resilient security infrastructures in the digital age.

7.2 Literature Review

With the development of automation, AI, ML, and cybersecurity have become much more sophisticated (Sarker, 2023) [8]. Digital immune systems are a new approach to cybersecurity, based on biological immune systems that autonomously detect, prevent, and respond to cyber threats. Digital immune systems utilizes AI-based anomaly detection, predictive analytics, and automated response systems to enhance security measures. However, DIS, while improving real-time threat detection and reducing human error, is not without limitations (Salmani *et al.*, 2024) [9]. Notably, AI-based security models are insufficiently trained to handle human-driven threats such as social engineering attacks, insider attacks, and behavioral anomalies that cannot be expected to follow predictable paths (Kommisetty *et al.*, 2022) [10]. Cybersecurity with human oversight means that human analysts, ethical decision makers, and security professionals are actively monitoring, interpreting, and responding to cyber threats. While most contemporary cybersecurity research focuses on technical solutions (Lu and Da Xu, 2018) [11], human decision-making, ethical oversight, and the psychological analysis of cyber risk management are still underexplored. Cybersecurity landscapes have become increasingly complex, the shift from pure automation to an integrated human-oriented deployment has become necessary. Both AI's and ML's over-dependence traditional cybersecurity approaches rely heavily on AI and ML for threat detection, analysis, and mitigation. Artificial intelligence has certainly made strides in security models, but the human element is vital in dealing with cyber risk specifically in recognizing abnormal behaviors and containing threats that leverage human weaknesses, according to research (Evans *et al.*, 2016) [12]. To combat such evolving cyber-attacks, the idea of the DIS has been introduced, one that combines automation powered by AI and human intervention. This literature review investigates the impact of human oversight in DIS in a behavioral forensic context to fill unmet needs with current automated cybersecurity mechanisms.

Digital immune systems are described as a cybersecurity paradigm that mirrors the innate and adaptive response of the biological immune system in detecting, neutralizing, and adapting to the emergence of new threats (Falowo *et al.*, 2024) [13]. The DIS detect cyber risks using real-time monitoring, AI-driven anomaly detection, and automated responses. These systems work using behavioral analytics, predictive threat-intelligence behavior, and self-learning algorithms to improve and strengthen the cyber protection systems. While DIS shows promising results in automating such threats and response systems, they face challenges in coping with adversarial approaches like social engineering, insider threats, and human-centered cyberattacks. Without understanding the intent, motivation, context and anomalies, AI-enabled security solutions are vulnerable to complex attacks that influence human behavior. These limitations underscore the need for human oversight in DIS to provide more effective decision-making, fewer false positives, and better adaptive responses. The AI-based cybersecurity solutions are built on predictable algorithms and conclusive models drawn from the data they are trained on, making them incapable of grasping the nuanced and evolving nature of cyber threats. However, there is nothing that replaces vast amounts of experience, which means human analysts provide intuition for security-business context to decisions. Human oversight enhances cybersecurity outcomes by facilitating judgment-oriented reasoning that is unattainable through artificial intelligence (Paul and Jana, 2021; Dehghan and Khosravian, 2024) [14, 15] especially in situations where intent is ambiguous, or threat indicators are not clear. Contextual signals such as variance in work schedules, attempted access to unauthorized files or systems, and erratic communication patterns guide human analysts to interpret user behavior and identify insider threats. These distinctions are vital to preventing cyber incidents within which AI models are blind and can lead to over-reliance on historical data patterns. The AI-driven security models can efficiently analyze huge amounts of data in order to find statistical anomalies, but they are incapable of evaluating the psychological and social components of cyber threats. Cybercriminals often use cognitive biases, emotional responses, and trust mechanisms to trick victims into exposing sensitive information. The AI systems, which are based mainly on pattern recognition, find it difficult to identify such social engineering tactics. Artificial intelligence, however, may misclassify behavioral anomalies as benign. For example, in the incident of spear-phishing attacks, in which attackers that uses tailored messages to trick individual targets, human analysts can consider factors like message tone, sender reputation, and recipient behavior to assess the authenticity of messages (Ghazi–Tehrani and Pontell, 2022; Francia *et al.*, 2024) [16, 17].

Behavioral forensics draws from fields such as psychology, criminology, and data analysis to examine human behavior in the digital realm. Distinct from traditional cybersecurity strategies that primarily target technical vulnerabilities, behavioral forensics investigates the cognitive and social determinants that drive cybercriminal actions and victim responses. Behavioral forensic strategies help discover insider threats, deceptive behavior, and risk behavior patterns in organizations. Integrating forensic analysis into cybersecurity operations allow the detection of threats and proactive responses to prevent cyber incidents. The application of behavioral forensics has navigated multiple areas of cybersecurity, including cyber fraud (Rich and Aiken, 2024; McClain *et al.*, 2015) [5, 18], insider threat, and social engineering. Cybercriminals have been shown to cover their tracks, but they do so in a way that produces characteristics over their behavior, including inconsistent login times, inconsistent access times and file types, and change in communication style, that can be used to indicate the start of a security incident. For instance, the Twitter Bitcoin Scam of 2020 saw attackers using social engineering to manipulate Twitter staff members into providing them access to internal systems. The AI-based security mechanisms did not trigger alerts of the attack since no malware or brute-force intrusion attempts were employed. The forensic analysis confirmed that employees could have noticed the signs of compromise by detecting behavioral inconsistencies in access patterns (Madarie *et al.*, 2025) [19]. Combining behavioral forensics with cybersecurity frameworks enables organizations to enhance their capabilities to identify and respond to human-driven cybersecurity attacks that may go unnoticed by AI systems. However, cybersecurity decision-making is subject to cognitive biases that can contribute to errors in threat assessment and incident response, despite the benefits of human oversight. Confirmation bias, overconfidence bias, and availability bias are some of the biases that have been recognized to affect cybersecurity professionals (Withanaarachchi and Vithana, 2022; Oppenheimer, 2024) [20, 21]. Confirmation bias, for instance, is when security analysts give more weight to evidence that reinforces their beliefs while dismissing countervailing evidence. This results in failure to recognize the security risks posed by new threat vectors or misinterpretation of authentic activities as security threats. It is important to address these biases through structured training, decision-support systems, as well as cross-functional collaboration to achieve objective cybersecurity. While augmenting human decisions in cybersecurity operations can be extremely beneficial, the introduction of human oversight brings about scalability issues, especially for organizations that operate significant digital structures. Human analysts have limited cognitive abilities, and there have been delays in complex security event analysis, but AI-powered security tools can analyze millions of data points in real-time. The optimal way to manage complexity in cybersecurity is to use a hybrid approach that blends AI automation with selective human intervention (Salem *et al.*, 2024) [22]. Artificial intelligence should handle incident routine threat detection and mitigation tasks, while human analysts should focus on high-risk incidents, forensic investigations, and ethical oversight. The use of behavioral forensics and human oversight in cybersecurity can raise ethical issues and lead to privacy concerns, particularly regarding the monitoring of employees, data collection and decision transparency. Despite the effectiveness of stronger security protocols in countering insider attacks, organizations are required to adhere to legal and ethical restrictions to safeguard personal privacy when surveilling individuals (Karale, 2021; Andrew and Baker, 2021) [23, 24].

This literature review shows why we still need humans to oversee cybersecurity complexity in digital immune systems. The AI-based security models are still incapable of understanding human behaviors, especially when dealing with human-driven cyber threats. The behavioral forensics is a useful framework to analyze cybercriminals due to social engineering attacks, as well as threat actors and improves cybersecurity for decision making. Though there are significant advantages to integrating human judgment into cyber defense, there are potential pitfalls stemming from cognitive biases, scalability, and ethical concerns that must be overcome to devise the best approach to embedding human oversight into cyber defense architectures. Incorporating a hybrid security methodology, that fuses AI automation with real-world skills, will support the evolution in organizations to withstand the persistent nature of cybercrime.

7.3 Case Studies Highlighting Human Oversight

7.3.1 Twitter Bitcoin Scam (2020)

In this scam, the attackers used social engineering techniques to gain access to internal systems and post false tweets. While AI-based security could not stop it, human intervention was necessary to manage the damage (Chandra *et al.*, 2024) [25]. This is one of the most high-profile examples of a social engineering cyberattacks. Attackers took control of prominent

Twitter accounts (including those belonging to @elonmusk, @BillGates, @JeffBezos, @BarackObama, and @Apple) and posted messages directing readers to a false Bitcoin scam. This event showcased the weaknesses of AI-powered security systems and illustrated the importance of human intervention in defending against cyber-attacks. This prominent cyberattack known as the Twitter Bitcoin Scam saw hackers take control of dozens of verified Twitter accounts owned by several celebrities such as Elon Musk, Bill Gates, Jeff Bezos, and Barack Obama. They utilized these accounts to advertise a fake Bitcoin scheme, convincing users to send cryptocurrency to a specified wallet with the false promise of doubling their initial investment. Instead of targeting software flaws, the attackers used social engineering tactics to get Twitter workers to give them access to internal customer service tools. This incident revealed the failure of AI-based security mechanisms to detect human tampering and highlighted the crucial importance of human intervention in cyber defense. Instead of relying on technical exploits common to hack attacks, the attackers targeted Twitter employees. The attackers bypassed conventional cybersecurity measures by deceiving internal staff, without ever hacking user accounts directly. The attackers impersonated Twitter IT personnel and reached employees *via* phone calls – a technique called voice phishing (vishing). They gained access to sensitive data by manipulating employees into revealing their login credentials through trust and authority. Under the pretense of adhering to security protocols, some employees entered their credentials including usernames and passwords into a fake login page that the attackers had set up. This gave the hackers access to Twitter's internal administrative tools. After they got into Twitter's system, the attackers reset the email addresses and passwords of high-profile accounts. They bypassed protections for two-factor authentication (2FA), which gave them full control of several accounts. The hackers could now post tweets, read direct messages, and manage linked email accounts. The hackers then hijacked the accounts and sent messages that promised users they would double their investment if they sent Bitcoin to a wallet. Users who fell for these tweets transferred Bitcoin to the attackers hoping to get a return. In a matter of hours, the scam earned more than $118,000 in Bitcoin until Twitter acted. The AI-driven security clearly did not prevent the attack Twitter's AI-powered security systems were primarily used to identify automated threats, malware, and brute-force hacking attacks. But, because this attack used social engineering rather than conventional hacking methods, AI found it difficult to identify it as a cybersecurity threat. Most AI security models are built around finding external cyber threats. But once the attackers had legitimate credentials, their activity was indistinguishable from any employee doing their work. Because the hackers broke into Twitter's system with valid logins, AI did not consider their actions suspicious. Human intent is a non-parameter that AI driven security tools cannot comprehend, rendering them ineffective at deception. Social engineering attacks like vishing can take advantage of trust and authority, something AI is not well-suited to analyze. And therefore, the AI system did not detect the event as a breach in progress. Shortly after the fraudulent tweets went viral, Twitter's security team noticed an unusual trend multiple top accounts posting the same Bitcoin scam message. And human analysts quickly evaluated the situation and saw the coordinated nature of the attack. While AI relies on pre-defined threat detection algorithms, human involvement brought in quick contextual understanding and response. Once Twitter verified the breach, the security team proactively locked the accounts attacked manually to prevent more fraudulent action. To prevent further platform hijacking, engineers took away tweeting about Bitcoin. To stop other accounts from being compromised, Twitter temporarily limited tweeting functionality for all verified accounts. The password reset requests were also turned off to stop attackers from recovering access to any taken over accounts. A forensic investigation revealed that the attack had been planned by a 17-year-old hacker in Florida, among others. Within weeks, law enforcement agencies arrested the perpetrators, emphasizing the crucial role of human-led investigations in the field of cybersecurity. Workers were trained on various aspects of safety, but security lessons learned were not abundant, as their security efforts were more robust post-attack. Organizations should provide training to help employees identify and resist social engineering attacks. This encompasses educating employees about phishing, vishing, and other deceptive measures employed by cybercriminals. Organizations should be tightening their access controls for internal administrative tools. Adopting a zero-trust security model adds layers of authentication and human verification for sensitive operations. The AI security models need to be improved to include behavioral forensics, enabling them to identify discrepancies in the employees' behavior. Explainable AI systems should be built so that unusual behaviors of accounts that could threaten an organization can be brought to the attention of its security team, should they be relevant in real time (Holder and Wang, 2021) [26].

It turned out that AI-driven security systems are still limited, as demonstrated by the Twitter Bitcoin Scam of 2020. Social engineering attacks, unlike standard cyber-attacks, target software flaws and take advantage of human psychology. They can be difficult for AI-powered cybersecurity tools to detect. This incident highlights the need for a hybrid security model that combines AI-driven automation with human supervision.

Digital immune systems are excellent at detecting automated attacks, but humans are needed to analyze human-driven attacks. Also, AI security models must include behavioral forensics for involvement in planning insider threats and social engineering attacks. Human involvement is still necessary for incident response, forensic analysis, and moral cybersecurity decisions. Combining AI-powered automation with humans by integrating AI-powered automation with human ingenuity, organizations can reinforce their cyber resilience and defend themselves against modern cyber threats more efficiently.

7.3.2 SolarWinds Cyberattack of 2020

It is dubbed as one of the most sophisticated supply chain cyberattacks in history. The attack was on SolarWinds' Orion software and affected thousands of organizations, including U.S. government agencies, Fortune 500 companies, and cybersecurity companies. This attack type was made possible by the compromise of trusted software updates that were distributed *via* trusted systems and bypassed traditional security defenses (Martínez and Durán, 2021) [27]. A good example of this occurred from a hack, where attackers capitalized on the native weakness in AI security systems to utilize legitimate credentials and trusted access points to be able to infiltrate systems on their victims. It would be over nine months before human eyes spotted the anomaly, the attack had gone undetected. Cybersecurity researchers conduct a process of critical review that demands human eyes, alerting them to stealthy, sophisticated computer intrusions that large security apparatuses overlook. The hackers had attacked after previously penetrating SolarWinds own software development environment. They assured that the compromised software would propagate to thousands of organizations through legitimate software update channels by inserting infected code eventually dubbed SUNBURST malware into Orion, a popular I.T. infrastructure management software platform later. After the malware was implanted, it was digitally signed by SolarWinds, making it appear legitimate and safe. More than 18,000 customers, including government agencies and big corporations, downloaded and installed the infected update, unknowingly leaving the door open for the malicious back door to their networks. Rather than applying brute force approaches or inserting malware as in a traditional cyberattack, the attack specifically targeted SolarWinds and used laterally within networks with stolen credentials and valid user rights. This plan circumvented anomaly-based AI security systems, since it gave the impression that the attackers were acting as users would. The attackers operated in stealth mode for over nine months, siphoning sensitive data from the government and corporations. Because they used valid access credentials, there were not any immediate red flags, and the attack continued undetected. Artificial intelligence-powered security models are primarily based on anomaly detection approaches for the detection of unauthorized access attempts. In this instance, however, the attackers were at least partially relying on trusted credentials, which means they were functioning within the usual access limits of authorized users. As a result, AI security tools deemed their movements as completely legitimate and harmless. Supply chain attacks represent challenges for AI-based security systems because they deliver malware through trusted channels. The SolarWinds Orion update was signed and released by the company itself, thus security models automatically did not see it as a threat. The AI systems are primarily trained to detect outside threats, meaning the systems were unable to identify the harmful code that was introduced into legitimate software updates. A large number of AI-based security tools monitor login locations, access patterns and behavioral characteristics to highlight anomalous activity. In this case, attackers monitored and mimicked the behavior of illegitimate users; they were careful to act with the patterns of behavior that had said above. As a result, no such deviance was detected, and it became possible to go undetected.

Eventually, the breach was discovered in December 2020 when cybersecurity company FireEye noticed unusual behavior in its internal network. FireEye's security team then discovered that several of their proprietary penetration-testing tools had been stolen, prompting an immediate forensic investigation. The cybersecurity firm FireEye's analysts studied system logs and network traffic patterns in detail, spotting unusual outbound communications starting from SolarWinds Orion software. Further examination revealed embedded malware, known as SUNBURST, in the software update. After the discovery, the U.S. Cybersecurity and Infrastructure Security Agency (CISA) worked with FireEye and private cybersecurity firms to ascertain the full impact of the breach. Affected organizations were quickly informed, and emergency security updates were released to stop further exploitation. To avoid a repeat of incidents like this, cybersecurity frameworks will need to implement hybrid models, where AI-based security tools are complemented by human-led forensic investigations. Threat hunting teams should routinely perform manual log reviews and behavior analysis to catch hidden anomalies that an AI might miss. To detect anomalous patterns of trusted users, AI security models need to incorporate behavioral analytics. It means organizations must implement a zero-trust security strategy, ensuring that software updates are thoroughly checked no matter where they are sourced from. Detection of deviations in the use of legitimate credentials should be incorporated into AI models even if no clear red flags are available. In that case, AI should integrate XAI so that human analysts can validate and verify the steps taken by AI to reach its conclusions. The AI security models of the oncoming future should raise an alert about even legitimate user credentials, whenever behavioral analysis shows the profile is not in sync with historical norms. Establish cybersecurity fusion centers security teams led by AI collaborate with forensic analysts in cybersecurity fusion centers, ensuring that threat detection and prevention are both comprehensive in scope and multi-layered in approach. The cyberattack at SolarWinds in 2020 highlighted the increasing sophistication of supply chain cyber threats and the shortcomings of AI-based security systems. Although AI is key to automating the need for threat detection, stealthy adversaries can circumvent these capabilities by taking advantage of trusted credentials and legitimate software pathways. This case shows the importance of human oversight in cybersecurity, highlighting that while DIS deliver real-time automation, human analysts are still essential to identifying and deterring more advanced, long-term cyber threats. To do this, behavioral forensics is to be merged into AI security models to be able to catch insider threats and non-traditional attack vectors. All software supply chains should begin adopting zero-trust security frameworks to protect against dependencies on trusted but maliciously compromised updates. Integrating the strengths of AI-based automation and human intellect enables firms to create proactive cyber defense strategies that meet the challenges of ever-evolving cyber risks in a multivariate digital world. Starting with the SolarWinds Cyberattack of 2020, sophisticated adversaries have demonstrated that they can defeat AI-driven security by exploiting trusted systems. Human oversight will always be necessary to identify stealthy breaches that AI may miss. This reinforces the need for a hybrid security model where DIS identify external threats and human threat hunters investigate internal anomalies. They lead to hidden risks because behavior forensics need to monitor even the legitimate users and credentials that exist in your network. Implement zero-trust security across every software supply chain cyber threat intelligence & human collaboration by combining AI-driven automation with human expertise, organizations can develop an agile cybersecurity capital to detect and mitigate sophisticated and extended cyber threats (Tanikonda *et al.*, 2022) [28].

7.4 Proposed Model

The increasing complexity of cyber threats requires a hybrid approach that combines DIS and human oversight. While DIS can handle real-time, large-scale threat detection, human intuition and behavioral forensics are essential for addressing insider threats, social engineering, and ethical concerns in cybersecurity decision-making. Based on the above case studies and literature review, the proposed framework blends three key components:

- Digital immune systems for automated, AI-driven threat detection.
- Behavioral forensics for identifying anomalies in user behavior.
- Human oversight for contextual analysis, ethical decision-making, and final validation.

The step wise functioning of the framework is as follows:

1. Threat detection by DIS:
    - Artificial intelligence models analyze network traffic, access logs, and behavioral patterns.
    - Suspicious activities (e.g., unusual login times, file access patterns) trigger alerts.

Table 7.1 highlights three key components in cybersecurity: Digital Immune Systems (AI-driven threat detection), Behavioral Forensics (analyzing human behavior to identify insider threats), and Human Oversight (reviewing AI decisions to ensure ethical, accurate responses). It emphasizes the role of technology in detecting threats and the importance of human analysis. Thus, combining AI with human expertise enhances security and reduces false positives.

Table 7.1 Shows the role in cybersecurity.

Component	Function	Role in cybersecurity
Digital immune systems	Artificial intelligence-driven anomaly detection	Detects threats based on predefined patterns, machine learning, and behavioral analytics
Behavioral forensics	Human behavior analysis	Identifies insider threats, social engineering tactics, and suspicious user activity
Human oversight	Decision-making and intervention	Reviews AI-generated alerts, prevents false positives, and ensures ethical responses

2. Behavioral forensics analysis:
   - Forensic techniques analyze user intent, deception indicators, and insider threats.
   - For example, if an employee suddenly downloads a large volume of files, behavioral forensics examines past behavior, motivations, and risk factors.

3. Human oversight decision-making:
   - Cybersecurity analysts review flagged incidents and decide whether it is a false positive or a real threat.
   - If needed, intervention steps such as account suspension, forensic investigation, or alert escalation are initiated.

Further, the Human-in-the-loop (HITL) security models enhance cybersecurity by ensuring human validation in key decision-making areas

Table 7.2 The HITL security model workflow.

Step	Process	Artificial intelligence role	Human role
1.	Threat identification	Artificial intelligence detects unusual activity and generates alerts	N/A
2.	Risk scoring and classification	Artificial intelligence assigns a risk score based on previous incidents and behavioral analysis	N/A
3.	Review and validation	Artificial intelligence suggests actions (block user, request MFA, flag for review)	Human analyst reviews and decides if AI's recommendation is correct.
4.	Action implementation	Artificial intelligence executes automated response (e.g., blocking access)	If required, a human makes high-risk decisions (e.g., terminating an employee).

where AI alone may fail. The HITL is a collaborative security model where AI-based systems flag potential threats, and human experts validate and act upon them. It ensures AI-driven security decisions align with business, ethical, and legal requirements.

Table 7.2 outlines the HITL (Human-in-the-Loop) security model, where AI and human analysts collaborate. AI handles threat identification, risk scoring, and suggests actions, while humans validate AI's recommendations and make critical decisions. In this model, AI automates low-risk responses, but human oversight is essential for high-risk actions, ensuring ethical and accurate outcomes.

7.5 Conclusion

Human oversight, DIS, and behavioral forensics are emerging technologies that herald the future of cybersecurity. The AI-powered security is all well and good, but it does not possess the ethical reasoning and human intuition needed and critical decision-making must involve human input. Adopting HITL security models, XAI, and behavioral cybersecurity techniques can lead to enhanced security on the one hand and ethically and legally compliant decision-making on the other. The future is to expect the cybersecurity workforce to make sure we build a cybersecurity infrastructure that is robust not just tomorrow but a century from now that can figure out the interplay between automation and the human touch. The ever growing sophistication of cyber threats has led to a paradigm shift in cybersecurity frameworks, where increasingly complex models of human-machine collaboration have replaced fully automated defense, thus constituting the need for integrated frameworks to leverage the fundamentals AI, DIS, and human safeguards. This study has delved into the shortcomings of AI-based security models and emphasized the need for human intervention to detect behavioral anomalies, protect against insider attacks, and minimize attacks that leverage human vulnerability. Behavioral forensics is a method that can provide valuable insights, enhance detection of deception, and strengthen decision-making processes in cybersecurity. With this in mind, the study has led to a number of key findings that point to the necessity of human oversight when it comes to cybersecurity and, in particular, within the purview of a DIS.

Although AI and ML allow for more efficient and faster identification of threats and an automatic response in cases of a crisis, these technological solutions fall short when it comes to sophisticated, social engineering type attacks. On the other hand, day-to-day cybercriminals can use tactics such as embezzling login credentials or using deception and psychological manipulation of the employees to bypass an automated defense unit if traditional AI models can only predict behaviors by relying on pattern recognition or anomaly detection. Case studies including the infamous Twitter Bitcoin Scam (2020) and SolarWinds Cyberattack (2020) show us that AI-based security systems used static algorithms, fixed attack signatures and a narrow range of behavioral intelligence that caused them to miss potential threats. Human review has an inherent advantage; it can make context- and intent-based decisions, something that AI-driven security systems struggle to extract conclusions from. Insider threats can be identified through human analyses, as are bizarre furious behavioral patterns, as well as ethical decision-making in security. This study highlights the fact that human intuition, ethical reasoning, and critical thinking cannot be duplicated in cybersecurity risk management. Behavioral forensics combines psychology, criminology, and forensic analysis to examine how human behavior pulls the strings when it comes to cybersecurity threats. This technique is useful in identifying social engineering attacks, fraud, and insider threats, where cybercriminals psychologically engineer people to compromise security protocols. While traditional cybersecurity frameworks concentrate on technical vulnerabilities, behavioral forensics operates on cognitive biases, decision-making processes, and deception indicators to provide a more holistic threat detection strategy we cannot create with AI alone.

Even though human involvement substantially improves cybersecurity, the research has found several intricacies that will need to be overcome to enable effective AI-human partnership. These include cognitive biases in human decision-making, overconfidence bias, confirmation bias, and availability bias that can cause errors in security analysis. Scalability issues, since human analysts cannot investigate every alert generated by AI-based security tools. This challenge highlights the importance of a selective, risk-based prioritization of human intervention in cyber operations, where the human analyst is not expected to verify every flagged anomaly, but to focus on high-priority threats. Ethics and privacy issues, especially around behavioral forensics and employee tracking. There is an ongoing need to balance security and privacy so that organizations do not implement cybersecurity strategies that violate individual rights or create undue surveillance mechanisms. This research proposes a hybrid cybersecurity landscape leveraging AI-based automation, behavioral forensic analysis, and Human-in-the-Loop to plan a significantly more flexible and sustainable security system. this strategy integrates AI-driven DIS for real-time visibility, anomaly detection, and automated response procedures. Behavioral forensic analysis for spotting insider threats, deception and manipulation-based cyberattacks. Human oversight for final decision-making, ethical programming, and strategic security design is very crucial.

7.6 Managerial Implications

This study provides managers with much-needed evidence regarding the role of human oversight in AI-based DIS, essential to support the evolution of cybersecurity frameworks in the industry. While AI and automation can enhance cyber defenses, managers should understand their limitations and the potential risks of neglecting human expertise in cybersecurity, focusing on behavioral risks, ethical concerns, and the impact of cybersecurity decisions. The major managerial implication of this study is that firms should not endeavor with cybersecurity from a technology perspective alone. The AI-based security solutions, however, do lack the ability to assess intent, interpret deceptive behavior, or detect insider threats that stem from human vulnerabilities. Managers need to understand that cybersecurity is not just a technical issue, it is a human problem and finding the right balance between automated defenses and human responses is key to dealing with this. This calls for the incorporation of behavioral forensics to understand combative tactics behind such an action, which AI systems cannot do alone, to mitigate the risk of social engineering. Since the data shows that AI security systems struggle with detecting social engineering attacks and insider threats, managers should also invest in workforce training programs that improve their employees' ability to recognize and respond to cyber threats. Employees are a common weak link in cybersecurity as they are typically unaware of phishing scams, credential theft, and other manipulation tactics employed by cybercriminals. Organizations need to adopt a security awareness, training, and education program that includes behavioral forensics and teaches employees what deception looks like and what biases, behaviors, and patterns can be defensive against potentially fraudulent ideas. By creating a culture of awareness of security, the chances of human error resulting in cyber incidents are significantly diminished. A further important application of this research is the need for a hybrid security model that combines AI with human decision-making. The human and AI collaboration within security tools is basically human experts thinking how to manage high-risk incidents that need contextual analysis and how AI-driven security tools can manage everything else including real-time threat detection. All security solutions, even this method, require the assumption of a threshold that, when exceeded, identifies an event as an alert to be investigated; cannot be predicted regarding the complete set of events. Excessive dependence on AI opens room for making mistakes in cybersecurity decisions for systems like we saw during high-profile cyber incidents such as the Twitter Bitcoin Scam and the SolarWinds attack. Incorporating human analysts into cybersecurity workflows can not only decrease response times but also increase resiliency against any advanced cyber-attacks through the reduction of misclassifications. An integration of human oversight in cybersecurity frameworks leads to another managerial consideration in terms of scalability and resource allocation. Human analysts face cognitive limitations and need time to investigate security alerts, compared to the capabilities of AI-based security tools that can analyze huge sets of data in a fraction of a second. So, managers will have to build a systematic cybersecurity operation enabling them to apply human oversight only where really needed. Adopting HITL AI models allow AI security systems to identify potential concerns, which can then be analyzed by a human analyst for further investigation.

Adopting a tiered security response model will help ensure that managers direct security team response efforts to the risk areas while leaving it to AI to report routine threats. According to the findings of this research, adopting XAI in cybersecurity management is imperative. One of the critical challenges in AI-driven security efforts is that it is difficult to tell what an AI model found suspicious in a behavior to generate an alert. A lack of understanding on the manager and security professionals' part results from the opaque nature of the decision-making process. The XAI addresses this gap by allowing the security analyst to interrogate and validate the reasoning of AI reporting a threat. Managers must therefore deploy security solutions with explanation capabilities to inform and streamline the decision-making process. The transparency would also help with accountability and meeting regulatory compliance, as it must be established that due diligence was undertaken to flag a threat. In determining the managerial implications, the ethical considerations must be considered, especially where the integration of behavioral forensics into cybersecurity management is concerned. For instance, this integration is bound to raise several privacy concerns, especially surrounding the monitoring of and data collection on employees. Therefore, managers must ensure that organizational security policies are within acceptable ethical standards and legal frameworks. It requires a delicate balance between security priorities and the rights to privacy. Over-intrusive monitoring and overreach in data collection on employees could lead to resistance and even legal complications. It is critical to have explicit guidelines on how behavioral data is collected, analyzed, and used in making security decisions. Additionally, there will be a need for managerial oversight to avoid the possibility of discrimination or bias being introduced in the security assessments using behavioral analytics. The findings also suggest that organizations must move towards zero-trust models to enhance access control and prevent insider threats. Traditional security that builds the defenses around the network perimeter is rapidly becoming ineffective as cyber adversaries increasingly rely on infiltration or abuse of trusted credentials to gain access. Thus, managers must implement identity verification tools, such as multi-factor authentication, role-based access controls, and maintaining close watch on the activity. The objective would be minimizing trust while minimizing access to reduce unauthorized access and instances of credential-based attacks. Finally, it would help to call for cross-functional collaborations between cybersecurity teams, human resources, legal departments, and behavioral analysts. As the findings suggest, cybersecurity is not an independent function but an interdisciplinary approach. Therefore, it would be critical for managers to involve legal and compliance teams in security decision-making. A close partnership between technical security teams and behavioral analysts could improve insider threats detection, awareness, and social engineering prevention.

It is also essential to future-proof cybersecurity strategies, as threats evolve in sophistication. Entities must remain proactive in implementing cybersecurity frameworks, as well as investing on emerging technologies. The study also emphasizes self-teaching security systems that use AI-based behavior analytics to detect new threats in real-time. But managers need to make sure they keep these systems transparent, accountable, and aligned with human decision-making processes. In summary, the research highlights the need for organizations to address the complexity of cybersecurity management with a solution that combines AI-based security automation, behavioral forensics, and human judgment. Adopting an AI approach to cybersecurity without acknowledging its limitations in combating human-driven cyber threats leaves organizations vulnerable to catastrophic security breaches. As cyber criminals become more advanced, managers should take it upon themselves to actively implement a cybersecurity framework that accounts for both the positives of technological war fighting and human intellect in tandem to commit security decisions that balance speed and ethics. Through building a security-aware culture, deploying AI-human collaboration frameworks that scale, and adopting XAI and zero-trust paradigms, organizations can strengthen their ability to withstand the ever-changing terrain of cyber threats.

AI disclosure statement: The author acknowledges the use of AI-based tools for minor language editing or grammatical correction. However, all intellectual contributions, analyses, and conclusions presented in this chapter are entirely the author's own.

References

1. Möller, D.P.F., Cybersecurity in Digital Transformation, in: *Guide to Cybersecurity in Digital Transformation. Advances in Information Security*, vol. 103, Springer, Cham, 2023, https://doi.org/10.1007/978-3-031-26845-8_1.
2. Aldhaheri, S., Alghazzawi, D., Cheng, L., Barnawi, A., Alzahrani, B.A., Artificial Immune Systems approaches to secure the internet of things: A systematic review of the literature and recommendations for future research. *J. Netw. Comput. Appl.*, *157*, 102537, 2020, https://doi.org/10.1016/j.jnca.2020.102537.
3. Tayyab, M., Hameed, K., Mumtaz, M., Muzammal, S.M.M., Mahadevappa, P., Sunbalin, A., AI-Powered Threat Detection in Business Environments: Strategies and Best Practices, in: *Generative AI for Web Engineering Models*, pp. 379–436, IGI Global, Hershey, PA, USA, 2025, http://doi:10.4018/979-8-3693-6230-3.ch013.
4. Nair, M.M., Deshmukh, A., Tyagi, A.K., Artificial intelligence for cyber security: Current trends and future challenges, in: *Automated Secure Computing for Next-Generation Systems*, pp. 83–114, 2024, https://doi.org/10.1002/9781394213948.ch5.
5. Rich, M.S. and Aiken, M.P., An Interdisciplinary Approach to Enhancing Cyber Threat Prediction Utilizing Forensic Cyberpsychology and Digital Forensics. *Forensic Sci.*, *4*, 1, 110–151, 2024, https://doi.org/10.3390/forensicsci4010008.
6. Hu, Y., Kuang, W., Qin, Z., Li, K., Zhang, J., Gao, Y., Li, K., Artificial intelligence security: Threats and countermeasures. *ACM Comput. Surv. (CSUR)*, *55*, 1, 1–36, 2021, https://doi.org/10.1145/3487890.
7. Sarker, I.H., AI-based modeling: techniques, applications and research issues towards automation, intelligent and smart systems. *SN Comput. Sci.*, *3*, 2, 158, 2022, https://doi.org/10.1007/s42979-022-01043-x.
8. Sarker, I.H., Machine learning for intelligent data analysis and automation in cybersecurity: current and future prospects. *Ann. Data Sci.*, *10*, 6, 1473–1498, 2023, https://doi.org/10.1007/s40745-022-00444-2.
9. Salmani, H., Nasiri, S., Ahmadi, M., The advantages, disadvantages, threats, and opportunities of electronic patient-reported outcome systems in cancer: A systematic review. *Digit. Health*, *10*, 20552076241257146, 2024, http://doi.org:10.1177/20552076241257146.

10. Kommisetty, P.D.N.K., Kuppala, B.M.S.R., Buvvaji, H.V., Transforming Cyber Defense: Anomaly Detection and Predictive Analytics for Automated Threat Response. *Int. J. Eng. Comput. Sci.*, *11*, 8, 25585–25600, 2022, https://doi.org/10.18535/ijecs/v11i08.4694.
11. Lu, Y. and Da Xu, L., Internet of Things (IoT) cybersecurity research: A review of current research topics. *IEEE Internet Things J.*, *6*, 2, 2103–2115, 2018, http://doi.org/10.1109/JIOT.2018.2869847.
12. Evans, M., Maglaras, L.A., He, Y., Janicke, H., Human behaviour as an aspect of cybersecurity assurance. *Secur. Commun. Netw.*, *9*, 17, 4667–4679, 2016, http://doi.org/10.1002/sec.1657.
13. Falowo, O.I., Botsyoe, L., Koshoedo, K., Ozer, M., Enhancing cybersecurity with artificial immune systems and general intelligence: A new frontier in threat detection and response. *IEEE Access*, 12, 123811–123822, 2024, http://doi.org/10.1109/ACCESS.2024.3454543.
14. Paul, R. and Jana, A.K., Credit Risk Evaluation for Financial Inclusion Using Machine Learning Based Optimization, 2021, Available at SSRN 4690773. http://doi.org/10.2139/ssrn.4690773.
15. Dehghan, M. and Khosravian, E., Advancing Situation Awareness Systems: Evaluating Decision-Making Methods with UAV Applications. *Manage. Strat. Eng. Sci.*, 6, 4, 122–133, 2024, https://doi.org/10.61838/kman.aitech.2.4.6.
16. Ghazi-Tehrani, A.K. and Pontell, H.N., Phishing evolves: Analyzing the enduring cybercrime, in: *The New Technology of Financial Crime*, pp. 35–61, Routledge, 2022, https://doi.org/10.1080/15564886.2020.1829224.
17. Francia, J., Hansen, D., Schooley, B., Taylor, M., Murray, S., Snow, G., Assessing AI vs Human-Authored Spear Phishing SMS Attacks: An Empirical Study Using the TRAPD Method, 2024, https://doi.org/10.48550/arXiv.2406.13049.
18. McClain, J., Silva, A., Emmanuel, G., Anderson, B., Nauer, K., Abbott, R., Forsythe, C., Human performance factors in cyber security forensic analysis. *Procedia Manuf.*, 3, 5301–5307, 2015, https://doi.org/10.1016/j.promfg.2015.07.621.
19. Madarie, R., Kranenbarg, M.W., de Poot, C., Examining the cyclical nature of crimes: A looped crime script of data theft from organizational networks. *Comput. Hum. Behav. Rep.*, *17*, 100548, 2025, https://doi.org/10.1016/j.chbr.2024.100548.
20. Withanaarachchi, A. and Vithana, N., Female underrepresentation in the cybersecurity workforce–a study on cybersecurity professionals in Sri Lanka. *Inf. Comput. Secur.*, *30*, 3, 402–421, 2022, https://doi.org/10.1108/ICS-08-2021-0129.
21. Oppenheimer, H., How the process of discovering cyberattacks biases our understanding of cybersecurity. *J. Peace Res.*, *61*, 1, 28–43, 2024, https://doi.org/10.1177/00223433231217687.

22. Salem, A.H., Azzam, S.M., Emam, O.E., Abohany, A.A., Advancing cybersecurity: a comprehensive review of AI-driven detection techniques. *J. Big Data*, *11*, 1, 105, 2024, https://doi.org/10.1186/s40537-024-00957-y.
23. Karale, A., The challenges of IoT addressing security, ethics, privacy, and laws. *Internet Things*, *15*, 100420, 2021, https://doi.org/10.1016/j.iot.2021.100420.
24. Andrew, J. and Baker, M., The general data protection regulation in the age of surveillance capitalism. *J. Bus. Ethics*, *168*, 565–578, 2021, https://doi.org: 10.1007/s10551-019-04239-z.
25. Chandra, K.K., Kalla, K., Bhatia, J., Jayaprakash, M., Dey, S.R., Detection and analysis of cryptocurrency scams on twitter, in: *International Conference on Algorithmic Aspects in Information and Management*, 2024, September, Springer Nature Singapore, Singapore, pp. 3–14, https://doi.org/10.1007/978-981-97-7801-0_1.
26. Holder, E. and Wang, N., Explainable artificial intelligence (XAI) interactively working with humans as a junior cyber analyst. *Hum.-Intell. Syst. Integr.*, *3*, 2, 139–153, 2021, https://doi.org/10.1007/s42454-021-00039-x.
27. Martínez, J. and Durán, J.M., Software supply chain attacks, a threat to global cybersecurity: SolarWinds' case study. *Int. J. Saf. Secur. Eng.*, *11*, 5, 537–545, 2021, https://doi.org/10.18280/ijsse.110505.
28. Tanikonda, A., Pandey, B.K., Peddinti, S.R., Katragadda, S.R., Advanced AI-Driven Cybersecurity Solutions for Proactive Threat Detection and Response in Complex Ecosystems. *J. Sci. Technol.*, 3, 1, 2022, http://doi.org/10.2139/ssrn.5102358.

8

Ontologically Structured Methods for Evaluating Semantic Textual Similarity in Security Applications

Atul Gupta, Rohit Saxena*, Vishal Nagar and Satyasundara Mahapatra

Department of Computer Science & Engineering, Pranveer Singh Institute of Technology, Kanpur, India

Abstract

In computer engineering and cognitive science, evaluating semantic textual similarity (STS) among phrases, paragraphs, and documents is crucial. Additionally, it has numerous uses in a variety of industries, including geomatics and bioinformatics. In this chapter, we analyzed the concept of semantic recognition of patterns and the utilization of the tool that is basically concerned about security domain. In this study, we give a review on several linguistic similarity techniques, as well as information on the existence of various STS-related tools and apps. For several tasks in natural language processing (NLP), including abstractive summarization, semantic features, short response grading, pattern recognition, and extracting, STS is a critical part. They categorize the conceptual similarity metrics into three main groups: knowledge-based similarity, corpus-based similarity, and string-based similarity. The techniques connected to the WordNet ontology are highlighted more. Structural approaches are crucial for deciphering the original meaning of ambiguous terms because they are exceedingly challenging for computers to analyze. We also suggest a novel outlook to gauging sentence semantic relatedness. This suggested approach combines the information into a language model while utilizing the benefits of taxonomy methodologies.

***Keywords*:** WordNet ontology, NLP, semantic similarity, tools-security domain, information content similarity, cosine similarity, jaccard similarity

**Corresponding author*: rohitt.saxenaa@gmail.com

Sujata Priyambada Dash, Vaibhav Mishra, Bijeta Shaw, Sandeep Kumar Panda and S. Balamurugan (eds.) Digital Immune System: Principles and Practices, (167–182) © 2026 Scrivener Publishing LLC

8.1 Introduction

Similarity measure is an important component in natural-language processing (NLP) and is a key job for several application domains and related disciplines. A measure called semantic textual similarity (STS) can be used to evaluate the semantic relatedness in between groups of texts. Both immediate and indirect connections between the papers are what determine how similar they are [1, 2]. The existence of semantic linkages between them can be used to quantify and identify these connections. The idea of STS recognition in text data was put forth in the works mentioned in [3, 4] in 2006. After that, attention was directed into lengthy texts or specific terms.

Following that, since 2012, the work of determining semantic relatedness has expanded to include creating a similarity score between 0 and 5 using various SemEval tasks [5–7]. In this test, a score of 0 denotes perfect semantic congruence and a score of 5 indicates unrelatedness. One of the main objectives of the STS task is to build a cohesive framework by fusing many disparate conceptual components to determine their influence on various NLP tasks.

Such a framework's development is a significant research challenge with various vital applications in NLP, including information extraction and electronic education, as well as text categorization [8, 9], question answering [10], significance feedback and text categorization [11], word sense ambiguity [3], and resource extraction [12].

Numerous meaningful web apps, such as entity identification, community extraction, and ontology building, all benefit from semantic similarity. It is also helpful for Twitter searches [12], where the capacity to precisely gauge semantic similarity between words or objects is necessary. Among the primary issues with IR is how to find a set of pictures and documents that are semantically linked to a particular search request in an internet search engine [13].

The methods listed below can be used to gauge how similar two texts are in terms of their semantics: topological-based similarity, statistical-based similarity, semantic-based similarity, vector space-based similarity, word alignment-based similarity, and machine learning-based similarity. Topological studies, which are among these techniques, are crucial for deciphering the intended meaning of ambiguous words because they are exceedingly challenging for computers to analyze.

The remainder of this essay is structured as follows: in Section 8.2, we discussed the relevant topological techniques research. We looked at the specific use of three similarity techniques in Section 8.3. Edge-based similarity metrics are presented in Section 8.3.2, while hybrid approaches is reported in Section 8.4. Character-based and term-based string similarity measurements were each presented in Sections 8.5 and 8.6. In Section 8.6, we also suggested a brand-new technique for identifying linguistic similarity between sentences based on the learning algorithm and WordNet taxonomy, and in Sections 8.7 and 8.8, we presented the findings of a brief experiment using the suggested technique. We presented a list of the tools and apps that are readily available for calculating resemblance in Section 8.9.

8.2 Related Work Based on Topological Methodology

It can be challenging for humans to interpret ambiguous words in many situations, and it can be even more challenging for computers to do so. The various connections between the terms or concepts can be used to resolve these uncertainties: hierarchical relationship, correlative (e.g., cause-and-effect), and congruence [14]. It has been proposed and used as a specific case of semantic relatedness of proximity the IS-A connection between the concepts [15]. The proximity between terms and concepts can be defined using taxonomies to calculate topological resemblance, which in turn can be used to evaluate similarity score.

A conceptual network that considered the semantic distance between nodes in the network was used to study the ambiguity of lexical item during page indexing [16]. In this research, the WordNet semantically structure was used to examine phrase sense during text indexing. The aggregation of ideas from a group of contiguous terms was found to disambiguate the distance between the input word's various senses. A strategy for identifying semantic similarity in a classification based on the idea of information content was put forth by Philip Resnik in another study [17].

Jiang and Conrath presented a novel method for determining the semantic similarity of words by combining corpus statistical data with lexical taxonomy structure. As a result, the taxonomy was used to generate the semantic distance among the nodes in the semantic space, which produces better results when compared to the computational evidence that was derived through a redistributive study of corpus data. Edge counting system was inherited and further improved by a node-based approach in this proposed method, which is a hybrid approach [14]. A random walk across a graph was suggested [18] as a way to discover the resemblance among words and sentences. In this effort, WordNet's ontological sources and local semantic data were merged. To get the matching score, the lexical pattern produced by random process was compared to another distribution of this type. It has been determined that a feature for identifying textual entailment tasks is the graph work similarity between texts.

8.3 Methods of Semantic Similarity Computation

8.3.1 Knowledge-Based Similarity

Content extraction, relying on the term semantic relatedness, has received a lot of attention in the field of data mining. All of these approaches take the semantic and logical connections between the terms into account. Therefore, using this knowledge, we may roughly classify the semantic similarity of items in ontologies into three groups: node-based similarity, edge-based similarity, and hybrid similarity, which mixes node and edge similarity.

8.3.1.1 Node-Based or Information Content Similarity

To compare the semantic similarity of ideas, node-based or information content (IC) techniques [17, 19] are utilized. Any idea or node represents IS-A in this approach. One set named C is used to store a classification, and each node in this set has a distinct notion. It makes intuitive sense that the degree to which two conceptions are similar depends on the knowledge they have in common. An edge counting approach may be used in classification to identify the actual relationship between two ideas. This approach requires moving higher in the hierarchy to get a minimum upper bound if the minimum pathway connecting pair of nodes is long. Figure 8.1 illustrates an instance of an IS-A connection between ideas, with the terms 'NICKEL' and 'DIME' each include 'COIN.' In this illustration, the super class MEDIUM OF EXCHANGE is shared by both NICKEL and CREDIT CARD [33].

$$\mathrm{IC} = log^{-1}\ p(c) \tag{8.1}$$

The quantity of word sense is an important component [17, 20], which also establish a straightforward category frequency formula:

$$\mathrm{freq} = \sum_{w \leftarrow word(c)} freq(w) \tag{8.2}$$

Probabilistic evaluation may be used to calculate the detection model, where N refers to the total number of measured nouns (excluding any that are not included in any WordNet classes, of usual).

$$p(c) = \frac{freq\,(c)}{N} \tag{8.3}$$

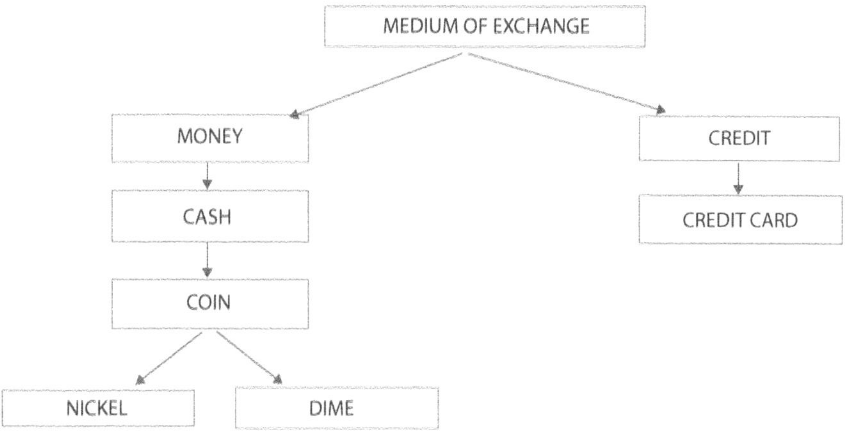

Figure 8.1 WordNet taxonomy [33].

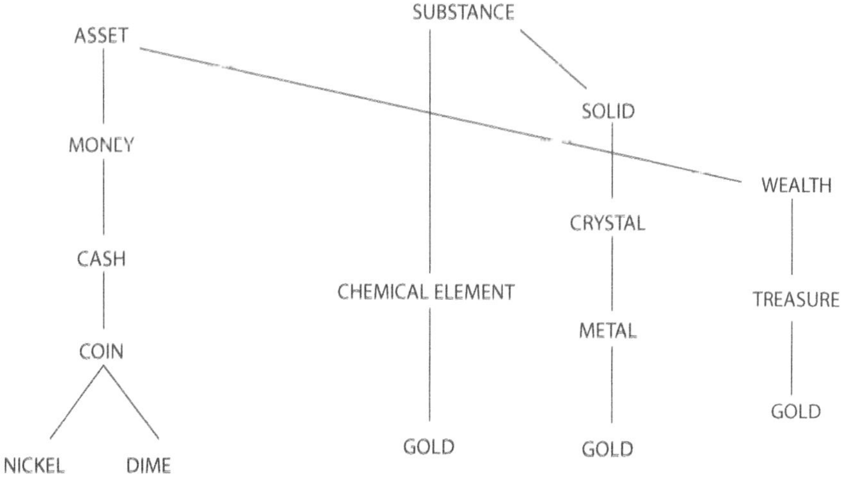

Figure 8.2 WordNet taxonomy of multiple inheritance [14].

NICKLE and GOLD, which contain additional parent classes, serve as examples of multiple inheritance notions in Figure 8.2. The highest similarity value across all the category pairings, which is related to their varied senses, may be used to assess the resemblance in this situation since one word has much more sense [14]:

8.3.2 Edge-Based Approach

The primary method of calculating semantic similarity in classification is the edge-based approach. It measures how many connections there are connecting two nodes that represent the ideas under comparison. They seem to be more identical, the shorter the route between two nodes [14].

It was noted that the proximity among nodes in a hierarchy classification should meet matrix qualities such as the 0 property, meaningful property, and favorable property. It is required to provide an edge linking two nodes weight since the distance between them should not always be equal. The following significant factors should be considered [15] when determining the weight:

(a) **Density in networks:** For instance, when calculating WordNet's network density, greater densities must consider the plant-flora portion. The length between connections is closest to the estimated local density [21].
(b) **Depth of nodes:** As one moves down a structure, it can be argued that distance decreases regarding its depth.
(c) **Link type:** It depicts how two nodes are related to one another. Merely IS-A links are considered in several edge-based models [15, 21]. The weight can also be determined using other relationships, such as Meronymy-Holonymy, which have distinct effects.

To calculate edge-based resemblance, edge count has indeed been studied [17]. By deducing the path length from the longest feasible path, the distance metric may be changed into the similarity measure as follows:

$$sim_{edge}\,(w1, w2) = 2\,\mathrm{d}_{\max}\text{-}\{\min(c1, c2)\; len(c1, c2)\} \tag{8.4}$$

where d_{max} is the taxonomy's greatest level of detail, and $c1$ and $c2$ correspond to the phrase's first and second meanings, correspondingly.

8.4 Hybrid Approach

There are significant distinctions between both the node- and edge-based approaches that were covered in the preceding sections. The edge-based approaches appear to be correct without any clear justification, whereas the node-based technique appears to be far more precise than distance-based. Although WordNet was used to create the layers rather than assess similarity, its distance measurement was based on the show's subjective perceptions.

On the contrary hand, information content is reliant on the taxonomy's design and was not relevant to the connection kinds [14]. Despite the fact that these two approaches are distinct from one another, edge-based was used to develop a combined approach that takes decision-making into account [17]. The conditional distribution of the child notion ci of its parent notions p was used in this manner to determine the connection improved strength:

8.4.1 Corpus-Based Similarity

Learning about statistical similarities from information, or a corpora, that is a compilation of spoken or written content. In this approach, a mathematical model was created initially, and closeness was then calculated. Over recent years, a number of models have been developed, resulting in discovered the following classification.

(a) **Latent semantic analysis (LSA):** With the help of a sizable text corpus, the relevant knowledge of phrases has been retrieved and expressed in this manner [22]. The distinctive phrases and text fragments are placed in rows and columns of a grid in the initial phase. Each item displays the number of times a character appears in the text [23]. A function that represents two meanings—the relevance of a phrase in a document and the extent to which a phrase type shares knowledge in the discussion domain—weights cell frequencies.

(b) **Generalized latent semantic analysis (GLSA):** Whenever word vectors are created from a diverse text corpus, the efficiency of LSA suffers [24]. Rather than using the bag-of-words content matrices used during LSA, the GLSA methodology is utilized to locate the terms and text vectors based on linguistically driven handful term commonalities [25].

It is a paradigm in which several approaches of dimensionality reduction are integrated with various metrics of the semantic relationships of concepts [26].

8.5 String-Based Similarity

8.5.1 Similarity Based on Character

The largest subset of a text may be found using this approach. According to the frequent patterns sequence of characters, it evaluates the two strings and determines how close they are. It is measurable as follows:

$$LC_{sub}(S_1, S_2) = LC_{suff}(S_1, S_{2,\text{--------}}) \tag{8.5}$$

LCSuff is a function that identify the frequent patterns suffix of potential S1 and S2 prefixes.

8.5.2 Similarity Based on Levenshtein Distance

It is a string measurement or gap between two strings that provides the amount of work needed to change one string into another. This alteration is accomplished by the insertion, deletion, replacement, or transformation of a specific character or two adjoining characters [28].

8.5.3 Similarity Based on Needleman–Wunsch

To align the sequence data, bioinformatics employs a particular sort of dynamical algorithm. The terms "ideal matching method" and "sequence alignment approach" are also used [29].

8.5.4 Similarity Based on Smith–Waterman

It is a variant of the Needleman–Wunsch method that uses localized structural alignment to compare the two texts, nucleotide sequences, or protein sequences. It analyzes the text segments inside to calculate similarity and then optimizes similarity. Due to its computationally difficult cubic structure, it is typically rarely employed in huge issues [34].

8.6 Similarity Based on Terms

8.6.1 Cosine-Based Similarity

It determines the angle cosine that exists between two separate vectors in an internal product space by comparing them. In any other inclination, the cosine is less than one and equals zero. Two vectors that are in the same direction have a cosine resemblance of 1, whereas those in 90 degrees have a resemblance of 0. To discover the cohesiveness among them, it is also data capturing extraction [30]. The Euclidean dot product can be used to calculate the cosine of two separate vectors.

$$a.b = ||a||\,||b||\cos\theta \tag{8.6}$$

$$\cos\theta = \frac{A.B}{||A||\,||B||} = \frac{\sum_{i=1}^{n} AiBi}{\sqrt{\sum_{i=1}^{n} Ai^2}\sqrt{\sum_{i=1}^{n} Bi^2}} \tag{8.7}$$

where Ai and Bi are the components of A and B.

8.6.2 Similarity Based on Euclidean Distance

It is the separation in Euclid spaces between two points. Here between two places s and t, the Euclidean distance is:

$$d\,(s, t) = d\,(t, s) = \sqrt{\sum_{i=1}^{n}(ti - pi)^2} \tag{8.8}$$

8.6.3 Jaccard Similarity

A statistical method for determining the closeness and variety among two finite lists is known as the Jaccard coefficient [31]. This is how it is explained:

$$J(A, B) = \frac{|A \cap B|}{|A \cup B|} = \frac{|A \cap B|}{|A| + |B| - |A \cap B|} \tag{8.9}$$

The Jaccard distance, abbreviated as J and derived by deducting the Jaccard Index from 1, is used to determine the disparity between two finite categories.

8.7 Proposed Methodology

To determine the lexical correspondence between two sentences, a linguistic prototype conceptual system has been suggested in this study. One of these two terms is regarded as the source text (S), and the other as the targeting text (T). Both S and T are taken to be conceptually and grammatically sound. The following phases can be used to break down the new method:

1. While beginning any similarity measure job in any language comprehension, it is crucial to eliminate all punctuation marks. All punctuation were initially placed in a Java list, and then all S and T words were individually evaluated for recognition. Despite the fact that stopping words are indeed the most frequently used terms, there is not one list that can be utilized for all psycholinguistic tasks. During the similarity step, these recognized stopped phrases are disregarded.
2. The phrases are initially given part-of-speech (POS) labels using the Penn Treebank texts [35], that is the most often utilized grammatical data. Additionally, the system gets such recognized labels and phrases to create the tree structure.
3. Top-down parser is used to create the parse tree after weighing its benefits over bottom-up parsing. Most English grammatical roles are taken into account while parsing. The top-down parsed tree is then created using the detected word structures.
4. The syntax tree and other statistical data from earlier stages are taken into account while designing a cross (equal to level of the tree) undirected weighted graph in this step. When building a graph, the following characteristics are taken into account:
   Step1: POS: When two entities are discovered to be identical in two tree structures at the same layer, all stop - word depending on their POS info are ignored.
   Step2: Depth of node: All potential routes are taken beginning at the root node S and continue until the search finds

a word or idea at a higher level (i.e., a leaf node) of the tree. Whenever a term is present in both the tree and the same POS tags at the same layer, the depth of the term is taken into account when comparing similarities.

Step3: Matching the String: If a phrase with the POS is discovered in the tree structure of S and T, a weighted value is added to the connection if the two nodes are identical.

5. The value here between the two graphs is evaluated once the structure creation step is complete. Weight is determined under the given circumstance:

   (a) Whereas if POS label differs between pair of nodes that share the same level, the WordNet classification connection is taken into account. The inverse logarithm of the probabilistic reasoning and the link prediction reasoning are taken into consideration when calculating the informativeness, or weight w_i, of the connection.

   (b) Two separate weighting values are created if the POS label is different but the contents match.

$$W_i = \text{sim}\ (C1, C2) \tag{8.10}$$

$$w_i^2 = \text{frequent}\frac{Ci}{N} \tag{8.11}$$

   where C1 and C2 stand for two ideas that are at the level of two tree structures. *N* stands for the word count and POS tags from a huge text corpus, and *Ci* stands for the total number of class C words. Lastly, weight is determined using the highest of w1 and w2.

   (c) Hardly a weight is calculated for the connection between the current value node and the proper value noun node if no requirement is met and the sentence is determined to be of noun class and the terms are proper nouns.

   (d) Finally, despite taking into account the weight limit of the connection, similarity is determined as the minimum distance path. The average is then determined by adding the scores of all linkages from start node S to the leaf node.

8.8 Results

Using the SemEval 2015 trained Dataset-3, a combination of 50 phrases is used to assess the textual similarity score. Two distinct runs are performed for this assignment. WordNet taxonomic connections are taken into account during the initial run, and a best match of 0.46 is provided. Word-Net 2.0 is taken into consideration for this work. In the second run, we used information content to raise the similarity score. The top rating for this challenge is 0.78. This approach, which beats previous approaches [14, 19, 32], calculates the IC score by merging the WordNet taxonomic and classifier learning algorithm.

8.9 Software Used for Computing Semantic Similarity

WordNet-based similarity: This is a WordNet-based Perl package that applies knowledge from the lexicon database WordNet over the information to detect semantic similarities and associated measures. Leacock–Chodorow, Jiang and Conarth, Wu–Palmer, Banerjee–Pedersen, Hirst–St. Onge, Patwardhan Pedersen, Rensik, and Lin are only a few of the measurements that it supports. For both nouns and verbs, a pairwise closeness component has already been generated.

a. **Unified medical language system (UMLS):** The UMLS is a free and accessible Perl package that determines semantic relationship and resemblance depending on vocabularies and taxonomies prevalent in the healthcare area. It provides a numerical number between two medical ideas to show how comparable they are.
b. **SEMantic SimiLARity (SEMI-LAR):** An integrated platform for users, academics, and programmers to obtain incorporated Java-based resemblance algorithms is called a SEMI-LAR toolkit. It offers a framework and a GUI-based interface for accessing resemblance techniques. To discover the resemblance, the methods available in this tool range from simple lexicon similarity metrics to word-to-word metrics to more complex methods that rely on unsupervised techniques like latent sentiment similarity and latent Dirichlet allocation to kernel-based techniques.

8.10 Conclusion

We describe four distinct STS metrics in this study. We separate the character-based and term-based string resemblance measurements into two classes. These two measurements compute the gap between two strings, groups, or vectors to determine the distinctions and similarities between string sequencing and character creations. In all, we provided 14 string similarity metrics divided into two categories. We also covered the three topographical method types of node-method, edge-method, and hybrid method, the last of which combines node and edge-based techniques. These topological analyses are mostly used to determine how different and similar phrases and ontological notions are.

AI disclosure statement: The author acknowledges the use of AI-based tools for minor language editing or grammatical correction. However, all intellectual contributions, analyses, and conclusions presented in this chapter are entirely the author's own.

References

1. Corley, C. and Mihalcea, R., Measuring the semantic similarity of texts. *Proceedings of the ACL workshop on empirical modeling of semantic equivalence and entailment*, Association for Computational Linguistics, pp. 13–18, 2005.
2. Rus, V., Lintean, M.C., Banjade, R., Niraula, N.B., Stefanescu, D., Semilar: The semantic similarity toolkit. *ACL (Conference System Demonstrations)*, pp. 163–168, 2013.
3. Li, Y., McLean, D., Bandar, Z.A., O'shea, J.D., Crockett, K., Sentence similarity based on semantic nets and corpus statistics. *IEEE Trans. Knowl. Data Eng.*, 18, 8, 1138–1150, 2006.
4. Mihalcea, R., Corley, C., Strapparava, C., Corpus-based and knowledge-based measures of text semantic similarity, in: *Aaai*, vol. 6, no. 2006, pp. 775–780, 2006.
5. Agirre, E., Banea, C., Cardie, C., Cer, D.M., Diab, M.T., Gonzalez-Agirre, A., Guo, W., Mihalcea, R., Rigau, G., Wiebe, J., SemEval-2014 Task 10: Multilingual Semantic Textual Similarity, in: *SemEval@ COLING*, pp. 81–91, 2014.
6. Agirre, E., Cer, D., Diab, M., Gonzalez-Agirre, A., Guo, W., * SEM 2013 shared task: Semantic textual similarity, in: *Second joint conference on lexical and computational semantics (* SEM), volume 1: proceedings of the Main conference and the shared task: semantic textual similarity*, pp. 32–43, 2013.

7. Agirre, E., Cer, D., Diab, M., Gonzalez-Agirre, A., Semeval-2012 task 6: A pilot on semantic textual similarity, in: ** SEM 2012: The First Joint Conference on Lexical and Computational Semantics–Volume 1: Proceedings of the main conference and the shared task, and Volume 2: Proceedings of the Sixth International Workshop on Semantic Evaluation (SemEval 2012)*, pp. 385–393, 2012.
8. Aliguliyev, R.M., A new sentence similarity measure and sentence based extractive technique for automatic text summarization. *Expert Syst. Appl.*, 36, 4, 7764–7772, 2009.
9. Steinberger, J. and Jezek, K., Using latent semantic analysis in text summarization and summary evaluation. *Proc. ISIM*, 4, 93-100, 8, 2004.
10. Mohler, M., Bunescu, R., Mihalcea, R., Learning to grade short answer questions using semantic similarity measures and dependency graph alignments, in: *Proceedings of the 49th annual meeting of the association for computational linguistics: Human language technologies*, pp. 752–762, 2011.
11. Rocchio, J., Relevance feedback in information retrieval, in: *The Smart retrieval system-experiments in automatic document processing*, pp. 313–323, 1971.
12. Salton, G., Singhal, A., Mitra, M., Buckley, C., Automatic text structuring and summarization. *Inf. Process. Manage.*, 33, 2, 193–207, 1997.
13. Coelho, T.A.S., Calado, P.P., Souza, L.V., Ribeiro-Neto, B., Muntz, R., Image retrieval using multiple evidence ranking. *IEEE Trans. Knowl. Data Eng.*, 16, 4, 408–417, 2004.
14. Jiang, J.J. and Conrath, D.W., Semantic similarity based on corpus statistics and lexical taxonomy, arXiv preprint cmp-lg/9709008, 1997.
15. Rada, R., Mili, H., Bicknell, E., Blettner, M., Development and application of a metric on semantic nets. *IEEE Trans. Syst. Man Cybern.*, 19, 1, 17–30, 1989.
16. Sussna, M., Word sense disambiguation for free-text indexing using a massive semantic network, in: *Proceedings of the second international conference on Information and knowledge management*, pp. 67–74, 1993.
17. Resnik, P., Using information content to evaluate semantic similarity in a taxonomy, arXiv preprint cmp-lg/9511007, 1995.
18. Choudhury, M., Hassan, S., Mukherjee, A., Muresan, S., Proceedings of the 2009 Workshop on Graph-based Methods for Natural Language Processing (TextGraphs-4), in: *Proceedings of the 2009 Workshop on Graph-based Methods for Natural Language Processing (TextGraphs-4)*, 2009.
19. Resnik, P., Wordnet and distributional analysis: A class-based approach to lexical discovery, in: *AAAI workshop on statistically-based natural language processing techniques*, pp. 56–64, 1992.
20. Richardson, R. and Smeaton, A.F., Using WordNet in a knowledge-based approach to information retrieval, 1995.
21. Lee, J.H., Kim, M.H., Lee, Y.J., Information retrieval based on conceptual distance in IS-A hierarchies. *J. Doc.*, 1993.

22. Landauer, T.K. and Dumais, S.T., A solution to Plato's problem: The latent semantic analysis theory of acquisition, induction, and representation of knowledge. *Psychol. Rev.*, 104, 2, 211, 1997.
23. Landauer, T.K., Foltz, P.W., Laham, D., An introduction to latent semantic analysis. *Discourse Process.*, 25, 2-3, 259–284, 1998.
24. Ando, R.K., Latent semantic space: Iterative scaling improves precision of inter-document similarity measurement, in: *Proceedings of the 23rd annual international ACM SIGIR conference on Research and development in information retrieval*, pp. 216–223, 2000.
25. Royer, C., Term representation with generalized latent semantic analysis, in: *Recent advances in natural language processing IV: selected papers from RANLP*, vol. 292, p. 45, 2005.
26. Matveeva, I., Farahat, A., Royer, C., Document representation with generalized latent semantic analysis, in: *Proceedings of the Conference On Research and Development in Information Retrieval (SIGIR 2005)*, 2005.
27. Bard, G.V., Spelling-error tolerant, order-independent pass-phrases via the Damerau-Levenshtein string-edit distance metric, Cryptology ePrint Archive, 2006.
28. Bagrow, J.P. and ben-Avraham, D., On the Google-fame of scientists and other populations. *AIP Conf. Proc.*, 779, 1, 81–89, American Institute of Physics, 2005.
29. Needleman, S.B. and Wunsch, C.D., A general method applicable to the search for similarities in the amino acid sequence of two proteins. *J. Mol. Biol.*, 48, 3, 443–453, 1970.
30. Tan, P.-N., Steinbach, M., Kumar, V., *Introduction to data mining*, Pearson education Inc., New Delhi, 2006.
31. Jaccard, P., Étude comparative de la distribution florale dans une portion des Alpes et des Jura. *Bull. Soc. Vaud. Sci. Nat.*, 37, 547–579, 1901.
32. Hughes, T. and Ramage, D., Lexical semantic relatedness with random graph walks, in: *Proceedings of the 2007 joint conference on empirical methods in natural language processing and computational natural language learning (EMNLP-CoNLL)*, pp. 581–589, 2007.
33. Tversky, A., Features of similarity. *Psychol. Rev.*, 84, 4, 327, 1977.
34. Smith, T.F. and Waterman, M.S., Identification of common molecular subsequences. *J. Mol. Biol.*, 147, 1, 195–197, 1981.
35. Marcus, M., Santorini, B., Marcinkiewicz, M.A., Building a large annotated corpus of English: The Penn Treebank, 1993.

9

Building Human-Centric Cyber Resilience – The Role of HR Practices

Preshita Neha Tudu*, **Aparna Rani, Steffi L. and Chavali Akhila**

Department of HR & OB, ICFAI Business School (IBS), Hyderabad, India

Abstract

In the rapidly evolving digital era, organizations face increasing vulnerability to cyber threats that can disrupt operations, compromise sensitive data, and harm firm's reputation. To mitigate these risks, it is prudent to foster cyber resilience, enabling firms to anticipate, withstand, and recover from cyberattacks with minimal impact. While cybersecurity focuses on prevention, cyber resilience emphasizes adaptability and recovery. Traditionally led by IT departments, the role of human resources (HR) has become indispensable in fostering a cyber-resilient workforce. Human resources play a pivotal role by integrating cybersecurity awareness into recruitment, training and development, policy development, employee compensation, employee off boarding and organizational culture. Through strategic employee engagement, continuous learning programs, and compliance enforcement, HR strengthens an organization's defense against cyberattacks. Aligning HR strategies with cyber resilience strengthens security, maintains business continuity, safeguards critical digital assets and digital infrastructure.

Keywords: Cybersecurity, cyber resilience, HRM functions, recruitment and selection, training and development, resilient organizational culture, compensation, communication

9.1 Introduction

The dynamic and increasing digitalization of organizations has revolutionized the way businesses operate including its systems, processes, and

**Corresponding author*: preshita@gmail.com

Sujata Priyambada Dash, Vaibhav Mishra, Bijeta Shaw, Sandeep Kumar Panda and S. Balamurugan (eds.) Digital Immune System: Principles and Practices, (183–210) © 2026 Scrivener Publishing LLC

culture. It helps organizations minimize costs, increase connectivity, optimize the efficient use of resources, improve automation, and fuel proactive decision-making (IBM Security, 2023) [16]. Undoubtedly, the digital revolution has a sturdier hold onto the business than ever before. While digitalization has opened mammoth opportunities for organizations, it has also made them vulnerable to various cyber threats such as malware, ransomware, spyware, phishing, Distributed denial of service (DDoS) attacks, Man-in-the-middle (MitM) attacks resulting in data breaches, data loss, data theft, system disruption, financial loss, fines, legal consequences and dent on the firm's reputation (CSRC NIST, 2024) [6]. Recently, Change Healthcare, a key processor of U.S. medical claims, suffered a ransomware attack (US HSS, 2024) [33]. The attackers breached the company's systems, extracted sensitive data, and deployed ransomware, severely disrupting healthcare operations nationwide. Medical claims processing and electronic payments stopped, which forced patients to pay out-of-pocket for medications and services. Similarly, a faulty update in CrowdStrike's Falcon Sensor software caused a massive worldwide disruption for Microsoft Windows users resulting in widespread system failures (The Hindu, 2024) [31]. Approximately 8.5 million devices crashed globally, displaying the infamous "Blue Screen of Death." Important sectors, including healthcare, banking, aviation, and manufacturing, faced severe operational setbacks. Even grocery stores, educational institutions, TV and radio stations, and fuel stations were affected. A similar attack happened in India where Indian consumer wearable brand boAt suffered a significant data breach, exposing the personal information of over 7.5 million users (Forbes India, 2024) [9]. The breach was allegedly coordinated by a hacker known as 'ShopifyGUY,' who leaked sensitive user data, names, phone numbers, addresses, email IDs, addresses, and customer IDs. Approximately 2GB of personally identifiable information was discarded on dark web forums, raising serious concerns about data security and privacy. Hence, it is imperative to understand, address, and safeguard organizations against cyberattacks. Traditionally, information technology (IT) departments and technical solutions spearhead cybersecurity initiatives. But to thrive in today's dynamic digital landscape, organizations must emphasize and prioritize the need for robust cyber resilience strategies (The Economic Times, 2023) [29].

While robust IT infrastructure and innovative technologies are critical for cyber resilience, the role of human resource management (HRM) in building and maintaining a resilient system has surfaced as an essential yet often overlooked component. Employees often serve as the first line of defense against cyber threats, and human resource (HR) practices play a vital role in arming and empowering them to protect organizations from ever-evolving cyber threats. Before understanding the roles of HR practices, let us understand what cyber resilience is and how it is different from cybersecurity.

With cyber threats spreading their wings all over and becoming more sophisticated, it is no longer a question of whether a business will be targeted and fall prey to. Thus, the organizations must be equipped to respond to and recover from such attacks. And here, the concept of cyber resilience comes to the fore. It has become a key to protecting the functionality, operational continuity, and integrity of organizations in the era of evolving cyberattacks. Cyber resilience refers to an organization's ability to anticipate, endure, bounce back, and adapt to cyber incidents, while ensuring minimal disruption to organizational operations (CSRC NIST, 2024) [6].

Unlike traditional cybersecurity, which aims at preventing cyberattacks, cyber resilience goes beyond having anti-virus software and firewalls; it emphasizes a more holistic approach and incorporates proactive risk management, incident response planning, and adaptability to emerging threats, thereby, facilitating the continued functioning of business operations even when security defenses fail (IBM Security, 2023) [16]. Take banking institutions that witness daily money transactions; a ransomware attack on a bank can interrupt its operations resulting in permanent loss of sensitive data and customer access. However, a cyber-resilient bank will have an incident response team, data backups, and a recovery strategy to restore operations quickly.

While cybersecurity is essential in defending against cyberattacks, true resilience is accomplished when an organization is capable of handling and minimizing the impact of these attacks and continues its operations with minimal disturbance. Thus, cyber resilience is not just about preventing attacks but also about ensuring that when the attack happens, the organization is equipped well to bounce back stronger, and more prepared, to handle such threats in the future (The Economic Times, 2023) [29]. Cyber resilience refers to an association's skill to formulate for and re-join to any and improve from cyberattacks or any species of occurrences. It includes executing vigorous security measures, proactive threat recognition, incident retort planning, and restoring systems and data rapidly. Responding to the increasing cyber threat requires an amalgamation of up-to-date security products, modern enterprise configuration, and trained employees to identify and respond to the threats before they cause disruptions. The Microsoft Incident Response Team helps organizations recover from security compromises and toughen their cyber defenses (Microsoft Security, 2024) [23]. They offer two types of incident responses, the onsite reactive incident response for active security incidents and the remote proactive investigations to detect potential threats before they cause harm. By harnessing Microsoft's strategic partnership with security organizations globally and Microsoft's product teams, they ensure thorough investigations for effective solutions. The team emphasizes proactive threat detection, and better security monitoring to identify perils in the organization's digital landscape.

9.2 Cybersecurity and Cyber Resilience – Different or Same?

Although often used interchangeably, cybersecurity and cyber resilience differ in their focus. While cybersecurity primarily aims at the prevention of cyberattacks by safeguarding data and systems from unauthorized access or breaches, cyber resilience goes further and emphasizes an organization's ability to withstand and recuperate from cyberattacks, ensuring operational continuity even after an attack (Linkov & Kott, 2019) [20]. Cyber resilience strengthens organizations' security strategies and prepares for the *'if'*, not *'when'* (European Commission, 2024) [8]. Let us first understand cybersecurity before we delve a little deeper into cyber resilience.

Technology has changed the way we work, communicate, and conduct business. But at the same time, it has opened doors for new cyber risks that are complex and dynamic (Schneier, 2020) [26]. In today's digital environment, cybersecurity is not just added protection but a key to safeguarding systems, networks, and data from unauthorized access, damage, and theft (Von Solms & Van Niekerk, 2013) [34].

Cybersecurity refers to the tools, technologies, and practices that protect networks, computer systems, data, software from cyber threats arising from unauthorized or malicious access, hackers, malware, phishing attacks, ransomware, or even unintentional human errors that compromise security (Bada, Sasse, & Nurse, 2019) [4]. The primary goal of cybersecurity is to proactively detect and mitigate these threats to ensure the integrity, confidentiality, and availability of the information (Anderson, 2020) [2]. Just like when we want to secure our house, we install locks, cameras, and alarms, to prevent break-ins, similarly, cybersecurity uses a combination of preventive measures, threat detection, and system resilience to keep digital environments safe (Ament & Haag, 2016) [1].

The key elements of cybersecurity are:

1. Prevention: Preventive cybersecurity identifies and blocks the threats before they can cause harm to the systems. It utilizes various tools to minimize the likelihood of a cyberattack. A financial institution encrypts customer data and uses multi-level authentication to avert unauthorized access to accounts (Herath & Rao, 2009) [12]. Preventive measures include:

- **Firewalls:** Act as a digital barrier to filter and block malicious traffic.
- **Encryption:** Secure sensitive data so only authorized users can access it.
- **Intrusion detection systems:** Monitor networks to detect suspicious activities in real-time (Gordon, Loeb, & Zhou, 2020) [10].

For example, to protect the sensitive information of the patients, hospitals may encrypt patients' records by converting them into an unreadable format. So even when their IT system is attacked by ransomware, it cannot access the encrypted patient records. And because hospitals maintain offline backups, they can restore data without paying the ransom (European Commission, 2024) [8].

2. Endurance: Even with strong preventive measures, cyberattacks may still occur. System hardening ensures that when a breach happens, its impact is minimized. This includes:

- **Regular software updates and patches** to close security loopholes.
- **Backup and disaster recovery plans** to restore lost data in case of a breach.
- **Network segmentation** to limit attackers from accessing critical systems (Linkov & Kott, 2019) [20].

For example, to check for outdated software or security gaps, hospitals may scan the system regularly using vulnerability assessment tool. They can update their software, including operating systems, applications, and network infrastructure, within a specified time (Ament & Haag, 2016) [1].

Cyber threats can disrupt businesses, steal sensitive information, and cause financial and reputational damage. We can conclude that organizations must invest in cybersecurity to protect customer data, intellectual property, and operational stability (Schneier, 2020) [26].

9.3 Does Cyber Resilience Bolster an Organization's Cybersecurity?

The answer is yes. A good cybersecurity plan includes cyber resilience practices. It goes further by spotting the inevitability of violations and encompasses both adversarial threats such as hackers and non-adversarial threats like human error (Linkov & Kott, 2019) [20]. It specializes in the functionality of systems and companies to resist, adapt to, and recover from assaults. A classic example of cyber resilience can be traced back to December 2020 when Winds Orion, a major infrastructure monitoring and management company, became the victim of cyberattacks. Hackers fed malicious code into Orion IT monitoring and management software which is used by many government agencies and private companies worldwide (IBM, 2024) [17]. When the company found that their system was hacked, it quickly followed the incident response plan, quarantined the affected systems, and mended vulnerabilities before proceeding to improve their security postures.

The key elements of cyber resilience are:

1. **Prevention**: Although entire safety is not possible, cyber resilience includes implementing proactive measures to stop cyber threats before they occur or minimize vulnerabilities (Von Solms & Van Niekerk, 2013) [34]. For example, a bank prevents cyberattacks with robust encryption and multi-factor authentication (MFA). It detects fraud using AI-based irregularity. If there is a breach, the bank immediately responds by freezing doubtful transactions and later restores customer accounts through secure backups (Gordon, Loeb, & Zhou, 2020) [10].
2. **Capacitation**: Cyber resilience focuses on learning from past events of cyberattacks and based on the lessons learnt (Schneier, 2020) [26], it continuously improves and updates their resilience strategies. For example, a technology company conducts a post-attack analysis to identify weaknesses and updates its cybersecurity policies accordingly. For example, a technology firm may improve its ability to predict and

respond to cyberattacks by conducting a post-attack analysis to identify potential vulnerabilities and continuously update its cybersecurity strategies accordingly with real-time data. Further, provide suggestions to response teams for proactive defense (Bada, Sasse, & Nurse, 2019) [4].

3. **Reconstruction**: Quick restoration of the systems and data after a cyberattack is vital for resilience, allowing businesses to resume usual operations. After a cyber incident, the firm restores its systems using secure backups and ensures all vulnerabilities are repaired. For example, a hospital becomes a victim of a ransomware attack that has encrypted its patients' personal information, and records, making them inaccessible to the hospital staff. So, instead of paying the ransom to the hackers to get back access, the hospital activates its cloud-based backup system and restores critical data, ensuring minimal data loss. Further, it patches affected systems and validates their security before reconnecting them to the network and then conducts post-recovery testing to check that systems are secure as well as operational while preventing future incidents (Ament & Haag, 2016) [1].

Table 9.1 Cybersecurity vs. cyber resilience.

Factors	Cybersecurity	Cyber resilience
Prevent	Attack prevention is a vitally important aspect, which includes installing firewalls and monitoring the network.	Assumes there would be breaches regardless and it is more focused on damage control; prevention is not ignored.
Withstand	Reduces the damaging impact resulting from a cyberattack.	Withstands attacks where normal business operations continue.
Recover	Recovery is the action taken after both good and bad prevention steps.	Puts emphasis on quick recovery after an attack starts, as well as during the active attack.
Goal	Ensure that attacks do not compromise systems and data.	Enable systems to cope with and recover from the adverse impacts caused by attacks or other significant disruptions.

One way to understand the difference is by acknowledging that no security system can provide complete protection against every type of cyberattack and even the well-guarded systems can be compromised. Therefore, organizations must integrate both cyber resilience and cybersecurity into their risk management strategy. While cybersecurity focuses on preventive measures to lessen the likelihood of a successful attack, a purely defensive approach is inadequate since cyber threats are continuously evolving. A robust cyber resilience strategy warrants quick detection of cyber threats, capacitation and adaptation with minimal disruption. We can conclude that cybersecurity involves locking the doors and the windows of the house along with installing security cameras to prevent thieves from breaking in and entering. However, cyber resilience admits that despite all the security measures those thieves could still break inside (Ament & Haag, 2016) [1]. So, it enables you to deal with ill-fated situations, ensuring there is sufficient damage control and that you lose as little as possible. Table 9.1 explains the difference between cyber security and cyber resilience.

9.4 The Evolving Role of Human Resources in Cyber Resilience and Data Protection

9.4.1 Human Resource's Digital Transformation in the 1990s and Early 2000s

The advent of technology began to reshape business operations, and companies started to embrace digital tools and digitize administrative processes (Johnson, Lukaszewski, & Stone, 2016) [18]. The focus was now shifted to automate and simplify tasks across departments, HR notwithstanding. The HR software such as People Soft and SAP revolutionized traditional HR functions. These software automated and streamlined HR core functions such as payroll, performance tracking, and record-keeping (TechTarget, 2019) [28]. Undoubtedly, these tools offered significant improvements with minimal manual intervention; but it also introduced new challenges, particularly in cybersecurity (Manoharan, 2024) [21].

During this period, cybersecurity was not yet a significant threat to HR operations and the focus was primarily optimization of the usability of digital tools rather than on protection sensitive employee data (Ubisend, 2020) [32]. However, cybersecurity issues arose, especially concerning the safety of sensitive employee data, forcing HR and IT to begin collaborating on access control and compliance (Inspired eLearning, 2021) [15]. As digitally transformed organizations moved forward, cybersecurity issues arose and protecting HR data began to highlight the vulnerability of these systems (Nica, Burcea, & Sabie, 2024) [24].

9.4.2 Digitally Focused Growth (Mid-2000s to 2010)

The mid-2000s to 2010 saw a digital change in HR practice through the proliferation of the human resource information system (HRIS) and cloud-based platforms to manage tasks, including employee recruitment, performance reviews, compensation, time tracking, and approval of leave requests (Deloitte Insights, 2017) [7]. These systems streamlined HR functions, brought a higher level of automation, enhanced the employee experience enabling the HR department to respond faster to organizational needs. However, with digitalization increased cybersecurity risks began to surface more prominently (TechTarget, 2019) [28]. Cyber criminals began targeting sensitive data and protection of these data, such as personal details, payroll information, salary data, became a growing concern for HR (Ubisend, 2020) [32]. To address the issue, HR and IT teams implemented stronger security measures such as data encryption, access control, and compliance with regulations (Inspired eLearning, 2021) [15]. The data breaches, fraudulent activity and identity theft led to new vulnerabilities that spurred HR departments to collaborate with IT teams to address the issue and implement stronger security measures such as data encryption, access control, and compliance with regulations (Chakraborty, Biswas, & Khan, 2022) [5]. This era marked a paradigm shift toward the need for stronger security protocols in HR systems.

9.4.3 Advanced Security Actions (2015 to 2020)

From 2015 to 2020, HR departments faced complex, more destructive, and ever evolving cyber threats as a result cybersecurity became the primary focus for HR departments (Inspired eLearning, 2021) [15]. During this period, cyber vulnerabilities were mainly employee data management, where cybercriminals would steal sensitive data of employees and manipulation of payroll systems, where cybercriminals would change payroll data to reroute employee wages and salary. Additionally, HR departments also had to deal with malware, social engineering tactics, and phishing attacks, where fraudsters targeted employees and deceived them to disclose their personal data such as their usernames, passwords, and social security numbers (Ubisend, 2020) [32].

The later years of this era witnessed a shift toward remote work, which added to the already existing list of challenges to cybersecurity. Now, employees were using external tools and cloud platforms and were accessing company data from their personal devices and home networks (Deloitte Insights, 2017) [7]. Traditional on-premises security measures were no longer sufficient, making it more complex for the company to maintain continuous safety protocols. To address the issue, HR and IT teams implemented MFA to protect sensitive data by requiring employees to verify their identity through multiple channels (e.g., password plus a mobile or an email verification) (TechTarget, 2019) [28]. This was one of the most significant steps toward strengthening cyber resilience. The HR teams increased their efforts manifold to create awareness in employees about cyber risks, cybercrimes, and safe data-handling practices (Nica, Burcea, & Sabie, 2024) [24]. Organizations also began embracing AI-driven tools to identify emerging threats and prevent fraudulent conducts, monitor system access, and safeguard companies' data from potential vulnerabilities allowing HR department to act proactively in case of cyber risks (Huang, Huang, & Zhu, 2021) [13]. In spite of these advancements, complex cyber threats persistently challenged HR.

9.4.4 Combining Cyber Resilience and Human Resource Strategies (2020 to Present)

The COVID-19 pandemic accelerated the shift toward remote, cloud-based, and hybrid work models, transforming the operation of various departments, with HR as no exception (Deloitte Insights, 2017) [7]. These changes brought workplace flexibility, increased productivity, decreased environmental impact, improved work-life balance but also aggravated the risk of data breaches and cyber threats as employees accessed company's data from home networks and personal devices (TechTarget, 2019) [28]. The HR had to adapt to these heightened threats. So, in response, HR and IT teams embraced a cyber-resilience approach and developed HR policies that aligned with cybersecurity strategies to safeguard employee data and protect organizational integrity (Aydin, Karaarslan, & Narin, 2024) [3].

The HR department focuses on cybersecurity training and incident management to inform employees about emerging cyber threats and importance of data protection (Ubisend, 2020) [32]. The HR are now increasingly using AI-based tools to detect, analyze, and preemptively mitigate cyber threats (TechTarget, 2019) [28]. These tools evaluate large size data, including network traffic, logs, and code repositories, to detect any deviations from normal behavior through patterns and anomalies that might indicate potential vulnerabilities (Deloitte Insights, 2017) [7].

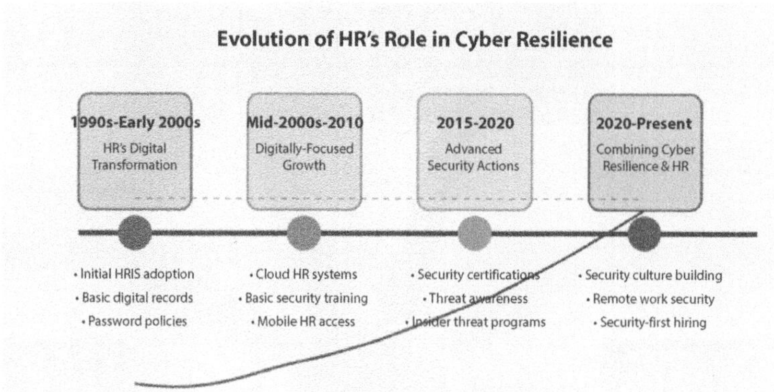

Figure 9.1 The evolution of HR's role in cyber resilience.

Similarly, predictive analytics allow HR teams to use data and analytical techniques to anticipate potential cyber risks in real-time and take pre-emptive measures (Schiliro, 2023) [27]. With data protection and data privacy rules becoming stricter, HR must remain vigilant and comply with evolving legal requirements and update company's HR and cyber resilience policies accordingly (Manoharan, 2024) [21]. Figure 9.1 exhibits the evolution of HR's role in cyber resilience.

9.5 The Role of Human Resources in Building Cyber Resilient Organizations

A dynamic cyber-resilient organization goes beyond the implementation of leading-edge technologies within the interconnected digital landscape of today. As organizations continue to navigate the challenges of the digital age, integrating cyber resilience with HR practices is no longer an option but essential. A comprehensive cyber resilient strategy goes further from implementing advanced and latest technologies and strong IT infrastructure to relying heavily on the human factor. After all, employees are a significant element for a resilient organization and serve as the first line of defense against cyberattacks, making HR practices a key to shaping a cyber-resilient workforce. Cyber threats often emerge within an organization, whether through negligence, human error, or insider threats. According to a report, 60 percent of employees who were fired steal important company data after leaving the position. Furthermore, an IBM study revealed that over 20 percent of breaches in organizations can be ascribed to careless employee mistakes (IBM Security, 2020) [14]. Hence, it

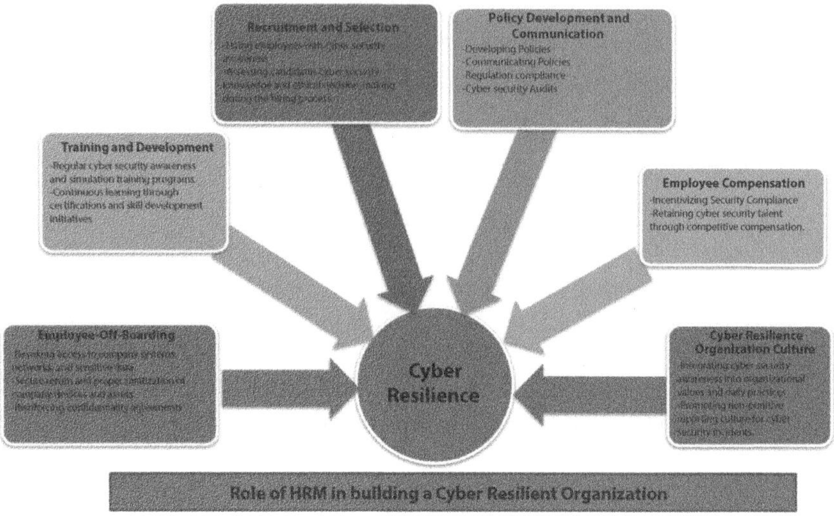

Figure 9.2 The role of HRM in building a cyber-resilient organization.

becomes important for HR teams to work in partnership with IT experts to develop training programs, strategies, and best practices that mitigate cyber threats. The HR department holds sensitive employee and organizational data, including names, date of births, bank details, and home addresses. These accounts are major targets for cybercriminals. Given the vulnerability of data, HR professionals must not only be knowledgeable in cybersecurity practices and protect their departmental data but also assist as promoters for security awareness across the entire organization. There is a need for HR to play a twin role—protecting the sensitive data of employees and instilling cyber awareness organizational culture through training, ethical guidelines, and proactive security measures. To build an effective cyber-resilient organization, it is imperative to incorporate cybersecurity into HR functions. By nurturing security-sensible employees and aligning HR policies with cybersecurity goals, organizations can strengthen their defenses, mitigate risks, and ensure operation continuity in a dynamic cyber threats age. Let us try to understand how various HR functions when integrated with cybersecurity bolsters a cyber-resilient organization. Figure 9.2 exhibits the role of HR in building cyber resilient organization.

9.5.1 Recruitment and Selection

The foundation of any cyber-resilient organization starts with gathering a workforce with the skills, expertise, and attitude to anticipate, prevent, and respond to cyber threats. Strategic recruitment and selection guarantee that the company has the right employees to maintain strong cybersecurity while promoting a culture of awareness and vigilance (IBM Security, 2023) [16]. Acquiring people with cybersecurity expertise for the roles of incident responders, security analysts, threat intelligence analysts, and security architects ensures a diverse skill set that can address numerous cybersecurity concerns, from threat identification and prevention to crisis response and system recovery (CSRC NIST, 2024) [6]. Apart from methodological competence firms must strive to hire those candidates who have the expertise to manage threats. A financial institution hires an incident response expert who has experience in handling real-time cyberattacks. During an unauthorized forced access to one of the accounts, the expert immediately froze the transactions. Thus, preventing the compromise of sensitive customer data (The Economic Times, 2023) [29].

Hiring people who hold the required knowledge, awareness, skills, and mindset to protect against cyber threats helps in constructing a cyber-resilient organization. Cybersecurity professionals such as information security analysts, ethical hackers, and IT risk managers strengthen an organization's defense mechanisms. Companies like Microsoft and Google actively seek candidates who have cybersecurity certifications to improve their cyber resilience (IBM Security, 2023) [16]. Interviewers can integrate cybersecurity awareness as an important measure during the hiring process. Questions related to data breaches, data safety, data privacy, etc. can be asked to the candidates to solicit their opinion and assess their knowledge and their attitude toward cybersecurity, which will result in creating a workforce that is proactive in detecting and mitigating cyber risks (CSRC NIST, 2024) [6]. Apart from hiring for these technical roles, selecting employees who exhibit strong ethical decision-making and compliance with security practices can curtail insider threats. For instance, financial and banking institutions conduct background checks and assess digital literacy before selecting a candidate to ensure he can safeguard sensitive financial data. The recruitment process can also include behavioral assessments to identify candidates who are adaptable to evolving cyber threats. Deloitte and IBM incorporate situational-based interviews to assess a candidate's response to cyber incidents (The Hindu, 2021) [30]. By including cybersecurity considerations in the recruitment and selection process, companies can develop a workforce that not only protects against cyber incidents but also promotes a culture of vigilance and resilience. Hiring the right person with the right skills is crucial not only for the growth of the organization but also for maintaining a strong cybersecurity posture.

9.5.2 Training and Development

The cybersecurity response teams are not solely responsible for fostering cyber resilience in an organization; every employee is central to safeguarding the organization from cyber threats. The digital environment is continuously evolving and training is vital to ensure that employees effectively combat emerging cyber threats. Building a cyber-resilient organization requires a structured and proactive approach to training and development, ensuring that employees at all levels are equipped with the knowledge and skills to prevent, detect, and respond to cyber threats effectively.

According to a report (IBM Security, 2020) [14], human error is one of the leading causes of data breaches. Conduction of regular cybersecurity awareness programs will educate employees, as well as refresh their knowledge on evolving cyber threats, which can significantly reduce the risk of accidental security lapses. In Google and Microsoft, cybersecurity training sessions are a mandate and include simulated attacks, tabletop exercises, and real-world examples to help employees recognize, report, and respond to suspicious activities. Further, continuous updates through newspapers, journal articles, short videos, and interactive quizzes can reinforce learning and keep cybersecurity as a priority.

Additionally, organizations can conduct role-specific training for IT professionals or customize training based on their job functions and level of cybersecurity to make them understand their duties and responsibilities in maintaining cybersecurity. The IT employees need extensive knowledge of penetration testing, network security, incident response, risk management, compliance, and decision-making skills during incidents of cyber-attacks (The Economic Times, 2023) [29]. Meanwhile, other employees need guidance on types of cybercrimes and ways to detect them, password management, secure handling of data, and safe internet browsing. Hence, Training programs can be tailored according to the roles in maintaining security to minimize the possibility of both intentional and unintentional breaches. Facebook Meta regularly conducts social engineering awareness trainings that train employees to recognize and prevent social engineering attacks.

Organizations can also encourage employees to pursue certification courses to enrich their knowledge and proficiency, as well as keep them updated on the best cyber incident practices. These training and development programs can develop a cyber-aware workforce that proactively contributes toward improving a company's cybersecurity posture (IBM Security, 2023) [16]. Furthermore, old-style classroom lecture training methods often do not prepare employees for real-world threats. Organizations can employ hands-on learning training methods like cyberattack drills and simulation training, which will let employees experience real-world scenarios and accordingly respond to cyber incidents. Deloitte regularly organizes cybersecurity war games where employees work through hypothetical breach scenarios that challenge them to think critically and act decisively under pressure. This experiential learning instills confidence and enhances preparedness so that employees can quickly respond in the event of a real cyberattack (CSRC NIST, 2024) [6]. Organizations can encourage their workforce to undergo continuous learning and certification courses to keep themselves abreast of evolving cyber threats, new security protocols, regulatory requirements, and best cyber mitigation practices to enhance their knowledge and strengthen defense capabilities. Companies such as Google, IBM, and Deloitte offer incentives or financial support to employees to complete these certification courses and provide access to online learning cybersecurity workshops, conferences, and professional networking bodies to reinforce employees' cybersecurity skills further.

Training and development strategies implementation can aid in building a workforce that is equipped well to handle cyber threats and their challenges, minimizing susceptibilities and strengthening resilience, thereby, helping businesses protect sensitive information, maintain data integrity, and respond to potential security breaches (The Hindu, 2021) [30].

9.5.3 Policy Development and Communication

When it comes to HR's daily operations, it plays a strategic role in developing policies that integrate cyber resilience into an organization's overall strategy. It is accountable for administering cybersecurity compliance by ensuring that policies related to security protocols, data protection, data handling, device management, secure remote work, password protection, and employee behavior are documented properly, communicated, and enforced. In collaboration with the IT department, HR ensures that each employee understands and obeys cybersecurity guidelines. Google has successfully integrated HR-driven cybersecurity policies to mitigate cyber risks and has one of the most cutting-edge cybersecurity compliance frameworks called the zero-trust security model (Google Works space, 2023) [11]. This framework is based on the idea that no person or device, whether inside or outside the organization, can be trusted and must undergo identity authentication and authorization to seek permission. Since financial institutions are frequent targets of cyber threats, HR at JPMorgan Chase in collaboration with its IT department continuously monitors employee activity to identify insider threats, and if any unauthorized access is detected the concerned employee faces consequences including suspension or termination (JPMorgan Chase, 2021) [19]. They also conduct regular cybersecurity compliance audits to ensure that employees comply with the company's security systems, laws, and regulations.

Organizations require dynamic cyber resilience policies that evolve simultaneously with emerging risks and HR plays a pivotal role in continuous policy updates and its adaptation to new cyber threats. It regularly reviews, analyses, and updates cybersecurity policies along with the IT team to align them with regulatory requirements and industry standards like the General Data Protection Regulation or the California Consumer Privacy Act. Such practices ensure that employees remain informed, updated, and compliant with the newest security protocols. For example, JPMorgan Chase frequently reviews and updates its cybersecurity policies to strengthen their financial cybersecurity by preventing insider threats, fraud, and cyberattacks (JPMorgan Chase, 2021) [19]. The HR department plays a crucial role in enforcing these policies and ensuring employee compliance. In Microsoft, regular phishing simulations are a mandate to assess employee awareness levels. If employees become victims of simulated phishing, HR sends them to undergo security training. Simultaneously, policies related to emerging phishing tactics are updated and communicated to employees to prevent real attacks. Human resources should regularly conduct cybersecurity audits to identify policy gaps and adjust policy accordingly. The updated policy should reach employees on time to ensure that every employee in the organization comprehends, adapts, and complies with the latest adjustments in cybersecurity policies. By continuously updating cybersecurity policies and incorporating them into HR practices, it enables businesses to address emerging challenges and foster a workforce that is vigilant, well-equipped, and compliant with evolving security measures.

However, just formulating and updating the cyber resilience policies will never suffice the purpose of building a cyber resilient organization; effective communication of policies to employees is the key. Human resources plays a major role in the dissemination of cybersecurity policies in an organized, comprehensible, engaging, and accessible way. Organizations can promote a security-conscious workforce that proactively contributes to cyber resilience. Without transparent communication, even the most methodical cybersecurity policies may fail due to a lack of awareness, ambiguity, or resistance from employees. Human resources documents cybersecurity policies with clarity and simplicity, avoiding complex or technical jargon that can be tough for non-technical employees to understand. For example, "ensure compliance with MFA protocols *via* centralized identity verification systems," can be difficult for employees to understand. Instead, HR communicates it as *"Always verify your login with a second step, like a mobile code or fingerprint scan."*

Another critical factor is regular and engaging training programs that reinforce policy updates and best practices. Simply issuing a policy document is not enough—organizations must ensure that employees internalize cybersecurity principles through interactive training sessions, real-world case studies, and scenario-based learning. Companies like Google and IBM use simulated phishing attacks to test employee awareness, followed by targeted training for those who fail the test. This approach effectively communicates cybersecurity risks and teaches employees how to recognize and respond to threats in real situations. Additionally, companies must have two-way communication channels, which allow employees to report security concerns, seek clarifications, ask questions, and provide feedback on cybersecurity policies. Transparent communication through calls or emails, help desks, and anonymous reporting tools can encourage and improve policy adherence and help identify potential vulnerabilities. To help its global defenders, Microsoft has initiated the Cybersecurity Champions Program where select employees from different departments take the role of advocates, ensuring that information and infographics related to cybersecurity are communicated effectively to each employee and also their concerns are addressed (Microsoft, 2024) [22]. Finally, multi-channel communication strategies enhance policy implementation. Lastly, cybersecurity policies should not be limited to lengthy documents; multi-channel communication strategies must be used to disseminate the guidelines. Policies should be communicated to employees through emails, seminars, intranet announcements, posters, video tutorials. Companies like Facebook Meta employ short, visually engaging infographics and micro-learning modules to coach employees about cybersecurity policies in an easy format.

9.5.4 Employee Compensation

A well-structured compensation strategy, aligned with cyber resilience goals, plays a crucial role in fostering a cyber-resilient workforce (Microsoft, 2024) [22]. Rewards and incentives encourage employee participation in cybersecurity, increase their commitment to cybersecurity, and develop a strong sense of conscientiousness and loyalty to protect organization from cyber threats (IBM, 2023) [16]. Cybersecurity practices can be reinforced by offering rewards, bonuses, appreciation, certificates, and recognition to employees for adhering to security protocols, reporting potential threats, or detecting vulnerabilities in the system (IBM Security, 2023) [16]. These incentives motivate employees to remain vigilant and create a culture where cybersecurity is not just an IT concern but a shared responsibility across the entire organization (JPMorgan Chase, 2021) [19]. For instance, tech giants like Google and IBM offer performance-based incentives to employees who contribute to cybersecurity initiatives, such as phishing detection challenges and security awareness training (Google Workspace, 2023) [11].

Organizations give incentives to their employees in the form of bonuses, rewards, and recognition for maintaining compliance by following the protocols or even identifying threats (Microsoft, 2024) [22]. Nowadays, companies offer financial support and encourage their employees to learn professional certification courses and also advance training courses so that the employee skills are developed and the organizations' cybersecurity also becomes much stronger (IBM, 2023) [16]. With amalgamation of compensation with the objectives of cyber resilience, HR can develop a workforce that vigorously contributes to the security framework of an organization (JPMorgan Chase, 2021) [19].

9.5.5 Cyber-Resilient Organizational Culture

The HR department has an important role in creating a cyber-resilient organizational culture where employees understand, prioritize, and act accordingly to protect the organization's digital infrastructure from cyber threats. Human resources organizes cybersecurity training and awareness programs for employees, which endow them with knowledge to recognize potential cyber threats like phishing, ransomware or malware, select best practice and play their role in protecting sensitive information (Gordon, Loeb, & Zhou, 2020) [10]. A well-informed workforce reduces human errors, which is the most primary source of cybersecurity violations. Google's Security Checkup program ensures employees are regularly trained and updated on the latest threats. Additionally, HR ensures that employees understand the organization's cybersecurity culture. In IBM, both HR and IT departments integrate cybersecurity awareness into their job descriptions, job specifications, and their hiring processes, thereby ensuring that cybersecurity is a shared responsibility (Von Solms & Van Niekerk, 2013) [34]. Human resources also ensure that clear cybersecurity policies are formulated, implemented, followed and embedded in the organizational culture rituals. For instance, at the induction process of Cisco, new hires are informed in detail of the firm's cybersecurity rules and practices to make certain best practices are followed from day one. Human resources also promotes a culture of vigilance and non-punitive reporting (Ament & Haag, 2016) [1]. Microsoft's robust incident-reporting structure encourages employees to report potential security breaches or mistakes without fearing punishment or repercussions. The role of HR in creating a cyber-resilient culture also involves protecting employees' mental health and promoting employee well-being by ensuring they are not inundated with cyber threats-related anxiety and stress. Human resources can create a psychologically safe environment where employees can seek help regarding cybersecurity issues (Bada, Sasse, & Nurse, 2019) [4]. Google promotes digital detox programs where employees are encouraged to go offline for some time and get themselves involved in non-screen activities such as games, exercise, face-to-face conversation to reduce employee burnout related to constant digital vigilance. Salesforce promotes digital detox through its "Ohana Culture." It provides fitness facilities, meditation spaces for employees and encourages digital breaks. Cyber resilience organizations embed strong governance, preparedness, and culture throughout the organization (Risk Logic, 2024) [25].

9.5.6 Employee Offboarding

A job change or retirement, where employees leave the current organization, is an important part in business life that requires managing the exit of employees in a manner that reduces risk to the firm's assets and sensitive data (Von Solms & Van Niekerk, 2013) [34]. This method is particularly important because when employees depart. They may have been, intentionally or unintentionally, exposed to security risks and vulnerabilities (Linkov & Kott, 2019) [20]. Therefore, the implementation of robust offboarding protocols can help mitigate this risk, and the HR department's involvement is crucial in facilitating the effortless and safe departure of employees, mitigating the possible cybersecurity risks. The primary responsibility of HR toward cyber resilient departure is to coordinate with the IT team and deactivate the departing employee's user accounts, the access to company networks and systems to check unauthorized access to sensitive data. Human resources must ensure this happens swiftly, often in collaboration with IT, as part of the company's offboarding policy. Human resources must inform the IT department about employees' resignation to ensure that the process of access removal is initiated instantly and additional surveillance during and after the offboarding process is put on the departing employees to monitor suspicious activity. Almost all companies, such as IBM, Accenture, Google, and Microsoft, adhere to such practices of swiftly disabling user accounts and credentials to prevent access to internal systems and networks. Uber, Facebook, and Amazon employ behavioral analysis tools to examine the online activities of exiting employees during notice period and beyond to avert breaches (Gordon, Loeb, & Zhou, 2020) [10].

Further, HR is responsible for data protection during offboarding and making sure departing employees do not save, retain, or transfer any confidential data in physical or digital form. The department collects laptops, desktop, storage devices, files, documents, phones, and other company-owned devices and meticulously checks for any unauthorized data collection or storage before they are deleted or returned (Bada, Sasse, & Nurse, 2019) [4]. Human resources must work closely with IT to make sure that all devices are accounted for and properly sanitized. If the departing employee had access to any shared accounts or systems, HR should coordinate with IT to change any passwords or access credentials to prevent unauthorized access after departure. Tesla and Apple have strict device collection processes where employees return all company-issued devices to get them checked for any unauthorized data storage. Exit interviews are not merely a tool to collect data from the existing employees but provide an opportunity to reinforce the significance of confidentiality and enhance security features. During exit interviews, HR reminds exiting employees of their responsibilities undersigned non-disclosure agreements and that they understand that mishandling or misusing firm's data can attract consequences. Organizations like Salesforce and Facebook conduct exit interviews to gather feedback on organizational processes and to detect weaknesses and areas of improvement as a departing employee can offer honest insights. Human resources can inquire about potential risks or security concerns the employee might have noticed, which can be used to improve the cybersecurity system (Ament & Haag, 2016) [1].

Moreover, HR is responsible for developing an offboarding checklist that ensures all mandatory steps are completed, from account deactivation accounts to collecting devices, before an employee leaves. These offboarding processes and checklist must be updated frequently to adapt to new cybersecurity threats and reflect improvements in the organization's cyber resilience to cyber risks (Von Solms & Van Niekerk, 2013) [34]. Human resources, IT, and other departments at IBM and Cisco collaborate to develop and update customized offboarding checklists to ensure that the offboarding process is streamlined, safe, and effective (Ament & Haag, 2016) [1].

9.6 The Future and Challenges of Human Resources and Cyber Resilience

The future of HR in creating cyber-resilient organizations lies in its capacity to adapt to evolving cyber threats and partner with IT departments to embed cybersecurity awareness and policies into everyday practices, operations, and the culture so that organizations can better protect their sensitive employee data while adapting to the dynamic digital landscape (Bada, Sasse, & Nurse, 2019) [4]. As organizations increasingly rely on digital technologies to operate and grow, HR departments face a significant challenge: integrating cyber resilience into their operations and ensuring the workforce is prepared to navigate cybersecurity threats. While cybersecurity is traditionally seen as the responsibility of IT departments, HR plays a crucial role in creating a security culture, safeguarding sensitive employee data, and fostering a proactive approach to cybersecurity across the entire organization (Herath & Rao, 2009) [12]. However, several challenges make this task particularly complex for HR.

9.6.1 Building Cybersecurity Awareness among Employees

The biggest challenge HR must deal with while creating a cyber-resilient organization is building a cybersecurity sensitive workforce (Schneier, 2020) [26]. Despite due importance being given to growing awareness of digital risks, people fail to acknowledge that they can be a victim of cyberattacks and do not perceive them as their personal concerns (Von Solms & Van Niekerk, 2013) [34]. They lack basic information to protect themselves and their companies from cyberattacks. This attitude is a challenge for HR to encourage proactive behavior among employees toward data protection. Furthermore, as cyber threats evolve constantly, HR must stay agile and update training methods, modules and materials continuously to develop engaging, effective, and updated content. Some employees view cybersecurity as problems for the IT department and do not practice proactive behavior toward safe handling of sensitive data. This again is a challenge for HR to make them understand that cybersecurity directly impacts them, and they should be aware of cybersecurity practices (Herath & Rao, 2009) [12].

Human resources lack technical expertise to completely comprehend the intricacies of cybersecurity, making it difficult to convey the vulnerabilities of cybersecurity to the workforce effectively. Furthermore, in large organizations, HR may struggle to tailor cybersecurity awareness programs to the specific needs of different departments or roles, making it harder to address the unique vulnerabilities each group faces. Lastly, as remote and hybrid work models gain momentum, HR's ability to maintain consistent and effective training is becoming a mammoth task. Some employees are working from the office using office devices, some are working outside secure office environments, using personal devices, and networks making HR struggle to tailor cybersecurity awareness programs to the specific need (Von Solms & Van Niekerk, 2013) [34].

9.6.2 Recruiting and Retaining Cybersecurity Talent

The next challenge is the recruitment and retention of cybersecurity talent who have expertise to address cyber risks. With the increasing demand and limited supply for cybersecurity professionals, HR struggles to attract the candidates with a blend of technical expertise and practical experience (Von Solms & Van Niekerk, 2013) [34]. It is often difficult to recruit for cybersecurity roles due to a shortage of qualified candidates. On the other side, as the requirement for cybersecurity specialists far exceeds the available talent pool, they have the luxury in choosing from several job offers, and the retention of talent is even harder (Anderson, 2020) [2]. Further, HR departments often do not have the required knowledge to evaluate the technical capacities of cybersecurity candidates, further adding to complexities of the hiring process. With the high costs of recruitment, attracting expertise should be the focal point, but HR should also focus on offering attractive compensation, career advancement opportunities, a supportive work environment, and work-life balance to retain these employees (Bada, Sasse, & Nurse, 2019) [4].

9.6.3 Ensuring Data Privacy and Data Protection

The HR department has the responsibility to manage the wealth of sensitive employee data and, the protection of this data from unauthorized access or breaches is of paramount importance (Schneier, 2020) [26]. It is more challenging to ensure this data remains safe when being used across workforce systems and platforms. The remote and hybrid work models further complicate this challenge of securing data as the workforce accesses sensitive files and systems from personal devices and unsecured networks (European Commission, 2024) [8]. A balance must be struck between the accessibility of employee data and its protection. Human resources must ensure that the authorized workforce can use the data they need, while unauthorized access is prohibited. It is also an uphill task for HR to keep itself abreast with the constantly evolving data privacy laws, which impose strict protocols on handling personal information, its storage, and sharing process. It is mandate for the HR departments to comply with these protocols, as well as attend to internal risks, such as employees unintentionally exploiting sensitive information or falling victim to cyberattacks (Herath & Rao, 2009) [12].

9.6.4 Creating a Cybersecurity Culture

The role of HR goes beyond implementing cybersecurity policies; HR helps build a culture of cybersecurity that permeates the whole firm. However, it has its own complexities. First, many employees may not perceive cybersecurity as part of their daily responsibilities but view it as the sole responsibility of the IT department. Dealing with such an attitude is a challenge for HR to promote a shared ownership and accountability when it comes to safeguarding company's data, especially in a company where cybersecurity is still not an essential part of the corporate culture (Gordon, Loeb, & Zhou, 2020) [10].

Cybersecurity best practices require awareness of potential cyber threats and consistent proactive behavior from all employees to deal with such threats, which can be challenging because employees have varying levels of technical knowledge. Human resources must also integrate cybersecurity into an organization's other core values such as productivity, innovation, and profit without disturbing the balance (Bada, Sasse, & Nurse, 2019) [4]. The dynamic nature of cyber threats is another challenge because HR must continuously update the training programs, methods, and modules to fit with the latest cyber risks (Von Solms & Van Niekerk, 2013) [34]. The resistance to change is again a major challenge faced by HR. Employees tend to resist security measures that are time-consuming or inconvenient for them. Additionally, with more workforce shifting to remote and hybrid work setups, HR must ensure that every employee, working at different locations and using different devices and networks, exercises the same cybersecurity practices thereby, creating a uniform cybersecurity culture.

9.6.5 Adapting to Regulatory Changes and Compliance Requirements

The landscape of cybersecurity regulations is continuously changing and adapting to these cybersecurity regulatory changes, and compliance requirements is a challenge for HR. It is the responsibility of the HR department to develop and implement cybersecurity policies that comply with regulations and further ensure employees adhere to these policies and regulations (Linkov & Kott, 2019) [20]. Updating the cybersecurity policies can be overwhelming for HR especially when it requires significant effort to continuously monitor new rules and regulations and adjust existing policies accordingly. When companies fail to conform to these cybersecurity regulations, it can attract legal penalties, data breaches, and damage to the company's reputation. Hence, it is imperative for HR to understand the regulations and integrate them into everyday operations successfully (Herath & Rao, 2009) [12].

9.7 Conclusion

To build a cyber-resilient organization, a holistic approach is needed to surpass technological safeguards and integrate human-centric strategies. While cybersecurity focuses on preventing cyberattacks, cyber resilience ensures organizations can withstand and recover from cyber threats with minimal disruption. This paradigm shift from a purely defensive approach to a more holistic, proactive stance highlights the necessity of integrating cyber resilience into everyday business operations. Employees often serve as the first line of defense against cyber threats, making the role of HR critical in fostering a security-aware workforce. By embedding cybersecurity considerations into HR practices such as recruitment, training, and policy development, organizations can strengthen their defense mechanisms against both external cyber threats and internal vulnerabilities caused by human error or insider threats. A well-informed and security-conscious workforce can significantly reduce the risks associated with data breaches, phishing attacks, and social engineering tactics, ultimately contributing to the overall cyber resilience of the organization.

Furthermore, HR plays a vital role in shaping a cyber-resilient culture by promoting ongoing cybersecurity education, implementing strict access controls, and ensuring compliance with evolving data protection regulations. Regular training programs, simulated cyberattack drills, and behavioral assessments help employees recognize and respond to potential cyber threats effectively. Additionally, HR collaborates with IT teams to develop and communicate cybersecurity policies that align with organizational goals and the industry's best practices. Employee well-being is also a crucial consideration, as cybersecurity-related stress can impact productivity and decision-making. By fostering a balanced approach that prioritizes both security and employee engagement, HR can create an environment where cybersecurity awareness becomes second nature. As cyber threats evolve, the collaboration between HR and IT will remain essential in safeguarding sensitive data, mitigating risks, and ensuring long-term organizational resilience in the digital age.

AI disclosure statement: The author acknowledges the use of AI-based tools for minor language editing or grammatical correction. However, all intellectual contributions, analyses, and conclusions presented in this chapter are entirely the author's own.

References

1. Ament, C. and Haag, M., Strengthening security awareness and reducing risk through continuous training. *J. Inf. Secur. Appl.*, 30, 1–7, 2016.
2. Anderson, R., Why information security is hard – An economic perspective, Information Security Group, University of Cambridge, 2020, Retrieved from: https://www.thelancet.com/pdfs/journals/lancet/PIIS0140-6736%2820%2930567-5.pdf.
3. Aydin, O., Karaarslan, E., Narin, N.G., Artificial intelligence, VR, AR and metaverse technologies for human resources management, 2024, https://arxiv.org/pdf/2406.15383.
4. Bada, M., Sasse, M.A., Nurse, J.R., Cybersecurity awareness campaigns: Why do they fail to change behavior? *Comput. Secur.*, 87, 101573, 2019.
5. Chakraborty, A., Biswas, A., Khan, A.K., Artificial intelligence for cybersecurity: Threats, attacks and mitigation, in: *Artificial intelligence for societal issues*, vol. 231, pp. 3–25, 2022.
6. CSRC (Computer Security Resources Center) NIST (National Institute of Standard and Technology), 2024, Retrieved from: https://csrc.nist.gov/glossary/term/cyber_resiliency.
7. Deloitte Insights, The digital transformation in HR, Deloitte Insights, 2017, Retrieved from: https://www2.deloitte.com/us/en/insights/focus/human-capital-trends/2017/digital-transformation-in-hr.html.
8. European Commission, The Cyber Resilience Act: Strengthening Cybersecurity for Digital Products and Services, European Union, 2024, Retrieved from: file:///C:/Users/lenova/Downloads/365-Article%20Text-552-1-10-20200723.pdf.
9. Forbes India, Hit with massive data breach, boAt loses data of 7.5 million customers, 2024, Retrieved from: https://www.forbesindia.com/article/news/hit-with-massive-data-breach-boat-loses-data-of-75-million-customers/92483/1.
10. Gordon, L.A., Loeb, M.P., Zhou, L., The impact of information security breaches: Has there been a downward shift in costs? *J. Comput. Secur.*, 28, 2, 163185, 2020.

11. Google Workspace, Expanding Google AI in Workspace with new zero trust and digital sovereignty controls, 2023, Retrieved from: https://workspace.google.com/blog/identity-and-security/accelerating-zero-trust-and-digital-sovereignty-ai.
12. Herath, T. and Rao, H.R., Protection motivation and deterrence: A framework for security policy compliance in organizations. *Eur. J. Inf. Syst.*, 18, 2, 106125, 2009.
13. Huang, Y., Huang, L., Zhu, Q., Reinforcement learning for feedback-enabled cyber resilience. *Annu. Rev. Control*, 53, 273–295, 2021.
14. IBM Security, Cost of a Data Breach Report, 2020, Retrieved from: https://www.ibm.com/security/digital-assets/cost-data-breach-report/1Cost%20of%20a%20Data%20Breach%20Report%202020.pdf.
15. Inspired eLearning, 20 Years of Cyber Security Awareness: Evolution of Security, 2021, Retrieved from: https://www2.deloitte.com/us/en/insights/focus/human-capital-trends/2017/digital-transformation-in-hr.html.
16. IBM Security, What is Cyber Resilience?, 2023, https://www.ibm.com/think/topics/cyber-resilience.
17. IBM, SolarWinds Orion (CVE-2020-10148), 2024, Retrieved from: https://www.ibm.com/docs/en/randori?topic=2022-solarwinds-orion-cve-2020-10148.
18. Johnson, R.D., Lukaszewski, K.M., Stone, D.L., The Evolution of the Field of Human Resource Information Systems: Co-Evolution of Technology and HR Processes. *Commun. Assoc. Inf. Syst.*, 38, 1, 533–553, 2016.
19. JPMorgan Chase, Fraud + Cybersecurity Stay Vigilant. Stay Protected, 2021, Retrieved from.:https://www.jpmorgan.com/content/dam/jpm/commercial-banking/insights/cybersecurity/899213-summer-21-fraud-cyber-mag_full-issue-final-ada-071221.pdf.
20. Linkov, I. and Kott, A., *Cyber Resilience of Systems and Networks*, Springer, 2019, https://arxiv.org/pdf/1806.02852.
21. Manoharan, P., A review on cybersecurity in HR systems: Protecting employee data in the age of AI. *Int. J. Adv. Res. Sci. Commun. Technol.*, 4, 605–612, 2024.
22. Microsoft, Cybersecurity Awareness Month: Securing our world—together, 2024, Retrieved from:https://www.microsoft.com/en-us/security/blog/2024/10/01/cybersecurity-awareness-month-securing-our-world-together/.
23. Microsoft Security, Microsoft Incident Response team ransomware approach and best practices, 2024, Retrieved from: https://learn.microsoft.com/en-us/security/ransomware/incident-response-playbook-dart-ransomware-approach.
24. Nica, E., Burcea, Ş.G., Sabie, O.M., The Critical Role of Human Resources in Mitigating and Managing Cybersecurity Risks in Modern Organizations: A Strategic Approach. *Psychosoc. Issues Hum. Resour. Manage.*, 12, 2, 2024.

25. Risk logic, Leading the Charge in Cyber Resilience: How Risklogic Empowers Organizations, 2024, https://risklogic.com.au/leading-the-charge-in-cyber-resilience/.
26. Schneier, B., Security and Survival in a Hyper-Connected World, W. W. Norton &Company, 2020, file:///C:/Users/lenova/Downloads/stevenwhittle,+DEESLR_2019_Vol16_Book_reports_finalv2.pdf.
27. Schiliro, F., Building a resilient cybersecurity posture: A framework for leveraging prevention, detection, and responsefunctions, 2023, https://arxiv.org/pdf/2303.10874.
28. TechTarget, ERP evolution sees major shifts in holistic view of business, 2019, Retrieved from TechTarget.: https://www.techtarget.com/searcherp/feature/ERP-evolution-sees-major-shifts-in-holistic-view-of-business.
29. The Economic Times, Technology Growing Complexity widening cyber inequity, 2023, https://economictimes.indiatimes.com/tech/technology/growing-complexity-widening-cyber-inequity-wef-report/articleshow/117204489.cms?from=mdr.
30. The Hindu, The world is hardly wired for cyber resilience, 2021, https://www.thehindu.com/opinion/lead/the-world-is-hardly-wired-for-cyber-resilience/article62105946.ece.
31. The Hindu, Microsoft CrowdStrike IT outage, Cause of Falcon sensor crash revealed, 2024, Retrieved from: https://www.thehindu.com/sci-tech/technology/microsoft-crowdstrike-it-outage-cause-of-falcon-sensor-crash-revealed/article68500078.ece.
32. Ubisend, The History of Technology in Human Resources, 2020, Retrieved from ubisend.: https://blog.ubisend.com/discover-chatbots/history-of-technology-in-human-resources.
33. US HSS, Change Healthcare Cybersecurity Incident, 2024, Retrieved from: https://www.hhs.gov/hipaa/for-professionals/special-topics/change-healthcare-cybersecurity-incident-frequently-asked-questions/index.html.
34. Von Solms, R. and Van Niekerk, J., From information security to cybersecurity. *Comput. Secur.*, 38, 97–102, 2013.

10

Blockchain-Based Cybersecurity: A New Era of Data Protection

Sagiraju Harinadharaju, Manjunadh Muvva, Bvv Satyanarayana, Rithish Abinav and Pooja Mishra*

Department of Computer Science and Engineering, Amrita School of Computing, Coimbatore, Amrita Vishwa Vidyapeetham, India

Abstract

Blockchain is introduced as a revolutionary solution to secure data with its decentralized architecture, secure cryptographic practices, and unalterable ledgers, and its advent is greeted as a game changer in digital security. Throughout this chapter, a comprehensive outline of blockchain fundamentals, such as its consensus algorithms and smart contract-based automation, is presented, with practical uses in health- care, finance, and supply chain management. These technologies, including emerging ones such as artificial intelligence and the Internet of Things, which are integrated into the blockchain, examine the economic, environmental, and regulatory implications in paving the future for research development. This study provides a full overview of the blockchain, from its basic concepts to advanced applications, enabling readers to seamlessly integrate blockchain solutions into their respective fields.

***Keywords*:** Blockchain, data security, decentralization, smart contracts, healthcare, finance, IoT

10.1 Introduction

10.1.1 Background and Motivation

In today's digital era, data is one of the most valuable assets for organizations and individuals. The rapid evolution of information technology,

**Corresponding author*: m_pooja@cb.amrita.edu

Sujata Priyambada Dash, Vaibhav Mishra, Bijeta Shaw, Sandeep Kumar Panda and S. Balamurugan (eds.) Digital Immune System: Principles and Practices, (211–228) © 2026 Scrivener Publishing LLC

coupled with the proliferation of interconnected systems, has led to an explosion in data generation and storage. However, this surge in digital data also introduces significant challenges in ensuring data integrity, confidentiality, and availability. Traditional security models, which are often centralized, have repeatedly proven vulnerable to cyber-attacks, data breaches, and malicious intrusions [8, 13].

Blockchain technology, originally introduced with Bitcoin [13], utilizes decentralization, cryptographic techniques [24], and irreversibility to create tamperproof records. The ability to cross the boundaries of traditional security models is quickly recognized [19]. This chapter further explores these advantages, as well as recent developments in blockchain applications [15, 16].

10.1.2 Limitations of Traditional Security Models

Traditional centralized data security models exhibit several inherent drawbacks:

- Single points of failure: Centralized systems store data in one or a few locations; a breach in these nodes can compromise the entire system [8].
- Data tampering: Without robust controls, centralized records can be altered without detection, undermining data integrity [1].
- Over-reliance on trust: Users must rely on a central authority to manage and secure data, which poses risks if that authority is compromised [5].

10.1.3 Scope and Objectives

This chapter aims to provide a comprehensive exploration of blockchain technology for data security by:

1. Detailing the fundamental components of blockchain technology, including its architecture, consensus mechanisms, and cryptographic foundations [13, 22].
2. Demonstrating how blockchain enhances data security through decentralized authentication, access control, and secure data sharing [2, 8].

3. Presenting real-world case studies from sectors such as healthcare, finance, and supply chain management [6, 14, 17, 21].
4. Exploring the integration of blockchain with emerging technologies such as artificial intelligence (AI) and the Internet of Things (IoT) [4].
5. Discussing the economic, environmental, and social implications, as well as regulatory challenges and future research directions [18].
6. Examining recent research on blockchain security enhancement using hybrid consensus algorithms and machine learning techniques [20], as well as a case study of blockchain technology in healthcare to explore the gaps and scope in India [12].

10.2 Fundamentals of Blockchain Technology

10.2.1 Historical Context and Evolution

Blockchain technology emerged in 2008 as the backbone of Bitcoin [13]. Initially developed for decentralized financial transactions, its applications have expanded significantly [19]. Over time, blockchain has evolved into a versatile technology supporting smart contracts, decentralized finance, and secure data management [21].

10.2.2 Core Components and Architecture

Blocks, chains, and cryptographic hashes: A blockchain is composed of sequentially linked *blocks*. Each block contains a header (time stamp, nonce, and previous block hash), the transaction data, and a nonce for consensus. Cryptographic hash functions (e.g., SHA-256) process each block's content to generate a unique, fixed-length hash. This design ensures that even minor modifications produce different hashes, securing the chain against tampering [8].
Decentralized ledger systems: In decentralized ledgers, multiple nodes maintain a full copy of the blockchain, enhancing fault tolerance and eliminating a single point of failure [3, 13].

10.2.3 Consensus Mechanisms

Consensus protocols are critical for ensuring that all nodes agree on the blockchain's state:

- Proof of Work (PoW): Miners solve computational puzzles to validate transactions. Though secure, PoW is energy-intensive [7].
- Proof of Stake (PoS): Validators are selected based on their stake, reducing energy consumption while maintaining security [9].
- Alternative protocols: Emerging models such as Algorand [10] further improve efficiency and security.

10.2.4 Cryptographic Security

Hashing algorithms: Hash functions like SHA-256 ensure data integrity by producing unique outputs for unique inputs. Their collision-resistant properties make tampering easily detectable [8].
Digital signatures: Digital signatures, based on asymmetric cryptography, allow users to sign transactions with a private key while others verify with the corresponding public key. This process guarantees transaction authenticity and non-repudiation [1].

10.2.5 Smart Contracts and Automation

Smart contracts are self-executing codes stored on the blockchain that automatically enforce the terms of an agreement when conditions are met. They reduce the need for intermediaries and minimize human error [2, 23].

10.2.6 Technical Diagrams and System Architecture

Figure 10.1 shows a color-enhanced diagram of a simplified blockchain security architecture, illustrating the flow among user nodes, smart contracts, blockchain nodes, and data stores.

10.2.7 Mathematical and Theoretical Models

Blockchain security is fundamentally underpinned by rigorous mathematical models and theories. These models include cryptographic primitives,

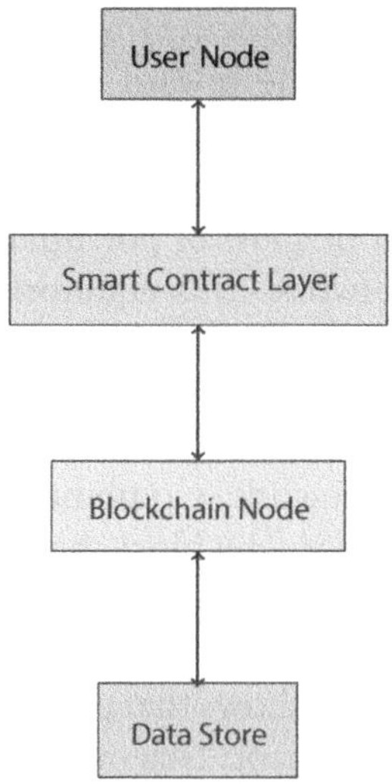

Figure 10.1 Simplified blockchain security architecture diagram.

probabilistic analysis, and game theory, which together form the theoretical basis for blockchain's robust security properties.

Cryptographic hash functions: At the heart of blockchain technology lies the use of cryptographic hash functions, such as SHA-256. These functions are modeled as random oracles, meaning they behave similarly to truly random functions. For any input x, the output $H(x)$ is a fixed-length string, and the probability that two different inputs produce the same hash (a collision) is negligible. For instance, with $n = 256$, the collision probability is around 2^{-256} [8].

Proof of Work and computational complexity: Consensus mechanisms like PoW rely on solving computational puzzles, which can be understood through probabilistic models. The process of finding a valid nonce that produces a hash with a required number of leading zeros is analogous to a random sampling problem. The number of attempts required to find a valid nonce follows a geometric distribution, where the expected number of trials is inversely proportional to the difficulty target. This inherently probabilistic process ensures that adding new blocks is computationally expensive, which in turn secures the network against attacks [7, 13].

Game theory and incentive mechanisms: Blockchain systems are designed so that participants (miners or validators) are economically incentivized to act honestly. Game theory provides the framework to analyze these incentive structures. For example, the reward mechanism in PoW systems is designed such that the Nash equilibrium is reached when all miners follow the protocol honestly. Deviating from the protocol (e.g., attempting double-spending) would result in a loss of potential rewards and an increased risk of rejection by the network. This equilibrium analysis demonstrates that rational actors are incentivized to maintain the security and integrity of the blockchain [1, 9].

Combined theoretical framework: Combined, these mathematical and theoretical models account for why blockchain systems are very resistant to various attack vectors. Cryptographic proofs provide data integrity; probabilistic analysis forms the foundation of the security of consensus mechanisms; and game theory shows that players have no economic incentive to collude against the protocol. This multi-layered model gives a solid theoretical underpinning to blockchain security, making it a strong technology against adversarial attacks. Overall, the intersection of cryptography, probability theory, and game theory not only explains the security characteristics of blockchain systems but also influences current research in making them more efficient and resilient [1, 8, 13].

10.3 Blockchain for Data Security

10.3.1 Decentralized Authentication and Identity Management

Cryptographic key management: Proper key control is crucial. Every user is given a separate key pair (public and private) to sign and verify transactions. This process guarantees the integrity of transactions and prevents unauthorized modifications [13].
Decentralized identifiers (DIDs): DIDs allow users to control their digital identities without depending on central authority. Coupled with public keys, DIDs form the basis for self-sovereign identity, minimizing risks of identity theft [21].

10.3.2 Access Control Mechanisms

10.3.2.1 Role-Based and Attribute-Based Controls

Access control in blockchain is applied through role-based access control (RBAC) or attribute-based access control (ABAC). Smart contracts enforce these models by automatically granting or revoking permissions based on user roles or attributes [8].

10.3.2.2 *Blockchain-Based Credential Verification and Access Control*

The following algorithm demonstrates how blockchain verifies user credentials to control access:

Algorithm 10.1 Blockchain-based access control.

Input: user credentials, blockchain ledger
Output: access granted / denied
Procedure:

1. Hash the user's credentials with a secure algorithm (for example, SHA- 256).
2. Look up in the blockchain ledger for equivalent hash.
3. If a match is found, grant access and log the event.
4. Alternatively, log the unauthorized access attempt and block access.

10.3.3 Intrusion Detection and Prevention Systems

Blockchain's immutable logging and distributed consensus play an important role in constructing secure intrusion detection systems.

Algorithm 10.2 Blockchain-based intrusion detection.

Input: network traffic logs, blockchain ledger
Output: intrusion alert / normal log
Procedure:

1. Calculate an anomaly score for each log entry based on predefined criteria.
2. Check the score against a threshold.
3. Mark entries with scores above the threshold as possible intrusions.
4. Log these events on the blockchain ledger to establish an immutable audit trail.
5. Raise an alert for investigation.

10.3.4 Secure Data Storage and Sharing

Blockchain can share data securely by authenticating user permissions and generating access tokens [25].

Algorithm 10.3 Secure data sharing using blockchain.

Input: user request, blockchain ledger, data identifier
Output: unique access token (or access denial)
Procedure:

1. Validate the user through cryptographic credentials authentication.
2. Get the access permissions of the user for the given data identifier.
3. If the user is authorized:
   a. Produce a unique access token using a secure random function.
   b. Record the token issuance with a timestamp on the blockchain ledger.
   c. Return the access token created.
4. Otherwise:
   a. Record the unauthorized access attempt.
   b. Return an access denial message.

10.4 Real-World Case Studies and Applications

10.4.1 Healthcare Data Security

Securing electronic health records (EHRs): In healthcare, safeguarding EHRs is important. Blockchain guarantees that each access or change is logged immutably, leaving a transparent audit history [21]. Furthermore, studies [11] have demonstrated the potential of blockchain in securing EHR systems in cloud environments.
Enhancing patient data privacy: By leveraging DIDs, patients can control access to their personal data, reducing the risk of unauthorized disclosures [8].

10.4.2 Financial Services and Fraud Prevention

Secure transaction processing: Blockchain enhances the security of financial transactions by eliminating centralized vulnerabilities. Each transaction is verified through decentralized consensus, reducing fraud risk [13]. Additionally, blockchain-based systems have been explored for fraud-resistant crowdfunding systems [14].

Anti-money laundering (AML) and compliance: Transparent blockchain records enable real-time monitoring and compliance with regulatory standards, aiding in the detection of suspicious activities [5]. Smart contract deployment for financial transactions has also been investigated [17].

10.4.3 Supply Chain and Internet of Things Security

Traceability and tamper-proof records: In supply chain management, the blockchain records every phase of the product lifecycle in an immutable ledger that drastically reduces the opportunity for counterfeiting [21].
Internet of Things device authentication and data integrity: Assigning unique digital identities to IoT devices enhances security. The following algorithm demonstrates how blockchain secures IoT devices:

Algorithm 10.4 Decentralized IoT device authentication protocol.

Input: IoT device ID, device credentials, blockchain ledger
Output: authentication status (authenticated / rejected)
Procedure:

1. The IoT device sends its ID and credentials to the blockchain network.
2. Each node verifies the credentials using digital signature verification.
3. Nodes participate in a consensus process to validate the device's authenticity.
4. If a majority confirm the credentials:
   a. Log the successful authentication on the blockchain ledger.
   b. Return "Authenticated."
5. Otherwise:
   a. Log the failed authentication attempt.
   b. Return "Rejected."

10.5 Integration with Emerging Technologies

10.5.1 Blockchain and Artificial Intelligence

Artificial intelligence-driven security analytics can leverage immutable data on the blockchain to detect subtle anomalies and potential threats. By integrating blockchain data with machine learning algorithms, organizations can achieve real-time threat detection and predictive analytics [21].

Figure 10.2 illustrates the integration between blockchain data and an AI analytics engine using a matrix layout for better alignment.

10.5.2 Blockchain and the Internet of Things

Blockchain can secure IoT networks by assigning each device a unique digital identity and recording all data exchanges immutably. This mitigates risks of unauthorized access and data manipulation [4, 6].

10.5.3 Blockchain in Cloud and Edge Computing

In cloud and edge computing, blockchain enhances data provenance and integrity by providing traceable records of every data interaction, thus improving the overall trustworthiness of distributed systems [21].

10.6 Economic, Environmental, and Social Implications

10.6.1 Cost-Benefit Analysis of Blockchain Security

While blockchain-based security systems require a significant initial investment, they offer long-term benefits including reduced breach costs,

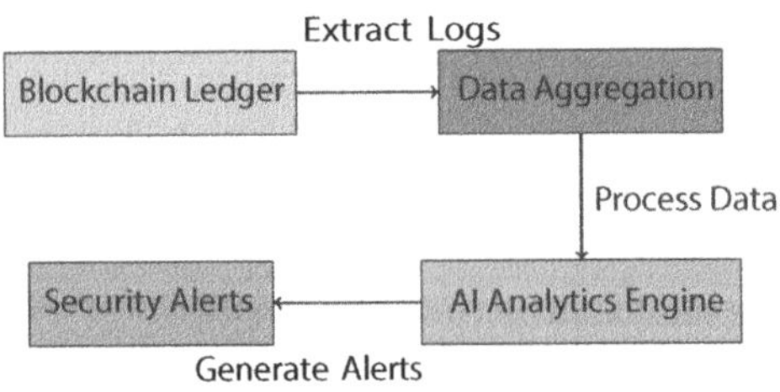

Figure 10.2 Integration of blockchain data with AI-driven security analytics.

Table 10.1 Comparative cost-benefit analysis: traditional vs. blockchain-based security.

Aspect	Traditional security	Blockchain-based security
Initial investment	Moderate to high	High (novel infrastructure)
Operational costs	high (manual processes)	Lower (automation *via* smart contracts)
Breach impact	significant	Reduced (immutable logs, rapid response)
Compliance efficiency	variable	Streamlined and transparent

improved operational efficiency through automation, and enhanced regulatory compliance [8].

Table 10.1 provides a comparative cost-benefit analysis.

10.6.2 Energy Consumption and Environmental Impact

Consensus mechanisms like Proof of Work (PoW) are energy-intensive, raising environmental concerns. Transitioning to energy-efficient models such as Proof of Stake (PoS) is essential for sustainable blockchain deployment [21].

Figure 10.3 compares energy consumption between PoW and PoS using colored nodes.

10.6.3 Social Trust and Decentralization Ethics

Blockchain's decentralized nature fosters greater transparency and accountability by distributing trust among network participants. However, ethical challenges remain regarding equitable access to technology and the digital divide [18].

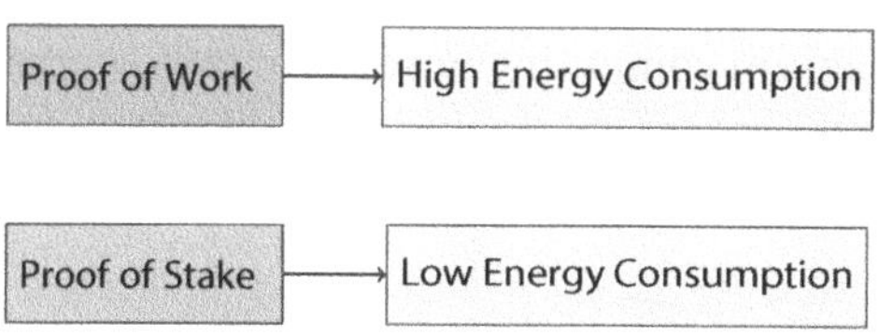

Figure 10.3 Energy consumption comparison: PoW vs. PoS.

10.7 Regulatory, Legal, and Compliance Considerations

10.7.1 Data Privacy Regulations and Blockchain

Blockchain's immutable nature may conflict with data privacy regulations such as the GDPR, particularly the right to be forgotten. Solutions like off-chain storage with on-chain hash pointers are being explored to resolve these issues [21].

10.7.2 Legal Frameworks and Governance Models

Decentralized networks challenge traditional legal frameworks. The enforceability of smart contracts and decentralized governance requires new legal models that balance innovation with accountability [8].

10.7.3 International Standards and Best Practices

Organizations such as ISO and IEEE are actively developing standards for blockchain technology. These standards aim to cover security, interoperability, and compliance protocols, thereby facilitating broader adoption in regulated industries [21].

10.8 Challenges and Future Research Directions

10.8.1 Scalability and Performance Issues

Blockchain must balance decentralization, security, and performance. Ongoing research into sharding, off-chain transactions, and layer-two protocols is critical to improve throughput and reduce latency [8].

10.8.2 Quantum Computing Threats and Post-Quantum Cryptography

The advent of quantum computing poses a threat to current cryptographic algorithms. Researchers are developing post-quantum cryptographic techniques to safeguard blockchain systems against future quantum attacks [21].

10.8.3 Integration with Legacy Systems

Integrating blockchain with existing legacy systems presents challenges in interoperability, data migration, and cost. Future solutions may involve middleware and standardized APIs to bridge these gaps [8].

10.8.4 Research Gaps and Open Questions

Several key research questions remain:

- How can different blockchain networks achieve seamless interoperability?
- What sustainable economic models can incentivize honest participation in decentralized systems [18]?
- How should ethical and regulatory challenges be addressed as blockchain evolves [5]?

Figure 10.4 illustrates the interrelationships among these challenges.

10.9 Conclusions and Future Outlooks

10.9.1 Summary of Key Findings

This chapter has demonstrated that blockchain technology, with its decentralized and immutable ledger, can significantly enhance data security. Key findings include:

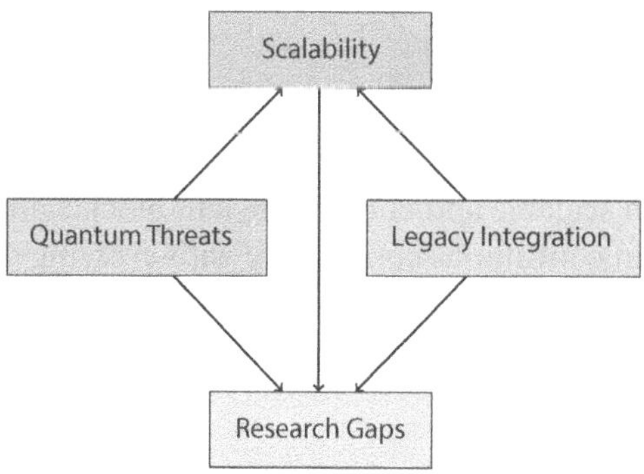

Figure 10.4 Interrelationships among key research challenges.

- Decentralization and immutability: Eliminates single points of failure and ensures data integrity.
- Enhanced security mechanisms: Blockchain-based authentication, access control, and secure data sharing provide robust security solutions.
- Integration with emerging technologies: Synergies with AI, IoT, and cloud computing improve threat detection and data provenance.
- Regulatory and ethical considerations: New challenges require evolving legal frameworks and standards.

10.9.2 The Future Role of Blockchain in Data Security

Blockchain will become increasingly integral in protecting digital data. Trends in the future are:

- Widespread use of scalable, energy-friendly consensus algorithms.
- Creation of quantum-resistant cryptographic algorithms.
- A blurring of lines between traditional systems and blockchain-based systems through hybrid architectures.
- Evolving legal and regulatory frameworks in favor of decentralized systems.

10.9.3 Recommendations for Practitioners and Researchers

Based on the findings, the following recommendations are proposed:

1. For practitioners:

   - Implement hybrid architecture that combine on-chain and off- chain storage.
   - Invest in scalable and energy-efficient blockchain solutions.
   - Maintain continuous compliance with evolving data privacy regulations.

2. For researchers:

   - Explore post-quantum cryptography to secure future blockchain systems.

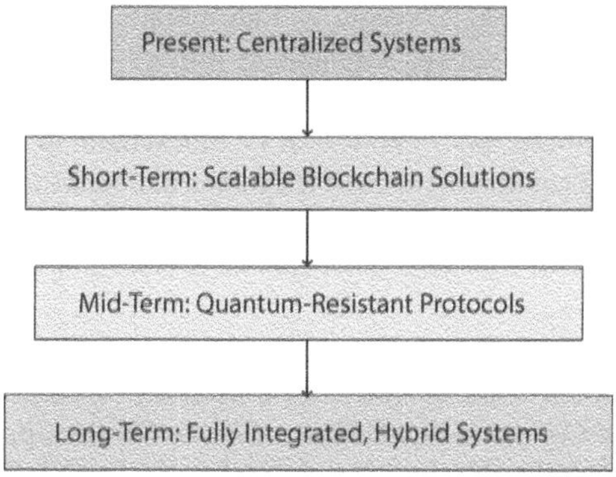

Figure 10.5 The projected timeline for future developments in blockchain-based data security.

- Develop interoperability standards between blockchain and legacy systems.
- Investigate sustainable economic models and ethical frameworks for decentralized networks.

Figure 10.5 shows the timeline.

AI disclosure statement: The author acknowledges the use of AI-based tools for minor language editing or grammatical correction. However, all intellectual contributions, analyses, and conclusions presented in this chapter are entirely the author's own.

References

1. Bonneau, J., Miller, A., Clark, J., Narayanan, A., Kroll, J.A., Felten, E.W., Sok: Research perspectives and challenges for bitcoin and cryptocurrencies, in: *2015 IEEE Symposium on Security and Privacy*, pp. 104–121, 2015.
2. Buterin, V., Ethereum whitepaper: A next-generation smart contract and decentralized application platform, 2014, Available at https://ethereum.org/en/whitepaper/.
3. Cachin, C., Architecture of the hyperledger blockchain fabric, in: *Proceedings of the 13th USENIX Conference on Operating Systems Design and Implementation*, pp. 1–6, 2016.
4. Christidis, K. and Devetsikiotis, M., Blockchains and smart contracts for the internet of things. *IEEE Access*, 4, 2292–2303, 2016.

5. Crosby, M., Pattanayak, P., Verma, S., Kalyanaraman, V., Blockchain technology: Beyond bitcoin, 2016, Available at https://www.ibm.com/downloads/cas/9RL3BDGJ.
6. Dorri, A., Kanhere, S.S., Panwar, R.J., Blockchain in internet of things: Challenges and solutions, in: *2017 IEEE International Conference on Internet of Things (iThings) and IEEE Green Computing and Communications (GreenCom) and IEEE Cyber, Physical and Social Computing (CPSCom)*, pp. 1–6, 2017.
7. Gervais, A., Karame, G., Capkun, V., Capkun, S., On the security and performance of proof of work blockchains. *Proceedings of the 2014 ACM SIGSAC Conference on Computer and Communications Security*, pp. 3–16, 2014.
8. Joshi, A.P., Han, M., Wang, Y., A survey on security and privacy issues of blockchain technology. *Math. Found. Comput.*, 1, 2, 121–147, 2018.
9. King, S. and Nadal, S., Ppcoin: Peer-to-peer crypto-currency with proof-of-stake, 2012, Available at https://peercoin.net/.
10. Micali, S., Algorand: The efficient and democratic ledger, 2017, Available at https://algorand.com/.
11. Murala, D.K., Panda, S.K., Sahoo, S.K., Securing Electronic Health Record System in Cloud Environment Using Blockchain Technology, in: *Recent Advances in Blockchain Technology*, S.K. Panda, V. Mishra, S.P. Dash, A.K. Pani (eds.), vol. 237, Intelligent Systems Reference Library, Springer, Cham., 2023.
12. Nair, V.K., Blockchain technology in healthcare-a case study to explore the gaps scope in india, in: *12th Annual ISDI conference, SP Jain Institute of Management & Research, SP Jain Institute of Management & Research*, 2018.
13. Nakamoto, S., *Bitcoin:* A peer-to-peer electronic cash system, 2008, Available at https://bitcoin.org/bitcoin.pdf.
14. Panda, S.K., Fraud-resistant crowdfunding system using ethereum blockchain, in: *Bitcoin and Blockchain*, pp. 237–276, CRC Press, 2020.
15. Panda, S.K., Jena, A.K., Swain, S.K., Satapathy, S.C., *Blockchain technology: applications and challenges*, Springer, Intelligent Systems Reference Library, 2021.
16. Panda, S.K., Mishra, V., Dash, S.P., Pani, A.K., Recent Advances in Blockchain Technology Real-World Applications. *Intell. Syst. Ref. Libr. (ISRL)*, 237, 1, 1–317, 2023. 978-3-031-22835-3.
17. Panda, S.K. and Satapathy, S.C., An investigation into smart contract deployment on ethereum platform using web3. js and solidity using blockchain, in: *Data Engineering and Intelligent Computing: Proceedings of ICICC 2020*, Springer, pp. 549–561, 2021.
18. Swan, M., *Blockchain: Blueprint for a New Economy*, O'Reilly Media, 2015.
19. Underwood, S., Blockchain beyond bitcoin. *Commun. ACM*, 59, 11, 15–17, 2016.

20. Venkatesan, K. and Rahayu, S.B., Blockchain security enhancement: an approach towards hybrid consensus algorithms and machine learning techniques. *Sci. Rep.*, 14, 1, 1149, 2024.
21. Wang, Y. and Kogan, M., Smart contract-based cybersecurity. *ACM Trans. Secur. Privacy*, 34, 2, 1–22, 2021.
22. Wood, G., Ethereum: A secure decentralised generalised transaction ledger, 2014, Available at https://ethereum.github.io/yellowpaper/paper.pdf.
23. Kumar, P., Dhanush, G.A., Srivatsa, D., Nithin, A., Sahisnu, S., A buyer and seller's protocol via utilization of smart contracts using blockchain technology, in: *Advanced Informatics for Computing Research: Third International Conference, ICAICR 2019*, Revised Selected Papers, Part I 3, p. 464–474, Springer, Shimla, India, June 15–16, 2019.
24. Mishra, P., Bhaya, C., Pal, A. K., Singh, A. K., A novel binary operator for designing medical and natural image cryptosystems. *Signal Process. Image Commun.*, 98, 116377, 2021.
25. Saiharsha, B., Sanjay Tharagesh, R.S., Nikish Kumar, S.V., Harini, N., Cloud based data integrity model for minimal human intervention using smart contracts, in: *2020 5th International Conference on Communication and Electronics Systems (ICCES)*, pp. 910–916, IEEE, 2020.

Part 3

DIGITAL IMMUNE SYSTEM: NOVEL PRACTICES

11

Blockchain Technology and Intelligent Networking for the Metaverse

Dileep Kumar Murala[1], Pradosh Kumar Gantayat[2], Sandeep Kumar Panda[2]* and K. Vara Prasada Rao[2]

[1]Department of Computer Science and Engineering, Faculty of Science and Technology (IcfaiTech), ICFAI Foundation for Higher Education, Hyderabad, Telangana, India

[2]Department of Artificial Intelligence and Data Science, Faculty of Science and Technology (IcfaiTech), ICFAI Foundation for Higher Education (IFHE), Deemed to be University, Hyderabad, Telangana, India

Abstract

People's lives have changed because of the imaginary world as technology improved. The internet, computers, artificial intelligence (AI), and electronics made it possible for the virtual world to open. There are a lot of new social networks connecting the real and virtual worlds called metaverses. They are growing rapidly as more people want to use them. It has been hard to keep privacy, stay safe, sync up well, and have low lag as the metaverse keeps changing and more data and value are added. These issues can be fixed as blockchain and smart networking technologies keep improving. The metaverse will then be able to meet its needs for safe building, constant data exchange, and computing. It is important to look at blockchain's role and rewards in detail to make metaverse encounters more real. The point of this poll is to talk about the metaverse's structure, growth, and general traits. This review chapter is one of a kind because it looks at the blockchain research that has already been done and lists its features, uses, and problems. We also went over the metaverse's uses and talked about how important they are and how they could be made better. The survey lets us discuss open questions, problems, and possible paths for future research.

***Keywords*:** Blockchain technology, artificial intelligence, metaverse, intelligent networking, cloud computing, extended reality (XR), privacy, security

**Corresponding author*: sandeeppanda@ifheindia.org

Sujata Priyambada Dash, Vaibhav Mishra, Bijeta Shaw, Sandeep Kumar Panda and S. Balamurugan (eds.) Digital Immune System: Principles and Practices, (231–268) © 2026 Scrivener Publishing LLC

11.1 Introduction

In recent years, humanity has entered an amazing era of technological explosion due to the rapid growth of several technologies, including communication networks, artificial intelligence (AI), computing technology, blockchain, and other technologies. How we engage with the material world that surrounds us is undergoing rapid transformation. The idea of the metaverse has just come back into existence [1]. The phrase "metaverse" first appeared in Neal Stephenson's 1992 science fiction novel "Snow Crash" [2]. The term consists of "meta" and "verse," which come from "universe." Some see the metaverse as a hypothetical internet. This version mixes physical and digital virtual worlds for perception and sharing utilizing XR [3]. An endless virtual digital universe connects the physical and digital worlds in the metaverse. Our avatar can immediately and thoroughly interact with the digital environment, independent of our field.

What technology is needed to support and manage such a complex ecosystem? It is possible to summarize the fundamental technologies that underpin the metaverse by using the word "BIGANT" [4]. For the sake of this discussion, the letters "B" stands for blockchain, "I" stands for interactivity, "G" stands for game, "A" stands for artificial intelligence, "N" stands for network and computing technology (network), and "T" is for the Internet of Things (IoT). Interactivity, AI, and games are among the technologies that have reached a somewhat mature stage after extensive development. For instance, many virtual reality (VR) devices and metaverse games have appeared [5]. High-speed, dependable connectivity and fast continuous computing are needed to process huge volumes of data created by the metaverse's many facilities and devices. For this reason, intelligent networking technology ensures good synchronization and minimal latency. We need these skills to give users immersive experiences.

In addition, when constructing the metaverse, it is impossible to disregard security concerns such as the protection of personal information, the management of trusted information, and the interchange of data [14, 83]. This is because the volume of data is increasing at a rapid rate, and the value of data is also increasing. Blockchain technology's decentralization, immutability, and transparency could secure the metaverse. This survey examines metaverse blockchain and intelligent networking implementation. Blockchain and intelligent networking may evolve the metaverse through virtual-real fusion and trustworthy management. This is the motivation for our decision to carry out this survey. The evolution of the metaverse was analyzed from four perspectives in an earlier extensive survey that was authored by Dionisio and colleagues [32, 37, 38, 84]. These four perspectives were actuality, universality, interoperability, and scalability about the metaverse. Not included in this are the most recent technological advancements, such as blockchain and 6G. An extensive metaverse survey by [23] highlighted six user-centric characteristics and a study plan. The survey addressed 14 metaverse components. Infrastructure, management technology, general technology, VR object interactions, and VR integration were investigated [6]. A large part of the poll examines nations' and businesses' metaverse actions. Metaverse-relevant wireless communication designs were examined in Reference [16, 39]. They discussed how the metaverse could improve wireless technologies. Metaverse privacy was briefly surveyed to keep VR users private while socializing [17, 40, 41]. References [10] studied metaverse blockchain applications.

This survey, unlike others, focuses on metaverse-secure intelligent networking. How blockchain and intelligent networking may strengthen ecosystems is examined. Before discussing the metaverse's development, traits, and structure, we provide the background. Readers can learn this direction and basic principles from this content. We then introduce the metaverse by explaining blockchain technology and intelligent networking, including communication and computing networks, and their advantages and disadvantages. We also study many metaverse ways to connect academic research to market products.

11.2 Blockchain for the Metaverse

Blockchain changed internet business transactions. Blockchain is crucial for data security and reliability. It fulfills metaverse data and asset exchange needs. Here is an introduction to blockchain and metaverse applications and issues. Information is scarce.

11.2.1 An Overview of Blockchain Technology

Blockchain, a jointly controlled and agreed-upon ledger, may efficiently record and monitor transactions and assets in a decentralized network. Satoshi Nakamoto invented blockchain to create a decentralized peer-to-peer (P2P) electronic cash payment system without a central bank [6, 42, 43].

11.2.1.1 What is the Significance of Blockchain?

Blockchain is an optimal option for transmitting and storing information. It provides enterprises with fast, transparent, tamper-proof, and shareable information [1, 12, 19, 44–47]. Three basic blockchain kinds are public, consortium, and private [2]. Blockchain transparency varies greatly. Authorized users can utilize the public blockchain without restrictions. Consortium blockchains are only accessible to registered nodes.

Private blockchains can only be used by a select group. External entities cannot access blockchain transaction data, but inside entities maintain transparency. In conclusion, the blockchain provides customized services to customers. Furthermore, the various uses of blockchain can be attributed to numerous pivotal components [7, 85].

- ***Distributed ledger:*** The transaction content stored in the blockchain can be accessed by the network members within the blockchain. After verification and blockchain storage, a transaction is immutable [8]. Due to the absence of any private information in the recorded transaction data, any participant in the network may easily monitor all transaction details, such as order sequence, timestamps, transfer details, and involved accounts. This ensures data transparency. A decentralized ledger-based certificate system [9] provides dependable and approved certifications. The process of verifying domain ownership and confirming the results are stored on a blockchain for validation, guaranteeing security and resistance to tampering [48, 49].
- ***Immutability of transactions:*** The immutability of transactions refers to the inability of any participant to alter or manipulate the recorded content of the blockchain once a transaction has been completed. Learning-based resource management was exhibited in public blockchain networks [10, 50, 51]. The immutability of blockchain prevents, attacks, and tracks data.
- ***Smart contract:*** A smart contract is a blockchain-stored collection of rules that are automatically executed along with transaction information [11, 52, 53]. Smart contracts expand the capabilities of the blockchain beyond virtual currency by facilitating transactions and searches for any valuable asset within the network. Smart contracts automate and verify

service transactions under [12]'s bargaining framework. Assurance is provided for both dependability and safety.

11.2.2 Benefit of Blockchain

- ***Trust:*** Participants inside the blockchain network can securely, precisely, and promptly record, transmit, and store data. Various types of blockchains can be developed to cater to varied application requirements, ensuring that data is accessible to users within specific regions [12, 54, 86].
- ***Security:*** All blockchain network participants must agree to validate transactions. Verifying the transaction as legal makes it unchangeable. Therefore, blockchain data will be forever recorded. Users cannot edit or remove transactions [13, 55, 56].
- ***Efficiency:*** The blockchain network enables the sharing of the ledger among its members, hence eliminating the need for repetitive reconciliations during member interactions. Moreover, smart contracts have the capability to autonomously implement the predefined rules recorded within the blockchain, thereby guaranteeing efficient and organized transactions [14, 57, 58].

11.2.3 Blockchain-Based Metaverse

The blockchain-based metaverse utilizes virtual currencies like Bitcoin to offer integrated digital asset services. The system can efficiently ensure the dependability and consistency of diverse transactions. Traditional centralized methods for metaverse data collection, exchange, and storage have a single point of failure and wasteful communication and processing. Interdisciplinary blockchain is ideal for metaverse data services. P2P storage and communication can secure and optimize metaverse bulk transactions. Blockchain cryptography, including asymmetric encryption and digital signatures, makes metaverse interactions secure and dependable. Finally, being a decentralized database, the blockchain can let metaverse entities build custom services. The blockchain can serve various metaverse applications [15, 59, 60].

- ***Data Sharing:*** Metaverse users can supply and request data. The blockchain's P2P data-sharing mechanism can meet numerous metaverse data service needs. Blockchain technology for information exchange may offer virtual and physical data services. Data requesters would distinguish shared data uniquely due to its nontamperability and security [16, 61, 62]. The metaverse includes adjustable needs and functions for constructing blockchain systems in different applications. Blockchain ensures physical and virtual consistency. Information sharing between worlds is accurate and consistent due to real-time consensus and audit of all nodes. Consistent and trustworthy blockchain information sharing helps solve application issues and prevent manipulation. To guarantee data is thoroughly examined before sharing, the author established a decentralized blockchain-based data-sharing network [17]. Natural language processing and a distributed data-sharing platform guarantee physical-digital coherence. In [26], the authors introduced blockchain-powered MEC for future vehicle networks. A blockchain-based data-sharing technique with configurable privacy protection was developed by Liu *et al.* [18]. The method adapts to system resources and user privacy. For the Internet of Vehicles (IoVs), Cui *et al.* presented a decentralized mechanism for exchanging vehicle driving data [28]. The system uses blockchain to establish a traceable V2V information-sharing technique, prohibiting anonymous data exchange. Therefore, the utilization of blockchain technology for data sharing could facilitate the metaverse in securely exchanging information between the virtual and physical realms, as well as between different applications. Therefore, data audit and quality may be assured. Due to blockchain technology's immutability, a well-designed consensus mechanism can prevent data fraud and economic disputes [18, 65, 66]. Moreover, the avatar will generate a substantial amount of data when entering the metaverse. Consequently, the disclosure of any personal information will significantly impact the users' level of trust and willingness to engage. Utilizing blockchain technology can prevent the compromise of centralized data storage. Blockchain's decentralization makes data sharing safer, faster, and more reliable [19, 63, 64].

➢ ***Data Storage:*** In the context of the metaverse, where all system functions are digital, finding a way to efficiently store, retrieve, and utilize data using blockchain technology is a crucial challenge. Blockchain technology uses distributed storage on a P2P network to assure data consistency, making metaverse data storage efficient. In response to high data update costs and vulnerable data storage methods of current centralized approaches, a blockchain-based data storage system was developed [20, 67] for incremental data updates. Smart contracts and fast data dissemination decrease unnecessary data and system overhead. To improve large-scale data storage access, splitting data was suggested [21] into continuous and state data. Storage engines store and manipulate data using indexes. A blockchain-based distributed data storage solution was developed to preserve data [22]. It fixes the trust issue created by centralized servers. There are suggestions of IPFS data storage [13, 23]. This technique solves the blockchain storage capacity problem by addressing content. Thus, blockchain technology for metaverse data storage can secure and reliably exchange data between users and apps. For instance, private sectors such as healthcare and real estate might be safely held within a private blockchain. Access to sensitive information is restricted to authorized entities only. In addition, utilizing blockchain for safe data storage can guarantee coherence and uninterrupted connection between the digital and physical realms, thanks to the distinctive design of consensus mechanisms tailored for specific applications. More precisely, the metaverse replicates real-life experiences in the physical world, while the blockchain securely stores data to guarantee its validity and verifiability, hence maintaining the consistency of data modifications. Secure data storage may also help people invest in the financial sector. Blockchain-based virtual money links metaverse assets to real-world goods [24].

- ***Virtual economy system:*** The metaverse must offer consumers a diverse and engaging interactive experience. Keeping the virtual and physical worlds coherent requires a reliable virtual economic system. Virtual resources like land and goods are crucial to capital circulation in the economy. Virtual images, wearables, and objects are profitable. Object ownership determines the avatar's virtual appearance and helps people integrate into the metaverse. The value of traditional game industry digital virtual assets is expected to approach $40 billion annually. Thus, the metaverse's virtual economy has great growth potential. The distributed nature of blockchain has recently made it popular. Satoshi Nakamoto introduced Bitcoin, a successful blockchain technology implementation. Subsequently, the blockchain-powered, P2P payment system has garnered significant interest from both academic and industrial sectors. The effects of blockchain-based economic systems on the global economy were examined [15]. A simple, effective blockchain-based virtual economic system was proposed [25, 68, 69], customizing a payment system for multiple applications. We examined whether distributed banking has a centralized management platform [26, 70]. Even with a centralized administration platform that enables more control, users' privacy may be compromised. This established a decentralized anonymous payment method with zero-knowledge evidence [27, 71, 72]. Point-to-point payments obscure the transaction's origin, destination, and amount. Simultaneously, the verification and examination of the proof are succinct and effective.

Like Bitcoin and other virtual payment systems, blockchain facilitates M2M and IoT payments [28, 73]. Increased research and algorithm programming fuel the machine interaction economy. A blockchain industrial market was launched [18]. The system's machines interact using smart contracts and have individual accounts. Decentralized industrial edge market on blockchain [29, 74]. This gives system members visibility and tracks edge device installations. Order processing *via* blockchain was proposed [30, 75]. Machine interface automation and system verification are improved by smart contracts. Currently, no blockchain-based solution unifies industrial business solutions into a unified market.

11.2.4 Difficulties and Discourse

Metaverse data sharing, storage, and transactions can be done with blockchain. However, two major issues remain: reliability and effectiveness.

- ***Users' privacy:*** This blockchain-based solution anonymizes users with a public-private key addressing mechanism, but network analysis can reveal their system history [30, 76].
- The access mechanism, which affects user privacy and security, depends on the blockchain's openness. Hence, conducting extensive study is still necessary to determine the

optimal approach for designing a blockchain architecture that is both extremely secure and trustworthy [31, 77].

- ***Centralization issue:*** The computer-powered consensus technique distributes nodes unevenly. Miners buy hardware to optimize profits, increasing the likelihood of mining pools with processing power greater than 51% of the world's total. Blockchain accounting privileges and data integrity are uncertain [32, 78].
- ***System robustness:*** Despite the blockchain-based scheme's cryptographic foundation, the network's privacy and security are still vulnerable. Can the system survive a network attack? Additionally, the blockchain system's capacity to quickly and reliably recover from attacks remains a major research challenge [33, 79].
- ***Audit complexity:*** Metaverse users' actions are carefully reviewed before being recorded on the blockchain. To protect user privacy and improve data security, data transparency must be reduced, making transaction audits more complicated [27, 80].
- ***Efficiency of blockchain:*** The efficiency of the blockchain is crucial due to the need for fast response times in the metaverse. This necessitates a highly optimized architecture for the blockchain consensus mechanism. The huge metaverse data mobility will conflict with blockchain-based data storage and efficient verification. Optimizing the system ensures effective storage and capture of enormous data sets [34, 81].

Blockchain, a distributed ledger, requires data openness to verify transaction content and authenticity. However, it is crucial to guarantee that transparent data does not reveal any sensitive information about transactions, thereby safeguarding transaction privacy. Hence, it is crucial to carefully address the issue of reconciling the conflict between data transparency and obscurity in the future metaverse for large-scale transactions. A blockchain concept that validates transaction details while hiding private information was introduced [3, 82]. Dual balance hides account and transaction balances. For account security, NIZK and public-key encryption were advised encryption [35, 36]. The NIZK-based paradigm can resolve the transparency-privacy dilemma by assuring that the proof does not reveal confidential information. A mixing approach eliminates the necessity for a trustworthy third-party to oversee the transaction [5]. Negotiations are evaluated for transaction details. Two outsourcing differential privacy approaches were offered [6], preprocessing and building blocks outsource differential privacy. Evaluators accessing transaction information ask several queries in a trusted execution environment. Energy trading and anonymous bargaining were secured with blockchain, multiple signatures, and encrypted chat streams [7].

However, metaverse transactions go beyond digital money. Complex transaction data will exacerbate information openness and privacy issues [8]. To protect users' personal data and transaction verification, diversification, and broad transactions must be investigated in the future. Ultimately, although blockchain offers features such as security, decentralization, immutability, and privacy preservation, there is still a need for further research to enhance its performance and customization for its implementation in the metaverse.

11.3 Review of Existing Literature

Multiple studies have examined blockchain-intelligent networking integration. Rivera presented an intent-based networking blockchain system to secure networks and enforce policies in 2023. In the paper [14], the author suggested using blockchain to build communication trust. Artificial intelligence systems can utilize this technology to ensure secure and transparent conversations. The user's input consists of a single character, specifically the letter "R." One major goal in 2022 was to investigate blockchain technology in 5G networks and IoT devices. The conference addressed decentralization, data interoperability, and security issues. Yu launched Anchor in 2021, a blockchain network that uses named-data networking to increase data transmission in blockchain systems. These studies show that blockchain technology and intelligent networking can improve communication network security, transparency, and efficiency. Table 11.1 describes the research on existing approaches to the integration of blockchain and intelligent networks.

Table 11.1 Integration of blockchain and intelligent networking research.

Ref.	Summary	Methodology	Drawbacks
Panda, S.K. *et al.* [2]	The paper discusses the inadequacy of traditional security measures in modern distributed systems, introduces contemporary paradigms like zero-trust networking and software-defined perimeters, highlights the role of intent-based networking in translating security policies, proposes the integration of IBN with blockchain for a single source of truth, and aims to achieve a zero-touch-and-trust network system.	The methodology involves automated policy management, continuous monitoring, data analytics, translation of security policies into network configurations, the use of Hyperledger Besu for blockchain implementation, integration of an IBN system for secure policy creation, an event listener mechanism for translating intents, and a synchronizer for maintaining alignment between network overlay configurations and policy intents.	Blockchain consensus mechanisms conflict with trust, integrity, and performance. Data sharing was not applicable in the study.

(*Continued*)

Table 11.1 Integration of blockchain and intelligent networking research. (*Continued*)

Ref.	**Summary**	**Methodology**	**Drawbacks**
Alja'afreh, *et al.* [1]	The paper explores the integration of blockchain and enterprise networks to enhance efficiency and mitigate risks, providing theoretical support and practical guidance for addressing barriers in complex enterprise networks.	The study conducted comprehensive literature research to analyze the theoretical history and application development of corporate networks and blockchains.	The paper suggests the need for global collaboration to address these challenges effectively.
Sakthi Kumaresh *et al.* [11]	The study explains how blockchain and AI might improve communication security, transparency, and privacy, revolutionizing secure communication.	The methodology involves focusing on security concerns related to communication networks, providing fundamental details of AI and blockchain, analyzing previous research works, emphasizing the need for awareness of integration benefits, and declaring no conflicts of interest.	The study highlights various challenges in the integration of blockchain and AI. The regulatory framework needs enhancement to bring more security and trust among users. Increasing awareness of the benefits of integrating blockchain and AI is crucial for further research efforts.

(*Continued*)

Table 11.1 Integration of blockchain and intelligent networking research. (*Continued*)

Ref.	Summary	Methodology	Drawbacks
Yu, S, *et al.* [35]	The paper discusses blockchain technology, its uses, the benefits of merging blockchain with edge computing, research hurdles, and current progress in enabling the integrated system.	The abstract does not provide a specific methodology, or a brief description of the methods used in the study. It focuses more on discussing the challenges, research issues, and vital aspects of integrating blockchain and edge computing systems.	Decentralized edge-computing management and security issues, blockchain scalability issue, scalability, self-organization, functionalities integration, resource management, and security challenges for integrated blockchain and edge computing systems.
J. J. Diaz Rivera, *et al.* [13]	The paper provides an elaborate investigation of how blockchain technology is integrated into intelligent networks, particularly focusing on 5G networks and 5G-based IoT, addressing challenges and offering solutions for spectrum management, data sharing, security, and privacy.	The technique analyzes the empowering of blockchain technology in intelligent networks, concentrating on 5G networks and 5G-based IoT, to overcome obstacles and constraints.	Implementing blockchain technology in intelligent networks presents decentralization, transparency, data interoperability, network privacy, and security threats. The effectiveness of blockchain technology in tackling these issues and associated downsides.

(*Continued*)

Table 11.1 Integration of blockchain and intelligent networking research. (*Continued*)

Ref.	**Summary**	**Methodology**	**Drawbacks**
Mahita Sri Arza, *et al.* [17]	The article examines blockchain and machine learning (ML) integration for communications and networking systems, including benefits, obstacles, and open issues to address before deployment.	The process entails surveying blockchain and ML efforts, identifying integration, benefits, and applications, and debating open difficulties and obstacles.	Before the widespread adoption of blockchain and ML in communications and networking systems, challenges in resource management, data processing, scalable operation, and security must be addressed.
Maksymyuk, *et al.* [18]	The study introduces Anchor, a named-data networking (NDN)--based blockchain network approach that propagates data more efficiently and securely than previous methods.	The methodology involved integrating blockchain and ICN through the introduction of a new technique called Anchor based on NDN, tailoring NDN, cascading two NDN systems, and conducting simulations for performance comparison.	High communication overhead and redundant traffic in existing blockchain networks. Security gaps from directly integrating blockchain and ICN.

(*Continued*)

Table 11.1 Integration of blockchain and intelligent networking research. (*Continued*)

Ref.	Summary	Methodology	Drawbacks
R. Yang, *et al.* [27]	For data propagation in blockchain systems, Anchor, an NDN-based blockchain network approach, is more efficient and safer than current methods.	The methodology involved integrating blockchain and ICN through the introduction of a new technique called Anchor based on NDN, tailoring NDN, cascading two NDN systems, and conducting simulations for performance comparison.	Current blockchain networks have high communication overhead and duplicated traffic. Security gaps from directly integrating blockchain and ICN.

11.4 Smart Network Architecture Using Blockchain

11.4.1 Network Design for Long Term Evolution

Current constraints include the fact that the long-term evolution (LTE)-based network structure is not well-suited for fully autonomous and intelligent functioning. First, the core network, which manages wireless data streams, must be reassessed. Hierarchically, every base station is connected to the MME and serving gateway. Connects to packet data network gateway. HSS stores all user data. It connects to the internet and other operators' P-GWs. Based on placement, the user's data must traverse the entire tree [8]. Docker containers can virtualize all system elements. While eNBs require different containers, evolved packet cores (EPCs) can be built in one. From a technical standpoint, it is possible to integrate the eNB and

EPC into a single container. Nevertheless, we maintain a clear distinction between our distributed mobile network model that relies on blockchain technology.

11.4.2 Smart Blockchain-Powered Distributed Mobile Network Infrastructure

Blockchain technology is mostly used in two main areas: cryptocurrency and smart contracts. Cryptocurrency is solely a financial market asset, whereas a smart contract enables two parties to establish specific economic connections in the physical world. We increase the technical and economic aspects of mobile network use using these two blockchain features. Figure 11.1 describes the next-generation wireless communications industry's future entities.

- **Spectrum owners.** Owners of the electromagnetic spectrum. The wireless spectrum is a crucial element of every wireless communication system. In the traditional mobile market, the government grants licenses for certain technologies (such as LTE, 5G, etc.) to use the spectrum. A mobile network operator can lawfully obtain such a license to offer

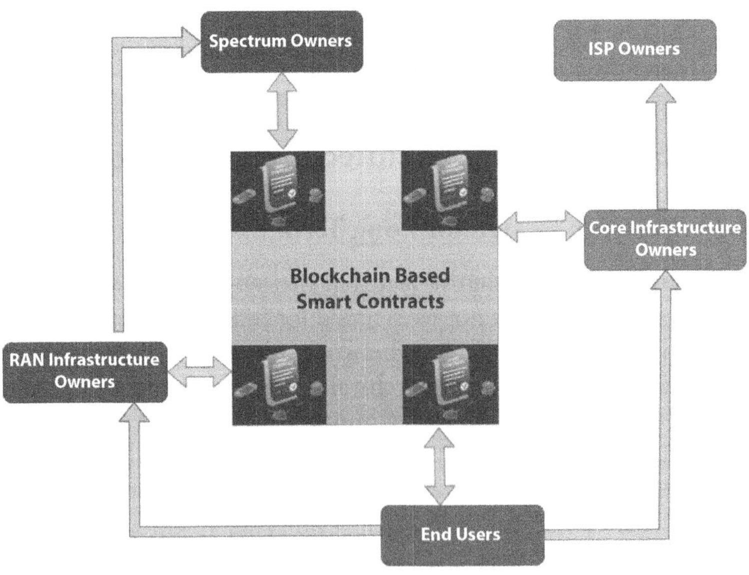

Figure 11.1 Distributed mobile network architecture using blockchain.

services to their subscribers. Our model assumes that the spectrum market is open, meaning that it is not possible for anyone to purchase it entirely. Instead, the government entity owns the complete spectrum and grants leases to infrastructure proprietors (such as mobile network providers) for a designated fee per unit of time. In a technical sense, it is possible to carry out these transactions by utilizing blockchain technology. As an illustration, the owner of the spectrum can create tokens (i.e., cryptocurrency assets) with a value equivalent to 1 Hz/second. The infrastructure owner can obtain spectrum based on their token balance.

- **Infrastructure owners.** Mobile networks invest considerably in infrastructure. An open infrastructure market allows anyone to invest in infrastructure and create a mobile virtual network operator. Individual companies can own wireless base stations and core networks. One can fund base stations, while another may fund servers that can host a virtual EPC with virtual machines or Docker containers to virtualize all necessary operations. They can distribute end-customer income in this case. The base station owner pays the spectrum owner for spectrum usage, and the core network owner pays the ISP so they can split end-user revenue proportionally.
- **ISP owners**. The ISP owner offers Internet connectivity to the owners of the infrastructure. Typically, these organizations provide monthly subscriptions at a set price based on a mutually agreed upon service level agreement. This choice is optimal since it is independent of the amount of traffic, which enables the creation of more adaptable data plans for the end customers.
- **End users.** End customers receive one or more USIM cards with IDs, account balances, and SLAs on normal mobile networks. Users are restricted to operator infrastructure. Our network model assumes the presence of numerous mobile virtual network operator (MVNOs), potentially ranging from tens to even hundreds, as opposed to the limited number often found in traditional mobile networks. Naturally, it would be impractical for end customers to handle agreements with such a multitude of diverse MVNOs. Thus, the implementation of blockchain smart contracts appears to hold great potential for this situation. Every user will be

assigned a distinct global identifier and financial account. In the future, it is quite probable that cryptocurrencies will be universally embraced, leading to the replacement of traditional invoicing systems with transactions involving cryptocurrency between users and infrastructure owners.

11.4.3 Mobile Network Smart Contract Application

Computer protocols called smart contracts speed up, verify, and enforce contract negotiations and execution. Smart contracts aim to foster trust and enable transactions without intermediaries [9]. Figure 11.2 describes the smart contracts that benefit 5G and 6G mobile networks.

- **Autonomy.** Users will no longer be constrained by the operator's offerings since they will no longer be compelled to select the most favorable data plan from a pool of unfavorable options. Typically, carriers provide a low-cost option with limited data and call allowances, as well as a high-priced

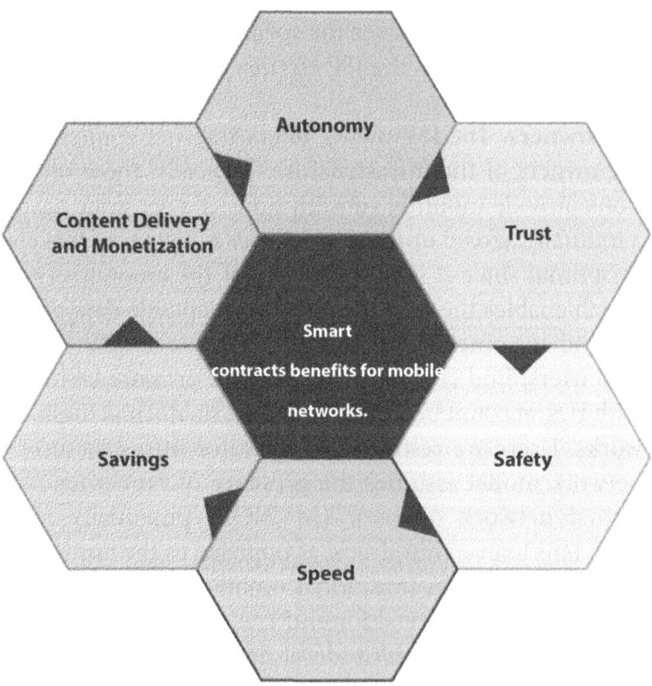

Figure 11.2 Smart contracts benefit for mobile networks.

one with a generous quantity of data and call allowances. Under these circumstances, numerous users are compelled to pay an elevated price for superfluous services. Each user equipment (UE) will be equipped with an intelligent agent using smart contracts. This agent will autonomously engage in real-time negotiations for price and service conditions, seamlessly switching between numerous operators. The user will remain unaware of these operations.

- **Trust.** After the user and infrastructure owner agree on particular needs, they remain unchanged throughout the smart contract. All conditions are encrypted on a shared ledger, so operators cannot change or violate them.
- **Safety.** Blockchain has great security against unauthorized access and fund theft because it verifies all transactions.
- **Speed.** Blockchain streamlines the process of negotiating terms and conditions among users, operators, and government entities by eliminating the need for documentation. The software code in a smart contract automates all procedures, resulting in significant time savings for all corporate processes.
- **Savings.** Smart contracts obviate the necessity for intricate and costly invoicing systems, thereby diminishing the CAPEX of MVNOs and significantly facilitating their market entry. Two varieties of smart contracts are delineated. The smart contract between the user and the MVNO (i.e., the infrastructure owner) is the first variety. The end-user can generate this contract by submitting a request for a mobile network connection, after which MVNOs provide their pricing to fulfill said request. Following this, an intelligent contact will be initiated so that the user is connected with the operator whose QoS requirements are met at the most economical cost. A smart contract between the owner of the infrastructure and the owner of the spectrum is the second variety. This contract is more straightforward due to the absence of any quality policies implied in its conditions. Whether or not the infrastructure proprietor makes timely payments for utilized spectrum is contingent on the terms outlined in a smart contract.
- **Content delivery and monetization.** Smart contracts can facilitate efficient content delivery and monetization for mobile networks:

Content Subscription: Automating subscription services for content such as music, videos, and news through smart contracts can ensure users are billed accurately and content providers are compensated promptly.
Micropayments: Enabling micropayments for small data transactions or pay-per-use content can be efficiently handled with smart contracts.

11.4.4 Blockchain-Based Unlicensed Spectrum Sharing

Unlicensed spectrum is widely used because of its unlimited and free resources. Mobile network provider competition makes unlicensed airwaves difficult. Before, we built a coalitional spectrum-sharing game with complete knowledge and updatable payoffs. Based on this, our current research develops a blockchain-based coalitional game among operators to share unlicensed spectrum. Since unlicensed spectrum is freely available, we suggest a virtual coin with no value in any traditional currency to ensure equal spectrum utilization. The suggested procedure follows this order.

Step 1. All mobile network operators sharing spectrum receive equal tokens at the start.
Step 2. Every operator using tokens from their account uses unlicensed airwaves.
Step 3. Blockchain transactions evenly distribute the operator's tokens to all other operators.

The proposed approach enables the explicit definition and execution of spectrum-sharing criteria while also preventing the operator from engaging in selfish behavior. If one operator uses more resources than others, their account will quickly run out, and they will have no tokens. Selfish operators cannot use the unlicensed airwaves until their balance rises because all operations are on the blockchain. Game theory may explain this predicament, where each operator is an autonomous player who chooses their unlicensed airwave strategy. The plan involves determining the amount of bandwidth that the operator intends to allocate for its subscribers. Given the scarcity of tokens, the optimal approach for the operator is to maintain an equilibrium between the inflow and outflow of tokens. To do this, the optimal choice is to utilize an equivalent or lesser amount of bandwidth compared to other operators.

11.5 Blockchain Meets Intelligent Networking in the Metaverse

Blockchain possesses several fundamental attributes, including robust security, unparalleled transparency, and absolute resistance to tampering, which give rise to novel opportunities in the realms of communication and computation. These features encompass the ability to share information safely, store data securely, and utilize trusted computing methods [9]. However, the blockchain has intrinsic consensus, broadcasting, and scaling issues [15]. Therefore, blockchain and intelligent networking technologies work together in the metaverse to build a secure and efficient ecosystem.

11.5.1 Blockchain-Enabled Communication

The metaverse requires communication networks with strict standards, and network resource sharing can address the exponential increase in network traffic. However, expenses, safety, and individualism can make resource sharing difficult. Blockchain technology can efficiently allow network entity interaction and resource sharing. There is improved 6G distribution, security, and automation with blockchain and AI dynamic resource sharing [10]. For 5G heterogeneous networks, [11] a blockchain-based spectrum-sharing architecture was created to address privacy and security concerns. This architecture ensures privacy, incentives, and spectrum efficiency. A blockchain-based two-stage secure spectrum intelligence sensing and shared auction system was built [12]. Secure auction transaction records are preserved on a blockchain. Blockchain-enabled network slicing is growing. A blockchain-based layered structure for 5G RAN autonomous resource slicing was presented [12]. Network-slicing systems and distributed blockchains can lease and assign resources in real-time [13]. B-RAN was announced for 6G secure wireless connectivity [14]. B-RAN wants to use blockchain for wireless connectivity. B-RAN's main concerns are cross-network collaboration, sharing, and intelligent group trusted access.

11.5.2 Blockchain-Enabled Computing

The metaverse requires lots of processing. Despite developments in cloud and edge computing, they cannot meet the metaverse's high experiential criteria. Furthermore, it is imperative to address the subsequent concerns of privacy and security, as well as the challenges associated with computing power compatibility, incentive systems, and other related matters. By integrating blockchain technology, a viable solution can be achieved in this scenario. Distributed computing makes matching demand with computer resources difficult due to the complexity of calculating each node's network contribution and the lack of incentive mechanisms. Blockchain technology can solve these problems. Golem2 is an Ethereum blockchain-based network that utilizes decentralized computer power. Users can purchase and trade computing power across the network. Users can use other users' machines to process power or sell their surplus power. Golem automatically connects computing power demands with sources. It compensates Ethereum-using computer users. Smart contracts describe computational resource attributes like memory capacity, CPU type, and disc space to match resource requests and provisions on the iExec blockchain. The classic centralized crowdsourcing system, privacy breaches, single points of failure, and exorbitant service prices were examined [16]. Blockchain-based incentive mechanism architecture was proposed. Smart agreements streamline system deployment, while the blockchain handles user reputation and incentives. Blockchain technology was suggested to improve participant registration, perceptual task execution, and reward distribution to safeguard user privacy and provide fair incentives [17]. Privacy, data security, and user distrust limit distributed computing. Blockchain can establish a safe, decentralized system. A blockchain-based smart grid entity management and safe resource connectivity solution were presented [18]. A blockchain-based automotive collaborative computing system was built [10] to address unscrupulous users. Distributed computing privacy requires federated learning [11].

Nevertheless, studies indicate that federated learning remains vulnerable to attacks, posing a potential danger of privacy breaches. A complete overview was provided [12] of the security and privacy problems encountered in federated learning. Blockchain offers robust privacy assurances and data protection for data interchange during the Federated Learning (FL) process. A digital twin wireless network (DTWN) paradigm improved end-user-edge server communication reliability and range [12]. Blockchain and FL improve parameter robustness and user model reliability, making edge intelligence safe and efficient. Federated learning participants received data security, computational auditability, and incentives from blockchain technology [14]. A hybrid blockchain architecture was suggested [11] for model parameter safety and dependability. A permissioned blockchain and locally directed acyclic network are used. Asynchronous FL ensures shared data reliability. The learning model is added to the blockchain and verified twice. Reputation was used [16] to assess mobile device dependability and trustworthiness and selected FL participants based on reputation. They ensure distributed reputation management with blockchain immutability.

11.5.3 Device Coordination

Future devices like computers, phones, and IoT devices can connect to the metaverse. These devices can collaborate on decision-making and computing [17]. In this scenario, many different gadgets raise the risk of untrusted devices and cyberattacks. Terminals and edge systems without proper protection can be attacked and tampered with. Tampering with device data affects system decision-making. Security specialists can deactivate these malicious programs and infected devices by identifying the centralized control center. Nevertheless, it is important to consider the aspects of security, latency, service availability, and the challenges associated with adjusting to intricate contexts and monitoring while considering the metaverse. Thus, blockchain technology can manage and coordinate networks and devices. Distributed architecture eliminates single points of failure, improving scalability and robustness [15, 18]. A blockchain-based device management architecture was presented [18] to solve heterogeneous network device security.

More precisely, the architecture offers distinct management and firmware update procedures that are tailored to the performance and needs of each device. This allows for the optimization of both network and device resources simultaneously. Furthermore, the use of blockchain and smart contracts for the purpose of managing equipment history and transmitting firmware guarantees the security, consistency, and verifiability of every device. To secure IoT device interoperability and communication, a blockchain-based firmware was devised [12], updating methods for embedded devices. By updating firmware from blockchain nodes, the device may safely authenticate the firmware version, ensure its accuracy, and download the latest embedded device firmware without unauthorized changes. Distributed IoT software update patches using blockchain technology [20]. They also used smart contracts to automatically reward patch transmission. Blockchain technology can solve identity verification and user trust issues in IoT systems [21]. This system allows decentralized tracking, identification, and authentication of user data, always ensuring its availability. Blockchain and smart contracts build trust among IoT participants. Blockchain's immutability was used [22] to improve network maintenance security and efficiency by monitoring equipment. Blockchain-stored device configuration files provide safe distributed management and fast accident recovery.

11.5.4 Efficient Consensus and Broadcast

The effectiveness of the blockchain's consensus and block broadcasting will be affected by the performance of the network. Network delay affects blockchain convergence, security, and transaction throughput, according to independent studies [12, 24, 25]. Assuming unlimited bandwidth, negligible network delay, and limitless computing capacity, the blockchain system can achieve an indefinitely high level of efficiency in consensus and transactions per second (TPS). Nevertheless, the majority of users possess restricted resources and capabilities. Hence, it is worthwhile exploring the enhancement of blockchain consensus and broadcasting efficiency by optimizing network performance. For instance, the exchange of information among blockchain nodes has consistently posed a challenging technical issue to resolve. The 5G networks offer broader coverage, faster data and information transfer rates, reduced communication latency, and the ability to accommodate a large number of connections, in contrast to 4G networks [26]. Hence, integrating blockchain technology can significantly enhance the overall communication rate and accomplish expedited transaction processing speed, all while preserving the decentralized nature of the blockchain. The paper [27] examined the way Bitcoin limits P2P networks to enhance data transfer capacity and reduce communication delay. The findings indicate that Bitcoin is unable to fully utilize network bandwidth and requires network architecture optimization to decrease blockchain network latency. A trust-enhanced blockchain P2P topology for fast and reliable blockchain broadcasting [28]. They considered transmission rate and dependability. This design improves the gearbox rate and dependability. It also reduces network stress with an effective node deactivation detection technique. The author [29] introduced BlockP2P, an optimized design that improves broadcast efficiency and security. To improve consensus time and increase network scalability, the P2P blockchain technology was modified [30] to a decentralized topology (especially a structured topology within a cluster).

11.5.5 Enhance Blockchain Scalability

To effectively implement blockchain systems, it is essential to integrate the three fundamental attributes of decentralization, security, and scalability. Scalability, in the context of blockchain systems, pertains to the system's capacity to handle transaction information. This capacity is primarily determined by the system's transaction processing performance, commonly measured as the TPS. The current blockchain systems, such as Bitcoin, face a major challenge in adapting to real application situations due to their inability to handle the growing number of transactions, which is known as scalability. The expense of blockchain participation and the need for consensus among all nodes drive this outcome. This metaverse has several user and service demands. The network updates transactions quickly and dynamically. Thus, scalability matters. Scaling the blockchain, especially TPS involves changing the consensus protocol, replacing the directed acyclic graph network, introducing cross-chain technology, and leveraging sharding technology [32]. The BTC uses Proof-of-Work (PoW), although there are additional methods, including Proof of Stake, PBFT, and improved iterations. These consensus processes try to fix PoW, but they involve trade-offs and compromises [27, 33].

A directed acyclic graph can turn the blockchain chain into a network. Each transaction in this structure is linked to several additional transactions, resulting in enhanced verification efficiency overall [34]. Cross-chain technology can be categorized into two types: multichain and sidechain. Both approaches involve the use of numerous chains to enable simultaneous transaction processing. The TPS is expected to increase as compared to a single chain. As the transaction volume grows, there will be constant growth in the demand for cross-chain data intercommunication. This will significantly raise the management complexity [35]. Sharding technology involves publishing each shard to the blockchain network after decomposing each transaction block. Each shard operates in parallel, allowing nodes to avoid downloading all transaction data. This considerably speeds up blockchain processing [12, 13]. Network technology improves blockchain scalability and reliability. Distributed computing network architectures can be scaled by using multiparty computer power and storage. As transactions increase, AI can speed up block creation, increasing throughput. Blockchain and edge computing provide dependable network access, storage, and distributed computation at the edges [13]. A distributed and trusted authentication system employing blockchain edge nodes and edge computing was created [12]. Improving authentication efficiency was the target. Edge computing-based caching had a good average delay and hit ratio. A decentralized big data-driven cognitive computing solution D2C [12] was created. This solution uses blockchain and federated learning. Blockchain increases federated learning participant verification and selection, increasing convergence and system robustness. BlockTDM [13] is a modular blockchain-based platform for secure, tamper-resistant data management. Being designed for edge computing makes it secure and credible.

11.5.6 Discussion, Challenges, and Massive, Distributed Computing

Large-scale distributed computing and application scenarios are problematic with the existing blockchain design, which limits calculations and node participation. Blockchain scalability limits the efficiency of processing any size resource in an ideal distributed computing system. Cross-chain structure, network technology, resource optimization, and other factors should be studied to maximize distributed computing power.

- ***Big data analysis:*** Blockchain and intelligent networking offer new perspectives on data analysis and storage with improved security. However, it is important to note that many applications have distinct data requirements and finding a solution for accomplishing multitask parallel processing is a significant difficulty. Furthermore, in practical use, the data within the network may lack labels or have incorrect labels, posing a significant difficulty for the processing of such unprocessed data. Thus, semi-supervised and device-collaborative learning may work.
- ***Resource optimization:*** To provide immediate services to metaverse users, communication, computation, and storage resources must be distributed and scheduled logically. After joining the blockchain system, designing appropriate coordination, consensus, and incentive mechanisms to optimize limited resources is a major research area.
- Furthermore, in a network environment that lacks security and is intricate, it is crucial to maintain a harmonious equilibrium between ensuring privacy and optimizing system performance.

11.6 Challenges and Future Scope

Many obstacles need to be solved if the metaverse is to be widely used. Technology will make it easier to experience the virtual and real worlds as they blend more and more. The desire for ever-better experiences and improved consumers' privacy pose problems even as supporting metaverse technology does. A study must be done in these fields, and potential remedies for these issues must be identified.

A. ***Dependable and effective transferring:*** Network performance depends on bandwidth, latency, and dependability. The shared metaverse requires low latency and excellent dependability for a seamless and coordinated experience. Mobility, varied sensing devices, and lots of data are network issues. Since 6G can improve metaverse communication, it has become a research center. With 6G technology, the metaverse will expand due to faster access rates, shorter access delays, faster motion speeds, and wider communication coverage, but efficient and reliable transmission will require communication and resource optimization protocols [47].
B. ***Computer performance:*** When the metaverse approaches a time of sensing, connection, and intelligence, meeting user needs and developing cutting-edge applications will require high processing power and a varied power supply. Furthermore, blockchain security and performance are tested in the distributed computer network. This implies the necessity of more studies on end-edge-cloud cooperation and distributed computing. Blockchain consensus mechanism design must meet low latency criteria for high-quality real-time user experience.
C. ***Architecture for unified communication-computing:*** Meeting the computational needs of the metaverse is challenging because communication and computing networks now function separately. The development of the metaverse depends on the integration of these networks. Intelligently operating, measuring, and scheduling these networks requires a unified communication and computing architecture. This requires the study and development of state-of-the-art technologies such as CFN, in-network computing (INC), and robust computing navigation [26]. The metaverse has challenges about resource usage and invocation since it blends the actual and virtual worlds. It will efficiently manage metaverse resources and allow users or systems to schedule them.

D. ***Building of networks:*** Successful deployment of the metaverse depends on a strong network infrastructure. This infrastructure must support edge computing, cloud computing, and high-speed communication networks to handle complex server computing tasks. The network should protect users from infrastructure compromise and decentralized network assaults by providing a secure link to the infrastructure. In an assault, it is imperative to protect virtual assets with both hardware and software. Furthermore, the need for wireless connectivity is growing. Thus, it is imperative to create safe wireless communication systems that can resist several centralized and decentralized operations. The reliability and security of the network infrastructure will make the metaverse more frictionless and safer.

E. ***Software development for metaverses:*** Because of the stringent performance, time, and personnel constraints, many software support sandbox games nowadays lack sophisticated modeling. To solve this problem, AI can produce basic materials and help with intricate creations. The removal of obstacles between blockchains must enable information transmission and software compatibility must be safely maintained on the blockchain.

F. ***Metaverse privacy and security***: Network, user, and environmental data make metaverse hostile behavior monitoring challenging [9]. Metaverse security and trust issues exist. Blockchain, AI, encryption algorithms, and protocols are key to identity management, trust, and security monitoring. Extended reality increases attack and infiltration chances. The DDoS and IP tracking attacks threaten user trust and financial and information security in the decentralized metaverse.

11.7 Conclusion

The progress of establishing a safe intelligent network for the metaverse is hindered by the need for precise coordination, secure and dependable transmission and processing of data, as well as the necessary equipment. In light of the evolving communication and processing demands, as well as the security challenges faced in the metaverse's development, we have examined the latest advancements in blockchain and intelligent networking.

To achieve the integration and interaction of the virtual and real worlds, the metaverse relies on a network that is both realistic and authentic. Therefore, we have examined the ways in which blockchain and intelligent networking may improve distributed computing, network and equipment management, and blockchain optimization to establish a more dependable, secure, and efficient ecosystem that will provide users with engaging experiences. In addition, we have addressed current challenges and identified potential areas of research in infrastructure, security, privacy, and the integration of communication and computers. This serves as a valuable reference for future studies conducted by researchers.

AI disclosure statement: The author confirms that no artificial intelligence (AI)-generated content or AI-assisted writing tools were used in the preparation of this chapter (including summaries and the abstract). All text, analysis, and conclusions are the result of the author's original work.

References

1. Alja'afreh, M., *et al.*, Metaverse through Blockchain and Intelligent Networking: A Comprehensive Survey. *2023 Fifth International Conference on Blockchain Computing and Applications (BCCA)*, IEEE, 2023.
2. Panda, S.K., Jena, A.K., Swain, S.K., Satapathy, S.C. (Eds.), *Blockchain Technology: Applications and Challenges*, Springer, Intelligent Systems Reference Library, https://doi.org/10.1007/978-3-030-69395-4.
3. Murala, D.K., METAEDUCATION: State-of-the-Art Methodology for Empowering Feature Education. *IEEE Access*, 12, 57992–58020, 2024, doi: 10.1109/ACCESS.2024.3391903.
4. Murala, D.K., Panda, S.K., Dash, S.P., MedMetaverse: Medical Care of Chronic Disease Patients and Managing Data Using Artificial Intelligence, Blockchain, and Wearable Devices State-of-the-Art Methodology. *IEEE Access*, 11, 138954–138985, 2023, doi: 10.1109/ACCESS.2023.3340791.
5. Dhaya, R. and Kanthavel, R., Elaborative Investigation of Blockchain Technology in Intelligent Networks, in: *Advancing Smarter and More Secure Industrial Applications Using AI, IoT, and Blockchain Technology*, DOI: 10.4018/978-1-7998-8367-8.ch004.
6. Murala, D.K. and Panda, S.K., Artificial Intelligence in the Development of Metaverse, in: *Metaverse, and Immersive Technologies: An Introduction to Industrial, Business and Social Applications*, pp. 407–436, John Wiley & Sons, Inc., 2023/10/20, https://doi.org/10.1002/9781394177165.ch15.
7. Murala, D.K. and Panda, S.K., Metaverse: A Study on Immersive Technologies, in: *Metaverse, and Immersive Technologies: An Introduction to*

Industrial, Business and Social Applications, pp. 1–41, John Wiley & Sons, Inc., 2023/10/20, https://doi.org/10.1002/9781394177165.ch1.
8. Murala, D.K. and Panda, S.K., The Internet of Things in Developing Metaverse, in: *Metaverse, and Immersive Technologies: An Introduction to Industrial, Business and Social Applications*, pp. 437–465, John Wiley & Sons, Inc., 2023/10/20, https://doi.org/10.1002/9781394177165.ch16.
9. Murala, D.K. and Panda, S.K., Blockchain in the Development of Metaverse, in: *Metaverse, and Immersive Technologies: An Introduction to Industrial, Business and Social Applications*, 28 September 2023, https://doi.org/10.1002/9781394177165.ch3.
10. Murala, D.K. and Panda, S.K., The Role of Immersive Reality (AR/VR/MR/XR), in: *Metaverse, Metaverse, and Immersive Technologies: An Introduction to Industrial, Business and Social Applications*, pp. 159–189, John Wiley & Sons, Inc., 2023/10/20, https://doi.org/10.1002/9781394177165.ch6.
11. Kumaresh, S. and Priya Iyer, K.B., Decentralised Artificial Intelligence Enabled Blockchain Network Model. *Turk. J. Comput. Math. Educ.*, 12, 10, 3797–3805, 2021.
12. Fu, Y., *et al.*, A survey of blockchain and intelligent networking for the metaverse. *IEEE Internet Things J.*, 10, 4, 3587–3610, 2022.
13. Diaz Rivera, J.J., Afaq, M., Song, W.-C., Blockchain and Intent-Based Networking: A Novel Approach to Secure and Accurate Network Policy Implementation. *2023 24th Asia-Pacific Network Operations and Management Symposium (APNOMS)*, Sejong, Korea, Republic of, pp. 77–82, 2023.
14. Varaprasada Rao, K., Murala, D.K., Panda, S.K., Blockchain: A Study of New Business Model, in: *Recent Advances in Blockchain Technology: Real-World Applications*, pp. 187–214, Springer International Publishing, 2023/2/12.
15. Kumar, K., Kumar, V., Seema, Sharma, M.K., Khan, A.A., Javed Idrisi, M., A Systematic Review of Blockchain Technology Assisted with Artificial Intelligence Technology for Networks and Communication Systems. *J. Comput. Networks Commun.*, 2024, 9979371, 2024, https://doi.org/10.1155/2024/9979371.
16. Lokre, S.S., Naman, V., Priya, S., Panda, S.K., Gun Tracking System Using Blockchain Technology, in: *Blockchain Technology: Applications and Challenges*, Intelligent Systems Reference Library, vol. 203, S.K. Panda, A.K. Jena, S.K. Swain, S.C. Satapathy (Eds.), Springer, Cham, 2021, https://doi.org/10.1007/978-3-030-69395-4_16.
17. Arza, M.S. and Panda, S.K., An Integration of Blockchain and Machine Learning into the Health Care System, in: *Machine Learning Adoption in Blockchain-Based Intelligent Manufacturing*, vol. 1, pp. 33–58, DOI: 10.1201/9781003252009-3.
18. Maksymyuk, T., *et al.*, Blockchain-based intelligent network management for 5G and beyond. *2019 3rd international conference on advanced information and communications technologies (AICT)*, IEEE, 2019.

19. Murala, D.K., Panda, S.K., Sahoo, S.K., Securing Electronic Health Record System in Cloud Environment Using Blockchain Technology, in: *Recent Advances in Blockchain Technology*, Intelligent Systems Reference Library, vol. 237, V. Mishra, S.P. Dash, A.K. Pani (Eds.), Springer, Cham, 2023, https://doi.org/10.1007/978-3-031-22835-3_4.
20. Nanda, S.K., Panda, S.K., Das, M., Satapathy, S.C., Automating Vehicle Insurance Process Using Smart Contract and Ethereum, in: *Advances in Micro-Electronics, Embedded Systems and IoT*, Lecture Notes in Electrical Engineering, vol. 838, V.V.S.S.S. Chakravarthy, W. Flores-Fuentes, V. Bhateja, B. Biswal, (Eds.), Springer, Singapore, 2022, https://doi.org/10.1007/978-981-16-8550-7_23.
21. Panda, S.K., Dash, S.P., Jena, A.K., Optimization of Block Query Response Using Evolutionary Algorithm, in: *Data Engineering and Intelligent Computing*, Advances in Intelligent Systems and Computing, vol. 1, V. Bhateja, S.C. Satapathy, C.M. Travieso-González, V.N.M. Aradhya (Eds.), Springer, Singapore, 2021, https://doi.org/10.1007/978-981-16-0171-2_54.
22. Panda, S.K., Rao, D.C., Satapathy, S.C., An Investigation into the Usability of Blockchain Technology in the Internet of Things, in: *Data Engineering and Intelligent Computing*, Advances in Intelligent Systems and Computing, vol. 1, V. Bhateja, S.C. Satapathy, C.M. Travieso-González, V.N.M. Aradhya (Eds.), Springer, Singapore, 2021, https://doi.org/10.1007/978-981-16-0171-2_53.
23. Panda, S.K. and Satapathy, S.C., An Investigation into Smart Contract Deployment on Ethereum Platform Using Web3.js and Solidity Using Blockchain, in: *Data Engineering and Intelligent Computing*, Advances in Intelligent Systems and Computing, vol. 1, V. Bhateja, S.C. Satapathy, C.M. Travieso-González, V.N.M. Aradhya (Eds.), Springer, Singapore, 2021, https://doi.org/10.1007/978-981-16-0171-2_52.
24. Panda, S.K., Mohammad, G.B., Nandan Mohanty, S., Sahoo, S., Smart contract-based land registry system to reduce frauds and time delay. *Secur. Privacy*, e172, 2021, https://doi.org/10.1002/spy2.172.
25. Panda, S.K., Elngar, A.A., Balas, V.E., Kayed, M. (Eds.), *Bitcoin and Blockchain: History and Current Applications*, 1st ed., CRC Press, 2020, https://doi.org/10.1201/9781003032588.
26. Panda, S.K. and Satapathy, S.C., Drug traceability and transparency in medical supply chain using blockchain for easing the process and creating trust between stakeholders and consumers. *Pers. Ubiquitous Comput.*, 2021, https://doi.org/10.1007/s00779-021-01588-3.
27. Yang, R., Yu, F.R., Si, P., Yang, Z., Zhang, Y., Integrated Blockchain and Edge Computing Systems: A Survey, Some Research Issues and Challenges. *IEEE Commun. Surv. Tutor.*, 21, 2, 1508–1532, Second quarter 2019, doi: 10.1109/COMST.2019.2894727.
28. Panda, S.K., Daliyet, S.P., Lokre, S.S., Naman, V., Distributed Ledger Technology in the Construction Industry Using Corda, in: *The New Advanced*

Society: Artificial Intelligence and Industrial Internet of Things Paradigm, https://doi.org/10.1002/9781119884392.ch2.
29. Sathya, A.R., Panda, S.K., Hanumanthakari, S., Enabling Smart Education System Using Blockchain Technology, in: *Blockchain Technology: Applications and Challenges*, Intelligent Systems Reference Library, vol. 203, S.K. Panda, A.K. Jena, S.K. Swain, S.C. Satapathy (Eds.), Springer, Cham, 2021, https://doi.org/10.1007/978-3-030-69395-4_10.
30. Niveditha, V.R., Sekaran, K., Amandeep Singh, K., Panda, S.K., Effective prediction of bitcoin price using wolf search algorithm and bidirectional LSTM on the internet of things data. *Int. J. Syst. Syst. Eng.*, 11, 3–4, 224–236.
31. Varaprasada Rao, K. and Panda, S.K., A Design Model of Copyright Protection System Based on Distributed Ledger Technology, in: *Computer Communication, Networking and IoT*, Lecture Notes in Networks and Systems, vol. 459, S.C. Satapathy, J.C.W. Lin, L.K. Wee, V. Bhateja, T.M. Rajesh, (Eds.), Springer, Singapore, 2023, https://doi.org/10.1007/978-981-19-1976-3_17.
32. Varaprasada Rao, K. and Panda, S.K., Secure Electronic Voting (E-voting) System Based on Blockchain on Various Platforms, in: *Computer Communication, Networking and IoT*, Lecture Notes in Networks and Systems, vol. 459, S.C. Satapathy, J.C.W. Lin, L.K. Wee, V. Bhateja, T.M. Rajesh, (Eds.), Springer, Singapore, 2023, https://doi.org/10.1007/978-981-19-1976-3_18.
33. Liu, Y., Yu, F.R., Li, X., Ji, H., Leung, V.C.M., Blockchain and Machine Learning for Communications and Networking Systems. *IEEE Commun. Surv. Tutor.*, 22, 2, 1392–1431, Second quarter 2020, doi: 10.1109/COMST.2020.2975911.
34. Chen, Y., Li, J., Liu, Z., Zheng, Z., Lin, P., Hu, R., Wang, M., A study of the theory of chain-network integration between blockchain and enterprise network. *Proc. SPIE 12079, Second IYSF Academic Symposium on Artificial Intelligence and Computer Engineering, 1207909*, 1 December 2021, https://doi.org/10.1117/12.2622717.
35. Yu, S., Ahmed, N., Wang, R., Anchor: An NDN-Based Blockchain Network, in: *Applied Cryptography in Computer and Communications, AC3 2021*, Lecture Notes of the Institute for Computer Sciences, Social Informatics and Telecommunications Engineering, vol. 386, B. Chen, and X. Huang (Eds.), Springer, Cham, 2021, https://doi.org/10.1007/978-3-030-80851-8_1.
36. Murala, D.K., Panda, S.K., Swain, S.K., A survey on cloud computing security and privacy issues and challenges. *J. Adv. Res. Dyn. Control Syst.*, 11, 1276–1290, 2019.
37. Murala, D.K., Panda, S.K., Swain, S.K., Secure dynamic groups data sharing with modified revocable attribute-based encryption in cloud. *Int. J. Recent Technol. Eng. (IJRTE)*, 8, 4, 2019, ISSN: 2277-3878.
38. Murala, D.K., Panda, S.K., Swain, S.K., A novel hybrid approach for providing data security and privacy from malicious attacks in the cloud environment. *J. Adv. Res. Dyn. Control Syst.*, 11, 1291–1300, 2019.

39. Panda, S.K., Swain, S.K., Mall, R., An investigation into usability aspects of E-Commerce websites using users' preferences. *Adv. Comput. Sci.: Int. J.*, 4, 1, 65–73, 2015.
40. Panda, S.K., Swain, S.K., Mall, R., Measuring Web Site Usability Quality Complexity Metrics for Navigability, in: *Intelligent Computing, Communication and Devices*, Advances in Intelligent Systems and Computing, vol. 308, L. Jain, S. Patnaik, N. Ichalkaranje (Eds.), Springer, New Delhi, 2015, https://doi.org/10.1007/978-81-322-2012-1_41.
41. Panda, S.K., A Usability Evaluation Framework for B2C E-Commerce Websites. *Comput. Eng. Intell. Syst.*, 5, 3, 66–85, 2014.
42. Bhalerao, V., Panda, S.K., Jena, A.K., Optimization of Loss Function on Human Faces Using Generative Adversarial Networks, in: *Machine Learning Approaches for Urban Computing*, Studies in Computational Intelligence, vol. 968, M. Bandyopadhyay, M. Rout, S. Chandra Satapathy (Eds.), Springer, Singapore, 2021, https://doi.org/10.1007/978-981-16-0935-0_9.
43. Panda, S.K. and Dwivedi, M., Minimizing Food Wastage Using Machine Learning: A Novel Approach, in: *Smart Intelligent Computing and Applications*, Smart Innovation, Systems and Technologies, vol. 159, S. Satapathy, V. Bhateja, J. Mohanty, S. Udgata, (Eds.), Springer, Singapore, 2020, https://doi.org/10.1007/978-981-13-9282-5_44.
44. Panda, S.K., Sathya, A.R., Mishra, M., Satpathy, S., A supervised learning algorithm to forecast weather conditions for playing cricket. *Int. J. Innov. Technol. Explor. Eng. (IJITEE)*, 9, 1, 2019.
45. Panda, S.K., Fraud-Resistant Crowdfunding System Using Ethereum Blockchain, in: *Bitcoin and Blockchain*, pp. 237–276, 2020.
46. Panda, S.K., Mishra, V., Balamurali, R., Elngar, A.A., *Artificial Intelligence and Machine Learning in Business Management Concepts, Challenges, and Case Studies*, pp. 1–278, https://doi.org/10.1201/9781003125129.
47. Joshi, S., Panda, S.K., Ar, S., Optimal Deep Learning Model to Identify the Development of Pomegranate Fruit in Farms. *Int. J. Innov. Technol. Explor. Eng.*, 9, 3, 2352–2356, 2020.
48. Puranam, K.S.RK., Gaddam, M.C.T., K, V.P.R., Panda, S.K., Reddy, G.S.M., Anatomy and Lifecycle of a Bitcoin Transaction. *Proceedings of International Conference on Sustainable Computing in Science, Technology and Management (SUSCOM)*, Amity University Rajasthan, Jaipur - India, February 18, 2019, Available at SSRN: https://ssrn.com/abstract=3355106 or http://dx.doi.org/10.2139/ssrn.3355106.
49. Panda, S.K. and Swain, S.K., Quality Assurance Aspects of Web Design, in: *Design Solutions for Improving Website Quality and Effectiveness*, pp. 87–129, IGI Global, 2016.
50. Panda, S.K., Bhalerao, V., Ar, S., A Machine Learning Model to Identify Duplicate Questions in Social Media Forums. *Int. J. Innov. Technol. Explor. Eng.*, 9, 4, 370–373, 2020.

51. Ahmareen, S., Raj, A., Potluri, S., Panda, S.K., Book Shala: An Android-Based Application Design and Implementation of Sharing Books, in: *Smart Intelligent Computing and Applications*, Smart Innovation, Systems and Technologies, vol. 159, S. Satapathy, V. Bhateja, J. Mohanty, S. Udgata (Eds.), Springer, Singapore, 2020, https://doi.org/10.1007/978-981-13-9282-5_28.
52. Panda, S.K., Das, S.S., Swain, S.K., S-Model for Service-Oriented Applications in Web Engineering. *Regional College of Management*, 10, 3, 38–46, 2013.
53. Panda, S.K., An Investigation into Usability and Productivity of ECommerce Websites.
54. Panda, S.K., Chandrasekhar, A., Gantayat, P.K., Panda, M.R., Detecting Brain Tumor Using Image Segmentation: A Novel Approach, in: *Data Engineering and Intelligent Computing*, Lecture Notes in Networks and Systems, vol. 446, V. Bhateja, L. Khin Wee, J.C.W. Lin, S.C. Satapathy, T.M. Rajesh, (Eds.), Springer, Singapore, 2022, https://doi.org/10.1007/978-981-19-1559-8_35.
55. Sanghi, P., Panda, S.K., Pati, C., Gantayat, P.K., Learning Deep Features and Classification for Fresh or off Vegetables to Prevent Food Wastage Using Machine Learning Algorithms, in: *Intelligent Data Engineering and Analytics*, Smart Innovation, Systems and Technologies, vol. 266, S.C. Satapathy, P. Peer, J. Tang, V. Bhateja, A. Ghosh, (Eds.), Springer, Singapore, 2022, https://doi.org/10.1007/978-981-16-6624-7_44.
56. Gantayat, P.K., Mohapatra, S., Panda, S.K., Secure Trust Level Routing in Delay-Tolerant Network with Node Categorization Technique, in: *Intelligent Data Engineering and Analytics*, Smart Innovation, Systems and Technologies, vol. 266, S.C. Satapathy, P. Peer, J. Tang, V. Bhateja, A. Ghosh, (Eds.), Springer, Singapore, 2022, https://doi.org/10.1007/978-981-16-6624-7_45.
57. Panda, S.K., Urkude, S.V., Urkude, V.R., Vairachilai, S., An investigation into COVID 19 pandemic in India, in: *The New Advanced Society: Artificial Intelligence and Industrial Internet of Things Paradigm*, vol. 1, pp. 289–305, Wiley.
58. Panda, S.K., Das, S., Swain, S.K., Web Site Productivity Measurement Using Single Task Size Measure. *J. Inf. Sci. Comput. Technol. (JISCT)*, 4, 3, October 12, 2015.
59. Hanumanthakari, S. and Panda, S.K., Detecting Face Mask for Prevent COVID-19 Using Deep Learning: A Novel Approach, in: *Smart Intelligent Computing and Applications, Volume 2*, Smart Innovation, Systems and Technologies, vol. 283, S.C. Satapathy, V. Bhateja, M.N. Favorskaya, T. Adilakshmi, (Eds.), Springer, Singapore, 2022, https://doi.org/10.1007/978-981-16-9705-0_45.
60. Panda, S.K., Sathya, A.R., Das, S., Bitcoin: Beginning of the Cryptocurrency Era, in: *Recent Advances in Blockchain Technology*, Intelligent Systems Reference Library, vol. 237, S.K. Panda, V. Mishra, S.P. Dash, A.K. Pani, (Eds.), Springer, Cham, 2023, https://doi.org/10.1007/978-3-031-22835-3_2.
61. Panda, S.K., Mishra, V., Dash, S.P., Pani, A.K., *Recent Advances in Blockchain Technology Real-World Applications*, Intelligent Systems Reference Library (ISRL, volume 237), vol. 1, pp. 1–317, 978-3-031-22835-3.

62. Panda, S.K., Mohapatra, R.K., Panda, S., Balamurugan, S., *The New Advanced Society: Artificial Intelligence and Industrial Internet of Things Paradigm*, vol. 1, pp. 1–512, John Wiley & Sons, DOI:10.1002/9781119884392.
63. Nanda, S.K., Panda, S.K., Das, M., Satapathy, S.C., Decentralization of Car Insurance System Using Machine Learning and Distributed Ledger Technology, in: *Intelligent Data Engineering and Analytics, FICTA 2022*, Smart Innovation, Systems and Technologies, vol. 327, V. Bhateja, X.S. Yang, J. Chun-Wei Lin, R. Das, (Eds.), Springer, Singapore, 2023, https://doi.org/10.1007/978-981-19-7524-0_52.
64. Nanda, S.K., Panda, S.K., Dash, M., Medical supply chain integrated with blockchain and IoT to track the logistics of medical products. *Multimed. Tools Appl.*, 82, 32917–32939, 2023, https://doi.org/10.1007/s11042-023-14846-8.
65. Panda, S.K., Jena, A.K., Panda, M.R., *et al.*, Speech emotion recognition using multimodal feature fusion with machine learning approach. *Multimed. Tools Appl.*, 82, 42763–42781, 2023, https://doi.org/10.1007/s11042-023-15275-3.
66. Panda, S.K. and Mohanty, S.N., Time Series Forecasting and Modeling of Food Demand Supply Chain Based on Regressors Analysis. *IEEE Access*, 11, 42679–42700, 2023, doi: 10.1109/ACCESS.2023.3266275.
67. Desai, D.D., *et al.*, Optimal Ambulance Positioning for Road Accidents With Deep Embedded Clustering. *IEEE Access*, 11, 59917–59934, 2023, doi: 10.1109/ACCESS.2023.3284993.
68. Lakshmi, L., Devi, K.D.S., Gupta, S., Reddy, K.A.N., Grandhi, S.K., Panda, S.K., WOMT: Wasserstein Distribution Based Minimization of False Positives in Breast Tumor Classification Using Deep Learning. *IEEE Access*, 11, 57831–57842, 2023, doi: 10.1109/ACCESS.2023.3279496.
69. Mishra, P. and Panda, S.K., Dependency Structure-Based Rules Using Root Node Technique for Explicit Aspect Extraction From Online Reviews. *IEEE Access*, 11, 65117–65137, 2023, doi: 10.1109/ACCESS.2023.3287830.
70. Routray, N., Rout, S.K., Sahu, B., Panda, S.K., Godavarthi, D., Ensemble Learning With Symbiotic Organism Search Optimization Algorithm for Breast Cancer Classification and Risk Identification of Other Organs on Histopathological Images. *IEEE Access*, 11, 110544–110557, 2023, doi: 10.1109/ACCESS.2023.3322222.
71. Agarwal, R., Pande, S.D., Mohanty, S.N., Panda, S.K., A Novel Hybrid System of Detecting Brain Tumors in MRI. *IEEE Access*, 11, 118372–118385, 2023, doi: 10.1109/ACCESS.2023.3326447.
72. Nayak, S.K., Garanayak, M., Swain, S.K., Panda, S.K., Godavarthi, D., An Intelligent Disease Prediction and Drug Recommendation Prototype by Using Multiple Approaches of Machine Learning Algorithms. *IEEE Access*, 11, 99304–99318, 2023, doi: 10.1109/ACCESS.2023.3314332.
73. Gupta, A., Gandhi, R., Jatana, N., Jatain, D., Panda, S.K., Ramesh, J.V.N., A Severity Assessment of Python Code Smells. *IEEE Access*, 11, 119146–119160, 2023, doi: 10.1109/ACCESS.2023.3327553.

74. Sethi, B.K., Singh, D., Rout, S.K., Panda, S.K., Long Short-Term Memory-Deep Belief Network-Based Gene Expression Data Analysis for Prostate Cancer Detection and Classification. *IEEE Access*, 12, 1508–1524, 2024, doi: 10.1109/ACCESS.2023.3346925.
75. Mahapatra, A., Majhi, S.K., Mishra, K., Pradhan, R., Rao, D.C., Panda, S.K., An Energy-Aware Task Offloading and Load Balancing for Latency-Sensitive IoT Applications in the Fog-Cloud Continuum. *IEEE Access*, 12, 14334–14349, 2024, doi: 10.1109/ACCESS.2024.3357122.
76. Mishra, P., Sharma, O., Panda, S.K., ADN-BERT: Attention-Based Deep Network Model Using BERT for Sarcasm Classification, in: *Evolution in Computational Intelligence, FICTA 2023*, Smart Innovation, Systems and Technologies, vol. 370, V. Bhateja, X.S. Yang, M.C. Ferreira, S.S. Sengar, C.M. Travieso-Gonzalez (Eds.), Springer, Singapore, 2023, https://doi.org/10.1007/978-981-99-6702-5_51.
77. Varaprasada Rao, K. and Panda, S.K., Initiation, Innovation, Implementation and Integration of CBDC in Digital Virtual Payment Systems, in: *Advances in Microelectronics, Embedded Systems and IoT, ICMEET 2023*, Lecture Notes in Electrical Engineering, vol. 1156, V.V.S.S.S. Chakravarthy, V. Bhateja, J. Anguera, S. Urooj, A. Ghosh, (Eds.), Springer, Singapore, 2024, https://doi.org/10.1007/978-981-97-0767-6_20.
78. Panda, S.K., Revolution of the Metaverse and Blockchain Technology, in: *Metaverse and Immersive Technologies: An Introduction to Industrial Business and Social Applications*, Wiley, Hoboken, NJ, USA, 2023.
79. Sahoo, S.K., Das, S., Panda, S.K., Alzheimer's Disease Classification Using Brain MRI Based on 2D CNN and Transfer Learning, in: *Proceedings of the 6th International Conference on Communications and Cyber Physical Engineering, ICCCE 2024*, Lecture Notes in Electrical Engineering, vol. 1096, A. Kumar, and Mozar, (Eds.), Springer, Singapore, 2024, https://doi.org/10.1007/978-981-99-7137-4_1.
80. Panda, S.K., Ramesh, J.V.N., Ghosh, H., Rahat, I.S., Sobur, A., Bijoy, M.H., Yesubabu, M., Deep Learning in Medical Imaging: A Case Study on Lung Tissue Classification. *EAI Endorsed Trans. Pervasive Health Technol.*, 10, 2024.
81. Paruchuri, V.N.L.L., Shaik, A.H., Murala, D.K., Panda, S.K., IoT-Enabled Neural Network Analysis for Early Detection and Prediction of Mental Depression, in: *Information System Design: Communication Networks and IoT, ISDIA 2024*, Lecture Notes in Networks and Systems, vol. 1057, V. Bhateja, J. Tang, D.K. Sharma, Z. Polkowski, A. Ahmad, (Eds.), pp. 257–268, Springer, Singapore, 2024, https://doi.org/10.1007/978-981-97-4895-2_21.
82. Paruchuri, V.N.L.L., Malaviya, M.P., Murala, D.K., Panda, S.K., Connecting IoT Sensors for Enhanced Dementia Disease Monitoring and Intervention, in: *Information System Design: Communication Networks and IoT, ISDIA 2024*, Lecture Notes in Networks and Systems, vol. 1057, V. Bhateja, J. Tang,

D.K. Sharma, Z. Polkowski, A. Ahmad, (Eds.), pp. 269–281, Springer, Singapore, 2024, https://doi.org/10.1007/978-981-97-4895-2_22.

83. Panda, S.K., Das, S., Sahoo, S.K., Predominant Music Genre Classification Using Machine Learning Approach, in: *Signal Processing, Telecommunication and Embedded Systems with AI and ML Applications, ICMEET 2023*, Lecture Notes in Electrical Engineering, vol. 1281, V. Bhateja, V.V.S.S.S. Chakravarthy, J. Anguera, A. Ghosh, W. Flores Fuentes, (Eds.), Springer, Singapore, 2025, https://doi.org/10.1007/978-981-97-8422-6_17.
84. Panda, S.K., Das, S., Sahoo, S.K., Vehicle Detection and Classification Using Intelligent Systems, in: *Signal Processing, Telecommunication and Embedded Systems with AI and ML Applications, ICMEET 2023*, Lecture Notes in Electrical Engineering, vol. 1281, V. Bhateja, V.V.S.S.S. Chakravarthy, J. Anguera, A. Ghosh, W. Flores Fuentes, (Eds.), Springer, Singapore, 2025, https://doi.org/10.1007/978-981-97-8422-6_18.
85. Chandrasekhar, A., Dodhiawala, Z., Panda, S.K., An Investigation into Chronic Kidney Disease Based-on Classification Model, in: *Signal Processing, Telecommunication and Embedded Systems with AI and ML Applications, ICMEET 2023*, Lecture Notes in Electrical Engineering, vol. 1281, V. Bhateja, V.V.S.S.S. Chakravarthy, J. Anguera, A. Ghosh, W. Flores Fuentes, (Eds.), Springer, Singapore, 2025, https://doi.org/10.1007/978-981-97-8422-6_19.
86. Chandrashekhar, A., Saheb, S.H., Panda, S.K., Balamurugan, S., Peng, S.-L., *Metaverse and Immersive Technologies: An Introduction to Industrial, Business and Social Applications*, John Wiley & Sons, 2023.

12

Role of AI in Digital Immune Systems

Sanjay Fuloria

Operations and IT, ICFAI Business School (IBS), Hyderabad, India

Abstract

This chapter explores the integration and critical role of artificial intelligence (AI) in digital immune systems, illustrating AI's transformative capabilities in contemporary cybersecurity practices. Drawing parallels between biological immune systems and digital defenses, it highlights how AI technologies, including machine learning (ML), deep learning, and natural language processing, enable real-time anomaly detection, rapid response, and adaptive threat mitigation. The evolution of digital immune systems, from early antivirus methods to advanced AI-driven cybersecurity frameworks, underscores AI's significance in addressing the increasing complexity and scale of modern cyber threats. The chapter further discusses the application of various ML approaches, including supervised, unsupervised, and reinforcement learning, alongside advanced deep learning models such as convolutional neural networks and auto encoders, in identifying sophisticated cyber threats. Practical examples from sectors like finance, healthcare, manufacturing, and public services illustrate both successes and challenges in deploying AI-driven cybersecurity. Finally, the chapter identifies critical implementation challenges, ethical concerns, regulatory constraints, and emerging research directions, highlighting the necessity for balanced governance and continuous innovation in AI applications within digital immune systems.

***Keywords*:** Artificial intelligence, digital immune systems, cybersecurity, machine learning, deep learning, anomaly detection, real-time threat intelligence, ethical AI

Email: sanjay.fuloria@ibsindia.org

Sujata Priyambada Dash, Vaibhav Mishra, Bijeta Shaw, Sandeep Kumar Panda and S. Balamurugan (eds.) Digital Immune System: Principles and Practices, (269–288) © 2026 Scrivener Publishing LLC

12.1 Introduction

Modern organizations are grappling with an unprecedented scale and sophistication of cyber threats. Traditional security methods—firewalls, antivirus applications, and signature-based detection—face significant limitations when encountering newer types of malicious intrusions (Harmer, Williams, Gunsch, & Lamont, 2002) [12]. Consequently, the analogy of a "digital immune system" has emerged, modelled after biological immune responses to harmful pathogens. The aim is to continuously monitor systems, detect abnormal patterns, and execute coordinated countermeasures.

Artificial intelligence (AI), encompassing technologies like machine learning (ML), deep learning, and natural language processing (NLP), has proven pivotal in supporting digital immune systems (Dasgupta, 1999) [7]. Unlike purely rules-based security methods, AI-driven solutions can grow more adept with experience. They can spot unconventional behavior, detect zero-day exploits, and quickly adapt to unpredictable attack vectors. For example, AI systems train on massive troves of log data and real-time signals from networks, giving them the ability to pinpoint suspicious deviations in user activity or process behavior (Forrest, Perelson, Allen, & Cherukuri, 1994) [9].

Looking back historically, the roots of digital immune strategies date to the 1990s when IBM first developed methods to automatically quarantine computer viruses, an early approach to continuous, self-updating threat defense (White, 1997) [33]. Over time, the sheer growth in network traffic and the complexity of malware demanded more powerful solutions. Artificial intelligence, by harnessing vast data sets and learning algorithms, has become the backbone of next-generation cyber defense platforms.

Given the explosion in cloud computing, remote work arrangements, and the Internet of Things (IoT), the "attack surface" has multiplied, making the job of human analysts nearly impossible to handle alone. The AI-driven digital immune systems respond by autonomously correlating threat information, isolating compromised endpoints, and enhancing detection by learning from every new attack (Kim, Bentley, & Timmis, 2008) [16]. Critics point to potential downsides, such as data privacy concerns, algorithmic bias, and the vulnerability of AI models to adversarial exploitation (Brundage *et al.*, 2018) [4]. Despite these critiques, AI's role in strengthening the capacity for real-time defense is widely recognized as transformative.

In this chapter, we will discuss how digital immune systems are organized, the role of AI and ML, real world examples, ethical issues, and trends in research. Based on both the achievements and failures, the present situation will be presented along with potential future developments. By the end of this chapter, it will be clear that while all the AI-based immune systems are not perfect, then again, their adaptive features are essential for any effective cybersecurity measure.

12.2 Origin of Digital Immune Systems

The idea of digital immune systems can be dated as far back as the 1990s, when researchers first experimented with translating ideas from immunology to computer security (Forrest *et al.*, 1994) [9]. The concept of IBM's early "digital immune system" was one of the first to propose the idea of a system that could detect and remedy computer viruses without human intervention (White, 1997) [33]. This was based on a feedback loop in which viruses could be quickly identified, analyzed, and removed — an approach, obviously, antedating the present concept of continuous threat monitoring.

Almost in parallel, the field of artificial immune systems (AIS) developed to focus on computational implementations of biological immune systems (Dasgupta, 1999) [7]. Research on AIS simulated biological responses to invasion and proposed negative selection, clonal selection, and immune network theories to mimic biological strategies for recognizing and responding to invasive threats. Within the context of cybersecurity, these ideas were applied to anomaly-based intrusion detection, where "non-self" patterns were flagged as potentially malicious.

By the early 2000s, the quantity and variety of cyber threats had grown to include DDoS attacks, spyware, and advanced types of malware. Since signature-based tools were often ineffective against new variants of threats as they became recognized even after the threat and its signature had been discovered leaving networks exposed (Kephart & Chess, 2003) [15]. To this end, researchers sought adaptive defenses—those that could learn from their environment and identify anomalies independent of known signatures.

This period also saw the growth of autonomic computing concepts, which suggested that systems should be capable of self-healing and self-protection. These ideas mesh well with the concept of a digital immune system. While theoretical frameworks were plentiful, practical applications often stumbled due to limited computing resources and the challenge of collecting and labelling large datasets for training (Harmer *et al.*, 2002) [12].

As advanced persistent threats (APTs) began to dominate headlines, the focus shifted to stealthy, continuous infiltration strategies used by attackers. In reaction, numerous security tools started integrating machine learning techniques to catch subtle anomalies. Even so, many early products operated in silos, for example, endpoint-focused solutions or network-centric sensors, rather than an integrated, immune-like structure across the entire organization.

Fast-forward to the current era, and we see a complex interplay of threat intelligence services, user behavior analytics, and automated response platforms (Shaukat & Zhu, 2022) [30]. These composite solutions reflect a growing ambition to emulate a biological immune system at scale: continuous detection, swift quarantine, thorough remediation, and reinforcement of defenses for the next wave of threats. By appreciating this evolution, we gain insight into both how far technology has come, and which limitations remain. As the following pages will be discussed, these underlying concepts directly illuminate the way AI intersects with modern digital immune systems, promising ever more dynamic and proactive security capabilities.

12.3 Underlying Principles of Digital Immune Systems

Drawing on parallels with human biology, digital immune systems hinge on a series of foundational principles that collectively foster resilience and adaptation. In immunology, the body recognizes its own tissues (self) and mounts a defensive response only when encountering foreign agents (non-self). Transposed onto cybersecurity, this translates to thorough modeling of "normal" behavior—such as baseline network activity and system usage—so that anomalies can be flagged (Forrest *et al.*, 1994) [9]. Just as the immune system adjusts its response after repeated exposures to a pathogen, a digital immune system must refine its threat detection algorithms over time. Machine learning allows for iterative improvements, continuously incorporating new insights to identify emerging exploit techniques and malicious signatures.

Biological immune responses are more effective after the first encounter. Analogously, digital systems aim to store threat patterns in a database so that similar attacks can be immediately identified. This function is reminiscent of caching known malicious indicators for prompt detection. Immune functions in the body occur within cells distributed throughout different organs. In a digital environment, sensors are likewise spread across endpoints, servers, and network layers. Each sensor independently identifies threats, enabling a collective feedback loop (Kim *et al.*, 2008) [16].

The human body uses various defenses—physical barriers, innate immunity, and adaptive immunity. Similarly, digital immune systems combine multiple layers: from perimeter firewalls and endpoint detection to behavioral analysis tools, ensuring redundancy in case one layer fails.

A hallmark of successful immune responses is swift, localized action before infection spreads. Translating that to cybersecurity, the digital immune system must isolate compromised endpoints and revoke suspicious credentials in near real-time to prevent lateral movement (Harmer *et al.*, 2002) [12].

Although these principles effectively bolster security, they rely heavily on automation and advanced analytics. Legacy methods that depend on static rules can identify known threats but falter in detecting zero-day or polymorphic attacks (Yin, Zhu, Fei, & He, 2019) [36]. This is where AI's ability to learn from evolving datasets becomes essential. As we shall see, each of these immunological concepts is amplified when combined with AI algorithms. The synergy enables more refined pattern recognition, faster identification of emerging threats, and a more coherent integration of different detection layers. Nonetheless, challenges like interpretability, potential biases in data, and adversarial attacks against AI models must be addressed. Consequently, adopting an immune-based model is not a one-time solution but a living system that calls for steady training, updates, and policy oversight.

12.4 Artificial Intelligence's Expanding Role in Cybersecurity

Artificial intelligence was a tech buzzword some years back. As on today it is very useful in dealing with cybersecurity. Speedy data analysis is possible to extract insights from large datasets that might otherwise have eluded traditional rules-based methods (Brundage *et al.*, 2018) [4]. In digital immune systems, the role of AI is to augment both the identification of threats and the automated responses.

Artificial intelligence is advanced in detecting patterns. This ability of AI helps with network traffic, application logs or device telemetry. The earlier systems were based on blacklists or static rules, machine learning algorithms—like Random Forests and Neural Networks—can filter anomalies from vast data. For example, they can detect an unexpected upward spike in data transfers to suspicious domains or unusual internal file access activities (Yin *et al.*, 2019) [36]. AI can anticipate breaches or vulnerabilities. Historical logs are studied and correlated with real time intelligence to estimate the probability of future attacks. This predictive power helps security teams address issues before they happen—like patching known flaws or tuning detection thresholds in high-risk areas. AI significantly simplifies the integration of external threat intelligence, such as lists of malicious IP addresses, known malware signatures, or attacker techniques, into local defense systems. Machine learning models can automatically merge these data streams and form a cohesive intelligence picture that evolves as new information arrives (Shaukat & Zhu, 2022) [30].

Some sophisticated cybersecurity tools now operate with minimal human oversight. Once the system flags a threat, AI can immediately block traffic, quarantine suspicious endpoints, and initiate forensic steps—like the self-healing functions in a biological immune system. This agility is crucial, given how quickly modern attacks can spread. AI helps unify data from numerous sources—user identity systems, network monitoring tools, and endpoint logs—to form a comprehensive view of user and system behavior. By detecting anomalies in context, AI can reduce false alarms and home in on genuine threats, whether they stem from external hacking attempts or insider misuse. Large companies generate terabytes of security-relevant data each day. This is because relying on these logs with only human analysts is impractical. They also scale better-than-manual approaches, providing consistent results even when the amount of data that comes in increases rapidly.

The advantages of utilizing AI in cybersecurity include its ability to accurately analyze threats in real-time, process vast amounts of data efficiently, quickly assess potential threats and their probabilities, and evaluate the likelihood and potential consequences of an attack. However, there are also drawbacks, such as biases in AI systems that may cause them to overlook certain threats or be deceived by advanced, sophisticated attacks. Additionally, ethical concerns, such as privacy invasion, must be addressed (Brundage *et al.*, 2018) [4]. Despite these challenges, AI remains an essential element for organizations aiming to defend against persistent and automated attackers. It supports the development of adaptive security policies that evolve dynamically, moving beyond static rule sets. This duality of promise and risk highlights the importance of exploring the specific machine learning techniques that underpin AI's role in digital immune frameworks.

12.5 Key Machine Learning Approaches in Digital Immune Systems

The heart of any modern AI-based cybersecurity system is ML. Various ML algorithms in digital immune systems enable the concept of continuous learning that is vital for effective and timely threat detection. Supervised learning is a category of training models on tagged data, where each sample is classified as either benign or malicious, is included. The models Logistic Regression and Gradient Boosted Decision Trees are trained on patterns of standard attack behaviors (Yin *et al.*, 2019) [36]. After being trained they can use their knowledge to classify new data and thus help in the real time detection of harmful activities, for instance, aggressive web requests that may contain structured query language injection attempts.

When it is not practical to exhaustively label the data, then methods like clustering or auto encoders become applicable. These methods are part of unsupervised learning. These algorithms reveal structure or anomalies in data (Kim *et al.*, 2008) [16]. This system can quickly focus on unusual or deviant behavior that might indicate a zero-day exploit by building up an understanding of what is 'normal' in the data. Semi-supervised learning combines the best aspects of both supervised and unsupervised learning techniques and uses a limited number of labelled examples and a large amount of unlabeled data. This approach is most effective when a user cannot afford the time or resources to label everything, especially since malware evolves constantly.

In reinforcement learning, an agent is trained to interact with an environment, receiving rewards or penalties as guidance. Applied to intrusion detection or response, it can iteratively improve actions for quarantining infected machines over time (Nguyen & Reddi, 2019) [24].

Transfer learning assists in accelerating model development by reusing features or entire models previously trained in a related domain. In cybersecurity, this might translate into adapting a model that has proven effective in detecting one form of malware to tackle another with overlapping indicators.

Ensemble methods amplify detection accuracy by integrating multiple ML models. Voting or stacking techniques are especially relevant in environments where data streams are diverse—like logs, network traffic, and endpoint telemetry. Each model specializes in one area, and their collective outputs create a more reliable verdict.

While these ML techniques are powerful, they also demand careful oversight. Without consistent retraining, models can suffer from "concept drift," a phenomenon in which malware behaviors evolve to evade detection. Additionally, challenges in data imbalance—where benign events vastly outnumber attacks—can skew model sensitivity (Batista, Prati, & Monard, 2004) [3]. Addressing these issues requires robust data management, continuous model updating, and vigilance against manipulation by adversaries. Still, the net result of integrating ML into digital immune systems is a far more nuanced, flexible, and responsive defense than any static rule set could achieve.

12.6 Deep Learning and Advanced Threat Identification

While classical ML algorithms have long served cybersecurity well, deep learning (DL) has emerged as a game-changer by enabling more sophisticated pattern identification and classification. Deep neural networks contain multiple layered transformations, allowing them to capture intricate correlations within large-scale data (LeCun, Bengio, & Hinton, 2015) [20].

Although convolutional neural networks (CNNs) are best known for processing images, they can be applied to network data that has been converted into matrix-like forms. By detecting subtle patterns in traffic payloads or command sequences, CNNs can unearth malicious activities concealed within otherwise legitimate-appearing data (Tobiyama *et al.*, 2016) [31].

Cyber intrusions often develop in stages, for instance, adversaries escalate their privileges or move laterally at a given time. Recurrent neural networks, especially those based on long short-term memory (LSTM) cells, are very good at processing sequential data because they can keep track of the ongoing context. These architectures are therefore very useful for identifying patterns of suspicious activity in user logins or system processes (Hochreiter & Schmidhuber, 1997) [14]. Auto encoders learn to compress normal data such that any input looks suspicious because of high reconstruction error (Sakurada & Yairi, 2014) [27]. This property is very useful in detecting zero-day attacks or any unusual data movement which may be a sign of a breach.

The two neural networks in a generative adversarial network oppose each other; one creates data and the other tells the difference between real and fake. On one hand, generative adversarial networks can expand the size of data sets with realistic examples for training. On the other hand, attackers can develop adversarial inputs to threaten the system, which has left researchers to find a way to counter such threats (Xie *et al.*, 2021) [34].

Although deep networks often require considerable processing resources, optimizations in inference (e.g., model pruning or graphical processing unit (GPU) acceleration) now enable real-time evaluation. In high-stakes settings, sub-second reaction times can stave off widespread system compromise (Madry *et al.*, 2018) [22].

Deep learning's complexity sparks concern around its "black box" nature, especially if false positives could disrupt critical infrastructure. Methods such as attention visualization or local interpretable model-agnostic explanations (LIME) aim to shed light on how neural networks reach conclusions, improving analyst trust (Samek, Wiegand, & Müller, 2017) [28].

By combining deep learning with established machine learning and rule-based systems, digital immune defenses gain a formidable arsenal (Xu *et al.*, 2018) [35]. Deep networks excel at capturing elusive patterns, while simpler models can remain more transparent and require fewer computational overheads. The synergy of these methods provides holistic coverage against a vast array of sophisticated, emerging, and even previously unknown threats (White, 1997) [33].

12.7 Artificial Immune Systems and Intrusion Detection

Before the ascendancy of mainstream AI, the field of AIS laid significant groundwork by adapting immunological strategies to cybersecurity (Dasgupta, 1999) [7]. Artificial immune systems emphasize specialized ideas like negative selection and clonal selection, which resonate with the core defenses of digital immune systems.

In biology, T-cells that react against self-peptides are eliminated, ensuring the immune system targets only foreign agents. Similarly, AIS methods develop "detectors" that differentiate normal system patterns from malicious activity. By carefully training these detectors to avoid flags on "self," AIS-based intrusion detection can cut down on false positives.

When the immune system detects a pathogen, certain cells replicate and mutate slightly, allowing a more targeted response. Translating this metaphorically, AIS-based cybersecurity solutions spawn multiple variants of a detector once it successfully identifies malicious behavior, broadening coverage against evolving threats.

Biological immune cells regulate and influence each other, maintaining a balanced response. In a digital immune model, detectors situated throughout various network points can share alerts, calibrate thresholds, and collectively refine detection accuracy.

Proposed by Polly Matzinger in immunology, danger theory posits those immune responses center on signals denoting actual harm. Within AIS, this concept can be applied by correlating anomalies with specific indicators of compromised functionality—high CPU usage, error spikes, or suspicious data transfers—thus reducing false alarms.

While AIS offers a compelling conceptual base, contemporary AI (especially ML and DL) supplies the computational rigor and scalability. Hybrid strategies thus evolve: AIS principles guide how the system organizes and refines its detection processes, while AI's algorithms handle the heavy lifting of real-time anomaly spotting and classification (Kim *et al.*, 2008) [16].

Some network intrusion detection systems apply AIS logic to monitor traffic at a packet level, distinguishing valid from suspicious flows. While many such tools remain experimental, they underscore the feasibility of immune-based designs. Combining AIS frameworks with other advanced methods, from user behavior analytics to deep learning, can yield an unusually robust, self-adapting security posture.

In this sense, AIS has influenced how cybersecurity specialists conceptualize self-adapting defenses. The synergy between AIS ideas—drawn straight from biology—and modern AI is central to constructing digital immune systems that relentlessly evolve alongside the threats they are meant to intercept.

12.8 Real-Time Threat Intelligence and Automated Orchestration

A digital immune system's value lies largely in its capacity to synthesize threat intelligence from numerous sources and respond almost instantly. Modern attacks can spread globally within minutes, leaving little room for manual triage. Consequently, emphasis has shifted to automated orchestration, tying together detection and response under a unified operational model.

Cybersecurity teams rely on diverse feeds from commercial vendors, governmental bodies, and open-source repositories that catalogue malicious IPs, emerging malware strains, and known attacker techniques. A digital immune system harnesses AI to reconcile these feeds with local logs, filtering out false positives and focusing on the most pertinent threats (Shaukat & Zhu, 2022) [30].

Security orchestration, automation, and response (SOAR) platforms act as the central hub for orchestrating and automating complex workflows. Once suspicious activity is flagged, a SOAR system can isolate the affected endpoint, gather forensic data, and notify relevant teams. Over time, these platforms refine their workflows using machine learning, enhancing accuracy and efficiency (Barocas and Selbst, 2016) [2].

Real-time threat data can cascade across multiple security components. If, for example, endpoint monitoring detects a stealthy PowerShell script, it can instantly inform the firewall to block further outbound connections. This interconnected approach reduces the intervals between discovery and response.

Honeypots bait attackers into revealing their methods. Artificial intelligence can dynamically reconfigure these decoys in line with the latest threat intelligence, making them more believable and more effective at gathering data. The findings from honeypot interactions then feed back into the digital immune system, incrementally improving detection logic (Kotenko & Stepashkin, 2006) [18].

12.9 Practical Examples and Case Studies

Many real-world deployments of AI-driven digital immune systems are now underway, offering insight into how these solutions fare in diverse environments. From banking to manufacturing, these examples underscore both the promise and the complexities of AI-centric security.

Financial institutions have been pioneers in AI-based fraud detection, analyzing transactional and authentication data in real time (Chandola, Banerjee, & Kumar, 2009) [5]. By swiftly isolating suspicious behavior, banks can pre-empt account takeovers and wire fraud. Some also deploy AI to monitor employee conduct, minimizing insider risk.

Medical centers are prime targets for ransom ware, given the value of patient data. The AI-based digital immune solutions in this realm typically involve anomaly detection across electronic health record systems and device communication channels. In a number of reported cases, early detection and swift containment have prevented widespread ransom ware infections (Harries, 2021) [13].

Manufacturing plants and supply-chain networks increasingly implement sensor-enabled devices for real-time process monitoring. Artificial intelligence can spot minor irregularities in these signals, detecting sabotage or operational malfunctions. Such immediate alerts help prevent both production slowdowns and data exfiltration (Lee, Bagheri, & Kao, 2015) [21].

Public-sector organizations grapple with highly varied data flows and legacy systems, making them susceptible to wide-ranging advanced persistent threats (APTs). By deploying AI to unify and assess data from different departments, some agencies have managed to spot stealthy infiltration attempts earlier. However, privacy and oversight remain key concerns in governmental contexts.

Chronicle, part of Alphabet, leverages massive-scale log analysis and AI to detect hidden threats (Alphabet Annual Report, 2019) [1]. Its platform integrates petabytes of historical data, enabling a form of "retroactive" detection—where recently uncovered threats can be traced back in time, illuminating potential infiltration points.

A cloud-based security information and event management (SIEM) and SOAR solution, Azure Sentinel uses AI to identify anomalies and orchestrate responses (Microsoft Documentation, 2023) [23]. Companies adopting Sentinel often remark on how AI has cut down false positives and accelerated incident resolution, echoing key digital immune principles.

These practical examples illustrate that AI, when harnessed effectively, can provide immense security benefits, from halting fraudulent banking transactions to fending off ransom ware in hospitals. Yet each scenario also highlights the need for thorough data governance, careful system tuning, and trained staff who can interpret and act on AI-generated alerts. Such implementations serve as tangible proof of concept for the digital immune system model.

12.10 Core Implementation Challenges

Despite their impressive features, AI-driven digital immune systems confront numerous hurdles during real-world deployment. Navigating these challenges is crucial to achieving robust, reliable protection.

Collecting, cleaning, and correlating data from multiple sources—endpoints, servers, network logs—can be overwhelming. Without standardized formats or consistent metadata, AI models may struggle to parse events accurately, causing detection gaps or confusion (Halevy, Norvig, & Pereira, 2009) [11].

Successful implementation often requires experts who merge cybersecurity knowledge with ML expertise. The intense demand for such professionals leads to staffing bottlenecks. Relying solely on vendor-based solutions might also prove expensive or lead to vendor lock-in.

High-end GPUs or specialized accelerators may be necessary for real-time deep learning. In the cloud, usage-based fees can spike, especially if models need continuous retraining. On-premises setups must handle not only hardware costs but also the complexities of maintaining data centers.

Most organizations already have firewalls, antivirus programs, and SIEMs. Artificial intelligence-driven digital immune systems must interoperate seamlessly with these solutions, exchanging data and orchestrating responses without conflicts. This integration can be nontrivial, particularly for older systems lacking robust application programming interfaces (APIs).

12.11 Regulatory Constraints

Financial, healthcare and critical infrastructure sectors follow strict compliance mandates that define how data can be collected, stored, and analyzed. The developers of AI must consider these mandates when developing everything from logging policies to data retention schedules. This is because of the penalties for noncompliance.

Shifting to an AI-first approach can frighten staff, who may worry that their job will be replaced or that they will have to work with new and complex tools. Organizational buy-ins are essential: employees must understand that AI augments, rather than replaces, human expertise.

The implementation of AI-based digital immunity is rarely a matter of flipping a switch. It needs holistic change – technological, procedural, and cultural. But for the entities willing to make these changes, the long-term security payoff can be significant. It produces a flexible and adaptive system that is much better than static perimeter-based defenses.

As AI-driven security gains popularity there is the need to establish governance. It ensures that the use of technology does not go against the organization's legal obligations, moral principles or business culture.

The European Commission's 'Ethics Guidelines for Trustworthy AI' (European Commission, 2019) [8] provide principles such as transparency, fairness and accountability for reference. These guidelines, however, are also relevant to the cybersecurity domain, which can sometimes focus unduly on certain groups and minorities.

A cross functional governance board comprising IT, security, risk management, legal and compliance representatives should oversee AI initiatives. They will establish what level of risk is acceptable, look at new and emerging regulations and make decisions on data protection and ethics. This is because training, updating, and deploying AI models leave a record of how the models were trained, updated, and deployed. These logs can be useful when investigating a breach or when trying to meet the requirements of a regulator or auditing firm. Some decisions, including turning off major systems, often require human input. Therefore, the use of the Human-in-the-Loop model ensures that there is always human oversight. This approach leverages the strength of AI for basic or time-critical incidents while having humans deal with the nuances and strategic issues. Organizations can restrict fully automated actions to clearly malicious behavior and implement phased responses. In cases where the stakes are higher, the system may seek human input. Such guardrails are important to limit the consequences of the AI's mistake. This is because AI-based defenses are dynamic and keep on evolving with the training; therefore, governance structures must be dynamic, as well. A governance board should regularly review emerging threats, new legislative guidelines and feedback from the internal environment to ensure that the digital immune system is properly functioning and is ethically sound.

In this way, organizations can mitigate the risks to their users, maintain public confidence and ensure legal compliance. When done properly, the resulting digital immune system is both effective and ethically sound, comprising of cutting-edge AI techniques combined with properly designed governance and oversight mechanisms.

12.12 Emerging Horizons and Research Directions

The interplay of AI and digital immune systems is still an emerging area that is driven by the evolution of security threats. Some potential trends and areas of research that may define the next generation of cybersecurity include.

12.13 Federated Learning and Edge-Based AI

Federated learning is a type of learning in which models get trained on different nodes and these nodes learn from the data without transferring the data (Konečný *et al.*, 2016) [17]. This is particularly of great importance in the context of IoT, which is characterized by a large number of edge devices that produce a large amount of security-related data. Based on the edge, the inference speed is enhanced through the fact that anomalies are processed on the device itself, thus reducing the reliance on cloud communication. As quantum computing develops, existing cryptographic measures may become obsolete. Focus is placed on quantum proof algorithms and

AI for attack detection (Chen *et al.*, 2016) [6]. Notwithstanding, AI may also develop a system to transition to new encryption methods when the old ones are compromised.

Advancements in interpretable AI, such as layer-wise relevance propagation, aim to clarify how deep models reach certain decisions (Samek, Wiegand, & Müller, 2017) [28]. In cybersecurity, increased transparency can foster trust, particularly in mission-critical realms like defense or finance.

Researchers are delving into continuous authentication measures—like keystroke dynamics, typing cadence, and screen interaction patterns (Patel, 2016) [26]. AI evaluating these biometrics can rapidly detect compromised or spoofed sessions.

Organizations must manage myriad data sources—log files, web traffic, device sensor data, and user actions. Multi-modal AI, which merges diverse types of inputs, could yield a more holistic threat picture, enhancing the digital immune system's overall detection capabilities.

With multiple international bodies—like IEEE, ISO, and Cloud Security Alliance—developing guidelines around ethical AI, future cybersecurity solutions may benefit from more formal standards. This could simplify regulatory compliance, foster interoperability, and clarify best practices (Goodman and Flaxman, 2017) [10].

Continued research will likely revolve around refining the balance between high-powered AI methods and the inherent complexity and resource costs they impose. Breakthroughs in hardware acceleration, algorithmic optimization, and cross-domain data sharing could further accelerate the capabilities of digital immune systems. Ultimately, the success of these systems relies on a combination of technological innovation, responsible data practices, and collaboration among industry, academia, and government.

12.14 Harmonizing Automated Systems and Human Expertise

One prominent theme in AI for cybersecurity is the partnership between cutting-edge automation and human intuition. Machines excel at scouring big data for anomalies, but humans contribute deeper context, critical thinking, and ethical discernment. Instead of framing AI as a replacement for security analysts, many enterprises treat it as an enabler—AI filters out everyday noise, freeing analysts to investigate the truly complex threats

(Sharma & Kacker, 2021) [29]. The synergy sees humans focusing on advanced threat hunting and strategic foresight.

To fine-tune this balance, organizations conduct war games simulating sophisticated breaches. These drills clarify how swiftly AI detects the intrusion and how effectively humans respond once critical alerts arise. Such exercises pinpoint skill gaps, refine standard operating procedures, and strengthen overall readiness.

As AI tools update their detection logic, security teams must continually update their understanding of how alerts are generated. This makes it possible for the system to become more accurate in its work over time, by having regular training sessions and open lines of feedback (where analysts flag false positives or suggest new detection rules).

It can help to increase the trust and speed of response by providing interpretable dashboards or short summaries of why a particular alert was triggered. If an alert says, "Unusual login time plus new device usage", then an analyst quickly knows what is meant by this and can make a quick decision on further actions.

Large or critical actions like shutting down an entire segment of the network may require a human sign off. Small, routine tasks like blocking a known malicious IP can happen automatically. This hierarchical approach ensures that disruptive actions only happen when they are absolutely warranted.

When the low-level work of menial alert processing is left to the AI, then the cybersecurity professionals can spend more time on the higher level work: analyzing threat actor trends, upgrading the architecture of the organization and championing user training. This results in a more proactive security organization that is always looking forward.

It is possible to achieve the best results when the levels of automated and human defenses are properly balanced. The function of real time monitoring is performed by AI, while the role of managing the nuance and judgment of advanced attackers is handed over to humans. This division of work not only optimizes the use of resources but also helps to make digital immune systems adaptive and strong in a world where threats are constantly emerging.

As AI-empowered digital immune systems become more widespread, they must conform to industry standards and regulatory requirements to maintain acceptance and credibility.

International Organization for Standardization/International Electrotechnical Commission (ISO/IEC) 27001 underpins information security management, setting a global benchmark for risk assessments and controls. Although it does not specifically address AI, organizations can expand the scope to include AI governance, ensuring that machine learning pipelines undergo similar risk evaluations and documentation.

National Institute of Standards and Technology (NIST's) guidelines (Identify, Protect, Detect, Respond, and Recover) remain a touchstone for U.S. businesses (NIST SP 800-53 Rev. 5, 2020) [25]. While not exclusively tailored for AI, it recommends foundational controls that easily map onto AI-driven approaches. The NIST also publishes specialized guidance on adversarial ML, spotlighting potential vulnerabilities (Kurakin *et al.*, 2017) [19].

The General Data Protection Regulation in Europe demands strict data handling procedures, explicit consent, and breach notifications (Voigt & Von dem Bussche, 2017) [32]. In the context of digital immune systems, it is crucial to ensure that personal data gleaned from log files or behavioral analytics is lawfully processed, stored securely, and used proportionately.

Industries like finance follow Payment Card Industry Data Security Standard (PCI-DSS) for payment security, while healthcare abides by HIPAA for patient confidentiality. The AI-based security methods must adapt to these domain-specific mandates. This may entail specialized encryption, role-based access to logs, or time-bound data retention.

Regions around the globe, such as the EU, have begun drafting new laws focusing on AI oversight. Proposed frameworks demand transparency in high-risk AI systems and lay out compliance obligations for providers. Digital immune systems operating in these jurisdictions may need disclaimers or implement formal risk assessments to meet legal obligations.

Private entities, including the Cloud Security Alliance, are also rolling out certifications that incorporate AI readiness. Earning these certifications can bolster an organization's credibility and reassure stakeholders that robust security practices are in place.

Convergence of AI, cybersecurity, and regulatory structures is inevitable, reflecting a broader shift toward formalizing digital trust. Being proactive—by designing compliance into AI-driven systems from the outset—saves time, prevents legal complications, and underscores an organization's commitment to safeguarding both data and user rights. Successfully walking this line means pairing top-tier security methods with rigorous accountability measures, ultimately yielding a more stable and secure digital ecosystem.

AI disclosure statement: The author acknowledges the use of AI-based tools for minor language editing or grammatical correction. However, all intellectual contributions, analyses, and conclusions presented in this chapter are entirely the author's own.

References

1. Alphabet Annual Report, Alphabet Inc., 2019, Retrieved from https://abc.xyz/investor.
2. Barocas, S. and Selbst, A.D., Big Data's Disparate Impact. *Calif. Law Rev.*, 104, 3, 671–732, 2016.
3. Batista, G.E., Prati, R.C., Monard, M.C., A Study of the Behaviour of Several Methods for Balancing Machine Learning Training Data. *ACM SIGKDD Explor. Newsl.*, 6, 1, 20–29, 2004.
4. Brundage, M., Avin, S., Clark, J., *et al.*, The Malicious Use of Artificial Intelligence: Forecasting, Prevention, and Mitigation, Future of Humanity Institute, University of Oxford, 2018, Retrieved from https://maliciousaireport.com.
5. Chandola, V., Banerjee, A., Kumar, V., Anomaly Detection: A Survey. *ACM Comput. Surv.*, 41, 3, 1–58, 2009.
6. Chen, L., Chen, Q., Jordan, S., Liu, Y.K., Moody, D., Peralta, R., Perlner Ray, A., Smith-Tone, D., Report on Post-Quantum Cryptography. NISTIR 8105, National Institute of Standards and Technology, 2016, doi: 10.6028/NIST.IR.8105.
7. Dasgupta, D., *Artificial Immune Systems and Their Applications*, Springer-Verlag, Berlin, Heidelberg, 1999.
8. European Commission, Ethics Guidelines for Trustworthy AI, 2019, Retrieved from https://digital-strategy.ec.europa.eu.
9. Forrest, S., Perelson, A.S., Allen, L., Cherukuri, R., Self-Nonself Discrimination in a Computer, in: *Proceedings of the 1994 IEEE Symposium on Research in Security and Privacy*, IEEE, pp. 202–212, 1994.
10. Goodman, B. and Flaxman, S., European Union Regulations on Algorithmic Decision-making and a "Right to Explanation." *AI Mag.*, 38, 3, 50–57, 2017.
11. Halevy, A., Norvig, P., Pereira, F., The Unreasonable Effectiveness of Data. *IEEE Intell. Syst.*, 24, 2, 8–12, 2009.
12. Harmer, P.K., Williams, P.D., Gunsch, G.H., Lamont, G.B., An Artificial Immune System Architecture for Computer Security Applications. *IEEE Trans. Evol. Comput.*, 6, 3, 252–280, 2002.
13. Harries, S., Ransomware Attacks on Hospitals and the Role of AI in Preventing Them. *Health Data Manage. J.*, 3, 2, 34–45, 2021.
14. Hochreiter, S. and Schmidhuber, J., Long Short-term Memory. *Neural Comput.*, 9, 8, 1735–1780, 1997.
15. Kephart, J.O. and Chess, D.M., The vision of autonomic computing. *Computer*, 36, 1, 41–50, 2003.
16. Kim, J., Bentley, P., Timmis, J., Artificial Immune Systems, in: *Handbook of Natural Computing*, pp. 259–299, Springer, Berlin, Heidelberg, 2008.
17. Konečný, J., McMahan, H.B., Yu, F.X., Richtárik, P., Suresh, A.T., Bacon, D., Federated Learning: Strategies for Improving Communication Efficiency, arXiv preprint arXiv:1610.05492, 2016.

18. Kotenko, I. and Stepashkin, M., Agent-based Modelling and Simulation of Cyber-warfare Between Malefactors and Security Agents in Internet, in: *International Conference on Computer Network Security*, Springer, pp. 186–197, 2006.
19. Kurakin, A., Goodfellow, I.J., Bengio, S., Adversarial Examples in the Physical World, arXiv preprint arXiv:1607.02533, 2017.
20. LeCun, Y., Bengio, Y., Hinton, G., Deep Learning. *Nature*, 521, 7553, 436–444, 2015.
21. Lee, J., Bagheri, B., Kao, H.A., A Cyber-Physical Systems Architecture for Industry 4.0-based Manufacturing Systems. *Manuf. Lett.*, 3, 18–23, 2015.
22. Madry, A., Makelov, A., Schmidt, L., Tsipras, D., Vladu, A., Towards Deep Learning Models Resistant to Adversarial Attacks, in: *International Conference on Learning Representations (ICLR)*, 2018.
23. Microsoft Documentation, Azure Sentinel Overview, 2023, Retrieved from https://docs.microsoft.com/azure/sentinel.
24. Nguyen, T.T. and Reddi, V.J., Deep Reinforcement Learning for Cyber Security. *IEEE Trans. Neural Netw. Learn. Syst.*, 30, 10, 3049–3061, 2019.
25. NIST SP 800-53 Rev. 5, Security and Privacy Controls for Information Systems and Organizations, National Institute of Standards and Technology, 2020, doi: 10.6028/NIST.SP.800-53r5.
26. Patel, V.M., Continuous User Authentication via Biometrics: Data, Models, and Metrics. *IEEE Signal Process Mag.*, 33, 4, 42–52, 2016.
27. Sakurada, M. and Yairi, T., Anomaly Detection Using Autoencoders with Nonlinear Dimensionality Reduction, in: *Proceedings of the MLSDA 2014 2nd Workshop on Machine Learning for Sensory Data Analysis*, pp. 4–11, 2014.
28. Samek, W., Wiegand, T., Müller, K.R., Explainable Artificial Intelligence: Understanding, Visualizing and Interpreting Deep Learning Models, arXiv preprint arXiv:1708.08296, 2017.
29. Sharma, S. and Kacker, R., Augmented Intelligence in Cyber security: A Review, in: *Cyber security Analytics, Technology and Automation*, pp. 27–45, Springer, Berlin, Heidelberg, 2021.
30. Shaukat, A. and Zhu, P., Integration of Threat Intelligence into AI-driven SOC Platforms. *Comput. Secur.*, 119, 102737, 2022.
31. Tobiyama, S., Yamaguchi, Y., Shimada, H., Ikuse, T., Yamagata, Y., Malware Detection with Deep Neural Network Using Process Behaviour, in: *2016 IEEE 40th Annual Computer Software and Applications Conference (COMPSAC)*, IEEE, pp. 577–582, 2016.
32. Voigt, P. and Von dem Bussche, A., *The EU General Data Protection Regulation (GDPR): A Practical Guide*, Springer International Publishing, Berlin, Heidelberg, 2017.
33. White, S.R., Open Problem: The Digital Immune System, in: *Virus Bulletin International Conference*, pp. 229–256, 1997.

34. Xie, T., Liu, C., Li, K., Li, K., A GAN-based Adversarial Method for Cyber Threat Intelligence Enhancement. *J. Inf. Secur. Appl.*, 58, 102831, 2021.
35. Xu, W., Evans, D., Qi, Y., Feature Squeezing: Detecting Adversarial Examples in Deep Neural Networks, in: *Network and Distributed System Security Symposium (NDSS)*, 2018.
36. Yin, C., Zhu, Y., Fei, J., He, X., A Deep Learning Approach for Intrusion Detection Using Recurrent Neural Networks. *IEEE Access*, 6, 21954–21961, 2019.

13

AI-Powered Cybersecurity for Next-Generation Threats

Suryadeep Kumar Mahto[1]*, Bharat Singh[1], Nidhi Kushwaha[2] and Rajiv Kumar[1]

[1] *Department of Computer Science, Indian Institute of Information Technology, Ranchi, Jharkhand, India*
[2] *Department of Computer Science, National Institute of Technology, Jamshedpur, Jharkhand, India*

Abstract

The digital immune system (DIS) idea is drawn from the human immune system to develop adaptive and self-learning cybersecurity systems. As companies dramatically adopt digital transformation, cyberattacks are evolving with sophistication, prompting rapid innovation in cybersecurity technology. Artificial intelligence (AI) has played a big part in making this possible, substituting old rule-based security solutions with more intelligent, adaptive systems fueled by generative AI. Though old AI models have succeeded in automating threats such as threat detection, malware analysis, and anomaly detection, they are mostly dependent on historical data and preset patterns. This makes them incapable of detecting and acting on fresh or changing threats. With the rise in sophisticated and unprecedented cyber-attacks, intelligent, self-aware systems capable of evolving together with emerging threats have become increasingly needed. These necessities have ensured that AI-powered cybersecurity technologies are now more important than ever. In this chapter, we provide the key technologies related to next-generation need for cybersecurity threats.

***Keywords*:** Digital immune system, intrusion detection system, artificial intelligence, anomaly detection, Nozomi Network, isolation forest, Q-learning, self-healing response

**Corresponding author*: suryadeep.2024pg107@iiitranchi.ac.in

Sujata Priyambada Dash, Vaibhav Mishra, Bijeta Shaw, Sandeep Kumar Panda and S. Balamurugan (eds.) Digital Immune System: Principles and Practices, (289–304)

13.1 Introduction

Artificial intelligence (AI) had become important for cyber security, with its capacity to learn, adapt, and anticipate threats making it indispensable for both defenders and attackers [1]. The attack and defense nature of AI has turned cyber security into a continuously evolving battlefield, where threat actors and security teams continuously refine their technique to one another [1, 2].

Artificial intelligence has moved from being an abstract dream to a reality of today. A Forbes report suggests that in 2021, 76% of companies spent some portion of their IT budget on AI and machine learning (ML) [3]. Furthermore, the market for AI-based cybersecurity is expected to increase at a 27.8% CAGR through 2030. This trend reflects the major role of AI in making digital defenses stronger against more complex cyber threats.

The digital immune system (DIS) will seek to deal with such needs by providing self-healing and adaptive security technologies that defend digital spaces actively. Its next-generational threat-resistance capability is why it stands out as the premier innovation in current cybersecurity [3–6].

13.2 Overview of Digital Immune Systems

In today's world, where cyberattacks are becoming increasingly frequent, DISs have emerged as advanced AI-driven solutions designed to detect and mitigate threats in real time while providing self-healing capabilities. As shown in Figure 13.1, the system identifies, responds to, and neutralizes pathogens, similar to the biological immune system. Thus, a DIS uses multiple AI techniques to analyze, predict, and counteract cyber threats [7]. It is a cybersecurity framework that protects digital networks by continuous monitoring, threat detection, and rapid response.

The core concept of digital immunity focuses on building a resilient defense that not only alleviates cyberattacks but also keeps evolving to be updated for the everchanging threat. With the help of AI, ML, automation, and analytics, DIS learns from the past incidents and improves its defenses so that it can combat new, more complicated threats. As cyber threats become more complex and persistent, traditional reactive security measures are no longer sufficient. A DIS adopts a proactive approach, reducing

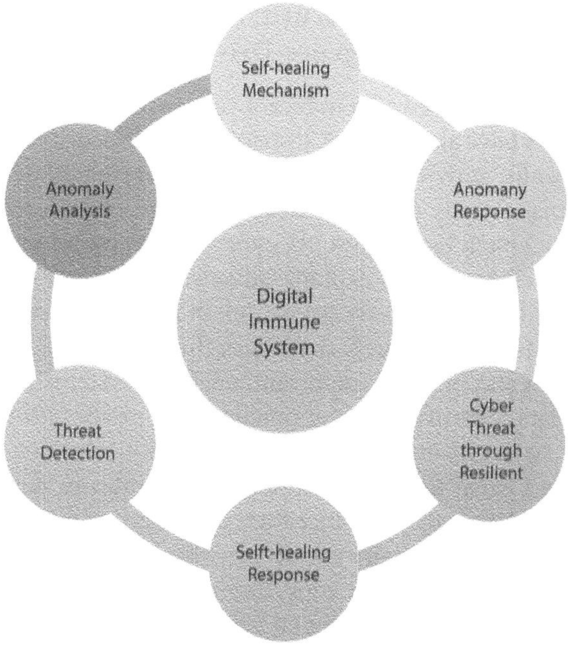

Figure 13.1 The framework of a digital immune system.

risk, strengthening resilience, and ensuring business continuity. Acting as an intelligent, ever-evolving shield, it helps organizations stay ahead of emerging threats and maintain robust protection in an increasingly hostile digital environment [5, 8].

13.2.1 The Role of Machine Learning in Enhancing Digital Immunity

Machine learning helps detect deviations in network traffic, user activities, or system processes, flagging potential threats in real time by using behavioral baselines. Also, the enhancement of threat intelligence by correlating data from diverse sources, refining detection accuracy, and reducing false positives is also done by ML. The need for ML-driven systems to provide adaptive and proactive defenses that evolve alongside emerging threats, fortifying organizations with a dynamic and resilient digital immune system has also increased as cyberattacks became more sophisticated [9, 10, 15].

13.2.2 Evolution of Cybersecurity: From Traditional to Artificial Intelligence-Driven Approach

Cybersecurity has changed a lot in recent years with the implementation of AI as the threats have also evolved. Previously used security models, which relied on firewalls, antivirus software, and signature-based detection, were effective against already existing threats but were not effective with rapidly advancing attack techniques. As cyber threats became more complicated—introducing zero-day exploits, advanced persistent threats (APTs), and polymorphic malware—traditional methods are not enough to combat these threats. Due to these challenges the integration of AI and ML in cybersecurity has become important, enabling systems to process vast amounts of data, identify subtle anomalies, and predict potential attacks in real time. Artificial intelligence-driven security solutions can autonomously evolve in real time to emerging threat patterns, automate threat response, and continuously enhance their defenses through iterative learning. This has led to the shift of cybersecurity from a reactive approach into a proactive, intelligent defense ecosystem, crucial for protecting today's continuously evolving complex digital landscape [11].

13.2.3 The Need for Intelligent Cybersecurity

Generative AI models give a good approach to cybersecurity as compared to traditional AI models. Generative AI analyzes vast amounts of unsupervised data to continuously refine its understanding of typical system activity and improve its ability to detect suitable or emerging anomalies that may indicate a cyberattack. This makes the system effective in identifying zero-day vulnerabilities and APTs, which can bypass conventional signature- or rule-based security systems. As cyber threats increase at an unprecedented rate, the requirement for adaptive, intelligent security systems has never been more critical. Moreover, static defense mechanisms are no longer needed to counter threats such as zero-day exploits, APTs, and polymorphic malware. In modern times, cyber environments require AI-driven solutions capable of continuously learning new data, adaptable to evolving attack patterns, and autonomously responding to potential risks in real time. These intelligent systems not only improve threat detection and incident response but also predict and mitigate future attacks. In a scenario where cyber adversaries constantly improve their tactics, organizations must adopt adaptive technologies to stay ahead and protect their digital ecosystems. In cybersecurity strategies increasingly incorporate techniques such as ML, deep learning, generative AI, behavior-based anomaly detection, threat intelligence integration, self-healing security systems, and federated learning. By improving methodologies, organizations can build security infrastructures but also capable of evolving alongside the ever-changing cyber threat landscape [12, 17].

13.2.4 Biological Inspiration for Digital Immune Systems

The DIS is modeled after the human immune system. As the human body goes through infections, it adapts and defends the body against infections through both adaptive and unlearned reactions. Similarly, DIS precaution digital systems from digital attacks, danger, system failures, and vulnerabilities by leveraging AI, automation, analytics, and ML. It ceaselessly monitors system health, detects anomalies, and replies to potential risks, like how biological immunity authenticates and neutralizes harmful pathogens. There are many similarities among the human immune system and the DIS; for example, in pattern recognition in which both depend on identifying between normal and abnormal behavior. The human immune system detects foreign encroaches upon using antigens and antibodies, while DIS employs behavioral analysis and anomaly detection to identify cyber threats [13]. Moreover, biological and digital immune systems exhibit adaptive learning where the first one shows biological immunity strengthens after exposure to pathogens, while the second one continuously improves through AI-driven self-healing mechanisms and threat intelligence. The core idea of a DIS was first introduced by IBM in the late 1990s as a method to fight computer viruses [13]. Over time, it has evolved into a comprehensive cybersecurity and reliability framework, designed to protect modern IT environments from malware, software failures, and sophisticated cyberattacks.

13.2.5 Real-World Applications in Network Security

A DIS protects cybersecurity by combining AI, automation, and analytics to detect and alleviate threats across various domains, including network security, endpoint protection, and cloud security. In cyber security, a DIS continuously monitors traffic, detects anomalies, and responds to cyber threats in real time. Inspired from biological immune responses, it employs intrusion detection systems (IDS) and intrusion prevention systems (IPS) to identify wrong activity and block attacks. Machine learning algorithms have played a crucial role for DIS in adapting to emerging threats, reducing false positives, and improving detection accuracy [14]. Endpoints such as laptops, mobile devices, and IoT devices are very often targeted for cyberattacks. To protect these devices, a DIS utilizes behavioral analysis, AI-driven antivirus solutions, and automated threat remediation. Self-healing mechanisms further increase the endpoint security by enabling devices to recover from infections without any manual intervention, like how the biological immune system neutralizes pathogens [13]. With the expansion of cloud computing, a DIS also protects cloud environments through AI-powered threat detection, automated compliance enforcement, and zero-trust architecture. It iteratively checks for misconfigurations, unauthorized access, and potential vulnerabilities, ensuring that the security of cloud workloads is working fine. By using these advanced capabilities, a DIS provides a proactive and adaptive cybersecurity framework that adapts alongside the ever-changing digital threat landscape.

13.3 Key Machine Learning Algorithms for Digital Immunity

The concept of a DIS leverages AI and ML to enhance resilience and adaptability. This chapter explores critical ML algorithms that empower digital immunity, enabling proactive threat detection, adaptive defense, and continuous learning [9, 24].

13.3.1 Anomaly Detection Algorithm

Anomaly detection is foundational to identifying irregular patterns that may signal potential threats. The following machine learning algorithms are used for the purpose [15]. Statistical methods use probability distributions to flag deviations. Other methods are based on clustering techniques (e.g., k-means, DBSCAN), which group data points to isolate outliers. We also use one-class support vector machines (SVMs) to separate normal data points from anomalies in high-dimensional spaces [16].

13.3.1.1 Isolation Forests

Isolation Forest is an unsupervised machine learning algorithm that detects anomalies by isolating data points through random partitioning across multiple decision trees. This approach makes it easier to distinguish outliers, as they require fewer splits to separate from the rest of the data. Isolation Forests are particularly effective for identifying rare, anomalous events. Tree-based Isolation use random partition data points; anomalies get isolated in fewer splits. Isolation Forests monitoring large dataset computational algorithm make it ideal for real-time. Isolation Forest is an unsupervised anomaly detection used for high-dimensional data. It works on the principle that anomalies are infrequent and unlike normal instances; hence, they are easier to separate from normal instances. Randomly splitting data points, the algorithm determines anomalies splits to separate, as they are further from dense, normal clusters. Isolation Forest is a binary tree-based technique optimized for anomaly detection [2]. Its time complexity is linear and low-memory. It is highly appropriate for handling large data. The technique achieves this through the construction of a collection of Isolation Trees from random data samples and summing the anomaly scores of each tree to derive a final anomaly score for each point. The Isolation Forest decides on behalf of similar and dissimilar anomalies that can be differentiated using fewer recursive splits [25].

13.3.2 Classification and Threat Identification

Classification models work on the division of data into multiple classes based on the same type of data. Classification techniques are Logistic Regression, Decision Trees, Random Forests, and SVMs, which have been used for threat identification. Among these techniques, Logistic Regression and Decision Trees are simple models for binary threat detection, Random Forests XGBoost utilized ensemble methods for high-accuracy threat classification. Additionally, SVMs is effective for complex, high-dimensional threat landscapes. These models enhance threat identification, helping systems distinguish between benign and malicious activities [3, 5, 12, 24].

13.3.3 Reinforcement Learning for Adaptive Defense

Reinforcement learning (RL) equips systems to dynamically learn optimal defense strategies, which includes the environment-action-reward paradigm and continuous adaptation. The first one interacts with its environment and learns through trial and error and the second one uses RL agents continuously refine defense tactics in response to new threats. This adaptive approach is invaluable for evolving attack surfaces and real-time threat mitigation [17, 18].

13.3.3.1 Q-Learning

Q-learning and its deep variant, deep Q-networks (DQN), are powerful RL algorithms for autonomous threat response. Q-learning uses a Q-table to map state-action pairs to rewards. Whereas DQNs extend Q-learning with DNNs to handle complex, high-dimensional states [19]. Reinforcement learning is a framework where an agent learns behavior through interactions with an environment, without prior knowledge of the task. The agent discovers optimal actions by balancing exploration and exploitation—a critical challenge in action selection. Exploitation helps the agent quickly converge with a locally optimal policy, while excessive exploration can degrade short-term performance but may enhance learning by avoiding suboptimal solutions [20].

13.4 Key Artificial Intelligence-Driven Capabilities in Digital Immune Systems

Artificial intelligence plays a pivotal role in enhancing the effectiveness of DISs by enabling intelligent, adaptive, and real-time threat management. Key AI-driven capabilities include anomaly detection, where ML algorithms identify unusual patterns of behavior that may indicate potential cyber threats. Predictive analytics help forecast vulnerabilities and emerging attack vectors, allowing organizations to proactively strengthen defenses. Automated incident replies reorganize threat suppression and mitigation that reduce reply times and minimize mutilation. Natural language processing supports in analyzing mammoth amounts of security data, finding the hidden things from the report, log files, and other outward sources. Incessant learning instruments confirm the organization progress by learning from previous occurrences, cleansing its finding and response approaches over time. In combination, these AI-powered features produce a dynamic and robust cybersecurity ecosystem that familiarizes to the developing threat landscape, empowering organizations to resolve the issues one step ahead of security bleachers.

13.4.1 Threat Detection and Anomaly Recognition

Cybersecurity involves threat detection and anomaly recognition. It aims to remove the potential threats by comparing the deviation from the standard norms. Anomaly functions as continuous monitoring of network traffic and detecting malicious activities by finding the unusual pattern [26]. This approach is helpful in identifying unknown threats, which are harmful to the network and may cause failure and degradation of network. Anomaly detection can raise a flag to a threat, which leads to further investigation and adds as a milestone in the security of the system. Common types of threat detections include:

- Spoofing is when the sender fails to prove itself as a trusted source.
- Impersonation is identifying the type of mail, which includes some words related to risk-taking actions.
- URL reputation provides the services by identifying whether the email body contains some URL, which redirects to any unsafe website.

13.4.1.1 Identifying Unusual Patterns in Network Traffic

To make the system error-free and free from any kind of suspicious activities, a comprehensive threat monitoring system is required. It involves behavior-based anomaly detection rather than rule-based threat detection.

- Rule-based threat detection involves effective approaches to identify the threat by monitoring network traffic. It involves the matching of network traffic with malicious-based network traffic by understanding and observing the URL, IP address, keywords, etc. Each signature serves as an indicator of compromise. While highly efficient, this method is limited to detecting known threats (such as documented CVEs) and relies on threat indicators being distinct and easily identifiable for effective detection.
- Operational anomalies and unknown threats that include zero-day vulnerabilities cannot be reliably detected through rule-based methods. The most effective way to identify them is through continuous monitoring with deep packet inspection (DPI), which analyzes industrial protocols within network traffic and compares current behavior against established baselines. Unlike dynamic enterprise networks, industrial control system (ICS) networks are relatively stable, making it easier to establish accurate behavioral baselines and spot deviations. However, this process requires advanced ML to understand the normal behavior of process variables extracted from network traffic. Once baselines are defined, behavior-based anomaly detection can flag unusual traffic patterns, abnormal sensor readings, and deviations

in flow parameters, helping to catch threats that traditional methods might miss.

The Nozomi Networks platform leverages ML to detect anomalies by learning the communication patterns of your industrial network and establishing a baseline of normal behavior as provided in Figure 13.2 [26]. This architecture illustrates a typical ICS security architecture, layering networks from field devices to enterprise IT, with integrated security features for threat detection, asset monitoring, and centralized management. It continuously monitors your environment, identifying deviations in communication or process variable values that may signal a cyber threat or a potential risk to system reliability. Our sensors use DPI to analyze over 250 industrial protocols, providing the detailed data necessary for in-depth behavioral analysis. This approach allows for the extraction of granular asset information, which include device-making, model, serial number, and firmware/OS version—for devices like industrial controllers, workstations, and servers. The platform can detect policy violations, equipment malfunctions and misconfigurations. Where policy violations mean actions like unauthorized programmable logic controller (PLC)

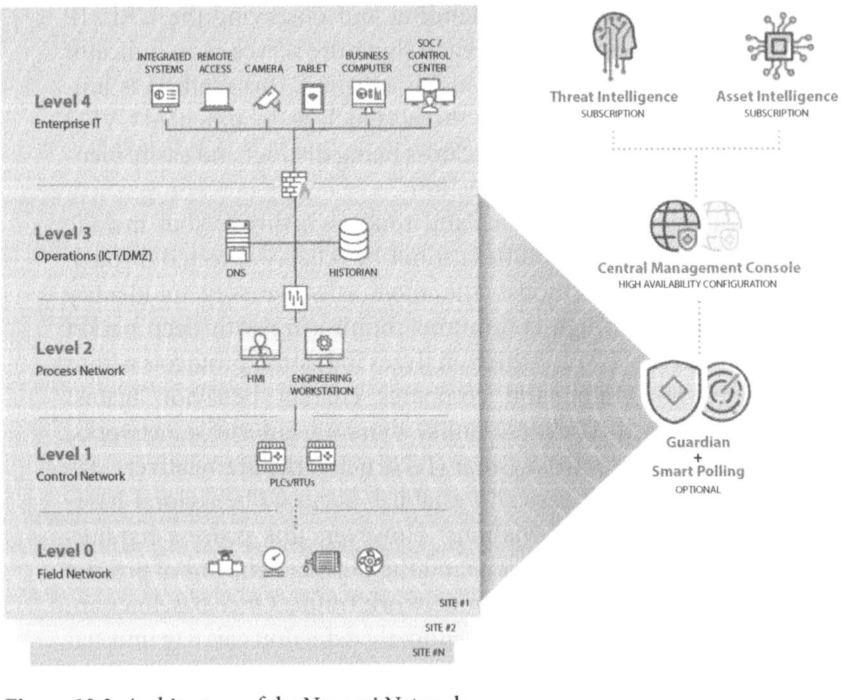

Figure 13.2 Architecture of the Nozomi Network.

program/firmware downloads, uploads, modifications, or PLC start/stop commands. Equipment malfunctions refer to issues, such as lost communication links, link resets, re-transmission errors, and simple network management protocol (SNMP) device health status failures. And misconfigurations signify the events like unauthorized protocol usage, PLC read errors due to invalid register addresses, and malformed supervisory control and data acquisition (SCADA) packet errors.

The Nozomi Networks platform delivers an advanced detection engine tailored for OT/IoT environments, blending rule-based and behavior-based techniques to identify and mitigate a wide range of threats. From resource spikes and zero-day vulnerabilities to stealthy living-off-the-land tactics that bypass signature-based methods, the platform effectively minimizes risk without overwhelming analysts with false positives.

For the previous known thread detection, the Nozomi threat intelligence provides cumulative data in-depth for research and analysis of thread, contribution ironic understanding into threat indicators. In the case of know-thread detection, Nozomi includes packet rules, YARA rules, threat definitions, STIX indicators, a complete threat knowledge base, and susceptibility signatures. The Nozomi platform's sensors accept incessant updates on developing malware and indicators of compromise (IOCs) detailed to industrial systems and IoT devices. This information draws from Nozomi's self OT/IoT research, as well as integrations with foundations like CISA's catalog, guaranteeing healthy and up-to-date threat treatment. This all-inclusive approach supports organizations proactively accomplish security, operational stability, and system integrity.

13.4.1.2 Detecting Zero-Day Attacks and Advanced Persistent Threats

Adversaries continuously looking for opportunities to attack and exploit the vulnerabilities of an organization's information systems are termed as APTs. It is a form of prolonged and targeted cybersecurity attack. Disrupting critical operations *via* insensitiveness data is its main motto. The major threat lies in endurance and strategic flexibility of cyber adversaries who consistently adjust their tactics to avoid detection and sustain access to the breached system, even though individual APT tactics may not always be technically complex [22].

A zero-day exploit is a powerful hacking tool that targets unknown flaws in software, hardware, or firmware. Hackers find these weaknesses through research, testing, or by taking advantage of the time gap between discovering the flaw and fixing it with a security update [21].

Zero-day exploits are highly dangerous because their unknown nature makes them hard to detect and stop with standard security tools. This highlights the importance of strong security practices, including a constant monitoring of cybersecurity software for unusual activity or suspicious files. In most cases, hackers used these vulnerabilities to divide small systems, which help to lower the risk by applying anti-fouling measures. For example, stern security rules and access, and encryption techniques are used. Basically, if zero-day weakness is available in the public domain, then hackers and experts of the securities can know all these weaknesses. They can utilize it to update the organization for new kinds of patches, which can be implemented as quicken as possible. If stern action was not taken for this weakness or some temporary arrangement has been made like tighter access control, network segmentation or traffic filtering to minimize the threat until a foolproof solution was not applied.

By holding all the previous security parameters, this multi-layered technique also traces zero-day attacks and APTs. Identifying and encountering unexpected patterns in network traffic and system security is the major task to take into consideration. To address the same condition, we employ techniques such as behavior-based anomaly detection and DPI. Machine learning and AI models can analyze vast datasets to spot subtle deviations from normal behavior, signaling potential threats. Threat intelligence feeds provide real-time updates on emerging attack tactics, while sandboxing allows suspicious files or code to run in isolated environments for analysis. Deception technologies, like honeypots, lure attackers into controlled environments, revealing their techniques. By combining these advanced detection methods, organizations can improve their ability to catch stealthy, evolving threats before they cause significant damage [10, 12].

13.5 Case Studies: Machine Learning-Powered Intrusion Detection Systems

Intrusion detection systems are being adopted across various sectors to enhance cybersecurity and resilience. The DIS frameworks are already being implemented across industries. In Figure 13.3, major portions of work related to ML-powered instruction detection is included with three industries like healthcare, finance, and critical infrastructure.

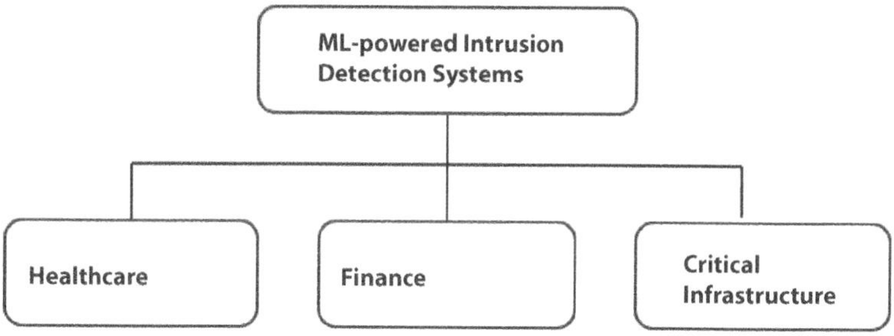

Figure 13.3 Intrusion detection system powered by an ML application.

13.5.1 Healthcare

Artificial intelligemce-driven DIS systems help protect sensitive patient data from ransomware and insider threats [23]. Mayo Clinic leverages AI and behavioral analytics to protect patient data. Their system continuously monitors network traffic for unusual patterns and uses automated responses to contain potential breaches—crucial for safeguarding sensitive patient records and complying with HIPAA regulations. Similarly, GE Healthcare has implemented cybersecurity solutions in medical devices, using anomaly detection to flag suspicious device activity and prevent tampering with critical equipment like MRI and CT scanners.

13.5.2 Finance

Financial institutions use DIS to detect fraudulent transactions and prevent data breaches. JPMorgan Chase uses AI-driven threat detection systems to monitor billions of transactions in real-time, identifying fraudulent activities and preventing cyberattacks. Combining cybersecurity and AI, we build a model to detect anomalies, combined with an automated incident response system to mitigate threats. Mastercard employs a global AI-powered fraud detection network.

13.5.3 Critical Infrastructure

The DIS uses an important defense system to protect critical infrastructure from cyber threats. This strategy is particularly important for protecting essential services, like power grids, financial systems, and healthcare networks. A regional power grid operator faced multiple cyberattacks on the grid system. The threats are ransomware attacks, distributed denial of service attacks, and attempts to manipulate control systems.

13.6 Conclusion

Artificial intelligence is used to power cybersecurity for next-generation threats. Artificial intelligence and cybersecurity are combined to develop a DIS with biological inspiration to threat detection, incident response, fraud detection, and behavior analysis. Artificial intelligence is performed to shape the next generation of defense tools and strategies. The threats are rapidly growing in the digital world, so too must increase our defenses with continuous innovation driving the future of autonomous digital security. Machine learning improves threat detection by making it more dynamic, adaptive, and precise. Artificial intelligence-powered DIS self-repair defenses to counter increasing future cyber threats. A smooth functioning of future threats for cybersecurity management must have optimal balance between automated systems and human coordination.

AI disclosure statement: The author acknowledges the use of AI-based tools for minor language editing or grammatical correction. However, all intellectual contributions, analyses, and conclusions presented in this chapter are entirely the author's own.

References

1. Baniecki, H. and Biecek, P., Adversarial attacks and defenses in explainable artificial intelligence: A survey. *Inf. Fusion*, 107, 102303, 2024, ISSN 1566-2535. doi: https://doi.org/10.1016/j.inffus.2024.102303. URL https://www.sciencedirect.com/science/article/pii/S1566253524000812.
2. Liu, F.T., Ting, K.M., Zhou, Z.-H., Isolation forest. *IEEE Trans. Knowl. Data Eng.*, 23, 6, 1–13, 2008.
3. Bishop, C.M., *Pattern Recognition and Machine Learning*, New York, Springer, 2006.
4. Shone, N., Ngoc, T., Phai, V., Shi, Q., A deep learning approach to network intrusion detection. *IEEE Access*, 6, 52843–52854, 2018.
5. Zheng, Y., Li, Z., Xu, X., Zhao, Q., Dynamic defenses in cyber security: Techniques, methods and challenges. *Digit. Commun. Netw.*, 8, 4, 422–435, 2022, ISSN 2352-8648. doi: https://doi.org/10.1016/j.dcan.2021.07.006. URL https://www.sciencedirect.com/science/article/pii/S235286482100047X.

6. Tounsi, W. and Rais, H., A survey on technical threat intelligence in the age of sophisticated cyber attacks. *Comput. Secur.*, 72, 212–233, 2018, ISSN 0167-4048. doi:https://doi.org/10.1016/j.cose.2017.09.001. URLhttps://www.sciencedirect.com/science/article/pii/S0167404817301839.
7. Waqas, M., Humphries, U.W., Chueasa, B., Wangwongchai, A., Artificial intelligence and numerical weather prediction models: A technical survey. *Nat. Hazard. Res.*, 2024, ISSN 2666-5921. doi: https://doi.org/10.1016/j.nhres.2024.11.004.URL https://www.sciencedirect.com/science/article/pii/S266659212400091X.
8. Ali, S., Wang, J., Leung, V.C.M., Ai-driven fusion with cybersecurity: Exploring current trends, advanced techniques, future directions, and policy implications for evolving paradigms– a comprehensive review. *Inf. Fusion*, 118, 102922, 2025, ISSN 1566-2535.doi: https://doi.org/10.1016/j.inffus.2024.102922. URL https://www.sciencedirect.com/science/article/pii/S1566253524007000.
9. Ahmad, R., Alsmadi, I., Alhamdani, W., Tawalbeh, L., A deep learning ensemble approach to detecting unknown network attacks. *J. Inf. Secur. Appl.*, 67, 103196, 2022, ISSN 2214-2126, doi: https://doi.org/10.1016/j.jisa.2022.103196. URL https://www.sciencedirect.com/science/article/pii/S2214212622000771.
10. Guo, Y., A review of machine learning-based zero-day attack detection: Challenges and future directions. *Comput. Commun.*, 198, 175–185, 2023, ISSN 0140-3664. doi: https://doi.org/10.1016/j.comcom.2022.11.001. URL https://www.sciencedirect.com/science/article/pii/S0140366422004248.
11. Por, L.Y., Dai, Z., Leem, S.J., Chen, Y., Yang, J., Binbeshr, F., Phan, K.Y., Ku, C.S., A systematic literature review on ai-based methods and challenges in detecting zero-day attacks. *IEEE Access*, 12, 144150–144163, 2024, doi: 10.1109/ACCESS.2024.3455410.
12. Kephart, J.O., A biologically inspired immune system for computers, in: *Proceedings of the Fourth International Workshop on Synthesis and Simulatoin of Living Systems*, R.A. Brooks and P. Maes (Eds.), pp. 130–139, MIT Press, Cambridge, MA, 1994.
13. Sommer, R. and Paxson, V., Outside the closed world: On using machine learning for network intrusion detection, in: *2010 IEEE Symposium on Security and Privacy*, pp. 305–316, 2010, doi: 10.1109/SP.2010.25.
14. Makani, R. and Reddy, B.V.R., Taxonomy of machine leaning based anomaly detection and its suitability. *Procedia Comput. Sci.*, 132, 1842–1849, 2018, ISSN 1877-0509. doi: https://doi.org/10.1016/j.procs.2018.05.133. URL https://www.sciencedirect.com/science/article/pii/S1877050918308652. International Conference on Computational Intelligence and Data Science.
15. Hu, W., Liao, Y., Rao Vemuri, V., Robust anomaly detection using support vector machines, in: *Proceedings of the international conference on machine learning*, vol. 6, p. 5, Citeseer University Park, PA, USA, 2003.

16. Kato, T. and Kobayashi, T.J., Understanding adaptive immune system as reinforcement learning. *Phys. Rev. Res.*, 3, 013222, Mar 2021, doi: 10.1103/PhysRevResearch.3.013222. URL https://link.aps.org/doi/10.1103/PhysRevResearch.3.013222.
17. Babalola, A.A., Belkacemi, R., Zarrabian, S., Craven, R., Adaptive immune system reinforcement learning-based algorithm for real-time cascading failures prevention. *Eng. Appl. Artif. Intell.*, 57, 118–133, 2017, ISSN 0952-1976. doi: https://doi.org/10.1016/j.engappai.2016.09.003. URL https://www.sciencedirect.com/science/article/pii/S095219761630166X.
18. Ji, Z., Wu, Q.M.J., Sid-Ahmed, M., An improved immune Q-learning algorithm, in: *2007 IEEE International Conference on Systems, Man and Cybernetics*, pp. 1636–1641, 2007, doi: 10.1109/ICSMC.2007.4414135.
19. Aslan, S. and Demirci, S., An immune plasma algorithm with Q-learning based pandemic management for path planning of unmanned aerial vehicles. *Egypt. Inf. J.*, 26, 100468, 2024, ISSN 1110-8665. doi: https://doi.org/10.1016/j.eij.2024.100468. URL https://www.sciencedirect.com/science/article/pii/S1110866524000318.
20. AlMahmeed, Y.S. and Al-Omay, A.Y., Zero-day attack solutions using threat hunting intelligence: Extensive survey, in: *2022 International Conference on Data Analytics for Business and Industry (ICDABI)*, pp. 309–314, 2022, doi: 10.1109/ICDABI56818.2022.10041568.
21. Rushdan, H., Shurman, M., Alnabelsi, S., Qutaibah, A., Zero-day attack detection and prevention in software-defined networks, 12 2019, doi: 10.1109/ACIT47987.2019.8991124.
22. Nasiri, S., Sadoughi, F., Tadayon, M.H., Dehnad, A., Security requirements of internet of things-based healthcare system: a survey study. *Acta Inform. Med.*, 27, 253–258, 12 2019, doi: 10.5455/aim.2019.27.253-258.
23. Singh, B., Kushwaha, N., Vyas, O., A Feature Subset Selection Technique for High Dimensional Data Using Symmetric Uncertainty. *J. Data Anal. Inf. Process.*, 2, 95–105, 2014, doi: 10.4236/jdaip.2014.24012.
24. Liu, F.T., Ting, K.M., Zhou, Z.-H., Isolation-Based Anomaly Detection. *ACM Trans. Knowl. Discov. Data*, 6, 3, 1–39, December 2008, doi: 10.1145/2133360.2133363.
25. Singh, B., Kushwaha, N., Vyas, O.P., Exploiting the anomaly detection for high dimensional data using descriptive approach of data mining. *2013 4th International Conference on Computer and Communication Technology (ICCCT)*, Allahabad, India, pp. 121–128, 2013, doi: 10.1109/ICCCT.2013.6749614.
26. Nozomi Networks, CITES Cybersecurity Solutions, Nozomi – Global Security Network.

14

Building Adaptive Digital Immune Systems: A Framework for Large-Scale Organizational Resilience

Shikha Gupta[1]*, Rajeev Kumar Ray[1], Amit Singh[2] and Anuj Pal Kapoor[1]

[1]*School of Management and Entrepreneurship, Indian Institute of Technology, Jodhpur, India*
[2]*Amrut Mody School of Management, Ahmedabad University, Ahmedabad, India*

Abstract

This study examines the scalability requirements of digital immune systems (DIS) for large organizations facing complex operational challenges. The research establishes five primary dimensions using an integrated framework: technical, operational, governance, knowledge, and regulatory scalability. The implementation model focuses on architectural principles including modularity, service-oriented design, and zero-trust approaches that enable enterprise-wide protection. We demonstrate how effective data governance and advanced analytics enhance threat detection capabilities across diverse business environments. This research addresses organizational structures that balance centralized oversight with distributed responsiveness, proposing federated governance models to optimize security operations. Implementation strategies highlight phased deployment, vendor integration, and cultural transformation to ensure adoption across complex organizations. Finally, the emerging challenges including AI-enhanced security, quantum computing threats, and evolving digital business models, providing a roadmap for organizations to build resilient digital immune systems that adapt to future technological shifts.

Keywords: Digital immune systems, enterprise scalability, cybersecurity integration, operational resilience, technology governance

**Corresponding author*: gupta.93@iitj.ac.in

Sujata Priyambada Dash, Vaibhav Mishra, Bijeta Shaw, Sandeep Kumar Panda and S. Balamurugan (eds.) Digital Immune System: Principles and Practices, (305–322) © 2026 Scrivener Publishing LLC

14.1 Introduction

The rapid growth of technological improvements, coupled with rising geopolitical tensions and increasing cyber threats, has created complex operational challenges for large organizations [1]. Modern operational requirements demand resilient technological capabilities that can scale effectively across multiple business units, geographical regions, and technology platforms [2, 3]. Digital immune systems (DIS) have emerged as an overall solution for safeguarding digital assets and mitigating IT risks across large-scale operations [4, 5]. Digital immune systems are an integrated protection methods, which unite processes with analytics and technologies to strengthen IT architecture alongside business operations and deliver assessments that measure technology ecosystem resilience [6]. These defensive systems function similarly to biological immune systems as they dynamically defend against threats while ensuring continuous operations [7, 8].

Market analyses highlight the increasing strategic relevance of DIS. The global DIS market was worth USD 25.30 billion in 2022 and is expected to grow at a compound annual growth rate (CAGR) of 12.7%, from 2023 to 2030 [9]. Significant growth in the market shows DIS is being recognized as a critical responsibility with strategic value for most organizations. Participating organizations implementing DIS strategies attain 80% downtime reduction leading to more effective customer satisfaction [4].

The implementation of DIS at an enterprise scale is particularly challenging for multinational corporations due to their complex organizational structures. These organizations must navigate technological, operational, governance, and cultural barriers. According to HCLTech [10], a robust DIS strategy begins with an evaluation of IT maturity levels, followed by the identification of gaps in security, observability, and automation. The assessment allows organizations to establish AI-driven observability capabilities in addition to AI-powered testing facilities and chaos engineering programs that perform system stress-testing. The Forbes Technology Council [11] further suggests that organizations should create security policies that are regularly reviewed, ensuring integration of tools, disaster recovery plans, and risk assessment practices to strengthen digital immunity.

Large organizations constructing scalable DIS need to follow specific guidelines during the systems' design phase. These organizations need monitoring frameworks that allow for oversight while enabling autonomous program implementation in their entire network system. This chapter

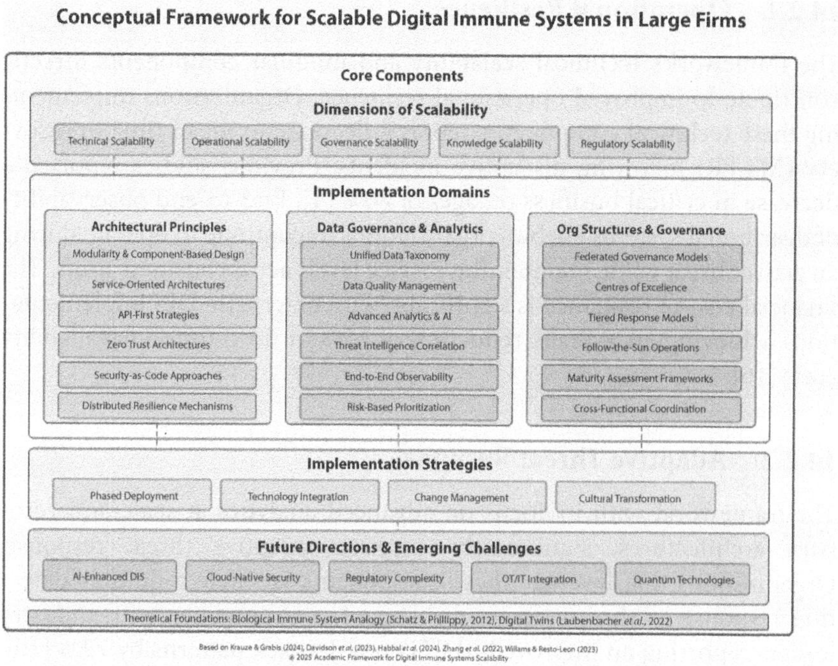

Figure 14.1 Conceptual framework for scalable DIS in large firms.

proposes a conceptual framework for scalable DIS in large firms, as shown in Figure 14.1, adopting studies [6, 12–15]. The chapter focuses on the key elements of scalability in DIS for large businesses through a strategic operational resilience framework. The study investigates key challenges faced by large businesses in developing their DIS and identifies effective methods for extending these systems across different business sectors, global locations, and varying regulations.

14.2 Framework to Outcomes: Measuring Digital Immune Systems Effectiveness

The proposed scalable DIS framework provides direct support for five key organizational outcomes that drive measurable value for large enterprises. This outcome-based framework enables organizations to quantify their success in implementation and return on investment (ROI).

14.2.1 Operational Resilience

The framework's technical scalability and modular components directly contribute to improved operational resilience. Organizations implementing these technical components report a decrease in mean time to recovery (MTTR) following disruptive incidents. Previous studies reported a decrease in critical business outages of 80% [4]. End-to-end observability of distributed systems enables organizations to continue to operate during an active threat while maintaining service levels across business units. The financial cost of resilience is significant, with enterprise DIS implementations achieving an average reduction of 65% in downtime/unavailability costs [16].

14.2.2 Adaptive Threat Response

The framework, with its focus on advanced analytics at scale and zero-trust architectures, significantly improves adaptive threat response. Organizations that leverage these components facilitate a quicker detection response to threats across distributed environments, with industry leaders reporting an improved MTTD novel attack patterns by 72% [10]. Additionally, distributed security operations models additionally facilitate cross-organization sharing of threat intelligence and security responses regardless of geographical region. These features result in significantly smaller breach scopes and less lateral movement for large enterprises [17].

14.2.3 Regulatory Compliance at Scale

The regulatory scalability dimension combined with overall data governance and federated governance models, directly supports streamlined compliance across jurisdictions. Organizations implementing these elements report reduced compliance-related findings and penalties, alongside accelerated adaptation to new regulatory requirements. Measurement and maturity assessment components enable consistent compliance performance across business units, leading to improved audit outcomes and regulatory relations. Studies indicate that mature implementations reduce compliance-related effort by 40% while improving conformance scores [18].

14.2.4 Sustainable Security Economics

Service-oriented architectures, vendor management integration, and technology rationalization components contribute to sustainable security economics. Organizations implementing these framework elements optimize security spending as a percentage in the IT budget, with leading implementations demonstrating reductions of 30% in operational security costs [19]. Skills development and cultural transformation initiatives improve resource utilization across security teams while enhancing strategic allocation of security investments. The cumulative effect is a lower total cost of security operations on a scale, providing sustainable economic models for security functions.

14.2.5 Digital Trust Acceleration

Knowledge scalability and cross-functional coordination components accelerate digital trust development. Organizations implementing these elements report increased customer confidence in digital services, accelerated adoption of new digital business capabilities, and enhanced partner integration. These outcomes directly translate to measure competitive advantage in digital transformation initiatives, with leading organizations leveraging their DIS as market differentiators [11].

The proposed framework is designed to produce these measurable outcomes through a structured implementation process. By linking each framework component to organizational outcomes, enterprises can establish baseline measurements, set targeted improvements, track incremental progress, demonstrate business value, and guide investment decisions throughout their DIS implementation journey.

14.3 Dimensions of Scalability in Digital Immune Systems

The DIS provides scalability that requires more than technical system capabilities. On a fundamental level, this approach integrates multiple important elements requiring complete organization-wide analysis to establish enterprise-wide resilience. Infrastructure as well as applications and security tools need to maintain performance levels even when processing growing quantities of data and users alongside escalating threats [19]. Operationally scalable systems maintain unified processes, response abilities, and control mechanisms, which function smoothly between various business sectors throughout different geographic locations [14]. The oversight processes paired with operational policies along with decision-making systems demonstrate efficiency as they spread through different organizational departments [18]. The organization uses knowledge scalability to distribute threat intelligence with best practices and study outcomes to all departments [16]. Organizations require a system that enables them to adapt security posture to multiple compliance demands in multiple jurisdictions [20]. An effective data governance, a critical component of DIS requires balancing centralization and decentralization, standardization and flexibility, and control and innovation [12]. This balancing act becomes increasingly complex as organizations scale, requiring thoughtful approaches that accommodate diverse organizational needs while maintaining coherence and effectiveness.

14.4 Architectural Principles for Scalable Digital Immune Systems

14.4.1 Modularity and Component-Based Design

Digital immune systems influence modular design as a core principle to enable scalability of the system by architecting system components into well-defined interface modules. Modular design provides operational advantages for organizations of any size by increasing efficiency in technologies, maintenance, adaptability, and speed of deployment [21]. Organizations that use modular design building tools can deploy a technology platform adaptable to international and domestic operation needs.

An example of modular and component-based design approach to digital immune system is the Security Adaptive Network Architecture (SANA) framework [22]. SANA is a network protection approach drawing on human immune principles through use of artificial immune cells as modular components supporting network security. The modular design provides flexibility and resilience to cyberattacks. In particular, the self-operating modules within the system concentrate on a specific security function, for example, intrusion detection and anomaly detection. The fact that individual components of the digital immune system can be maintained or upgraded as maintenance actions during routine operational service without a full system outage is a key operational benefit of the modular design.

14.4.2 Service-Oriented Architectures and Application Programming Interface-First Strategies

Service-oriented architecture (SOA) and application programming interface (API)-first methods facilitate interoperability at scale while supporting modular design principles. As these approaches enable organizations to combine different functional areas, security services become part of the business functions. They also provide automation capabilities with more clearly defined APIs for automated workflows that enable threat detection, incident response, and compliance monitoring. A DIS relies on standardized interfaces, which allows external partners, suppliers, and security service providers to be included in the framework at any scale. The mechanisms utilize data communication technology to provide real-time awareness of organizational connections [10, 17].

HCLTech [10] describes resilient DIS that rely on primary elements: observability, AI-augmented testing, chaos engineering, auto-remediation, and site reliability engineering (SRE), and software supply chain security. The approach incorporates security capabilities into business operational processes so that applications can continue to function as intended.

14.4.3 Zero-Trust Architectures at the Global Scale

Modern business expansion across international borders has reduced the effectiveness of traditional perimeter security methods. Zero-trust technologies establish verification protocols for all access requests, granting authentication-based permissions across all physical locations [23]. Digital immune systems benefit significantly from this security approach, as it ensures consistent protection regardless of whether resources are accessed from an office, the cloud, or a remote location. Access controls are standardized when authentication and authorization mechanisms function uniformly across multiple business units and various technology environments. A key advantage of zero-trust security is micro-segmentation, which reduces attack vectors, preventing internal network penetration attempts even as the network expands. Furthermore, it simplifies merger and acquisition integration, allowing new business units to be incorporated into the enterprise security posture without requiring complete infrastructure standardization.

Microsoft [19] states that 80% of all cyberattacks focus on vulnerabilities that existing updates could have addressed. Cloud computing technologies deliver automatic security updates, according to their research, which functions as an important protection method in an environment where cyber threats are constantly evolving. Microsoft allocates 1 billion USD annually to security expenditures, which illustrates why implementing cloud services within DIS strategies deliver value in maintaining effective protection. A global technology enterprise demonstrates how applying zero-trust security principles brings practical benefits when merging several acquisitions. Instead of attempting to force standardization on acquired business network infrastructure, which would require significant time, the company rapidly established standard identity management guidelines, data classification systems, and access controls.

14.5 Data Governance and Analytics at Scale

Organization requires effective data management methods to implement DIS across their larger structures [24]. Enterprises must build strong governance frameworks that allow for central oversight while maintaining distributed operational capabilities, as the volume, variety, and speed of security-related data continue to rise [12, 13]. A data management system for DIS needs standardized data classification schemas, data quality control policies, interoperability designs, permission rules, data storage protocols, and systems to address national jurisdiction concerns. With a unified data taxonomy, security data can be analyzed and reported across business units, ensuring consistency in classification and labelling [21].

Such principles are demonstrated by a global communications service provider through its established data management system. The system consists of a security telemetry data lake at its core, along with universal data collection agents deployed across all business units, supported by automated systems for ensuring the consistency of security monitoring data. Local security teams could access the relevant portions of enterprise data, analyze them, and share their results, fostering continuous enhancement of information exchange and DIS effectiveness. This case illustrates how strong data governance enables large companies to achieve complete organizational visibility and supports the scalability of digital immune systems.

As DIS expand, they generate security data sets that exceed human analysts' capacity to manage them effectively. Advanced analytics techniques and ML technologies assist organizations in detecting threats and anomalies on a large scale, prioritizing critical security risks [15, 23]. Digital immune systems require four core functions from their advanced analytics implementation: user behavior analysis, entity behavior analysis, threat intelligence correlation, and the scoring and ranking of security risks. A system for user behavior analytics provides an explanation for detection of irregular access behaviors that can represent external breach, or internal exploitation attempts at compromising multiple user accounts [10]. Entity behavior analytics identification of anomalous movements in and between systems across different applications and networks can identify signs of cyberattacks or operational failures [4]. The technology evaluates observation data associated with threat intelligence databases to identify organizations simultaneously detecting attacks while they are still within the kill chain phase of the attack [16]. The combination of threat assessment tools lets organizations allocate their resources with maximum efficiency through their capability to rate vulnerabilities based on evidence [14, 25]. An extensive study on AI trust, risk, and security management (AI TRiSM) frameworks evaluates their current applications while identifying existing challenges and potential future research opportunities [15]. Using risk-based operational methods together with ethical regulatory procedures AI TRiSM offers organizations a complete method for safeguarding their AI systems. The National Institute of Standards and Technology has provided the AI RMF 1.0 [23] as a structured guidance system for organizations developing security systems with AI enhancements. Organizations implementing AI for DIS must maintain standards of valid performance and reliability with precautions for safety and security [23].

In complex enterprise environments, observability is essential for system administrators to detect internal processes through external output monitoring. Scaled DIS require comprehensive observability to address threats effectively [6, 10]. It relies on instrumentation for monitoring, distributed tracing, contextual logging, and real-time dashboards and visualizations. Applications, business processes, and infrastructure systems incorporate instrumentation to embed monitoring functionalities, producing exclusive telemetry data [10]. Distributed tracing tracks transactions from origin to destination across system boundaries, enabling complex scenario analysis and the detection of system failure points [4]. Monitoring systems record essential metadata and events, producing results critical for accurate analysis and establishing connections between entities [11]. Real-time technical dashboards provide data visualizations tailored to different user groups, from security analysts to executive management [14]. Organizations are encouraged to incorporate AI analytics into their observability solutions to enhance full-stack monitoring, enabling them to identify security issues before they disrupt business operations, especially as companies expand and their system complexity increases [10]. A global pharmaceutical company implemented an enterprise observability platform, successfully managing operations by aggregating measurements from on-premises data centers, cloud setups, and factory systems. The platform matched data analytics with business information to differentiate between non-threatening fluctuations and real business threats, improving incident triage capabilities and reducing alert fatigue. This solution not only enhanced the scalability of the DIS but also ensured effective management of complex technological environments.

14.6 Organizational Structures and Governance for Scaled Digital Immune Systems

Large enterprises face an essential trade-off between concentrating control over DIS for efficiency and distributing control for localized responsiveness during scale-up. Organizational structures and governance frameworks play a crucial role in balancing centralized and decentralized forces that shape digital systems [14]. The mediation between centralization and decentralization in DIS is facilitated by federated governance structures, which ensure distributed responsibility while maintaining centralized accountability. This includes the establishment of experts and practice communities. A federated model of organization-wide governance establishes central teams to oversee standards, frameworks, and shared services, while local teams manage capabilities within defined boundaries [21]. Enterprise security functions maintain oversight and offer support to business units, which retain responsibility for security outcomes within their domains under distributed responsibility with centralized accountability [11].

Organizations use centers of excellence to specialize in distinct aspects of DIS before sharing valuable insights across all business units [10]. Systems of practice facilitate cross-functional teams from various divisions working together to solve organizational problems and distribute optimal solutions throughout different departments [26]. Business impact analysis must be prioritized in continuity planning [14]. They present a structured approach to identify essential business operations and their reliance on information technology infrastructure, stressing that "the primary purpose of a business impact analysis is to understand the effect a disruptive event can have on the organization." Digital security resources are allocated through risk assessments to protect primary business operations, strengthening the overall performance of the enterprise's DIS.

Global organizations require security systems designed to monitor continuously and take speedy action across their multinational territories and different regulatory domains [16, 27]. Successful incident response at scale requires operations that cover multiple time zones, multi-tier incident handling protocols, automated playbooks, and coordinated involvement across departments. Distributed security operations centers can collaborate across time zones through follow-the-sun operations, providing 24/7 security services without overburdening personnel [10]. The International Organization for Standardization [27] explains how tiered response models provide clear incident response paths and team responsibilities for global incident handling teams. Automating playbooks enables standardized response protocols and levels of automation, ensuring that common incidents are addressed uniformly across all locations [11].

Cross-functional coordination brings defined interfaces between security teams and other stakeholders, supporting unified incident management across organizational structures [14]. A DIS protects organizations from operational failures and enables continuous business operations by implementing advanced cybersecurity measures. Perri's [4] analysis reveals that ERP system downtime can cost up to USD 300,000 per hour, highlighting the business impact of disruptions and the need to integrate DIS functions with key enterprise applications to reduce operational instability. The International Organization for Standardization [27] presents ISO 22301:2019, which outlines a comprehensive system for business continuity management during disruptive incidents. According to this standard, "the purpose of business continuity is to ensure that an organization can continue to deliver products and services at acceptable predefined levels following a disruptive incident." A global financial institution applies a three-step incident response framework that follows these principles. Tier 1 analysts, operating from regional security operation centers, handle alert triage and routine incidents. Typical Tier 2 incident response teams handle sophisticated incidents by coordinating multiple locations, but Tier 3 specialists assist with crucial threats and create new detection systems for global threat monitoring. Large enterprises can establish overall threat response capabilities across diverse operational environments by using structured incident response models, which optimize minimal security expertise as a vital capability for effective DIS scaling. As organizations grow and become more complex, measuring the effectiveness of DIS becomes increasingly challenging. To assess their readiness and prove their value to stakeholders, organizations employ comprehensive measurement tools that seek opportunities for improvement [6, 17]. Evaluating DIS maturity requires assessment at three levels: capability maturity, outcome-based metrics, and leading indicators, along with benchmarking methodologies. Capability maturity assessments conduct standardized evaluations of DIS components by using maturity levels that help organizations establish baseline improvements [21]. Outcome-based metrics concentrate on minimizing damage from attacks along with enhancing speed of recovery instead of measuring pure technical achievements [14]. Leading indicators, through forward-looking metrics, enable organizations to find security risks or capability shortfalls ahead of time so they can execute preventive protection measures [15]. The benchmarking evaluation methods enable organizations to measure their performance against industry competitors and established standards, which help them identify growth opportunities for future development [17].

The National Institute of Standards and Technology [17] delivers the Cybersecurity Framework 2.0, which serves as an extensive method to manage cybersecurity risks through functions for Identify, Protect, Detect, Respond, and Recover. The scheme clarifies that cyber risk management remains a continuous operation, which directs organizations toward appropriate security designs that operate as digital shields. The multinational manufacturer uses its 12 business units to demonstrate these principles through its deployment of maturity assessment frameworks. The assessment showed that regions possessed varying observability levels since some had progressed with their capabilities, but others faced delays. The company dedicated resources to improve observation capabilities throughout its whole operation while building robust digital immune functionality at an enterprise level. Organizations with extensive operations should employ complete measurement systems to find gaps in capabilities, which enable them to strengthen digital defense mechanisms throughout their organization.

14.7 Implementation Strategies for Enterprise-Scale Digital Immune Systems

Implementing DIS at an enterprise-scale requires strategies that balance present risk reduction with future capability enhancement objectives. A successful deployment strategy involves the phased implementation of capabilities, demonstrating initial successes before expanding further [10, 11, 16]. Organizations typically follow four main strategies in their phased implementation: prioritizing vital assets and capabilities, achieving multiple initial project successes, incrementally increasing complexity, and conducting proof-of-concept programs. Protecting key assets and capabilities begins with implementing basic capabilities that lay the groundwork for further protection of digital assets with risk mitigation [14]. The first proof of digital transformation success through initial projects is that it addresses significant risks and pain points, allowing outreach to gain organizational support for further investment [11]. The implementation process starts with building step-by-step sequences of increasing complexity, ensuring prerequisites are met before adding advanced capabilities [10].

HCLTech [10] recommends that organizations' first step is to assess IT maturity by identifying whether there are areas that can be improved to develop observability, security, and automation, which will allow the effective implementation of a DIS. The assessment provides an understanding of basic DIS capabilities to deploy, particularly isolating critical items first. The development involves establishing security policies alongside surveillance systems, integrating multiple security components, and implementing comprehensive disaster response protocols. In addition to these foundational elements, there is a requirement for continuous security assessment to verify resilience, as noted by the Forbes Technology Council [11].

Large organizations manage a variety of technical environments, typically connecting their legacy systems with both commercial and custom software applications. The successful implementation of a DIS experiences unique circumstances across technical environments, resulting in the need for integration approaches to overcome operational and vendor management processes [19, 23]. Successful technology integration with vendors requires sound processes comprised of integration architecture design, strategic partnerships, vendor evaluations, and system rationalization programs. Integration architecture facilitates the seamless connection of different security technologies through data exchange, avoiding operational complexities across multiple environments [10]. Security vendor evaluations using standardized frameworks help organizations assess both technological expertise and organizational compatibility before making purchasing decisions [11]. Organizations may leverage a strategic partnership to work with key security vendors, influencing product development and gaining privileged technical support for a sustained operational advantage [19]. Scheduled evaluations concerning security technologies promoted by rationalization programs address redundancies, fill capability gaps, and maximize investment in infrastructure [14].

Microsoft [19] explained that organizations may work with established cloud vendors to leverage their advanced security measures designed for protecting data at rest and in transit. Partnerships with proven security vendors play a crucial role in building successful DIS. A multinational retail organization conducted an enterprise security integration platform that provided a real-world example of the principles of enterprise security design. By integrating API gateways with data normalization services and workflow automation, the platform enabled security tools to operate as a unified system. Their integration architecture preserved safeguarding entire security functions across technology, leading to the effective scaling of DIS within various organizational configurations.

Digital immune systems require more than technology; they require a change in organization culture and human behavior, along with comprehensive change management processes [16, 26]. Implementing DIS involves four key change management components: stakeholder involvement, skills development, educational programs, and performance-based compensation strategies. Leadership support from business stakeholders, IT leaders, and security professionals is essential for planning and governing the DIS through effective stakeholder engagement [14]. Skills development ensures that security teams and relevant stakeholders are properly trained to use DIS components, ensuring operational success [10]. Awareness programs educate all employees on their role in organizational resilience and the proper utilization of DIS to enhance security standards [19]. Organizations that align incentives with performance metrics can motivate behaviors that enhance resilience and encourage desired practices [26]. Digital transformation aims to create sustainable organizations by aligning technological, organizational, and cultural factors [26]. The authors emphasize the importance of conceptual models of digital transformation to achieve sustainability amid rapid technological change, highlighting the need to address both technical and non-technical aspects during the implementation of DIS.

A global professional services organization exemplified this by creating a network of "resilience champions" to implement these principles. The organization deployed security champions within business units, ensuring that enterprise security requirements were adapted to local practices and pursued necessary cyber investment funds. This approach accelerated the adoption of DIS by directly linking business outcomes to local executives, proving that cultural transformation efforts were effective in implementing DIS across diverse organizational environments. This case demonstrates that change management strategies help large organizations adopt DIS in various business settings, providing the necessary functional capability to effectively implement these systems within complex operational environments.

14.8 Adapting Digital Immune Systems to Future Challenges and Technological Shifts

Organizations must develop flexible security frameworks that not only address immediate cyber risks but also sustain long-term resilience against future vulnerabilities. Large enterprises that successfully integrate emerging technologies with human-centric security strategies will be better positioned to defend their operations effectively against both current and future cyber threats [18, 21].

A key challenge in the evolving cybersecurity domain is the necessity for quantum-resistant cryptography. According to the National Institute of Standards and Technology [17], all data protected by contemporaneous public-key encryption will be vulnerable to attacks once quantum computing advances to a practical level. To prepare for this shift, forward-thinking organizations are conducting "crypto-agility" and are evaluating their histories to produce transformation mechanisms until there is more widespread adoption of quantum-resistant cryptographic standards [17].

Social engineering attacks present another growing concern, leveraging more advanced techniques, including deepfakes, advanced phishing, and business email compromise [11, 19]. Digital immune systems will need the integration of behavioral analytics, human-responsibility assessments, and adaptive training to mitigate these threats. Security awareness initiatives, including simulated phishing exercises and policy reinforcement, play a critical role in enhancing employee resilience against social engineering tactics [11]. Microsoft [19] further highlights that human dynamics remain a significant risk in security and that a security-by-design approach is necessary for control measures to be aligned with cognitive behaviors.

14.9 Conclusion

This chapter explores how large enterprises may deliberately implement DIS to improve their operational resilience. Digital immune systems incorporate analytics, automation, and cybersecurity controls to safeguard the digital assets of the organization and enable business continuity. As technology has advanced rapidly and the circumstances of cybersecurity threats have multiplied, large enterprises are increasingly devoted to accelerating and scaling DIS deployment across their multinational facilities. Thus, this chapter has identified architectural principles that introduce service-oriented, modular design approaches, which serve to improve system agility and resilience. Effective large-scale cybersecurity solutions leverage advanced analytics, machine learning, and threat intelligence. These principles will enable organizational leadership to design and scale digital systems while ensuring operational readiness.

AI disclosure statement: The author acknowledges the use of AI-based tools for minor language editing or grammatical correction. However, all intellectual contributions, analyses, and conclusions presented in this chapter are entirely the author's own.

References

1. Luo, Y., A general framework of digitization risks in international business. *J. Int. Bus. Stud.*, 53, 2, 344, 2021.
2. Irfan, I., Sumbal, M.S.U.K., Khurshid, F., Chan, F.T., Toward a resilient supply chain model: critical role of knowledge management and dynamic capabilities. *Ind. Manage. Data Syst.*, 122, 5, 1153–1182, 2022.
3. Liu, R., Long, J., Liu, L., Seeking the resilience of service firms: a strategic learning process based on digital platform capability. *J. Serv. Mark.*, 37, 3, 371–391, 2023.
4. Perri, L., What Is a Digital Immune System and Why Does It Matter?, Gartner, 2022.
5. Schatz, M.C. and Phillippy, A.M., The rise of a digital immune system. *Gigascience*, 1, 1, 2047–217X, 2012.
6. Krauze, B. and Grabis, J., A Conceptual Model of Digital Immune System to Increase the Resilience of Technology Ecosystems, in: *International Conference on Research Challenges in Information Science*, Cham, pp. 82–96, 2024.
7. Laubenbacher, R., *et al.*, Building digital twins of the human immune system: toward a roadmap. *npj Digit. Med.*, 5, 1, 64, 2022.
8. George, A.S., George, A.H., Baskar, T., Digitally immune systems: building robust defences in the age of cyber threats. *Partn. Univers. Int. Innov. J.*, 1, 4, 155–172, 2023.
9. Grand View Research, Digital immune system market size, share & trends analysis report, 2023, [Online]. Available: https://www.grandviewresearch.com/industry-analysis/digital-immune-system-market-report.
10. HCLTech, Digital immune system: Demystifying implications, 2023, [Online]. Available: https://www.hcltech.com/trends-and-insights/digital-immune-system-demystifying-implications.
11. Forbes Technology Council, How organizations can create a digital immune system, Forbes, 12 December 2023, [Online]. Available: https://www.forbes.com/councils/forbestechcouncil/2023/12/12/how-organizations-can-create-a-digital-immune-system/.
12. Zhang, Q., Sun, X., Zhang, M., Data matters: A strategic action framework for data governance. *Inf. Manage.*, 59, 4, 103642, 2022.
13. Davidson, E., Wessel, L., Winter, J.S., Winter, S., Future directions for scholarship on data governance, digital innovation, and grand challenges. *Inf. Organ.*, 33, 1, 100454, 2023.

14. Williams, T. and Resto-Leon, M., Cracking the code: The keys to a successful business impact analysis. *J. Bus. Contin. Emergency Plann.*, 16, 4, 313–319, 2023.
15. Habbal, A., Ali, M.K., Abuzaraida, M.A., Artificial Intelligence Trust, risk and security management (AI trism): Frameworks, applications, challenges and future research directions. *Expert Syst. Appl.*, 240, 122442, 2024.
16. Forbes Technology Council, Digital immune systems: Assurance in the midst of volatility, Forbes, 15 May 2023, [Online]. Available: https://www.forbes.com/councils/forbestechcouncil/2023/05/15/digital-immune-systems-assurance-in-the-midst-of-volatility/.
17. National Institute of Standards and Technology, The NIST Cybersecurity Framework 2.0, NIST, Gaithersburg, MD, 2023.
18. European Commission, The EU's Cybersecurity Strategy for the Digital Decade, European Commission, Brussels, 2020, [Online]. Available: https://digital-strategy.ec.europa.eu/en/policies/cybersecurity-strategy.
19. Microsoft, How cyber security can become the immune system of your company's digital transformation, Microsoft News, 4 August 2016, [Online]. Available: https://news.microsoft.com/en-xm/2016/08/04/how-cyber-security-can-become-the-immune-system-of-your-companys-digital-transformation/.
20. European Parliament & Council of the European Union, Directive (EU) 2022/2555 on measures for a high common level of cybersecurity across the Union, Official Journal of the European Union, 2023, [Online]. Available: https://eur-lex.europa.eu/legal-content/EN/TXT/?uri=CELEX:32022L2555.
21. International Organization for Standardization, ISO/IEC 27001:2022, Information security, cybersecurity and privacy protection - Information security management systems – Requirements, 2022.
22. Hilker, M. and Schommer, C., Sana-security analysis in internet traffic through artificial immune systems, arXiv preprint arXiv:0805.0909, 2008.
23. National Institute of Standards and Technology, Artificial Intelligence Risk Management Framework (AI RMF 1.0), U.S. National Institute of Standards and Technology, 2023.
24. Tresp, V., Overhage, J.M., Bundschus, M., Rabizadeh, S., Fasching, P.A., Yu, S., Going digital: a survey on digitalization and large-scale data analytics in healthcare. *Proc. IEEE*, 104, 11, 2180–2206, 2016.
25. Kandasamy, K., Srinivas, S., Achuthan, K., Rangan, V.P., IoT cyber risk: A holistic analysis of cyber risk assessment frameworks, risk vectors, and risk ranking process. *EURASIP J. Inf. Secur.*, 2020, 1–18, 2020.
26. Mohamed Hashim, M. A., Tlemsani, I., Duncan Matthews, R. A sustainable university: Digital transformation and beyond. *Educ. Inf. Technol.*, 27, 7, 8961–8996, 2022.
27. International Organization for Standardization, ISO 22301:2019 Security and resilience – Business continuity management systems – Requirements, 2019.

15

Blockchain-Based Drug Authentication: Leveraging zk-SNARKs and IPFS for Enhanced Security

R. M. Sabriesh Ram Kumar, L.R.S. Harjith, Binil Rohaan, Raghul Gandhi and Pooja Mishra*

Department of Computer Science and Engineering, Amrita School of Computing, Coimbatore, Amrita Vishwa Vidhyapeetham, India

Abstract

The pharmaceutical industry is confronted with enormous challenges in maintaining drug authenticity, regulatory compliance, and supply chain openness. Counterfeit drugs, ineffective record-keeping, and security weaknesses are critical risks to public health and industry stakeholders. This chapter outlines a blockchain-based drug traceability system that combines zero-knowledge proofs (zk-SNARKs), verifiable credentials (VCs), and the interplanetary file system (IPFS) to improve privacy, security, and efficiency. Utilizing Ethereum smart contracts, decentralized storage, and cryptographic verification mechanisms, this system provides end-to-end traceability while upholding data confidentiality. The chapter delves into blockchain basics, security mechanisms, practical applications, and regulatory issues while it discusses the future of blockchain-based pharmaceutical supply chains.

***Keywords*:** Blockchain, drug traceability, zk-SNARKs, verifiable credentials, IPFS, smart contracts, data security

**Corresponding author*: m_pooja@cb.amrita.edu

Sujata Priyambada Dash, Vaibhav Mishra, Bijeta Shaw, Sandeep Kumar Panda and S. Balamurugan (eds.) Digital Immune System: Principles and Practices, (323–342) © 2026 Scrivener Publishing LLC

15.1 Introduction

15.1.1 Background and Motivation

Guaranteeing the authenticity and traceability of medicines [1] is an important issue across the world health sector. The use of spurious drugs, inefficiencies within the supply chains, and secrecy [2] have resulted in serious health implications and economic loss [2]. Conventional supply chain networks utilize centralized authorities [3], thereby exposing them to fraud, data alteration, and inefficiency [3].

Blockchain technology, being decentralized, immutable, and naturally transparent [4], offers a hopeful answer for safe drug traceability. Using zero-knowledge proofs (zk-SNARKs), verifiable credentials (VCs), and an interplanetary file system (IPFS), this project makes drugs authentic, securely traceable, and efficiently handled without revealing confidential information.

15.1.2 Limitations of Traditional Supply Chain Models

Traditional pharmaceutical supply chains suffer from several challenges:

- **Counterfeit drugs**: Fraudulent medicines enter the supply chain due to inadequate verification mechanisms [5].
- **Lack of transparency**: Centralized tracking systems make it difficult for stakeholders to verify a drug's journey from manufacturer to consumer [6].
- **Data tampering**: Centralized databases are vulnerable to unauthorized alterations [7].
- **Regulatory compliance challenges**: Governments and regulators struggle to enforce compliance due to fragmented record-keeping systems.

15.1.3 Scope and Objectives

This project seeks to deploy a blockchain-based pharmaceutical supply chain that improves security, traceability, and efficiency by:

- Creating a decentralized supply chain model based on Ethereum smart contracts for transparent and unalterable transactions.

- Adding zk-SNARKs for private authentication so that users can authenticate their supply chain role without exposing sensitive identity information.
- Issuing VCs as non-fungible token (NFT)-based digital certificates to authenticate users and transactions securely.
- Utilizing interplanetary file system (IPFS) for decentralized storage, ensuring tamper-proof record- keeping while maintaining cost-efficiency.
- Enhancing role-based access control, ensuring only authorized participants can update or track medicine status.
- Ensuring regulatory compliance by providing real-time auditing capabilities through blockchain transactions.

This project provides an innovative, privacy-preserving, and highly secure approach to pharmaceutical supply chain management, ensuring trust and efficiency across all stakeholders.

15.2 Understanding Blockchain

Blockchain is a decentralized and distributed ledger technology that enables secure and transparent transactions. It ensures data integrity, immutability, and trust without the need for a central authority. Originally introduced as the underlying technology for Bitcoin [8], blockchain has since evolved to support various applications across industries, including supply chain management, healthcare, and finance [4, 9].

15.2.1 Key Features

- **Decentralization**: No central body governs the blockchain; it runs on a peer-to-peer network, guaranteeing that transactions are replicated across multiple nodes, removing a single point of failure.
- **Immutability**: Data, once written, cannot be modified or removed. This characteristic guarantees trust and precludes fraudulent activity.
- **Transparency**: Every member possesses a copy of the ledger, making real-time tracking and auditing transactions possible.
- **Security**: Cryptographic methods like hashing and digital signatures guard transactions against tampering.

- **Consensus mechanisms**: Transactions are confirmed by network participants using consensus protocols to ensure the integrity and correctness of data.

15.2.2 Components of Blockchain

- **Blocks**: The building block of a blockchain with transaction data, a timestamp, and a cryptographic hash pointing to the prior block.
- **Nodes**: Machines that join the blockchain network and keep copies of the ledger. Nodes validate transactions and maintain network integrity.
- **Smart Contracts**: Computer programs that automatically execute contracts based on set rules without the involvement of intermediaries.
- **Consensus mechanisms**: Mechanisms that allow network participants to confirm the validity of transactions, avoiding double-spending and fraudulent behavior.

15.2.3 Consensus Mechanisms

Consensus mechanisms play a crucial role in validating and securing blockchain transactions [10]. Some of the widely used mechanisms include:

- **Proof of Work (PoW)**: Requires computational effort to validate transactions and add them to the blockchain. Used in Bitcoin, PoW enhances security but consumes high energy.
- **Proof of Stake (PoS)**: Validators are chosen based on the number of tokens they hold, reducing energy consumption compared to PoW.
- **Delegated Proof of Stake (DPoS)**: Stakeholders vote for delegates who validate transactions, improving efficiency and scalability.
- **Byzantine fault tolerance (BFT)**: Ensures consensus even in the presence of malicious nodes, enhancing network security and trustworthiness.

15.3 Security in Digital Systems

Security in computer systems is necessary to safeguard data and resources against unauthorized access [11], incidents, and cyberattacks. The contemporary digital landscape requires strong security infrastructures to protect sensitive data and preserve operational integrity.

15.3.1 Confidentiality, Integrity, and Availability

- **Confidentiality**: It provides that confidential information is made available only to authorized individuals, preventing unauthorized disclosure.
- **Integrity**: It ensures that information does not change and is reliable, ensuring that records and transactions cannot be altered without being detected.
- **Availability**: It guarantees that systems and data become available when necessary, averting disruption of services and maintaining uninterrupted operations.

15.3.2 Common Security Threats

- Malware and ransomware attacks: Malicious software that encrypts or steals data, demanding ransom payments.
- Phishing and social engineering: Cyberattacks that trick individuals into revealing sensitive information.
- Denial-of-Service attacks: Overloading a system to render it unavailable to legitimate users.
- Man-in-the-Middle attacks: Intercepting communication between two parties to steal or manipulate data.

15.4 Data Security in Blockchain

Blockchain technology enhances data security through cryptographic techniques and consensus mechanisms.

15.4.1 Cryptographic Hashing

Blockchain uses cryptographic hash functions (e.g., SHA-256) to secure transactions. Hashing ensures data integrity and prevents tampering by generating unique digital fingerprints for each block of data [10].

15.4.2 Encryption and Digital Signatures

- **Encryption:** Ensures secure data transmission by converting plaintext into ciphertext using cryptographic algorithms [22], protecting sensitive information from unauthorized access.
- **Digital signatures:** Authenticate the sender and ensure message integrity, preventing unauthorized modifications to data.

15.4.3 Consensus Mechanisms for Security

Blockchain employs consensus algorithms to validate transactions, making unauthorized modifications nearly impossible. This ensures trust and eliminates the need for intermediaries in sensitive operations like pharmaceutical supply chains [12].

15.4.4 Challenges in Blockchain Security

- **Fifty-one percent attack:** A scenario where a malicious entity gains control over the majority of the network's computational power, enabling them to manipulate transactions.
- **Private key security:** Loss of private keys leads to loss of access to assets, highlighting the need for secure key management practices.
- **Scalability issues:** High computational costs and slow transaction speeds can limit blockchain's widespread adoption.

15.5 Introduction to Interplanetary File Systems

An IPFS is a decentralized file storage system designed to address limitations in traditional cloud-based storage solutions.

15.5.1 How Interplanetary File Systems Work

An IPFS uses a content-addressed storage model [23], where each file is assigned a unique hash. Instead of relying on centralized servers, files are distributed across multiple nodes, ensuring redundancy and security.

15.5.2 Benefits of Interplanetary File Systems over Traditional Storage

Decentralization: Eliminates single points of failure and enhances data resilience.
Efficiency: Reduces bandwidth costs and enhances data retrieval speed by using a peer-to-peer model.
Tamper-resistance: Ensures data integrity through cryptographic hashing, preventing unauthorized modifications.

15.5.3 Integration of Interplanetary File Systems with Blockchain

An IPFS can be integrated with blockchain to store large files off-chain [13] while maintaining data integrity and access control through cryptographic hash references. This is particularly useful for storing pharmaceutical records and tracking drug authenticity.

15.6 Introduction to Zero-Knowledge Succinct Non-Interactive Arguments of Knowledge

Zero-knowledge succinct non-interactive arguments of knowledge or zk-SNARKs are cryptographic proofs that enable one party (the prover) to convince another party (the verifier) of a statement's validity without revealing any underlying data. This ensures both privacy and computational efficiency, making zk-SNARKs highly useful in blockchain-based applications like secure pharmaceutical supply chains.

15.6.1 How Zero-Knowledge Succinct Non-Interactive Arguments of Knowledge Work

Zero-knowledge succinct non-interactive arguments of knowledge function through a combination of mathematical proofs and cryptographic keys. Instead of directly sharing transaction details, the prover generates a proof that confirms their eligibility without exposing confidential data. The verifier can then check this proof in constant time.

Statement encoding: The problem (e.g., "Is this user authorized to order medicine?") is converted into an arithmetic circuit.
Trusted setup: A cryptographic setup phase generates public and private keys.
Proof generation: The prover uses private inputs and a proving key to generate a zk-SNARK proof.
Verification: The verifier checks the proof against the verification key to confirm validity.

15.6.2 Benefits of Zero-Knowledge Succinct Non-Interactive Arguments of Knowledge over Traditional Verification

Privacy-preserving: No need to reveal sensitive data (e.g., user roles, order history).
Efficiency: Proofs are short and verified in constant time, reducing on-chain computation.
Security: Ensures integrity while preventing data leaks in a decentralized supply chain.

15.6.3 Integration of Zero-Knowledge Succinct Non-Interactive Arguments of Knowledge with Blockchain in Pharmaceutical Supply Chain

Zero-knowledge succinct non-interactive arguments of knowledge work are integrated into blockchain-based pharmaceutical supply chains to enhance role-based authentication and transaction privacy:

- **Private role verification:** Users prove they have the correct role to order or process medicine without exposing role details.
- **Secure order processing:** Medicine orders require zk-SNARK proofs to verify authenticity, reducing fraud.
- **Tamper-proof tracking:** Ensures only authorized entities can update medicine statuses without revealing transaction details.

By leveraging zk-SNARKs, the system maintains trust, security, and privacy while ensuring regulatory compliance in pharmaceutical distribution.

15.7 Need for Blockchain in Drug Traceability

The pharmaceutical industry faces significant challenges in ensuring drug authenticity [5] and regulatory compliance. Blockchain offers a secure and transparent solution for tracking drugs throughout the supply chain.

15.7.1 Problems with the Existing Drug Supply Chain

- **Lack of end-to-end visibility:** The lack of end-to-end visibility in drug tracking leads to inefficiencies and counterfeiting risks, which can be addressed by integrating the Internet of Things (IoT) with blockchain [14].
- **Complex and fragmented processes:** Multiple intermediaries increase risks of errors and counterfeiting.
- **Inefficiencies in record-keeping:** Paper-based or centralized digital systems are prone to tampering and data loss.

15.7.2 Counterfeit Drugs and Their Impact

Counterfeit drugs pose a major risk to the healthcare system, and blockchain has been explored as a solution for improving security [15].

- **Health risks:** Counterfeit drugs may contain harmful or ineffective ingredients, endangering patient lives.
- **Economic losses:** Billions of dollars lost due to fraudulent drugs, affecting pharmaceutical companies and economies.
- **Erosion of trust:** Undermines consumer confidence in the pharmaceutical industry.

15.7.3 How Blockchain Solves these Issues

- **Immutable records:** Ensures that drug transaction data cannot be altered.
- **Enhanced traceability:** Tracks drugs from manufacturer to consumer with real-time updates.

15.8 Implementation of Blockchain-Based Drug Traceability System

Blockchain technology is integrated into the pharmaceutical supply chain to enhance transparency, security, and efficiency in drug tracking.

15.8.1 System Architecture Overview

The architectural diagram as shown in Figure 15.1 integrates smart contracts, zk-SNARKs, Web3, and a react-based frontend. The core functionalities include role-based access control, immutable order tracking, and decentralized verification of transactions.

15.8.2 Smart Contracts for Drug Verification

Ethereum-based smart contracts [21] are written in Solidity to automate medicine tracking [16, 17]. The SupplyChain.sol contract includes the following features:

- **Roles-based access:** Only authorized roles (manufacturer, distributor, etc.) can interact with specific functions.
- **Medicine ordering:** Users can order medicines based on predefined listings.
- **Tracking transactions:** Each update in the supply chain is recorded as a blockchain transaction.

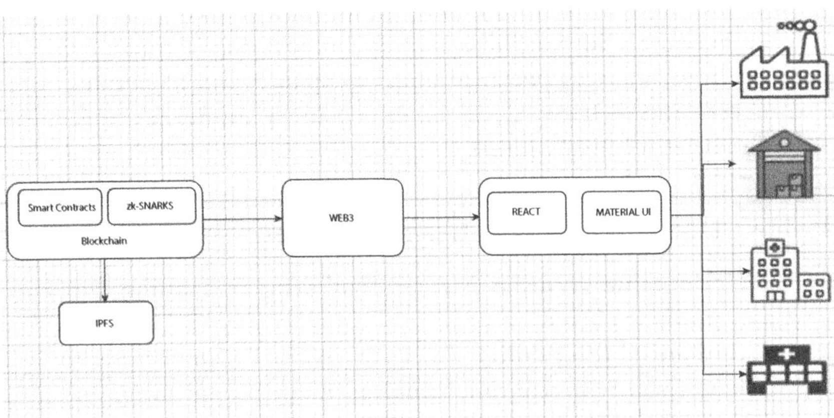

Figure 15.1 Architecture diagram.

- **Zero-proof knowledge verification:** Users must prove role ownership without exposing identity.
- **Interplanetary file systems storage:** Order details and transaction records are stored in IPFS to ensure decentralized access.
- **Verifiable credentials:** Users receive VCs upon successful order verification, ensuring authenticity.

Figure 15.2 shows the initialization of a local blockchain using Hardhat. It displays a list of test accounts with their corresponding private keys, which can be used for development and testing.

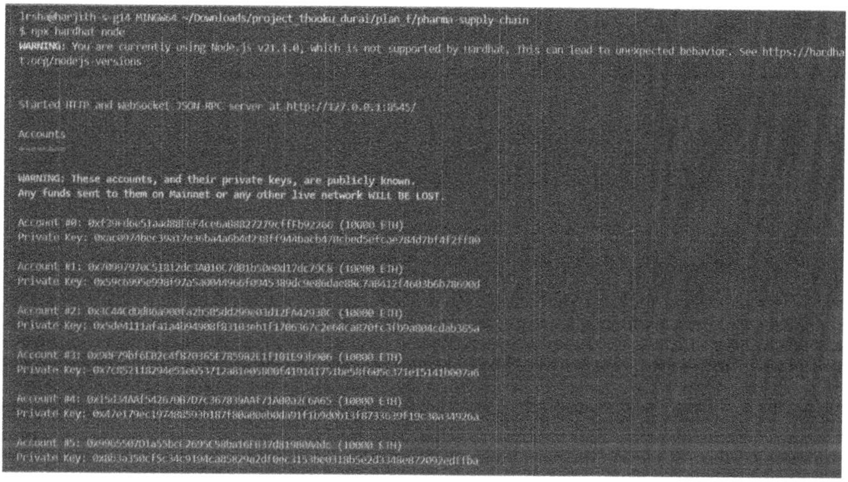

Figure 15.2 Hardhat accounts.

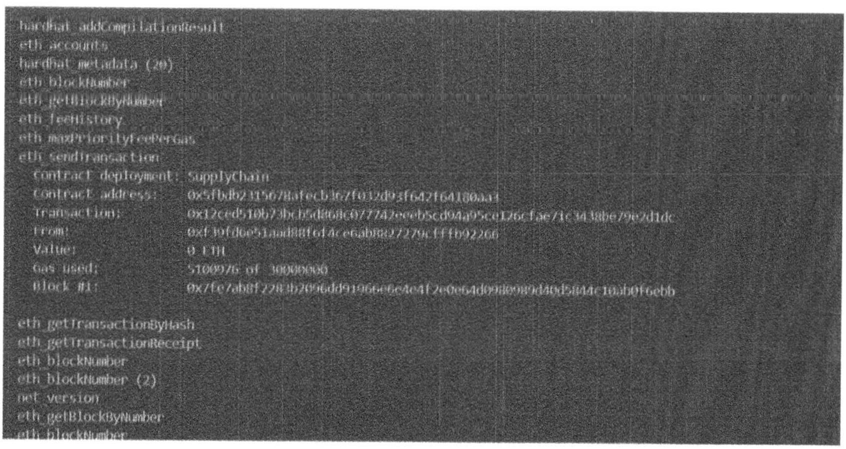

Figure 15.3 Deploying the supply chain smart contract.

Figure 15.3 confirms the successful deployment of the supply chain smart contract on the Hardhat network. It includes details such as the contract address, transaction hash, and gas usage.

15.8.3 Frontend and Web3 Integration

The frontend is developed using React.js and Material-UI, interacting with smart contracts through Web3.js. The user interface allows stakeholders to verify credentials, track orders, and update medicine statuses.

15.8.4 Integration of Zero-Knowledge Succinct Non-Interactive Arguments of Knowledge, Verifiable Credentials, and Interplanetary File Systems

15.8.4.1 Algorithm for Secure Order Processing

The algorithm for secure order processing has been given in algorithm 15.1.

15.8.4.2 Zero-Knowledge Succinct Non-Interactive Arguments of Knowledge (zk-SNARKs)

Zero-knowledge succinct non-interactive arguments of knowledge (zk-SNARKs) allow users to prove that they have the right credentials without revealing sensitive data. In this project, it ensures:

- **Order Verification:** Users must prove they have a valid role before ordering medicine [18].
- **Status Updates:** Users prove ownership of the VC NFT for a specific order before processing it to the next stage [19].

Algorithm 15.1 Blockchain-based order processing.

1: User requests to order medicine.
2: Generate zk-SNARK proof (inputs: user role, valid VC).
3: Smart contract verifies proof; proceed if valid.
4: Generate VC with user role, order details, and signature.
5: Store VC on-chain and issue NFT to user.
6: Store order details on IPFS; save hash on blockchain.
7: Users must prove VC ownership for order processing.

8: Order progresses from manufacturer to consumer.
9: Consumer verifies product authenticity using IPFS record.

15.8.4.3 Verifiable Credentials

Verifiable credentials are used to authenticate transactions without revealing unnecessary details. Each medicine order generates a VC NFT, which is stored on-chain and linked to the user. The VC contains:

- User Role & Identity Proof
- Order Details (Medicine Name, Quantity, Order ID)
- Digital Signature for Authenticity

15.8.4.4 Interplanetary File System

The Interplanetary file system ensures decentralized storage of order details. The order record is stored on IPFS, and the hash is saved on the blockchain. This allows:

- Tamper-Proof Storage of Order Details
- Efficient Retrieval Using the IPFS Hash Stored On-Chain

15.8.5 Supply Chain Workflow

The drug supply chain involves multiple stakeholders, ensuring the authenticity, quality, and security of pharmaceutical products. Blockchain technology enhances this process by providing an immutable, transparent, and decentralized ledger for tracking transactions at each stage. Figure 15.4 show workflow of the supply chain.

- **Supplier**: The process starts with the supplier providing raw materials for drug manufacturing.
- **Regulatory check**: Regulatory agencies inspect and ensure that the supplied materials meet quality standards.
- **Manufacturer**: After receiving raw materials, manufacturers produce drugs and verify compliance with quality standards.
- **Blockchain transaction**: The manufacturer records the production details as a transaction on the blockchain.
- **Distribution**: The finished drug batches are sent to distributors for further supply.

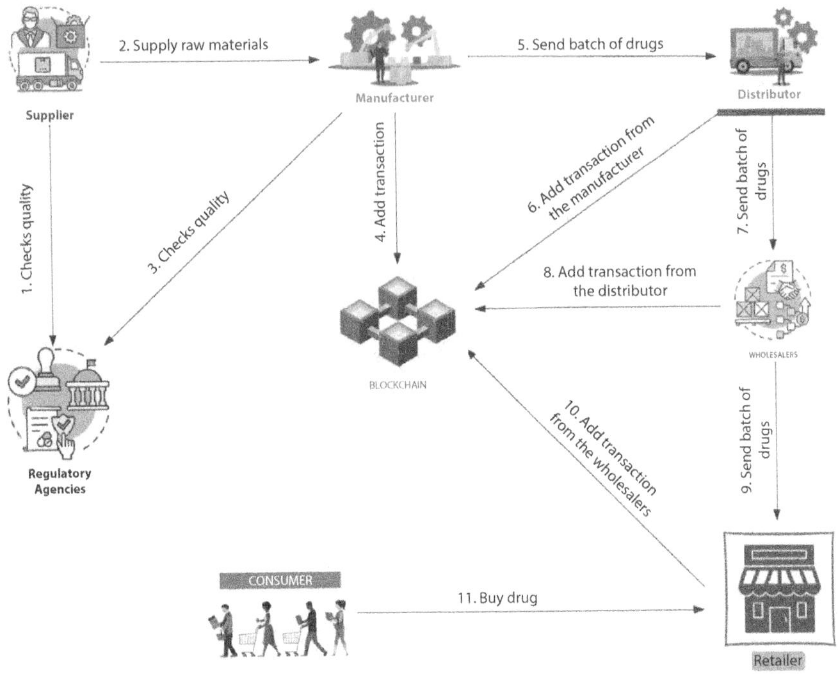

Figure 15.4 Blockchain-based supply chain workflow.

- **Blockchain transaction from manufacturer**: The manufacturer adds the transaction details of dispatched drugs to the blockchain.
- **Wholesalers**: Distributors send batches of drugs to wholesalers.
- **Blockchain transaction from distributor**: The distributor records transaction details on the blockchain.
- **Retailers**: Wholesalers supply the drugs to retail pharmacies for sale to consumers.
- **Blockchain transaction from wholesalers**: The wholesalers add transaction records to the blockchain, ensuring transparency.
- **Consumer purchase**: Finally, consumers buy the drugs, and the blockchain maintains a record of the entire supply chain journey.

15.9 Advantages and Challenges of Blockchain in Drug Traceability

Blockchain technology offers numerous benefits for drug traceability but also presents challenges in adoption.

15.9.1 Efficiency and Performance Metrics

To assess the efficiency of the blockchain-based system for drug traceability, several efficiency indicators and hyperparameters are compared in Table 15.1.

15.9.2 Benefits

- **Transparency**: Immutable records grant complete transparency of the supply chain.
- **Security**: Encrypted data and consensus mechanisms secure against unauthorized changes.
- **Efficiency**: Smart contracts make verification automatic, eliminating paperwork.
- **Counterfeit prevention**: Follows drug origin and movement to guarantee authenticity.
- **Regulatory compliance**: Facilitates audits and compliance with government regulations.

15.9.3 Challenges

- **Scalability**: Large volumes of transactions can slow down processing and raise storage requirements.
- **Cost**: Upfront investment in blockchain infrastructure and smart contract development.
- **Adoption barriers**: Pharmaceutical companies' resistance due to lack of blockchain knowledge.
- **Regulatory hurdles**: Adherence to international pharmaceutical regulations could necessitate blockchain adjustments.
- **Data privacy concerns**: Keeping sensitive information private while being transparent.

Table 15.1 Comparison of zk-SNARK + NFT-based supply chain vs traditional supply chain.

Metric	Zero-knowledge succinct non-interactive arguments of knowledge + NFT-based supply chain	Traditional supply chain (centralized)
Security	High (immutable records, zk-SNARK privacy)	Low (prone to tampering, data breaches)
Privacy	User proves role without revealing details	Role and user data stored in databases, prone to leaks
Data integrity	Blockchain prevents unauthorized changes	Relies on database security, can be altered
Efficiency (proof generation time)	Higher (500ms for zk-SNARK proof generation)	Faster (10ms role verification in databases)
Verification Speed	Instant (100ms, on-chain zk-SNARK verification)	Instant (Database lookup, 10ms)
Storage requirements	Higher (zk-SNARK proofs and NFT metadata stored on-chain and IPFS)	Lower (Centralized databases store roles and transactions)
Blockchain block size impact	Large (zk-SNARK proof and NFT metadata increase block size)	Small (No blockchain data stored)
Gas cost (Ethereum network)	High (200K gas for zk-SNARK proof verification)	No gas cost (centralized storage and verification)
Scalability	High (Decentralized, no single point of failure)	Limited (server bottlenecks, scaling issues)
Resilience to attacks	High (No centralized authority, zk- SNARKs prevent data leaks)	Low (centralized database can be hacked)
Regulatory compliance	High (on-chain verifiable credentials)	Risky (centralized control, lack of transparency)

In spite of these challenges, blockchain technology can revolutionize to facilitate drug traceability, to guarantee safety, efficiency, and consumer confidence in the pharmaceutical sector.

15.10 Future Scope

The application of blockchain to traceability of drugs is continually under development, and future improvements can amplify its functionality even more. Potential development areas are:

15.10.1 Artificial Intelligence-Based Analytics

Merged blockchain with AI can assist predictive analytics for forecasting of drug demand [20], anomaly detection, and supply chain optimization.

15.10.2 Integration with the Internet of Things

Utilizing IoT devices to monitor real-time conditions of drug storage (e.g., temperature, humidity) and processing this information onto blockchain for increased monitoring.

15.10.3 Advanced Smart Contracts

Creating more advanced smart contracts to automate verification of compliance, recalls, and regulatory reports, minimizing human intervention.

15.10.4 Cross-Industry Collaboration

Increased blockchain use across multiple players, such as healthcare providers, insurers, and regulators, is needed to develop an integrated and open ecosystem.

15.10.5 Scalability and Efficiency Improvements

Exploring new consensus mechanisms and layer-2 solutions to enhance blockchain's scalability and lower transaction costs for broad adoption.

AI disclosure statement: The author acknowledges the use of AI-based tools for minor language editing or grammatical correction. However, all intellectual contributions, analyses, and conclusions presented in this chapter are entirely the author's own.

References

1. Narayana, S. and Mishra, P., Blockchain technology for secure pharmaceutical supply chains. *J. Emerg. Technol.*, 12, 134–145, 2021.
2. Gupta, R. and Patel, A., Counterfeit drugs and blockchain: A systematic review. *Healthc. Inf. J.*, 15, 89–102, 2022.
3. Parmar, J., *et al.*, Blockchain-based drug supply chain security system. *IEEE Trans. Blockchain*, 6, 89–102, 2020.
4. Swan, M., *Blockchain: Blueprint for a new economy*, O'Reilly Media, 2015.
5. W. H. O. (WHO), Counterfeit drugs and their global impact, WHO Reports, 2021.
6. Berke, A., How blockchain could help the food industry increase transparency and reduce waste, MIT Sloan Review, 2017.
7. Nguyen, H. and Tran, Q., Regulatory challenges in blockchain-based pharmaceutical supply chains. *Regul. Aff. J.*, 5, 65–80, 2020.
8. Nakamoto, S., *Bitcoin: A peer-to-peer electronic cash system*, 2008. https://bitcoin.org/bitcoin.pdf.
9. Panda, S.K., Mishra, V., Dash, S.P., Pani, A.K., *Recent Advances in Blockchain Technology Real-World Applications*, vol. 237, Intelligent Systems Reference Library (ISRL), Springer, 2023.
10. Gervais, A., *et al.*, On the security and performance of proof of work blockchains. *ACM Conference on Computer and Communications Security*, 2016.
11. Bonneau, J., *et al.*, Sok: Research perspectives and challenges for bitcoin and cryptocurrencies. *IEEE Symposium on Security and Privacy*, 2015.
12. Venkatesan, K. and Rahayu, S.B., Blockchain security enhancement: An approach towards hybrid consensus algorithms and machine learning techniques. *Sci. Rep.*, 14, 1, 1149, 2024.
13. Benet, J., Ipfs - content addressed, versioned, p2p file system, arXiv preprint, 2014.
14. Nanda, S., Panda, S., Dash, M., Medical supply chain integrated with blockchain and iot to track the logistics of medical products. *Multimed. Tools Appl.*, 82, 32917–32939, 2023.
15. Nair, V.K., Blockchain technology in healthcare: A case study to explore the gaps and scope in india, in: *12th Annual ISDI Conference*, 2018.
16. Ak¸ca, E. and Karayılmaz, G., The role of blockchain in digital identity and supply chain management. *Blockchain Res. J.*, 3, 78–94, 2021.

17. Panda, S. and Satapathy, S., An investigation into smart contract deployment on ethereum platform using web3.js and solidity using blockchain, in: *Data Engineering and Intelligent Computing*, vol. 1, Advances in Intelligent Systems and Computing, V. Bhateja, S. Satapathy, C. Travieso-González, V. Aradhya (Eds.), Springer, Singapore, 2021.
18. Bitansky, N., *et al.*, Snarks for c: Verifying computations without reexecuting them. *CRYPTO*, 2013.
19. Gao, J. and Huang, P., Zero-knowledge proofs for scalable and private blockchain transactions. *Cryptogr. Adv. J.*, 9, 37–54, 2021.
20. Arza, M.S. and Panda, S.K., An integration of blockchain and machine learning into the health care system, in: *Machine Learning Adoption in Blockchain-Based Intelligent Manufacturing*, vol. 1, pp. 33–58, 2022.
21. Kumar, P., Dhanush, G.A., Srivatsa, D., Nithin, A., Sahisnu, S., A buyer and seller's protocol via utilization of smart contracts using blockchain technology, in: *Advanced Informatics for Computing Research: Third International Conference, ICAICR 2019*, Revised Selected Papers, Part I 3, p. 464–474, Springer, Shimla, India, June 15–16, 2019.
22. Mishra, P., Bhaya, C., Pal, A. K., Singh, A. K., A novel binary operator for designing medical and natural image cryptosystems. *Signal Process. Image Commun.*, 98, 116377, 2021.
23. Saiharsha, B., Sanjay Tharagesh, R.S., Nikish Kumar, S.V., Harini, N., Cloud based data integrity model for minimal human intervention using smart contracts. In *2020 5th International Conference on Communication and Electronics Systems (ICCES)*, pp. 910–916, IEEE, 2020.

16

Privacy-Preserving and Scalable Authentication Using zk-SNARK-Based ZKP Blockchain PKI

Amrutanshu Panigrahi[1]*, Bibhuprasad Sahu[2], Abhilash Pati[1] and Subrata Chowdhury[3]

[1]Department of CSE, Siksha 'O' Anusandhan (Deemed to be University), Bhubaneswar, Odisha, India
[2]Symbiosis Institute of Technology, Hyderabad Campus, Symbiosis International University, Pune, India
[3]Department of Computer Science & Machine Learning, Sreenivasa Institute of Technology and Management Studies, Chittor, India

Abstract

Public key infrastructure (PKI) establishes secure communication over digital interfaces and authorized access to technology resources. Traditional PKI systems have weaknesses such as key compromise, trust management failure, escalated vulnerabilities due to a unitary point of failure, and other shortcomings, unlike basic PKI Models, which operate with a certificate authority (CA) centrally. The study proposes blockchain PKI based on zero-knowledge proofs (ZKP), which, with the use of zk-SNARKs, strives to make existing frameworks more efficient and secure. Enhanced privacy guarantees from zk-SNARKs, alongside distributed blockchain, facilitate this. The blockchain acts as an all-encompassing store for certificates where personal privacy is maintained while validation is conducted. Humans can be less dependent on smart contracts, which automate the issuance, validation, and revocation of certificates, enhancing privacy. These characterize the system with ideal universal deployment along with control for execution speed, storage requirements, network responsiveness, and performance. In addition to the performance assessment for those factors, the system was evaluated for scalability, storage, throughput, and the overhead of communication and computing resources, all measured against efficiency. Research validated the operational

**Corresponding author*: amrutansup89@gmail.com

Sujata Priyambada Dash, Vaibhav Mishra, Bijeta Shaw, Sandeep Kumar Panda and S. Balamurugan (eds.) Digital Immune System: Principles and Practices, (343–368) © 2026 Scrivener Publishing LLC

correctness of the system regarding authentication within corporate, financial, Internet of Things, and distributed systems identity management frameworks. Adding zk-SNARKs enhances future advancements in scalability, cost-efficient contract execution, and privacy-boosted security through machine learning. The blockchain PKI constructed on zk-SNARKs offers a distributed and scalable solution to authentication without compromising the privacy of the users, thus solving the problems of existing PKI frameworks.

Keywords: Blockchain, public key infrastructure (PKI), certificate authority (CA), zero-knowledge proof (ZKP), zk-STARK

16.1 Introduction

Blockchain is considered a distributed ledger system with blocks that need to be cryptographically secured and connected. Through such technologies, one guarantees decentralization, transparency, and immutability, thus providing a strong tool to manage several security and digital trust-related issues. One of the main features separating blockchain technology from other similar technologies is decentralization [1]. Blockchain operates on a peer-to-peer architecture wherein several nodes maintain and verify the ledger, unlike normal centralized systems whereby one business has sole control over the data. Reducing points of failure adds to security [2]. The immutability of the blockchain restricts data modification in the distributed ledger, which is yet another advantage. Consensus and cryptographic hashing are two additional crucial elements for blockchain technology to be a growing technological tool. Any user may see transactions recorded on a public ledger, thereby eliminating user trust problems and supporting blockchain dependability *via* transparency and traceability. Consensus mechanisms include Proof of Work (PoW) and Proof of Stake (PoS), which verify transactions, and network security helps to preserve system integrity in part. Moreover, the development of smart contracts—contracts with pre-defined clauses—will boost efficiency and reduce the demand for middlemen for security and automation [3].

Blockchain's operation consists of a set of linked procedures guaranteed to verify transactions and safeguard data storage. Using cryptographic methods, a user starts a transaction first verified by network nodes. Later on, among other things, the transaction gets blocked. Every block has a unique cryptographic hash based on the one before that builds an interconnected construction to forbid illegal data changes [4]. Once a block is created, network users confirm its legitimacy using PoW or PoS, therefore completing the consensus method. The PoS depends on consumers staking money to guard the network; PoW depends on miners to verify transactions by solving difficult mathematical problems. After verification, the block is added to the current blockchain, permanently documenting the transaction. Such a system that is deployed concurrently and unchangeable offers security and confidence all over the network [5].

Among the main benefits of blockchain technology is security. As was already noted, the distributed character of the system reduces single points of failure, therefore reducing the possibility of hacking or illegal access. Turning transaction data into fixed-length hash values is almost difficult to reverse-engineer guarantees cryptographic hash, ensuring data integrity. Blockchain encryption and digital signatures help to better protect the user's transaction information and identity. Every user in the blockchain network has two cryptographic keys—public and private. Signing transactions using private keys achieves claim authentication and denial avoidance. Multi-signature wallets, zero-knowledge proof (ZKP), and Merkle Trees enhance anonymity and the safety of private blockchains' sensitive personal data. The public key infrastructure (PKI) enables authentication and safe information transfer using asymmetric cryptography, which first defines the security of a blockchain. The PKI consists of public and private keys used both ways; it comprises techniques for encryption, decryption, and digital signatures. The PKI is used in blockchain systems to provide validity of transactions, user verification, and information secrecy. Most PKI systems have centralized certificate authorities (CAs) in charge of managing and printing digital certificates. This leads to many security issues, including illegal access and certificate forging. Blockchain-based PKI changes the whole trust concept to handle these problems. Blockchain PKI distributes trust across many nodes, therefore reducing dependence on a single CA and so improving security by helping to manage risks [6, 7].

Notwithstanding its benefits, conventional PKI has some shortcomings: it is not scalable, it does not give enough regard to user privacy, and it lacks confidence. One of the main issues is the probable risk personal data might pose to security when logging into an account. Using ZKP to show knowledge of a secret without revealing any information about it, one person might provide a legitimate response. Using blockchain-augmented PKI with ZKP guarantees private data will not be leaked during identity verification procedures by strengthening the improvement of data security and privacy. Blockchain-based PKI might be helpful in areas like identity management, financial transactions, and secure communication; it could eliminate central authority, enhance auxiliary networks, and control access to personal information *via* ZKP. The verification of identification by users who may hide private data enables ZKP-based blockchain PKI to enhance the safety and confidence of online transactions. Fixing security and privacy calls for a new PKI using blockchain technology together with ZKP, hence advancing it. Because they depend on a single external trusted authority, classic PKI systems run the danger of having a single point of failure, therefore negating the effectiveness of conventional PKI. By using blockchain technology, we guarantee that no one institution can monopolize control over the verification process and hence remove reliance on a central authority to build a distributed PKI. Users of ZKP may verify their identity without revealing any personal information, therefore supporting data privacy. Following current privacy standards, such as the General Data Protection Regulation (GDPR), improves system security. Blockchain, along with smart cryptography ZKP, might drive developments in digital security and identity management. Privacy is a problem even now; however, this may be resolved by building a new PKI system grounded on blockchain and ZKP. Considering issues like these will help us to develop trust on the internet, which is simpler and better. The desire for an easy-to-use blockchain framework protecting privacy and the necessity of more security systems resulting from increasing digital interconnectivity indicate the need for a thorough investigation of new options that combine blockchain and encryption [8].

The current research aims to develop a blockchain-based PKI using ZKP consensus with zero-knowledge succinct non-interactive arguments of knowledge (zk-SNARKs). The proposed PKI is implemented over the Ethereum blockchain platform along with the Ganache truffle. In addition, the proposed PKI is evaluated using different evaluative parameters such as storage usage, gas utilization, and computational time required to implement different processes of the PKI.

16.2 Literature Survey

Among the many efforts researchers have made is using the Web of Trust (WoT) to solve the exceptional difficulties related to PKI based on CA-based systems. Research on the WoT has been conducted ever since it was initially founded in 1992. Caronni [9] established a technique for assessing trust using the web of trust by means of an examination of the network. Unlike previous methods with exponential expenses, a heuristic approach has since been proposed that allows computation to be done at a time that is sub exponential. The design of the WoT determines the temporal complexity of this special method; in certain cases, the WoT may be linear. The fact that the strategy that has been offered is not effective everywhere, nevertheless, is a major weakness. The method shows a great degree of optimism in cases where the trust paths show a considerable degree of interconnectedness or looping. Applying and assessing both on small WoT setups, a comparison was performed between the proposed heuristic method and the exponential-cost strategies that had been used in the past.

Researchers have tried to make CA-based PKI more secure by means of log-based PKI. In 2012, Google introduced certificate transparency (CT), a notable use of log-based PKI. This was done in response to the vulnerabilities revealed after breaches in CAs, particularly the attack targeted against DigiNotar in 2011. Certificate transparency logs provide an extra public ledger of transport layer security (TLS) certificates. This is carried out with the aim of raising the TLS ecosystem auditability. Chrome implemented CT for all recently issued certificates in April of 2018, therefore providing a complete view of the TLS ecosystem. This openness makes it easy for owners to inspect globally issued domain certificates, hence improving security and facilitating the discovery of illegal issuances. Conversely, there is more chance that hitherto unexplored fields and businesses might be revealed [10].

Certificate transparency aims to raise awareness of these certificates by posting certificates provided by CAs to CT logs, ideally kept by third parties. This helps to simplify the fast detection and distribution of mis-issuances. Logs are confined to appending only; Merkle hash trees help to detect any changes that could have taken place in the log history. Every certificate logged generates a signed certificate timestamp, often referred to as an SCT. Using the public key linked to those certificates allows one to verify the promise of inclusion that this SCT represents. Signed certificate timestamps may be delivered by means of a TLS extension, an online certificate status protocol (OCSP) response stapled, or even by being contained in the certificate itself. A CA may integrate an SCT into a certificate in the following way: a precertification is sent to a CT log, obtains an SCT in return, and then appends it to complete the certificate.

Researchers find that their interest in log-based PKI has not changed with time. Chuat *et al.* [10] offered the suggestion to improve web PKI by introducing trust flexibility for consumers and domain owners. They claim that as the current web PKI depends on a trust model uniform across all CAs, it suffers from issues. This method renders the system vulnerable to attack, as even the least secure CA may possibly compromise the entire framework. By enhancing the capacity of CT with a flexible trust framework, the created technique—F-PKI—forms a new kind of web PKI. A mapping server is included in F-PKI's design. This server oversees always getting sets of certificates from the CT log server to ensure their constant updating. By giving domain owners, the option to impose limitations on which CAs may provide certificates, one may build an ecosystem with varied degrees of confidence. Any and all certifications may still be verified using this framework, therefore allowing stakeholders to voice their different points of view about trust problems. The F-PKI also advocates for CAs to raise security standards so as to attract domain owners. This will finally result in better internet security and robust industrial competitiveness. Within the field of web PKI, F-PKI is a significant development that is differentiated by its strong security aspects, including backward compatibility and protection against downgrade events.

Basin *et al.* [11] underlined the need for a methodical design to solve this complexity. This is a result of the many conceivable attack paths, which include breaches of private keys and insufficient key revocation protocols. They put up an innovative PKI architecture called the advanced reliable public key infrastructure (ARPKI). Through better transparency and responsibility for certificate operations, including issuing, revocation, and validation, this system increases security. To guarantee the fundamental security characteristics of ARPKI, which is a formal model seldom used in the design of systems, TAMARIN prover [12] was used. The fact that ARPKI's methodological rigor makes it resistant to complicated assaults helps one to argue that Man-In-the-Middle attacks can still be readily carried out even if up to n−1 trustworthy entities are compromised. Since it enables public openness of all activities carried out, this is a major ARPKI discovery. Certificate authorities are prohibited from acting unethically. Hence, they assist in establishing confidence with clients and domain owners.

The loss or compromise of a domain key is a major occurrence capable of seriously compromising safe communications. Nonetheless, the ARPKI was designed to effectively manage such ultimate events. The authors proved that ARPKI offers a seamless user experience by showing how well it can correctly certify users without adding additional latency to TLS operations. The ARPKI system provides the path for a digital infrastructure that is both more secure and more flexible, therefore addressing the flaws of the current PKI. This is achieved by balancing the two processes exactly.

Based on blockchain technology, Kubilay and associates published CertLedger in their paper [13] as a PKI solution. To keep track of certification procedures, revocations, and actions connected with authority, this specific system uses the blockchain—a public ledger. This function helps to provide security against split-world attacks, as customers may examine

TLS certificates by looking at logs following the confirmation of the most recent block. CertLedger claims that this does not stop CAs from printing certificates with harmful material. Suggested [14] with an eye toward openness is decentralized public key infrastructure openness (DPKIT). This approach guarantees the verifiability of certificates from the moment they are issued until they are revoked when they become invalid. If the public could find it easier to audit the government agency than it already is, the DPKIT's capacity to validate the authenticity of certificates and spot dishonest actions may be enhanced. By means of a semi-decentralized PKI system, Hwang *et al.* [15] solved the scalability issue resulting from a high number of certificates. Their technique, in concert with cryptographic evidence and smart contracts, allows one to build an automated indemnification system. A TP-Merkle tree data structure helps one to do this. Moreover, it changes the proof-of-violation (POV) process so that neither the participant nor the CA can deny the other, and it gives the CA the capacity to act in a domain monitoring-related manner by this change.

To improve the degree of security, a kind of PKI, often referred to as a "cloud-based public key infrastructure" (CBPKI), combines blockchain technologies with cloud computing [16]. Moving CA operations to the cloud greatly strengthens the protection against assaults depriving the targeted system of services. Still, the removal of a certificate revocation list (CRL) is just one more strategy it employs to reach its aim of increasing efficiency. Since the compromised CA is still responsible for the certification process, there is still potential for false certificate issuing when one uses it. This is so because CA keeps observing the evolution of the certification process. Built on Ethereum, CertChain [17] is yet another auditing tool that is naturally decentralized and impossible to control. Referred to as CertOper, the new data structure is meant to hold all the information relevant to operations connected with certifications. The part of the text that follows proposes the creation of a new entity bookkeeper, mostly in charge of supervising all related actions connected to network certificates. The need of consumers to confirm the validity of certificates with the help of the bookkeeper enables an unethical bookkeeper to use their position to produce false certificates. One may consider this to be a security issue. Should Certcoin [18] be successful in creating a totally decentralized verification system, it will not rely on trusted people or companies to retain user identities. Using the proof-of-work idea—also used by Bitcoin, Namecoin, cryptographic accumulators, and distributed hash tables—this approach generates Following a comparable logical process, Qin *et al.* [19] suggested Cecoin, which avoids the Achilles' heel of the Bitcoin network's certificate method. Unlike human miners generating the bitcoin, the institution issuing certificates for Cecoin is the cryptocurrency authority. If you decide to go this route, the already tough procedure of license removal will get an unwelcome degree of complexity.

16.3 Background Study

16.3.1 Public Key Infrastructure

Public key infrastructure offers secure digital communication and over-network authentication. These functions can be performed with the aid of cryptography technology. Cybersecurity revolves around the safeguarding of authenticity, integrity, and confidentiality, especially related to transactions on the Internet. With the use of trusted third parties, digital certificates, and public and private key pairs, PKI ensures safe transactions between systems, people, and applications. In light of online banking, e-commerce, and secure communications, which enhance the protection of data and cyber-attack prevention, PKI's importance is on the rise. Public key infrastructure functions as electronic credentials depending on the CA, which is a trusted organization that manufactures and manages digital certificates. These certificates enable identity verification of individuals, websites, or technical devices. User authentication is done by the registration authority (RA), which, besides the CA, holds responsibility for vetting users prior to certificate issuing. Companies can establish encrypted communication and use digital signatures to authenticate messages once digital certificates are received [20]. PKI also includes an OCSP for tracking and managing compromised and otherwise dysfunctional certificates, as well as a CRL. Whenever an individual or a corporation applies for a digital certificate from a CA, the PKI system comes into action. The CS guarantees the verification that the identity of the person who is requesting the certificate is indeed authentic. This certificate contains the public key of the person being described; hence, other entities can use it to encode messages or to authenticate digital signatures that they issue. The entity retains the private key corresponding to the public key, which allows it to securely sign digital documents and decrypt received messages [21].

When a certificate is compromised, the CA might revoke it and add it to the CRL, invalidating the certificate's validity. Public key infrastructure is very beneficial in many different areas of cybersecurity. The SSL/TLS certificates assure users have secure internet access because they help encrypt website traffic. For example, email security solutions encrypt and sign messages and rely on a PKI. Companies may verify the validity of software using code-signing certificates, discouraging efforts at malware installation. While PKI is used by multi-factor authentication systems to provide secure user access, digital signatures on papers ensure legal legitimacy. In the modern digital world, PKI is essential to maintain security and trust. Offering a controlled, uniform system of encryption and identity authentication, PKI ensures internet connection integrity and helps safeguard private data from intruders. Figure 16.1 shows the working of PKI.

Public key infrastructure is a security technique that offers certified and safe communication using digital certificates and cryptographic keys. Many businesses—including CA, RA, verification authority, sender, and receiver—ensure trust and security in data flow working together. The process begins when the sender requires a digital certificate—which is necessary for identity verification and safe correspondence. The sender goes to the RA to get this certificate; an intermediary is responsible for confirming the sender's identification, and certificate approval is obtained. The request passes to CA once the RA has painstakingly validated it. The responsibility of a reliable CA is to generate digital certificates. After receiving the validated demand of the RA, the CA generates a certificate public key for the sender and securely stores the corresponding certificate private key. Receivers can access the public key for encryption and validation; the sender maintains ownership of the private key and uses it for signature needs. Once the certificate is generated, the sender can sign

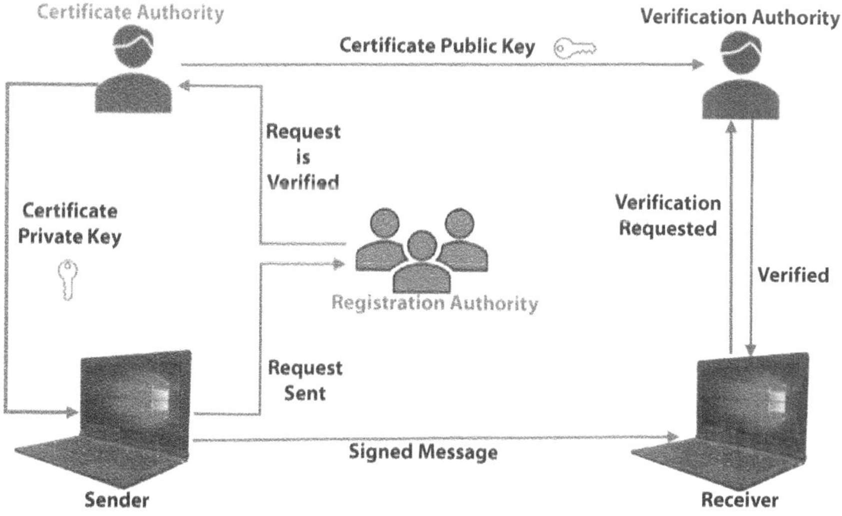

Figure 16.1 Working of PKI.

communications using their private key and then pass them to the recipient. The recipient must verify, unaltered and legitimate, the legitimacy of the signed correspondence they acquired from the sender. Once the recipient requests the sender's digital certificate to be validated by the VA, she can act as needed. The VA checks the certificate using the public key the CA gave. Should the certificate be valid and not revoked, the VA verifies its legality to the recipient. Once the receiver gets correct evidence, they might think the sender is being honest. This ensures encrypted, validated, encrypted correspondence safety against illicit developments. Safe email, online transactions, and data transfers are among the numerous ways the PKI system is changing cybersecurity by enabling digital signatures, identity validation, and encryption. Modern digital security depends on PKI if we want to halt cyber-attacks, fraud, and illicit access.

Although PKI offers safe communications and consistent authentication, its restrictions make it still challenging to use and maintain. One of these constraints is the centralizing one; PKI relies mostly on a reliable CA to produce and validate digital certificates. Should a CA behave in bad faith or self-destruct, the whole security system becomes open for attack. Because of this single point of failure, PKI is very susceptible to several kinds of attacks, including invalid certificate claims, CA breaches, and certificate forging. The administrative burden involved in certificate administration adds even another constraint. Companies using PKI must aggressively control certificate distribution, issuing, renewal, and revocation. Constant monitoring helps to save costs and resource investment by avoiding security threats from unprotected hacked or old certificates. Keeping a CRL and doing real-time OCSP verification incur little expense. Due to out-of-date revocation lists, certain systems might keep accepting a revoked certificate, therefore creating a major security risk. Apart from the listed problems, PKI has other difficulties with scalability. The need for certificate issuing and validation rises greatly as network users and device count rises. Conventional PKI implementation could provide a set of difficulties for big-size projects.

One other weakness of a conventional PKI system is centralizing. Earlier systems trusted a small number of CAs to issue and validate certificates. The whole trust network made feasible allowed one to address a flaw in the cryptographic authority: a single point of failure attack. The helplessness over authentication forces users to rely on other people for validation. Blockchain-based PKI is being sought by users who are worried about data breaches. Blockchain technology offers a distributed and permanent substitute relative to certificate administration and identification. The need for a trustworthy third party is eliminated as blockchain PKI distributes confidence across network nodes. Public keys and certificates must be kept on a permanent, unchangeable blockchain ledger: this helps to guard the data from access once recorded. A blockchain-based on PKI cannot be revoked as no changeable authority confirming issued certificates exists. Doing this eliminates the need for a central CA. The main strength of this approach is the prevention of problems connected to fraud and illegal certificate issuance. By simplifying the procedures of revoking and renewing the certifications, smart contracts may help to reduce administrative responsibilities even further.

One further benefit is the more sense of security that results. Once registered, the unchangeable character of blockchain data makes it very difficult—if not impossible—for any hostile party to generate or modify a certificate. This will make it rather tough for hackers to pass off as respectable companies or engage in impersonation campaigns. Still, another benefit of PKI based on blockchain technology is scalability. Unlike traditional PKI, which makes it hard for CAs to control millions of certificates, distributed networks allow blockchain-based solutions to grow naturally. This is really helpful for the security of IoT-enabled devices.

16.3.2 Blockchain-Based Public Key Infrastructure

The blockchain-based PKI system is a peculiar example of innovation as it seeks to replace centralized CAs with Blockchain's immutable, transparent, and distributed features that lead to digital security. Traditional PKI systems are far less convenient as digital certificates could be issued, maintained, or revoked by a single party and true trust. These structures still exist today, and their use persists. The consequence of an available CA is falling victim to a cyberattack, which leads to identity theft, phishing attempts, or data breaches. Incorporating blockchain technology into PKI solves these problems by guaranteeing a much more secure and reliable method for identity authentication and communication encryption. In PKI based on Blockchain, a distributed ledger eliminates the need for a central authority, thus managing the issuance and validation of certificates [22]. Contrary to traditional PKI, where the CA handles the issuing and managing of certificates, blockchain-based PKI forgoes putting digital certificates and public keys on an unchangeable blockchain ledger. Instead of relying on a central authority to monitor the authenticity of certificates, various blockchain network members collectively verify and maintain the system's integrity [23]. There is a high level of security against counterfeit and illegal revisions, as certificates that are issued and stored on the blockchain cannot be destroyed or modified without agreement from the entire network [24].

Among the various advantages blockchain presents for PKI is the elimination of vulnerabilities. Once CAs take over conventional PKI systems using bogus certificates, hackers will have simpler access to them. Attackers will never have an easy time establishing digital identities or certificates on the blockchain, as there is no unilateral authority at all. Furthermore, as blockchains are unchangeable, all certificate-related transactions—issuing, renewing, canceling, and modifying—have already been finished and will stay so. Using traditional PKI as a means of certificate verification, one might have to search for the CRLs or, worse, wait for the manipulated OCSP services for certificate validation, which is slow and unreliable. With certificates stored on a blockchain, all certificates can be stored publicly on a ledger, which enables the absence of middlemen when it comes to quick verification; this improves security and lowers operating costs without needing expensive infrastructure or administrative overhead. While blockchain-based PKI does come with a heavy dose of advantages, there are some cons to it as well. The sheer volume of certificate data causes inefficiencies in PK systems and raises intense concerns about scale. So, new hybrid approaches are being developed where some certificates are kept off-chain while the rest only contain the necessary information needed to access them.

Integrating existing frameworks with PKI is a different difficulty altogether. The existing infrastructure must be compatible with blockchain technology for many organizations that still rely on traditional PKI to adopt it. The essence of governance is heightened since employing either a public or permissioned blockchain significantly affects the construction of trust amongs users of the blockchain technology. As the World Wide Web becomes more ubiquitous and cyber invasions become more advanced, identity management and protection through blockchain technology is proving to be a more effective solution than traditional methods. Digital transactions, identity management, and distributed software provide a framework for trust by governments, companies, and software developers. With the latest developments in blockchains' scalability, smart contract automation, and self-sovereign identity solutions, blockchain-based PKI is positioned to change the face of cyber security. Identity management suggests propositions powered by immutable and transparent systems while controlled by no authority.

16.3.3 Zero-Knowledge Proof Consensus Mechanism

A ZKP is a technique used in cryptography wherein one party may verify the validity of a statement without disclosing the underlying facts to the other side. By using ZKP, one can persuade a verifier of their knowledge or the accuracy of a finished calculation without offering any accompanying documentation. While preserving the anonymity of private data, cryptographic evidence helps a claimant guard case-sensitive information that can be pertinent to the claim. The claimant is guaranteed that the defender does not find any material relevant to the claim as their trust in the statement's veracity rises. Zero-knowledge proof solutions protect user privacy while preserving transaction security and integrity, benefiting developers. Zero-knowledge proof consensus mechanism assures private and safe transaction acceptance by mixing zero-knowledge cryptographic proofs with blockchains and limiting any participant from access to transaction information. By means of PoW and PoS, these approaches enable the validation of the whole transaction datasets in blockchain systems. This connects the stated user anonymity with the growing system transparency. By means of ZKP with a consensus mechanism, nodes may hide the controlling integrity of the transaction data, thus facilitating efficient transaction validation. These techniques secure significant contracts, identity records, and other sensitive financial data to handle problems of scattered verification. Zero-knowledge proof in blockchain networks allows privacy in distributed systems, therefore simplifying system problems. Features of the ZKP consensus mechanism build system obscurity and confidence. Unlike other more typical consensus systems, ZKP removes data that is seen as crucial for transaction validation along with important transaction metadata [25].

In addition, ZKP allows efficient verification since the proofs are small and require significantly less computing power than more complex solutions such as PoW. The protective features of the system, however, ensure that rigorous monitoring of all claimed transactions is performed. This results in a far greater chance of a breach in data security. These advanced predictive AI algorithms exacerbated the consequences for ZKP-based consensus algorithms, which allow blockchain networks to become more scalable with a reduced chance of network traffic. Older PoW methods are still applicable in larger-scale scenarios where they rely on the effort of miners to unlock intricate cryptographic puzzles. On the other hand, PoS has the opposite stance in that its energy consumption is lower; however, it has no elements of privacy whatsoever. Validators without identity verification need to own and blindly validate the transactions that they stake. Byzantine fault tolerance (BFT) and delegated proof of stake (DPOS) are two additional strategies in the pseudo-anonymous realm that need to publicly validate transactions to pseudonymize the identity. ZKP decentralizes systems; for example, veil contracts and opaque financial systems enable the concealment of attributes such as identity. Much more foster these applications a distributed secure private consensus system enhanced with ZKP. Privacy guarantees enable blockchain consensus systems enhanced with ZKP to undergo fundamental transformations that allow the integration of privacy technologies into distributed networks. All the sensitive details related to health care, banking, and other commercial activities are far better protected using ZKP-based blockchain consensus due to added security in data protection during transactions. There's growing interest from the public in blockchain technology, while ZKP is helping create secure and clear frameworks for building scalable, privacy-preserving distributed systems [26].

16.4 Proposed Methodology

While constructing a PKI with ZKP, one may use cryptographic privacy techniques to add distributed trust, security, privacy, and economic components, thus expanding the present standard PKI systems. Implementing ZKP-based PKI requires a few crucial steps, including selecting an appropriate cryptographic technique and a ZKP-based verification process. The ZKP-based PKI aims to enhance privacy and security while still following the trust paradigm. The initial prerequisite towards a ZKP-based PKI system is the whole system architecture, including all fundamental components of PKI, including CA, RA, VA, and a distributed trust management ledger using blockchain technology. Under normal PKI, RAs are expected to confirm users' identification before issuing the relevant digital certificates; CAs oversee the issue of the certificates. Applying zero-knowledge proofs helps these ZKP-based PKI systems to improve, as no sensitive data relevant to the user ID verification needs to be exposed. The PKI system becomes relevant if many nodes examine and regulate certificates, leading to further decentralization and the elimination of single-point failures using a permissioned or hybrid blockchain network. While checking digital identities and certificates using an unchangeable record of cryptographic evidence, this ledger does not expose private information. To verify the given ZKPs throughout the certification stages of certificates and identities, all ZKP vergers must be integrated into the system logically.

16.4.1 Zero-Knowledge Succinct Non-Interactive Arguments of Knowledge

Using the sophisticated cryptographic proof system called zero-knowledge succinct non-interactive arguments of knowledge (zk-SNARKs), one can show another person that they know something or have done a calculation correctly without revealing any details about that information or calculation. Many privacy-preserving blockchain protocols, secure identity verification systems, and decentralized apps (dApps) use zk-SNARKs because of their efficiency, trustworthiness, and private verification capabilities. Protected transactions, made possible by zk-SNARKs, allow users of privacy-focused blockchains like Zcash to confirm the authenticity of their transactions without revealing the identity of the sender, recipient, or the amount exchanged. Ethereum Layer 2 scaling solutions, such as zk-Rollups, also make use of them to reduce gas costs and increase throughput [27]. The working of zk-SNARK can be represented in Figure 16.2. The main steps in the zk-SNARKs function are:

- Crucial to the cryptographic setup process is the trustworthy production of public parameters used in evidence creation and verification. This setup must be done securely to prevent backdoors.

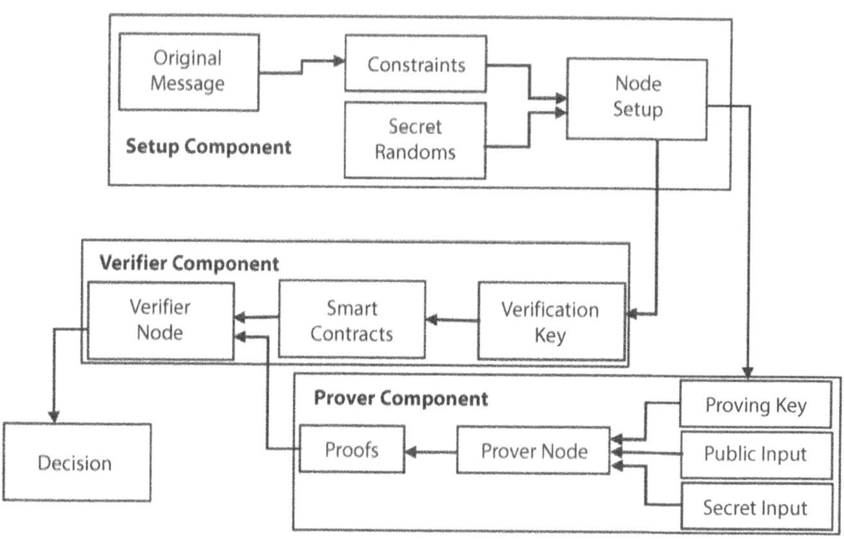

Figure 16.2 Working process of zk-SNARKs.

- To ensure that a statement is true—for example, to affirm the legality of a transaction without revealing its details—the prover constructs a cryptographic proof.
- By using the evidence and the public parameters, the verifier ensures that the assertion is valid while protecting any sensitive information from being learned.

16.4.2 Zero-Knowledge Succinct Non-Interactive Arguments in Zero Knowledge Proof-Based Blockchain Public Key Infrastructure

Zero-knowledge succinct non-interactive arguments of knowledge implemented into a blockchain PKI using ZKP significantly increases its efficiency, security, and privacy. Traditional PKI systems are vulnerable to certificate compromise, privacy breaches, and single points of failure as digital certificates are issued, handed, and evaluated by centralized CAs. One may solve the challenges by building a scalable, distributed, and user privacy-protecting authentication system from zk-SNARKs combined with blockchain-based PKI. Here, zk-SNARKs mostly secure sensitive data and confirm the legitimacy of certificates. Zero-knowledge succinct non-interactive arguments in zero knowledge enable users to offer cryptographic proof verifying their certificate instead of disclosing the certificate or private key during authentication. Unlike conventional PKI, in which users are urged to provide these details, this is in contrast. Crucially for providing secure digital identity verification in fields such as financial services, IoT security, and distributed identity management, this method guarantees authentication while retaining anonymity. Zk-SNARKs offer great advantages in blockchain-based PKI because of their simplicity and efficiency, which are devoid of interaction. Because they need numerous rounds of communication between the prover and verifier, traditional zero-knowledge proofs often produce increased computational and network overhead. Rapid confirmation of minimal size and absence of interaction make zk-SNARKs ideal for use in blockchain smart contracts. This increases the authentication method's scalability and helps reduce transaction expenses. Furthermore, zk-SNARKs enhance PKI safety and revocation processes dependent on blockchain technologies. Blockchain records of zk-SNARK proofs help validate digital certificates. This produces an unchangeable, distributed system.

16.4.3 Ganache Truffle Suite

Ganache allows one to quickly create, evaluate, and apply smart contracts—like a customized Ethereum blockchain. This is included in the Truffle Suite and has an Ethereum network replicated. Faster tests needing safety do not call on any external Ethereum or primary Ethereum connections. For developers using distributed applications and smart contracts, testing procedures, including Ethereum, are therefore simplified. Ganache UI and Ganache CLI are the two variants of Ganache. The former lets developers that need a user-friendly interface showing blockchain activities utilize specially created graphical user interfaces. The latter version, Ganache CLI, is better suited for automation as it is smaller in weight and more terminal orientated even if it preserves the same features as its cousin. Testing becomes much more efficient when immediate block mining using Ganache removes network confirmation-related transaction delays [28].

Furthermore, given test Ethernet accounts with Ether balances, it does not need to acquire tokens from outside testnets like Ropsten or Goerli. This explains why we must compile tokens from several tests. By changing block intervals and fuel pricing, developers may replicate many network circumstances. This helps people to better grasp how their contracts may really work. Many of Ganache's logs, along with their error alerts, allow smart contracts to go through extensive testing, revisions, and polishing before they are brought live on the Ethereum network. This takes place prior to the smart contract deployment. This useful tool helps one to do debugging chores much more easily. Using Ganache guarantees the public blockchain's pre-deployment assurance of app operation, minimization of costs from live testing, and process optimization. By offering a proactive strategy to apply secure testing environments for blockchains as they are versatile and simple, ganache helps greatly accelerate Ethereum's growth. Applied holistically, the instrument demonstrates in-depth degrees of control with the current tasks at hand and remarkable power and simplicity of usage [29].

16.5 Workflow of the Proposed Public Key Infrastructure

The first step produces the basic requirements required for communication. The key generation follows the crucial one of user certification. Digital certificate CA, as a reliable third party, must first verify the user. This certificate confirms the user is a so-called real user and enables one to use the authentication system. Once the approval of a certificate is attained, zk-SNARK proof will allow one to reveal an understanding of the facts without detailing them. Those involving blockchains, privacy, and authentication systems especially use this technique since revealing any irrelevant information could prove harmful. By means of zk-SNARK proofs, a person ensures the capacity to identify, safeguard, and protect sensitive information from being made public. The Blockchain industrial sector accepts data compiled after generation. The Blockchain provides a distributed immutable ledger, which ensures the safety and authenticity of the authentication information. Keeping zk-SNARK proofs on blockchains accessible later during the authentication process demands the maintenance of enduring, reliable records of verifiable authentication. This stage focuses on minimizing reliance on centralized power and increasing security control. Well-protected information increases user data. Pursuing user authentication enables the user to try to enter a particular system, platform, or service. Accessing these requires prior confirmation of Identification to fulfil the need. For fulfilment, the user needs to submit proof of claim from zk-SNARK. This information is an authenticated credential that legally certifies the holder's possession of relevant documents while not divulging any confidential information. Smart contract validation is also in progress, which is the fundamental component of the authentication framework.

A smart contract is a computer code that is implemented on the blockchain, which operates as an independent application capable of conditionally executing a predetermined sequence of steps. A smart contract performs zk-SNARK user proof checking. If the proof meets accepted standards for validation, the smart contract marks the validation as completed and enables user access. A user is considered authenticated after the authentication process is securely completed. Although the endeavor is said to have failed, should the smart contract discover fraudulent evidence or inadequate satisfaction of authentication criteria, the outcome will be different. Access is, therefore, denied. Distributed applications, privacy-preserving login systems, and other platforms requiring a secret analytic process all depend on this sort of authentication, which is clearly beneficial. Smart contract validation mixed with zk-SNARKs greatly improves system security and eliminates the need for private data-dispensing validation methods. This provides a logical response to contemporary cybersecurity issues focused on secrecy and safety. Figure 16.3 and Algorithm 16.1 show the proposed PKI working.

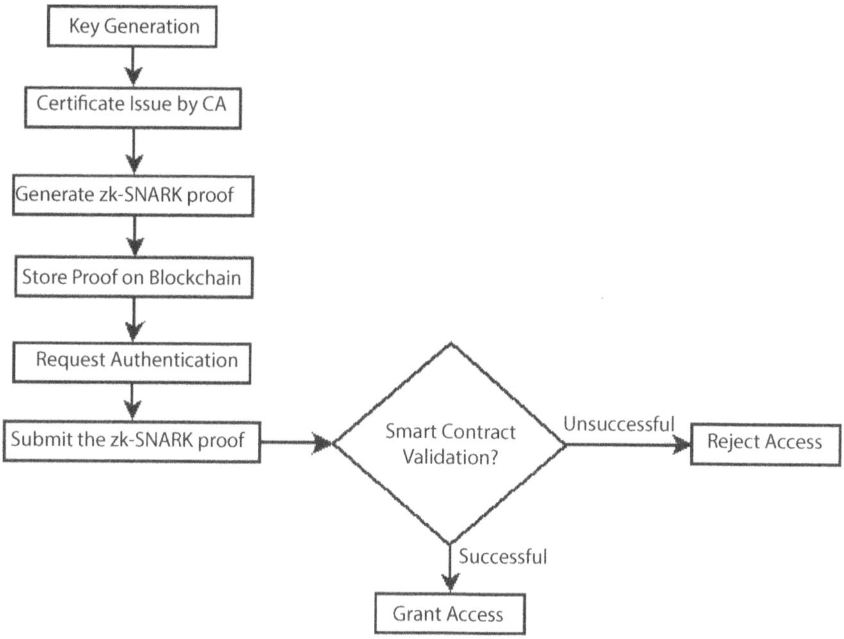

Figure 16.3 Working on proposed PKI.

Algorithm 16.1 Working of Proposed KPI.

```
Initiate Transaction
function GENERATE_KEY_PAIR
    Private_key ← generate_private_key()
    Public_key ← derive_public_key(Private_key)
    return (Private_key, Public_key)
end function
function ISSUE_CERTIFICATE(User_Public_key,
  CA_Private_key)
    Certificate ← Sign(User_Public_key, CA-Private_key)
    return Certificate
end function
function GENERATE_ZK_PROOF(User_Private_key,
  Certificate)
    Proof ← zkSNARK_prove(User_Private_key, Certificate)
    return Proof
end function
function STORE(Proof, Blockchain)
```

```
    Blockchain.add_transacrion(Proof)
    Blockchain.commit()
end function
function AUTHENTICATE_USER(User_Proof, Blockchain)
    if Blockchain.verify_zk_Proof(User_Proof) then
        return "Access Granted"
    else
        return "Access Denied"
    end if
end function
function REVOKE_CERTIFICATE(Certificate, Blockchain)
    Blockchain.revoke_certificate(Certificate)
end function
```

16.6 Result and Analysis

Assessing a ZKP-based blockchain PKI utilizing zk-SNARKs involves balancing four primary criteria: computational efficiency, storage, and memory consumption, communication and networking overhead, as well as scalability and throughput metrics. Under computational efficiency, monitoring the pace of cryptographic operations performed and resource consumption ensures timely proof generation, verification, and certificate issuing. Blockchain storage required to retain certificates and provide evidence of authentication is incorporated by the above-mentioned model of storage. Modification of zk-SNARKs scope may help reduce the excessive data volume. The networks and communication overhead complete the assessment of bandwidth and latency consumed by blockchain transaction activity and evidence transfer. This ensures continuous execution of the authentication procedures. Ultimately, scalability and throughput evaluate the extent to which the system can efficiently handle an increased volume of authentication requests. This ensures that large-scale deployment of the system utilizing PKI with zk-SNARK will remain feasibly optimal. With all these factors, there is an insightful view of the operation, security, and adaptability of the system's effectiveness in a real-world setting.

A ZKP-based blockchain PKI's efficiency is indicated by the time and resources used for cryptographic proof generation, validation, and computation using zk-SNARKs. A system's authentication proof validation and delivery mainly signify the user experience level. Generally taking 250 ms, efficiency and proof creation define zk-SNARKs. This time can and is usually cut around 7 milliseconds, which allows blockchain nodes or authentication systems to successfully validate credentials. Additionally, the rate of acceleration in the production and distribution of cryptographic keys is greatly impacted by the strategic pivotal timing of crucial generation and certificate expiration. By employing these optimized tactics made available through zk-SNARKs, the PKI can handle a myriad of authentication requests with marginal processing effort. Solutions based on blockchain PKI require substantial storage because the network incessantly archives all transactions. One disadvantage of Zk-SNARKs is the aggregate of their proofs: Approximately 384 bytes are regarded as too little. This reduces the overall expense of other storage cryptography techniques and decreases the area needed to be stored. Every digital certificate claim, based on evidence and verification, must comply with the 1.5 KB of allocated storage on the blockchain. Furthermore, the reduced storage cost of smart contracts enhances collateral retrieval—approximately 1 KB per control item retained.

The absence of flaws in the authentication process is achieved by means of a well-organized blockchain system and appropriate communication between users and verifiers. With a data transfer capacity of around 1.5 KB in PKI implemented with zk-SNARKs, the technique is lightweight enough to enable real-time transmission across a dispersed network. The blockchain ensures quick processing of transactions with an average latency of around 0.8 seconds. Because PKI systems allow zk-SNARKs,

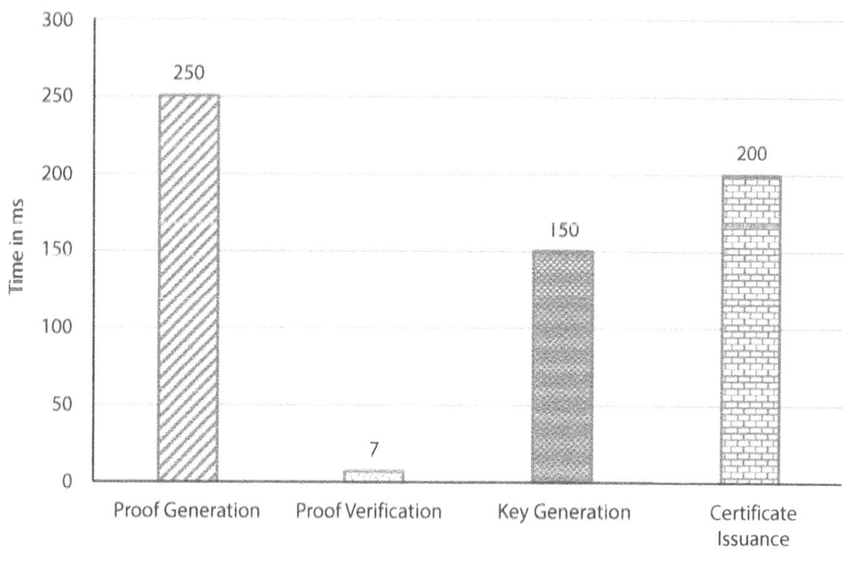

Figure 16.4 Computational efficiency of the proposed PKI.

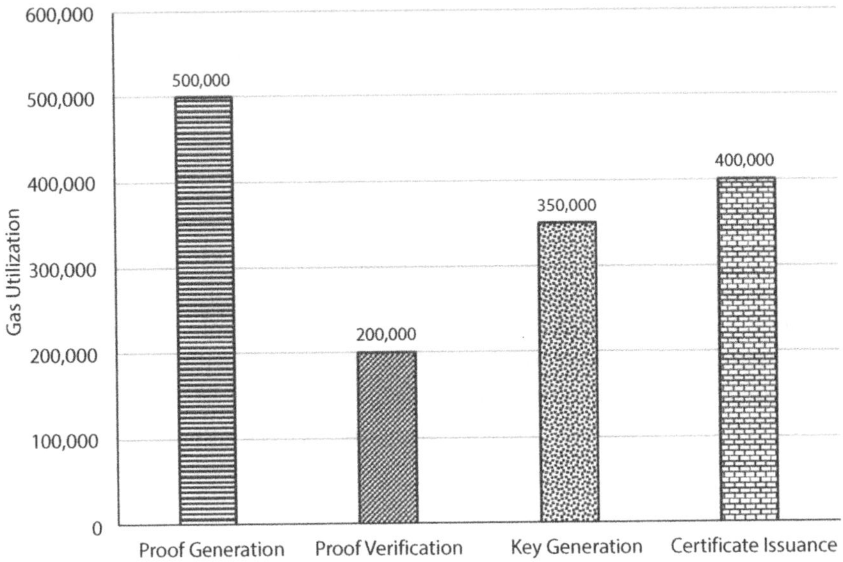

Figure 16.5 Gas utilization for different processes of proposed PKI.

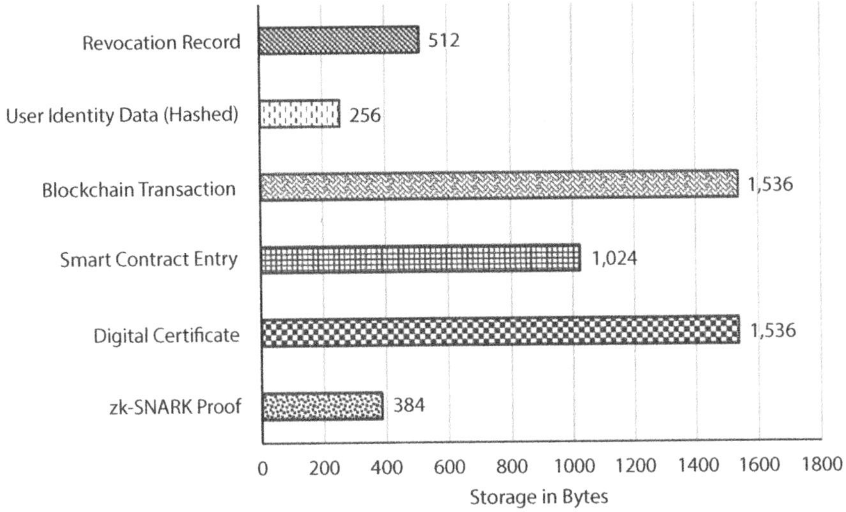

Figure 16.6 Storage overhead for the proposed PKI.

the transaction processing speed is a major consideration. The typical transaction processing speed is around 75 TPS, depending on the blockchain type. Due to the tiny proof size and minimal verification cost, a blockchain-based PKI that uses zero-knowledge proofs with zk-SNARKs has excellent scalability. What this means for digital device authentication, corporate identity validation, and borderless e-ID checks is that the system can handle a large number of transactions at once, according to the given text. So, it is true what they say: blockchain performance is almost unaffected by a 0.5% increase in processing load, guaranteeing low latency and great throughput. Figure 16.4 shows the computational efficiency of the proposed PKI. Figure 16.5 shows gas utilization for the proposed model. Figure 16.6 shows the storage overhead of the proposed PKI.

16.7 Conclusion

Zero-knowledge proof blockchain PKI based on suggested zk-SNARK provides safe, rapid, scalable decentralized authentication. The concept provides secure, private authentication free of centralized trust authority by the use of zk-SNARKs. The technology reduces processing delays by means of fast evidence generation and verification. Compact proof sizes and maximum blockchain storage promise lower storage overhead, therefore promoting sustainable data management. Lack of network or communication overhead enables perfect authentication with little bandwidth use. The system handles multiple authentication requests without slowing down, so it expands well, too. Regarding financial transactions, IoT security, distributed identity management, and corporate authentication systems, these characteristics make the suggested approach exceptional. Future advances might improve the model's performance and relevance. By replacing zk-STARKs for zk-SNARKs, scalability is enhanced, and the necessity of a trustworthy environment is thus avoided. Ethereum and Layer 2 blockchain systems might assist in reducing expenses by optimizing smart contract execution and gas prices. Combining multi-factor authentication, zk-SNARKs, and biometrics under hybrid authentication could improve security. Moreover, the anomalies and fraud detection using machine learning of blockchain-based PKI systems might boost reliability and trust. Finally, scalable, privacy-oriented, safe authentication provided by the Zk-SNARK-based ZKP blockchain PKI is shown. This architecture's development and optimization might help satisfy the needs for decentralized identity management and blockchain security.

AI disclosure statement: The author acknowledges the use of AI-based tools for minor language editing or grammatical correction. However, all intellectual contributions, analyses, and conclusions presented in this chapter are entirely the author's own.

References

1. Belotti, M., Božić, N., Pujolle, G., Secci, S., A Vademecum on Blockchain Technologies: When, Which, and How. *IEEE Commun. Surv. Tutorials*, 21, 4, 3796–3838, Fourthquarter 2019, doi: 10.1109/COMST.2019.2928178.
2. Guo, H. and Yu, X., A Survey on Blockchain Technology and its security. *Blockchain: Res. Appl.*, 3, 2, 100067, Feb. 2022, doi: https://doi.org/10.1016/j.bcra.2022.100067.
3. Panigrahi, A., Nayak, A.K., Paul, R., HealthCare EHR. *Int. J. Inf. Syst. Supply Chain Manage.*, 15, 3, 1–15, Jul. 2022, doi: https://doi.org/10.4018/ijisscm.290017.
4. Panigrahi, A., Pati, A., Dash, B., Sahoo, G., Singh, D., Dash, M., ASBlock:An Agricultural based Supply Chain Management using Blockchain Technology. *Procedia Comput. Sci.*, 235, 1943–1952, Jan. 2024, doi: https://doi.org/10.1016/j.procs.2024.04.184.
5. El Koshiry, A., Eliwa, E., Abd El-Hafeez, T., Shams, M.Y., Unlocking the power of blockchain in education: An overview of innovations and outcomes. *Blockchain: Res. Appl.*, 4, 4, 100165, Nov. 2023, doi: https://doi.org/10.1016/j.bcra.2023.100165.
6. Faisal, M. and Zulkernine, M., DKS-PKI: A Distributed Key Server Architecture for Public Key Infrastructure, pp. 23–43, Jan. 2022, doi: https://doi.org/10.1007/978-3-031-23690-7_2.
7. Panigrahi, A., Nayak, A.K., Paul, R., A Blockchain Based PKI System for Peer to Peer Network, Lecture Notes in Networks and Systems, pp. 81–88, 2022, doi: https://doi.org/10.1007/978-981-16-4807-6_9.
8. Panigrahi, A., Sahu, B., Panigrahi, S.S., Khan, M.S., Jena, A.K., Application of Blockchain as a Solution to the Real-World Issues in Health Care System. In: *Blockchain Technology: Applications and Challenges, Intelligent Systems Reference Library*, S.K. Panda, A.K. Jena, S.K. Swain, S.C. Satapathy (eds.), vol. 203, Springer, Cham, 2021. https://doi.org/10.1007/978-3-030-69395-4_8.
9. Caronni, G., Walking the Web of trust, pp. 153–158, Jun. 2000, https://doi.org/10.1109/enabl.2000.883720.
10. Chuat, L. *et al.*, F-PKI: A Flexible End-Entity Public-Key Infrastructure. In: *The Complete Guide to SCION. Information Security and Cryptography*. Springer, Cham, 2022. https://doi.org/10.1007/978-3-031-05288-0_18.
11. Basin, D., Cremers, C., Kim, T.H.-J., Perrig, A., Sasse, R., Szalachowski, P., Design, Analysis, and Implementation of ARPKI: An Attack-Resilient

Public-Key Infrastructure. *IEEE Trans. Dependable Secure Comput.*, 15, 3, 393–408, May 2018, doi: https://doi.org/10.1109/tdsc.2016.2601610.

12. Meier, S., Schmidt, B.R., Cremers, C., Basin, D., The TAMARIN Prover for the Symbolic Analysis of Security Protocols, pp. 696–701, Jul. 2013, doi: https://doi.org/10.1007/978-3-642-39799-8_48.
13. Kubilay, M.Y., Kiraz, M.S., Mantar, H.A., CertLedger: A new PKI model with Certificate Transparency based on blockchain. *Comput. Secur.*, 85, 333–352, Aug. 2019, doi: https://doi.org/10.1016/j.cose.2019.05.013.
14. Boyen, X., Herath, U., McKague, M., Stebila, D., Associative Blockchain for Decentralized PKI Transparency. *Cryptography*, 5, 2, 14, May 2021, doi: https://doi.org/10.3390/cryptography5020014.
15. Hwang, G.-H., Chang, T.-K., Chiang, H.-W., A Semidecentralized PKI System Based on Public Blockchains with Automatic Indemnification Mechanism. *Secur. Commun. Netw.*, 2021, 1–15, Oct. 2021, doi: https://doi.org/10.1155/2021/7400466.
16. Khieu, B. and Moh, M., CBPKI. *Proceedings of the 2019 ACM Southeast Conference*, Apr. 2019, doi: https://doi.org/10.1145/3299815.3314433.
17. Chen, J., Yao, S., Yuan, Q., He, K., Ji, S., Du, R., CertChain: Public and Efficient Certificate Audit Based on Blockchain for TLS Connections. *IEEE INFOCOM 2018 - IEEE Conference on Computer Communications*, Honolulu, HI, USA, pp. 2060–2068, 2018, doi: 10.1109/INFOCOM.2018.8486344.
18. Fromknecht, C., Velicanu, D., Yakoubov, S., Certcoin: A namecoin based decentralized authentication system, Massachusetts Inst. Technol., Cambridge, MA, USA, Tech. Rep, 6, pp. 46–56, 2014.
19. Qin, B., Huang, J., Wang, Q., Luo, X., Liang, B., Shi, W., Cecoin: A decentralized PKI mitigating MitM attacks. *Future Gener. Comput. Syst.*, 107, 805–815, Jun. 2020, doi: https://doi.org/10.1016/j.future.2017.08.025.
20. Boldyreva, A., Fischlin, M., Palacio, A., Warinschi, B., A Closer Look at PKI: Security and Efficiency, Springer eBooks, pp. 458–475, Jun. 2007, doi: https://doi.org/10.1007/978-3-540-71677-8_30.
21. Slagell, A., Bonilla, R., Yurcik, W., A survey of PKI components and scalability issues. *2006 IEEE International Performance Computing and Communications Conference*, Phoenix, AZ, USA, pp. 10–484, 2006, doi: 10.1109/.2006.1629442.
22. Panigrahi, A., Nayak, A.K., Paul, R., Sahu, B., Kant, S., CTB-PKI: Clustering and Trust Enabled Blockchain Based PKI System for Efficient Communication in P2P Network. *IEEE Access*, 10, 124277–124290, 2022, doi: 10.1109/ACCESS.2022.3222807.
23. Panigrahi, A., Nayak, A.K., Paul, R., Smart contract assisted blockchain based public key infrastructure system. *Trans. Emerging Telecommun. Technol.*, Oct. 2022, doi: https://doi.org/10.1002/ett.4655.
24. Panigrahi, A., Nayak, A.K., Paul, R., Impact of Clustering technique in enhancing the Blockchain network performance. *2022 International Conference on*

Machine Learning, Computer Systems and Security (MLCSS), Bhubaneswar, India, pp. 363–367, 2022, doi: 10.1109/MLCSS57186.2022.00072.

25. Diro, A., Zhou, L., Saini, A., Kaisar, S., Hiep, P.C., Leveraging zero knowledge proofs for blockchain-based identity sharing: A survey of advancements, challenges and opportunities. *J. Inf. Secur. Appl.*, 80, 103678–103678, Feb. 2024, doi: https://doi.org/10.1016/j.jisa.2023.103678.
26. Kuznetsov, O., Rusnak, A., Yezhov, A., Kanonik, D., Kuznetsova, K., Karashchuk, S., Enhanced Security and Efficiency in Blockchain With Aggregated Zero-Knowledge Proof Mechanisms. *IEEE Access*, 12, 49228–49248, 2024, doi: 10.1109/ACCESS.2024.3384705.
27. Koulianos, A., Paraskevopoulos, P., Litke, A., Papadakis, N.K., Enhancing Unmanned Aerial Vehicle Security: A Zero-Knowledge Proof Approach with Zero-Knowledge Succinct Non-Interactive Arguments of Knowledge for Authentication and Location Proof. *Sensors*, 24, 17, 5838, Sep. 2024, doi: https://doi.org/10.3390/s24175838.
28. Panigrahi, A., Pati, A., Sahu, B., Dash, B.B., Chowdhury, S., Patra, S.S., Cluster-Driven CA Selection Space Optimization in Blockchain with POA for Trust Calculation. *2024 International Conference on IoT Based Control Networks and Intelligent Systems (ICICNIS)*, Bengaluru, India, pp. 251–256, 2024, doi: 10.1109/ICICNIS64247.2024.10823131.
29. Kaur, S. and Singh, J., Designing and Deploying Blockchain with Truffle and Smart Contracts, Lecture notes in networks and systems, pp. 327–336, Jan. 2025, doi: https://doi.org/10.1007/978-981-97-8051-8_26.

Index

Also of Interest

Check out these published and forthcoming titles in the "Leading-Edge Breakthroughs in Artificial Intelligence" series from Scrivener Publishing

Digital Immune System
Principles and Practices
Edited by Sujata Priyambada Dash, Vaibhav Mishra, Bijeta Shaw, Sandeep Kumar Panda, and S. Balamurugan
Published 2025. ISBN 978-1-394-38375-7

Adaptive AI
Fundamentals, Challenges, and Applications
Edited by P. Pavan Kumar, G. Suresh Kumar, Ajay Kumar Jena, Sandeep Kumar Panda and S. Balamurugan
Published 2025. ISBN 978-1-394-38904-9

AI Trust, Risk and Security Management
Framework, Principles, and Practices
Edited by R. Karthick Manoj, S. Senthilnathan, S. Arunmozhi Selvi, T. Ananth Kumar, S. Balamurugan
Published 2025. ISBN 978-1-394-39299-5

Forthcoming 2025/2026

Neuro-Symbolic AI: Concepts and Applications
Decision Intelligence: Concepts, Applications, and Case Studies
Human-Centered AI: Frameworks and Applications
Responsible AI: Principles and Practices
Platform Engineering: Concepts, Challenges, and Applications
Composite AI: Fundamentals, Challenges, and Applications
Visual AI: Fundamentals, Challenges, and Applications
Causal AI: Fundamentals and Applications
Embodied AI: Concepts, Challenges, and Applications
Agentic AI: Concepts, Applications, and Case Studies
Data-Centric AI: Concepts, Applications and Case Studies
Sovereign AI: Frameworks, Principles, and Practices
Accelerated AI: Energy Efficient Computing Systems for Large Language Models (LLMs)
Actionable AI: Powered by Large Action Models (LAMs)
Affective AI: Concepts, Applications, and Case Studies
AI-Augmented Software Engineering: Principles and Practices
Ambient Invisible Intelligence: Fundamentals, Challenges, and Applications
Artificial Cognition: Technology, Applications, and Challenges
Artificial General Intelligence: Principles and Practices
Autonomous AI Agents: Foundations and Applications
Principles of Confidential Computing
Disinformation Security for Generative AI Applications: Concepts, Methodologies, and Use Cases
Embedded AI: Concepts, Challenges, and Applications
Graph Neural Networks (GNNs): Concepts and Applications
Industry Cloud Platforms: Fundamentals, Applications, and Case Studies
Multi-Modal Generative AI: Frameworks, Principles, and Practices
Objective-Driven AI: Concepts, Applications, and Case Studies
Physical AI for Robotics and Automation: Concepts, Techniques, and Applications
Predictive AI: Concepts, Applications, and Case Studies
Prescriptive AI: Concepts, Applications, and Case Studies
Shadow AI: Concepts, Applications, and Security
Small Language Models (SLMs) for Compact AI: Architectures, Principles, and Applications